# FINNS
IN THE UNITED STATES

# FINNS
IN THE UNITED STATES

A History of Settlement, Dissent, and Integration

Edited by Auvo Kostiainen

Michigan State University Press | East Lansing

Copyright © 2014 by Michigan State University

♾ The paper used in this publication meets the minimum requirements
of ANSI/NISO Z39.48-1992 (R 1997) (Permanence of Paper).

Michigan State University Press
East Lansing, Michigan 48823-5245

Printed and bound in the United States of America.

20  19  18  17  16  15  14    1  2  3  4  5  6  7  8  9  10

LIBRARY OF CONGRESS CATALOGING-IN-PUBLICATION DATA
Finns in the United States : a history of settlement, dissent, and integration /
edited by Auvo Kostiainen.
pages cm.
Includes bibliographical references and index.
ISBN 978-1-61186-106-8 (pbk. : alk. paper)—ISBN 978-1-60917-398-2 (ebook)
1. Finnish Americans—History. I. Kostiainen, Auvo.
E184.F5F55 2014
305.894'541073—dc23
2013012249

Book design by Charlie Sharp, Sharp Des!gns, Lansing, MI
Cover design by Erin Kirk New
Cover art is of the Red Lodge, Montana, Finnish American gymnastics society, 1910,
from the photo collection of the Department of General History, University of Turku.

Michigan State University Press is a member of the Green Press Initiative and is committed to
developing and encouraging ecologically responsible publishing practices. For more information
about the Green Press Initiative and the use of recycled paper in book publishing, please visit
*www.greenpressinitiative.org.*

Visit Michigan State University Press at *www.msupress.org*

# Contents

PREFACE .................................................................... vii

**Part 1. Introduction**

Updating and Rethinking the Finnish American Story, *Jon Saari* ............................ 3
Interest in the History of Finnish Americans, *Auvo Kostiainen* ........................... 13

**Part 2. Colonial Settlement of the Swedes and Finns**

The Delaware Colonists and Their Heritage, *Auvo Kostiainen* ............................ 29

**Part 3. Seamen, Masses, and Individual Migrants of the Nineteenth and Twentieth Centuries**

Migration from Finland to North America, *Reino Kero* ................................ 41
Finnish Settlements in the United States: "Nesting Places" and Finntowns, *Arnold R. Alanen* ........ 55
Ambiguous Identity: Finnish Americans and the Race Question, *Peter Kivisto*
    *and Johanna Leinonen* ....................................................... 75

**Part 4. Finnish Communities Organized**

Fighting for Temperance Ideas, *Paul George Hummasti* ................................ 91
Religious Activities of the Finns: An Examination of Finnish Religious Life in Industrialized
    North America, *Gary Kaunonen* ............................................... 107
Politics of the Left and the Right, *Auvo Kostiainen* ................................. 131
"Sooner or Later You're a Cooperator": The Finnish American Cooperative Movement,
    *Hannu Heinilä* ............................................................ 157

## Part 5. The Multitude of Cultural Life

Finnish Identity in Immigrant Culture, *Keijo Virtanen* ............................................. 173
Papers and Publications, *Auvo Kostiainen* ............................................. 205

## Part 6. Finland's Minority Emigrants

Finland-Swedes in North America, *Mika Roinila* ............................................. 221

## Part 7. Connected to Finland

Distant Dreams, Different Realities: North American Immigrants Revisit Finland, *Erik Hieta* ........ 243
Help among Nations: The Humanitarian Impulse in American–Finnish Relations, *Erik Hieta* ....... 253
The Return Migration of Finns from North America, *Keijo Virtanen* ............................... 263
Deported Finns, *Auvo Kostiainen* ............................................. 273

## Part 8. Acculturation and Generations

One Culture, Two Cultures? Families of Finns in the United States in the Twentieth Century,
   *Johanna Leinonen* ............................................. 285
The Transnational Practices of Finnish Immigrants, *Peter Kivisto* ............................................. 297
Who Is a "Real" Finn? Negotiating Finnish and Finnish American Identity in the Contemporary
   United States, *Johanna Leinonen* ............................................. 309

## Part 9. Turning to Americans

Adjustment and the Future, *Mika Roinila* ............................................. 319

FOR FURTHER REFERENCE ............................................. 327

CONTRIBUTORS ............................................. 333

INDEX ............................................. 335

# Preface

The history of the Finns in North America has been a target of interest for more than 100 years. In the 1920s, the number of first- and second-generation Finns in the United States reached circa 350,000. Today there are more than 600,000 persons in the United States who recognize their Finnish ancestry, while in Canada their number is more than 100,000. The main movement of Finns to the United States was cut down to only a few hundred per year in the 1920s by quotas in the immigration laws, while Canada remained an important destination during the interwar years. After World War II emigration from Finland resumed, with perhaps 50,000 new immigrants landing in North America until present day.[1]

Scholarly interest in the history of Finns in North America started in the early decades of the twentieth century, and gained strength especially from the 1960s onward. Scholars working in both Finland and North America researched and published extensively during the 1960s to 1990s, and the work continues today, with rising interest in new ethnic groups and multicultural features in societies. Interest in Finnish heritage in the United States has been sustained mainly by second- and third-generation descendants, post–World War II immigrants, and migration scholars.

The story of the Finns and their descendants in America is worth writing. This book is only the second comprehensive historical volume on the topic published in the English language; it follows in the footsteps of A. William Hoglund's *Finnish Immigrants in America 1880–1920*.[2] Hoglund, a second-generation Finnish American from rural upstate New York, wrote as an insider and as a professional historian. He saw the Finnish American story as a gritty and inventive survival tale, whose final chapter would inevitably be assimilation and integration into the larger American society. He had no use for fileo-pietistic interpretations that emphasized ethnic pride and positive contributions to mainstream American life. This current book builds upon Hoglund's insights into the immigrant story but also adds research and perspectives that extend beyond Hoglund's chosen timeline, 1880–1920. It enriches the story of the second and third generations, and documents Finnish American dissent from, as well as integration into, mainstream American society and politics.

This volume is not a narrative history of Finnish immigration with a single voice, nor is it an encyclopedic compendium of all things Finnish American. It explores from a variety of perspectives the collective experience of one specific ethnic group in the United States. It consists of nine parts and twenty chapters, each one reflecting aspects of the specific experiences of Finnish Americans. The book is organized in approximate chronological order, with thematic parts and chapters. The authors of this volume have been influenced by the vast body of work produced by social historians from the 1960s forward, with its emphasis on history from the bottom up and attention to class, race, and gender. Relatedly, they have been influenced by recent developments in history and the social sciences such as multiculturalism, transnationalism, and whiteness studies. Consequently, this volume offers a fresh and up-to-date analysis of the history of Finnish Americans, one that will permit comparisons with other ethnic experiences in the United States.

The Finns were late-arriving immigrants during the Great Migration (ca. 1880–1924), although there had been a prelude in the colonial era of the 1600s. They are, comparatively speaking, a small immigrant group. Nevertheless, because of their geographic concentration in regions such as the upper Midwest, their local and regional impact was pronounced. They differed from many other new immigrant groups from Europe in a number of ways, including the fact that their language was not Indo-European, and many Old Country cultural and social features reflected their geographic location on the northern borderlands of Europe.

The book begins with an introductory section that offers historiographical analyses of the study of the Finnish American history, followed by a compact overview of the overall composition and settlement patterns of these newcomers. Major topics in the book include explorations of the particularly vivid ethnic organizations Finns created, as well as the cultural life they sought to preserve and enhance while also fitting into their new homeland. One part examines the special significance of political dissent, in particular widespread participation in the full range of leftist organizations (except anarchism) and cooperative activities. At the same time, many Finns were religious, some perhaps seeing immigration as, to borrow from Timothy Smith, a "theologizing experience." The institutional life of these "Church Finns" will be counterposed to that of their "Red Finn" counterparts.[3]

The Red (left)/White (conservative) divide had major implications for the various forms of political engagement and immigrant culture that arose, the legacy of which impacted the entire ethnic group and its identity for decades. As significant as the internal division were various manifestations of transnationalism as immigrants sought to remain connected to the Old World. Noteworthy here was the exodus of many North American radical leftists to Soviet Karelia in the 1930s, and right after that the homeland politics that mobilized the larger Finnish American community to support Finland during the Winter War (1939–40) and Continuation War (1941–44). One chapter, influenced by whiteness studies scholars, also discusses the question of whether Finns belonged to the Mongol race; this question had a surprisingly long-lasting and vexing impact on the ethnic community.

The Canadian experience of Finnish immigration is not of special interest in this volume. There are a few reasons for this: Finnish American history in the United States is an older phenomenon and therefore more thoroughly analyzed, while many features of the Finnish experience in Canada still await researchers. And even though Canada and the United States are in many respects similar and cross-border contacts were frequent, the two histories of immigration are hardly identical. It was decided that this volume should concentrate on the history of Finnish immigration in the United States. Canadian Finns are noted in certain sections of the volume for comparative analysis. Finnish Canadian experiences are worthy of a volume of their own.

# PREFACE

The idea of writing this book as a joint effort was actually born during the scholarly and lay gatherings at FinnForums and FinnFests of the late 2000s. These meetings brought together people with a general interest in Finnish American history. More concrete discussions took place at the FinnForum in Eskilstuna, Sweden, in 2007; the project was given a push at the FinnFest of Duluth, Minnesota, in 2008; and finally materialized at the conference called "Finnish-American Immigrants in Transition" in Turku, Finland, in June 2009. The authors of the present volume are all active researchers in the history and society of Finns in North America and in Finland and represent different disciplines.

Special thanks go to each writer for great patience and spirited teamwork. Several individuals in Finland helped along the way, such as students and researchers at the University of Turku—Rauli Elenius, Johannes Huhtinen, Jaakko Mäntylä and Aleksi Huhta. Their efforts were covered by the FiDiPro project of the University of Turku and the Academy of Finland entitled "Multiculturalism as a New Pathway to Incorporation," with Peter Kivisto as the lead scholar. The language editing and commentaries by Helena Halmari were very useful. Finally, our volume in hand also contributed in the founding process of the John Morton Center for North American Studies at the University of Turku.

## NOTES

1. Quite speculative estimates counting all possible descendants with "Finnish blood" arrive even to millions of Finns in North America. Cf. S. C. Olin, *Finlandia: The Racial Composition, the Language, and a Brief History of the Finnish People* (Hancock, Mich.: Book Concern, 1957), 153.

2. A. William Hoglund, *Finnish Immigrants in America* (1960; repr. Salem, N.H.: Ayer, 1992).

3. Timothy L. Smith, "Religion and Ethnicity in America," *The American Historical Review* 83, no. 5 (1978): 1175.

PART 1
# Introduction

# Updating and Rethinking the Finnish American Story

*Jon Saari*

As written history is a collaboration of the living and the dead, it behooves us to examine the essential elements—the actors, the sources, the narrative themes, and the context for the stories—with a sharp eye on the living historians, who after all shape the tale and give it significance. The story told thus far—almost entirely by Finnish North Americans and Finnish nationals—of Finnish–North American history is rich and distinctive, enough to whet the appetite of all kinds of readers; a wider appeal to non-Finns, transcending the smaller and narrower ethnic audience, may yet secure the relevance of this story for the future.

### Actors: The Dead and the Living

The past is stored in archives as well as artifacts and living human memories. And at least for the immigrants of the Great Migration (1880–1924), it is now a story told by the living about the dead. Once most past actors are gone, there is no more back talk, no more in-your-face argument about the meaning of the past. At a Finnish American conference in Duluth, Minnesota, in 1974, young scholars in their thirties could still engage strong personalities, often second-generation Finnish Americans who knew the past directly through lived experience. I recall a conference at Northern Michigan University in the 1970s where Ernie Koski, the *Työmies* (Workers) editor and unrepentant Stalinist, faced off with Raymond Wargelin, a former president of Suomi College and the Suomi Synod. I also befriended Carl Ross, a former Finnish American Communist who did repent and turn his attention to historical studies of labor and women. They are all gone now, leaving traces in writings for us survivors to decipher and reinterpret.

*Finns in the United States: A History of Settlement, Dissent, and Integration* is an updated history of Finnish North America. It culminates the stage of historical writing begun in the 1960s and 1970s, when large numbers of professional historians engaged seriously with the immigrant past. A virtue is that the editor, Auvo Kostiainen, enlisted work from both established scholars and emergent younger voices; a sadness is that the number of scholars is shrinking, both among the old and the new. In its beginnings, this new professional history had active centers in Finland among graduate students at the universities of Turku and Helsinki and among third-generation scholars in the United States. A troika represents the original core of Finnish scholars: Reino Kero, Keijo Virtanen, and Auvo Kostiainen, all from the University of Turku, specializing respectively in emigration demographics and settlement patterns, return migration, and leftist organizations. One other Finnish scholar was later a graduate student at the University of Turku: Hannu Heinilä (cooperative movement). Representing North American scholars are a group of senior researchers (Arnold Alanen, landscape historian; Peter Kivisto, sociologist; and the late Paul George Hummasti, cultural historian), as well as several younger researchers (Gary Kaunonen, labor historian; Erik Hieta, cultural historian). Several Finland-born researchers with extensive North American experience round out the contributors: Johanna Leinonen and Mika Roinila.

As evidenced by their surnames, all of these scholars have some direct personal tie to this Finnish–North American story; even among Finnish nationals, North American family connections are common. All are to a degree insiders via shared ethnicity. But this personal and shared ethnic identification with the story obscures the degree to which they are all outsiders as well. Access to primary materials, both linguistically and culturally, is problematic. Older Finnish scholars have excellent Finnish-language skills, and can learn Finglish and bureaucratic Finnish as well through their research; but they sometimes struggle to convey those skills in idiomatic written or spoken English, and are less conversant with the later nonimmigrant generations. North American scholars, unless they are immigrants or bilingual bicultural members of the second generation, have more aggravated problems researching in Finnish and communicating their results in Finnish. Old Country languages typically are lost in the third generation, and lacking Finnish-language skills, one can do only the most rudimentary research on any aspect of the story before 1940.[1]

When one looks beyond language to cultural experience, the outsider predicament is even more acute. No contemporary scholar, Finnish or North American, can reconstitute the actual immigrant experience, even if they themselves are immigrants of a post–World War II vintage. Historians project their imaginations onto past actors and use present-day theories and ideologies to make sense of things. Let me illustrate the problems with the work of Gary Kaunonen, who wrote on religious activities of the Finnish immigrants for this volume. Kaunonen is a labor historian who wrote an honors thesis on Communist leader Gus Hall in 2002 and thereafter his M.A. thesis and Ph.D. dissertation on the mining conflicts in the Copper Country of Michigan that led to the big strike of 1913. In his *Finns in Michigan*,[2] Kaunonen said he wanted to avoid a whitewashed ethnic history and tell the good, the bad, and the ugly. But when the conceptual framework used is a bottom-up approach appropriate for labor history (class, industrial setting, power relationships, resistance), the resulting perspective on religion can be distorting. In his article in this volume, the Suomi Synod fails at an attempted "power grab" in America, and its "soul saving" is basically a subterfuge. This outsider's perspective is an awkward fit for those who view this history through the eyes of religious faith. Kaunonen often cites Douglas Ollila Jr. in his account. Ollila, an ordained Lutheran pastor, wrote a history of the synod in 1963 in rich detail and nuance, from primary sources in Finnish, and he was often very critical of the Lutheran church from the inside. Kaunonen, as an outsider to this church history, understandably does not match Ollila in his nuance nor sources, but is he a fair-minded critic? When access to primary sources and actual experience is minimal, the storytelling easily tilts toward the ideological or theoretical leanings of the teller, even with a professionally trained historian.

The issue of a "whitewashed ethnic history" points to the historian's responsibility to tell the story whole, not only in a positive light. In the 1910s and 1920s, the felt need to bend the storyline toward positive contributions to the newly adopted countries in North America was born out of intense pressure to assimilate and be good citizens. In reaction to the Mongolian descent issue, to popular images of bar fighting and knife wielding, and to the prominent role of Finnish Americans in the radical labor movement from 1900 into the 1930s, some Finnish American writers produced works that emphasized the positive contributions of the ethnic group to American life. Assimilation was swift, they argued, and troublemakers few. By the 1950s this "fileo-pietistic view," as it was later derogatorily labeled, dominated, and the leftist tradition had been eclipsed from history. It returned with a vengeance in the 1970s, however, as the Red Finns were rediscovered by the third generation, led by Michael Karni, among others. In an ironic twist, the positive contributions of Finnish Americans to American labor history were touted. The story was rebalanced, but the contribution-to-American-life framework only slowly receded. The *commemoration* of past actors and actions—nurtured by a sense of belonging personally to this story—was still a strongly felt need by third-generation Finnish American historians, less by Finnish historians.

### Sources: The Saved, the Lost, the Untapped

Without external sources there can be no history except what is dredged out of our own unreliable memories. These external sources are principally two types: documents and artifacts. The ravages of time and weather must be held at bay: paper ages, log buildings collapse, letters are tossed, monuments wear away, rag rugs are recycled to the sauna. Timely maintenance and selective preservation are in order. Professional and amateur historians have assumed this responsibility over the last sixty years; the essential record of documents and artifacts is there for the viewing, and is increasingly more accessible over the internet.

In his historiographical essay, Auvo Kostiainen has ably documented when preservation became a sustained effort, starting with the Minnesota Finnish American Historical Society and its twenty branches in 1945–50. *History of the Finns in Minnesota*[3], compiled by a Finnish journalist in Finnish, followed in 1957; *Michiganin Suomalaisten Historia*[4], also in Finnish, appeared a decade later, and was written by the archivist at Suomi College. The college created the first archive of Finnish American records and artifacts in 1932, but they were properly maintained only after the establishment of the Finnish American Heritage Center at what later became Finlandia University. By then the Immigration History Research Center (IHRC) at the University of Minnesota had become an important repository for twentieth-century Finnish American materials, with the help of research assistants Michael Karni and Timo Riippa.

In Finland, research into migration history got its start in the Department of General History at the University of Turku. A strong materials acquisition program, focusing on letters sent home from North America as well as genealogical information from steamship records and official documents, provided the foundation for this research. Finnish ministries actively participated in funding these efforts. From these seeds emerged in 1974 the Institute of Migration in Turku, an independent institution designed to document and publish research on worldwide migration-related issues, but particularly on the Finnish diaspora.

Motivated individuals were important to all these early efforts. John I. Kolehmainen did pioneering bibliographical work in the 1940s at Suomi College, and donated his extensive Finnish book collection to Northern Michigan University in the 1970s. A. William Hoglund, whose 1960 narrative history set important themes for the Finnish American story (1880–1920), was a tireless collector of books, pamphlets, plays, and newspapers from the immigrant generation during the 1970s and 1980s. He promoted the microfilming of perishable print sources and stressed collaboration among the collection-builders in Turku, Minneapolis, and Hancock, Michigan. He donated his own massive collection to the IHRC several years before his death in 2008. Vilho Niitemaa, in Turku, corralled promising Ph.D. graduate students in the 1970s and enlisted them to research the largely untold story of the Finnish emigrants in a world diaspora, whose most significant destination outside Europe was North America. These graduate students, among them Reino Kero, Keijo Virtanen, and Auvo Kostiainen, in turn, as professors in their own right, have overseen seventy-two M.A. theses (sixty-four on the history of Finns in the United States) and nine doctoral dissertations. An extensive and ongoing collection of books and articles, many of them untranslated, continues to be generated in Finland on migration history.

The preserved primary historical record, including the interpretive books built upon it, is large enough to tell the Finnish American story well, with detail and nuance. In this volume, many types of sources are used, from fictional accounts to oral interviews, from newspapers to census data, from organizational records to photographs. But one must ask if this volume is the final hurrah for a generation that has created a new professional history for Finnish America. Will the successor scholars, future readers, and funding patrons be there for this story to continue to be told and retold in North America? While this volume is an important achievement, years in the making, the prospects for the future are worrisome. A personal note from a regional university in an old settlement area illustrates the problem. I taught history at Northern Michigan University (NMU) in Marquette for thirty-four years and developed a course called The Finnish Immigrant in America. The course was eliminated after my retirement in 2005, and replaced by a general immigration history course. The situation is similar with two NMU colleagues—the sociologist and filmmaker Michael Loukinen and the mathematician and music patron John Kiltinen: few if any successors with an interest in Finnish America. Together over the past forty years we three, among others in the community, have been catalysts for much Finnish American activity, including two large Marquette FinnFests in 1996 and 2005. If these trends are widespread, what do they portend for the future?

### Narratives: The Separation of Finnish and Finnish–North American History

A history is not a chronology of events, not a scrapbook of activities, nor an encyclopedia of everything known about a subject. It is a mind creating patterns of meaning out of surviving sources from the past. These patterns of meaning over time tend to reflect deep and intractable predicaments that constrained all the past actors, and it is the historian's task to find those predicaments and to make them the heart of the storyline. In United States immigration history, the predicaments during the Great Migration focused on the uprooting of individual immigrants and their subsequent conflicted feelings about the old and new countries; on the creation of organizations that would serve their felt needs as well as meet the pressures and constraints of the new land and society; and upon the inevitable adaptations caused by children and grandchildren within the ethnic community through generational succession and the absence of new immigrants in large numbers after 1924.

Fundamental to this perspective is that there were no Finnish clones in North America. From the beginning there were two histories in the making: Finnish history on the margins of northern Europe, and Finnish American history in the settlement areas of North America. There were of course interconnections, comings and goings, and as Peter Kivisto demonstrates, even *transnational communities* in some aspects of Finnish American religious and industrial life where the two histories were joined temporarily together. I would argue that hybridization, however, was continuous because immigrants could not avoid strangers in an unfamiliar new world. They knew those of other tongues up close—suspicious officials, contemptuous mine bosses, other foreigners in their multiethnic communities—who made claims on their daily reality. They were inventive in creating their own institutions, finding and using spaces in an open society to serve their own ends and needs as workers, believers, consumers, readers. They created a new language of Finglish alongside the language of the Old Country. They watched their descendants quickly turn into partial strangers.

Johanna Leinonen minimizes these adjustments in drawing a portrait of early twentieth-century family life. Then, it is true, most ties that defined Finnish immigrants passed through ethnicity: national origin in Finland, Finnish spouses (84.3 percent), Finnish American institutions, Finnish friends and neighbors, and above all the medium of the Finnish language. But they were still hybrids, not clones, and with succeeding generations fewer and fewer ties passed through ethnicity. By the 1940s, the ethnic community was a shadow of its former self. The children and the grandchildren of the immigrants were moving into the American mainstream, both in terms of geographical mobility and occupational choice. For the third-generation descendants and beyond, ethnicity has become a dispensable aspect of identity characterized by elective, chosen behavior: learning or relearning the Finnish language, traveling to and reading about Finland, joining a Finnish American organization, writing or teaching about the Finnish American past, sending children to language camp, building a sauna in the basement. And the great majority of Norman Westerberg's one million "missing Finns," who have vanished according to projections in the census data, have opted out of Finnishness. It may be in their genetic makeup, but they do not care to self-identify as Finnish Americans. As Mika Roinila says in his concluding chapter, with understatement, the "missing Finns" present a formidable research problem.

Not so the Finnish Americans Leinonen interviewed to compose her portrait of early twenty-first-century family life. Her sample, however, is not drawn from descendants but from Finland-born migrants who moved to the United States since 1970 for work, study, and/or marriage. Highly mobile, cosmopolitan professionals, they could not be more different than the immigrants of the Great Migration. They are self-consciously hybrids who pick and choose their beliefs and lifestyle from both Finnish and American offerings. They chose to have little to do with Finnish American descendants, whom they find old-fashioned, but have formed their own support circles, music groups, and *suomi koulu* (schools). It is more accurate to call them transnational individuals, for they retain significant ties to Finland, often having a second home there as well as dual citizenship. They have not been pressured to become Americans, but have been able to shape their own identities in a globalizing world.

What is not yet fully appreciated is the extent to which this group of new immigrants is slowly supplanting descendants as the activist leaders within Finnish America. The 2011 FinnFest in San Diego was the first one run entirely by Finland-born "expatriates" or transnationals; its program had a very strong emphasis on introducing contemporary Finland, especially its innovations in education and technology, to American audiences. And in 2010 ten of the eighteen members of the Finlandia Foundation National

(FFN) board were Finland-born, making it evident that future programs will be negotiated between the two groups.[5] One striking feature of the Finland-born new immigrants is an ignorance, sometimes willful, of the earlier history of Finnish America. The wackiness of invented traditions such as St. Urho's Day is off-putting, and they don't see much authenticity in Finnishness without the Finnish language. Yet some finally "get it" that Finnishness in the descendant tradition is simply different. One Finland-born FFN board member had such a moment of revelation at a small rural cemetery in northern Minnesota, where rows upon rows of Finnish names testified to the thousands of her countrymen and women who had devoted their lives to survival on the harsh midwestern cutover lands.

In his finely crafted essay "Finnish Identity in Immigrant Culture," Keijo Virtanen offers some help in sorting out Finnishness in different generations and eras. He illustrates how schools, theater and music groups, and sports associations thrived during the immigrant era (1895–1930); a sense of Finnish national culture was kept alive through the Finnish language as well as through traveling Finnish playwrights, musicians, composers, and athletes. Thereafter groups needed to find pathways into the social reality of North America to survive; above all they had to address the English-speaking preferences and recreational and vocational needs of the immigrants' children and grandchildren. Activities dependent upon language, such as in the Finnish theater, faded faster than those in music and sports. For Virtanen, *liveliness* counted in sustaining Finnish culture, not ideology; temperance and labor halls as well as co-ops and church congregations all exhibited such liveliness during the immigrant era, and to varying degrees thereafter. For our own contemporary scene, liveliness is also perhaps a better standard than authenticity. Who is to say whether a support circle of Finland-born transnationals exhibits more Finnishness than a descendant-organized FinnFest in the Copper Country of Michigan, a St. Urho festival in Minnesota, or a kantele orchestra performing in San Diego?

Many complain that the pool of cultural images about Finnishness is becoming ever more shallow and simplified, where even *sisu* (gutsy persistence), sauna, and Sibelius seem like overreaching when projected into the Nth generation. Ethnic heritage inevitably becomes weaker in a land where all eventually become hybrids, fractional men and women, with identities spread across a whole range of partial selves. The post–World War II new immigrants/transnationals/expatriates will not be spared this reality with their own descendants. Is this a sad outcome? From the point of view of those who have chosen to be ethnically Finnish Americans, yes: a source of rich meaning has been lost. But from the point of view of the "lost ones," a cautious judgment is in order; they may have found other sources of meaning, in gender, in work, in the arts, in causes and in nature, in travel and in study, and even in other ethnic traditions and languages. Ethnic affirmers have for too long thought of identity as something rooted in an ancestral plot; yet identity forming in today's world is an inventive process marked by an unprecedented mixing of traditions and by an explosion of mobility through electronic communications, tourism, internal migration, and movements across borders. There are few places left—perhaps the western Upper Peninsula of Michigan?—where a self-identified ethnic insider can withdraw into an ethnic nest, let alone an ethnic fortress. For Finnish Americans, a lively four-day national FinnFest or a regional festival must suffice, and who can say for how long.

## Context: Assimilation and Integration in North America, Ethnic Cleansing in Europe

If the assimilation and integration of the descendants of Finnish immigrants proceeded inevitably in North America, the assimilation of ethnic minorities has not been an inevitable pattern elsewhere, particularly in Central and Eastern Europe in the twentieth century. Broader comparisons help us see the implied assumptions within the narrative story, which often go undetected. What was peculiar about North America? What was unusual about Finnish Americans? The story starts with racial classification.

The Finns, Peter Kivisto noted, were the only European-origin group denied naturalization in the United States on the grounds that they were of Mongolian race. Kivisto has a long record of turning nuggets of the Finnish American experience into larger meanings, starting with book-length studies of the socialist, Industrial Workers of the World (IWW), and Communist Finns; then the concept of generational succession; and in this volume, the ideas of transnational communities and race. From 1790 to 1952, naturalization in the United States was limited to free white males (with blacks added after 1870), so groups whose origins were racially clouded had to win their whiteness in court. A 1908 case of eighteen striking Finnish miners on the Mesabi range, who were to be deported on racial grounds, was overturned on appeal, with the argument that the Finns had been uplifted to whiteness through intermarriage and racial mixing and should not therefore be deported as Asiatics (Chinese had been the first group to be excluded entirely in 1882). Finns in America thus became white Europeans and the beneficiaries of white privilege, which eased their assimilation and integration.

Finland, as a borderland area in northern Europe, followed a long circuitous route before it was integrated into the European Union in 1995 as a modern Nordic nation. Centuries-long associations with Sweden and Russia in subordinate relationships led to a vigorous late nineteenth-century national awakening, unconfused by Finno-Ugric linguistic origins or Finland's reputation as a primitive northern forest folk. With its small and relatively homogeneous population, Finland secured its nationhood in 1917, despite a class-based civil war, and held its independence through World War II, despite bruising wars from the Soviet Union that cost the country dearly in casualties, territory, and refugees. Finland was nonetheless spared the fate of the countries of Central and Eastern Europe in a century marked by brutal ethnic cleansing. The ethnic patchwork of that region was mismatched with its political structures. With the collapse of the multicultural dynastic empires in Turkey and Austro-Hungary after World War I, politicians advocated the ideal of the homogeneous nation-state: one people, one country. The new ruthless empire-states of the USSR in Russia and the Third Reich in Germany turned the borderlands between them into killing fields of the worst type. Based on hierarchical theories of race and class, whole populations were segregated in ghettos and camps, deported en masse, and subjected to pogroms and persecution. The "final solution" in the Third Reich witnessed the extermination of "undesirable" people and groups, without regard to prior levels of assimilation and integration.

Some of the same dynamics existed in the United States during the Great Migration for American Indians and blacks, the former having been segregated on reservations and the latter subordinated under Jim Crow laws in the South. The Finns, like the Irish, were subjected to prejudice, but it never rose to the level of legal discrimination (except under the immigration quotas from 1924 to 1965). Labor activists were sometimes run out of town, and one was even hanged in Duluth in 1918, but Finns as an ethnic group were never targets for systematic lynching and vigilante action. Deportations, probably less than 200 Finns, occurred within the law and were applied to all ethnic groups.

Certain conditions marked the United States as a non-Europe. As a settler society, where everyone came from elsewhere (except Native Americans), there could be no exclusive claims as in Europe to an ethnic homeland. As a land of immigrants, the United States understood itself as a multicultural society within a constitutional framework of law and guaranteed civil liberties. The immigration cutoff in 1924 had the effect of accelerating the assimilation of different peoples through generational succession, intermarriage, and the predominance of the English language, at a time when Europe was descending into a killing field. A democratic Europe since the fall of the Iron Curtain in 1989 is trying to achieve something similar to the United States but even more difficult: a transnational European Union with twenty-seven newly linked nations, each now more or less homogeneous within fixed borders. The 1990s war in the former Yugoslavia may or may not have been the last of the ethnic killing fields; many issues of peaceful assimilation and integration remain in Europe, as they do in the United States.

If the Finnish American story is an illuminating foil for understanding the broader context of race and integration in the United States, this is only one of many ways in which this story may prove interesting to non-Finnish Americans in North America. The Red Finn story has attracted the interest of labor historians since the 1970s, most recently in the award-winning book by Gary Kaunonen on the background of the 1913 Copper Country strike, entitled *Challenge Accepted: A Finnish Immigrant Response to Industrial America in Michigan's Copper Country*.[6] The broader story is one of the rare instances in American history of a radical political culture with deep grassroots support in rural America built around Finn halls and co-op stores; it faded in the 1930s, but its activism, in concert with other groups, helped (in the phrase of labor historian David Montgomery) "to re-channel the American political mainstream through the New Deal."[7] Another bridge to non-Finns is the vernacular log architecture of the Upper Midwest, perhaps the richest legacy of a historic rural landscape in the country. Not just individual buildings have been preserved, but in some cases whole farmsteads (Hanka Finnish Homestead Museum near Arnheim in Michigan's Upper Peninsula) and even whole townships (Embarrass, Minnesota). Landscape historian Arnold Alanen has documented this historic Finnish American landscape in numerous articles spanning the entire range of Finnish settlements in the United States and Canada.[6]

The vitality among third-generation Finnish Americans, expressed through the annual national FinnFests since 1983, is itself a significant bridge to non-Finns. The festivals encapsulate Finnish American history with its intense interest in learning, whether from the Bible, Karl Marx, or the *Kalevala* (national epic); its hall culture of socializing and coffee drinking; its cultural interest in the performing arts and athletics; and its interest in maintaining ties with Finland. As an example, consider the fourteenth festival, held in Marquette, Michigan, in 1996. Three years in the making, it drew 6,500 registrants to five days of activities that included a medical conference on health and ethnicity; a parade down main street; 140 lectures, workshops, and panels; an integrated arts program with over 100 artists at thirteen sites; three plays, many musical performances, and two nightly dances; the world's largest sauna, heated by aircraft engines in a tent; athletic events; and various creative collaborations between Finns from Finland and Finnish Americans.[9] The small city of Marquette was taken over for a week, its residents invited into the festival by over a thousand blue-and-white painted chairs lining the venues to the events. Who wouldn't be interested in being a Finn for a day?

Although FinnFests continue to be held annually, one of them in 2009 on a cruise ship to Alaska, the vitality may fade with the passing of the third generation. But this passing should be more an occasion for reflection than mourning. The New Ethnicity (1970–2010) has already left its mark on history for Finnish America, and it is perhaps time to move past ethnicity toward a more inclusive identity. At least in America, ethnicity is a way station to other dreams, not a final destination. Two signs awaken in me this sense of closure: the publication of the anthology *Finnish–North American Literature in English: A Concise Anthology*,[10] and the newly initiated proposal for a Museum of the American People.

This unusual anthology is the work of editor Beth Virtanen, with a preface by Börje Vähämäki. It features twenty American and Canadian writers, all of whom have published at least two substantive works of fiction or poetry, and all of whom express a sense of Finnishness in their writings, either explicitly or implicitly. Although the oldest was born in 1915 (Emil Petaja) and the youngest in 1962, it is significant that all but the works of Petaja were published in the 1970s, 1980s, and 1990s during the period of the New Ethnicity. The support network of FinnFests, FinnForums, publishing outlets and journals, and writers groups seems to have been more important than what generation the writers came from. Seventeen of the twenty were second (three) or third generation (eleven) or in-between (three). All had higher education; at least five came out of interethnic mixed families; and at least ten had mixed marriages themselves. If such an anthology is compiled again in twenty years, with new writers and equally concise, it is likely that the book will be much thinner. The support structures of the New Ethnicity will be weaker, the Finnishness even more attenuated. The best of these writers will have merged into North American literature, without any justification to add "Finnish."

The new museum near the Mall in Washington, D.C., is in the planning stages, looking for congressional support for a presidential commission. No taxpayer dollars will be used for the commission or the museum, and promoters are gathering bipartisan support. The idea is to take all the ethnic and national groups that helped form what is now the United States and create a museum where historians can tell individual group stories as well as the collective national story of immigration.[11] In a land where many have claimed that immigration *is* our history, it is an idea long overdue. So how will the Finnish ethnicity fare in such a museum? Quite well, I would argue. Finnish immigrants were there at the beginning in colonial times in New Sweden (1638–55); although Finland was then part of Sweden, Finnish Americans in 1938 for the tercentenary succeeded in having Finland recognized as a "founding nation" along with Sweden. During the Great Migration, Finnish immigrants created a vibrant hall culture and fought for a place of dignity in industrial America, often as dissenters. Descendants after 1924 experienced both the assimilation of the melting pot, as the second generation merged with American life, and the multicultural integration of the salad bowl during the third-generation-led New Ethnicity. They also laid the basis for telling their own history, and making it relevant to other Americans. It is after all an ethnic story worth telling, and yes, commemorating.

### NOTES

1. I am a third-generation Finnish American, trained as a China historian, and I never acquired spoken or written Finnish-language skills. My writing in Finnish studies has been limited to historiography (the study of what and how others have written) and to the history of the Finlandia Foundation National (FFN) (Jon L. Saari, *Black Ties and Miners' Boots: Inventing Finnish-American Philanthropy—A History of Finlandia Foundation National 1953–2010* [Pasadena, Calif.: Finlandia Foundation National, 2010]). The foundation was an important organization created by immigrants

and second-generation Finnish Americans in 1953; ninety-five percent of its records are in English. I have been an FFN board member since 1999.
2. Gary Kaunonen, *Finns in Michigan* (East Lansing: Michigan State University Press, 2009).
3. Hans R. Wasastjerna, *History of the Finns in Minnesota,* ed. and trans. Toivo Rosvall (Duluth, Minnesota: Minnesota Finnish-American Historical Society, 1957).
4. Armas K. E. Holmio, *Michiganin suomalaisten historia* (Hancock, Michigan: Michiganin Suomalaisten Historia-Seura, 1967); English translation by Ellen M. Ryynänen. *History of the Finns in Michigan.* Detroit: Wayne State University, 2001.
5. Saari, *Black Ties and Miners' Boots,* 117–27.
6. Gary Kaunonen, *Challenge Accepted: A Finnish Immigrant Response to Industrial America in Michigan's Copper Country* (East Lansing: Michigan State University Press, 2010).
7. Montgomery was a labor historian at Yale. He was a keynote speaker at FinnForum IV held in Minneapolis in 1991, when this comment was made.
8. A recent example of Alanen's work is "Little Houses on the Prairie: Continuity and Change in the Finnish Vernacular Architecture and Landscapes of Canada," in Pauliina Raento, ed., *Finnishness in Finland and North America: Constituents, Changes, and Challenges* (Toronto: Aspasia Books, 2005), a special issue of *the Journal of Finnish Studies* 9, no. 2 (December 2005). Alanen was also the Third Finlandia Foundation Lecturer of the Year in 2009; he traveled throughout the United States lecturing on how and why the immigrants' ideas of landscape and buildings changed once they landed in North America.
9. Program booklet, FinnFest USA 1996. I was chair of the Cultural Programs Committee for this FinnFest in Marquette.
10. Beth L. Virtanen, ed., *Finnish–North American Literature in English: A Concise Anthology* (Lewiston, N.Y.: Edwin Mellen Press, 2009).
11. Information on the museum can be gathered at the following website: www.nmap2015.com. The periodization of the story envisions four chapters: I. The First Peoples Come, Prehistory to 1607; II. The Nation Takes Form, 1607–1820; III. The Great In-gathering, 1820–1924; and IV. And Still They Come, 1924–present. Finlandia Foundation National is thus far the only organization representing Finnish Americans on this national project.

# Interest in the History of Finnish Americans

*Auvo Kostiainen*

Historical interest in Finnish immigration to the United States may be divided into a few phases. First, in the early twentieth century the Finnish American past was examined through the genre of travel descriptions. Then, from the 1910s to the 1940s followed a period of historical interest that was characterized by strong national romantic overtones and an emphasis on the role of Finns in America. The Finnish American past was examined as a showcase for the achievements of Finns in North America. Justifications for their presence there were also sought. The next period consists of the two decades after World War II, during which historical interest often took the form of commemorating. The 1960s witnessed a strong recovery of historical interest in Finnish Americans, combined with the creation of new ethnic history in the entire Western world.

### National-Romantic Histories Prior to World War II

Early writing about Finnish American history included reporting, the purpose of which was to explain the heavy emigration to America.[1] At this time in Finland there was a lot of interest in emigration in general and, more specifically, interest in the emigrated Finns who now lived in North America. A number of accounts or travel descriptions were printed, but not anything that could be called modern historical writing. One of the first major commentaries of the Finnish emigrants in the United States was composed by the well-known Finnish writer and newspaperman Akseli Järnefelt, who described Finns in America in 1898.[2] It was based on his extensive travel in "Finnish" locations in North America. Järnefelt described the living conditions, work, and everyday life of the immigrant Finns. However, Järnefelt did not attempt any scholarly analysis; his work was descriptive. During later decades, and even in the beginning of the twentieth century, a number of similar descriptions appeared in Finland and received a large readership. One of the best known is the travel book of columnist and folklore analyst Sakari Pälsi. Published in 1926 with the title *Suuri, kaunis ja ruma maa* (The Great, Beautiful and Ugly Country),[3] it describes a journey across the continent on the Canadian side of the border. Also, a number of short stories were published in newspapers and various journals.

In the United States, one of the influential commentaries on immigration questions was the U.S. Immigration Commission, or Dillingham Commission, report from 1910,[4] in which the nature of incoming migrants was presented. Particular attention was at that time directed to the racial and linguistic features of the newcomers. As examined later in this volume, the "scientific racist" issues came to the fore and entered everyday discussions. As an example, there was a long-lasting debate on the possible Asiatic—and therefore undesirable—origin of the Finns.

The switch of focus toward the Finns' role in North America and its impact was mainly the result of the changing sociopolitical environment. During the second and third decades of the twentieth century, the U.S. domestic and foreign policy questions also had an influence on the interest and debate on the Finns in America. Main reasons included the participation of the United States in World War I, the reflections of the Russian Revolution in 1917, and the consequent limitations of immigration to the United States in 1921 and 1924, which strongly affected the number of Finns who could migrate to the United States. During preceding years, there had ensued heavy pressure towards particularly "new immigrants" including Southern and Eastern Europeans along with the Finns. Therefore, the quest for Americanization and assimilation often entered the discussions. The validity of immigrant groups and their status and role in the country were questioned.

On the other hand, new problems and debates arose regarding the historical status of the Finns in America. Were the Finns actually one of the founding nations of the United States? Also, the Finnish Americans were able to make use of Finland's reputation as the sole country of World War I period which had paid its debts to the United States. Finally, Finnish Americans adopted the image of the defender of democratic values in their fight against the aggression of the Soviet Union during the Winter War. These three factors were positive from the point of view of the Finnish American self-esteem and their image in the eyes of the others.

In the wake of trying to improve the reputation of Finnish Americans, Clemence Niemi followed the effort to establish the good reputation of Finnish Americans in the United States, as a response to the notoriety of so-called radical Finns. Apparently a geographer by education, Niemi made a 43 page study on the Houghton County, Michigan, which was a strong concentration of Finnish ethnic group in the Midwest. Niemi argued that in general, the Americanization process advanced well among the Finns, and they were raw material for good Americans. Finns were by no means troublemakers. They had preserved some of their traditions, but these traditions were vanishing gradually. This apparently referred to the hall activities, which will be discussed later. According to Niemi, the Finns' amalgamation and assimilation processes were so swift that Finns would not present any conflicting racial problem in the future.[5]

A Finnish American religious leader, John Wargelin, was very interested in the status of Finns in the United States. His book titled *The Americanization of the Finns* came out in 1924. The book was actually a commentary on the pressure toward the Finns as an ethnic group. He argued that despite some radical Finns, the majority of Finns were good people, although they had "some Mongol heritage." They were hard-working people and provided good material for American society.[6]

Another commentary on the role of Finnish Americans came from E. A. Louhi, who was not a historian either. His book on the colonial U.S. history and the New Sweden colony aimed at showing that the Finns were one of the real founding nations of the United States, actually because they made up a majority of the white population in the colony.[7] Louhi's book was naturally important for the self-respect and identity of Finns in America, although it was quite heavily nationally romanticized.

Another Finnish Lutheran priest in the United States, Salomon Ilmonen, had a great impact on historical visions of Finns in America. He may be called a "data collector" whose interest was directed to Finnish American history as a whole, but also to the Delaware colonial period and especially to John Morton, the signer of the U.S. Declaration of Independence in 1776. Some of Ilmonen's books were printed even in Finland, and the short John Morton biography was printed both in Finnish and in English.[8]

A new kind of effort was undertaken by F. J. Syrjälä, a newspaperman and the editor of the *Raivaaja*, a Finnish American socialist daily established in 1905 in Fitchburg, Massachusetts. Like many socialist leaders, he was interested in the history of the Finnish American labor force and its efforts to organize American industrial society, as well as to establish itself in that society. He wrote a history of the Finnish American labor movement in 1925. This history served as a leftist interpretation of the Finnish migration history to America as well as an account of the lives of Finnish immigrants in the United States.[9]

During the years between World War I and World War II, academic commentators started to write about Finnish American topics. The first professional historian of Finnish American ancestry at Columbia University, John H. Wuorinen wrote studies about Delaware, Finland, and Scandinavia.[10] John Syrjamaki, another researcher of Finnish background, published in 1940 his study of the Mesabi mining communities in the northern Minnesota iron range. It was mainly an analysis of the population and labor relations in the region, apparently a pioneering scholarly effort of its kind.[11] A geography professor, Eugene van Cleef from Ohio State University—not of Finnish ancestry, however—became interested in the Finns and Finland. He published several minor studies on the Finnish American population in Ohio and Minnesota and on the West Coast in the 1920s and the 1930s. Van Cleef also published a large volume on Finland in 1929.[12] In 1937, a second-generation Finn, John I. Kolehmainen (1910–95), earned his doctorate from Western Reserve University in Cleveland with his study "A History of the Finns in the Western Reserve." As later discussed, he became a prominent figure among Finnish American historians during the post–World War II decades.

Historians of Finnish ancestry became involved in a kind of "history war" or "tug of war" on the interpretations over the Delaware colony's tercentenary celebration in 1938, which took the form of discovering the Finnish American role in the history of the United States. This, in fact, turned into a competition between Finns and Swedes about who the real settlers were and from where they came. Who were the people of the New Sweden colony, and from where did they come? In addition to laypeople, many historians mentioned above commented on the 1938 Delaware New Sweden tercentenary celebrations; particularly Wuorinen and Ilmonen had leading roles.[13] The efforts of Finnish Americans were successful, and the Finns were officially recognized as a "founding nation" in the United States.[14]

### Commemorating the Finnish Experience—1940–1960

Remembering the Finnish experience during the two decades following World War II forms the next phase of historiography. The role of the older immigrant generation in the past was an interesting topic, and a variety of interpretations were created. This period was also characterized by the production of a number of so-called state histories of Finns in America. A generational change occurred with the decrease of migration from Finland because of the immigration laws in 1921 and 1924. Both academic writers and amateurs were involved in these debates.

There was preserved interest in Finnish American developments both in Finland and the United States. The scholarly interest in Finland actually increased in the 1960s. However, semischolarly interest was seen, for example, in the activities of Suomi Seura (Finland Society). Rafael Engelberg was the executive leader of this society from 1934 to 1959 and was intent on increasing cooperation between Finns abroad and in Finland. He compiled a massive volume in 1944 titled *Suomi ja Amerikan suomalaiset*.[15] Actually it was a collection of information from a large number of immigrant settlements around the continent, somewhat in the vein with Ilmonen's numerous volumes mentioned earlier.

Many significant developments occurred among amateur historians who promoted interest in Finnish American ethnicity and heritage. Finnish American historical societies were founded. The Finnish-American Historical Society (FAHS) was founded on March 15, 1920, apparently in New York City. Its chair was K. Aaltio, consul of Finland, and its vice-chair was the journalist Kalle Potti. The board members were also well known within the immigrant community: Salomon Ilmonen, John Wargelin, Antero Riippa, K. Arminen, and J. Lempiö. Ilmonen was a member of the nationwide American Historical Society.[16] The founders of the FAHS may be characterized as assimilationists and conservatives.

The FAHS was in contact with Finland's Historical Society (Suomen Historiallinen Seura), which was chaired by history professor Lehtonen. It seems that at the time the FAHS tried to achieve a firmer professional status. However, the society gradually became inactive. The rebirth of historical interest occurred during the preparations for the Delaware New Sweden colony tercentenary celebrations in 1936–38. At that time, the Delaware Tercentenary Committee was founded. Its goal was to coordinate the Finnish American efforts for commemoration of the colony.[17]

"State histories" of Finnish Americans were compiled. *The History of the Finns in Minnesota* came out in 1957 under the editorship of Hans R. Wasastjerna, at that time a young historian from Finland. The history was published both in English and in Finnish. Another important state history book was compiled in Hancock, Michigan, by the Reverend Armas K. E. Holmio in 1967.[18] Its English-language edition did not come out before the year 2001. Similar histories have been compiled on the Finns in the greater New York area[19] and on the Finns in Ohio and Pennsylvania.[20] Smaller historical accounts have been published as well, for instance in the Pacific Northwest region and in Canada. Accounts on special organizations such as many religious, cooperative, and temperance leagues have also appeared.

A number of local historical societies were founded. The creation and life span of Finnish American historical societies are somewhat unclear, although a few still exist. The Minnesota Finnish-American Historical Society (MFAHS), chaired by well-known Duluth, Minnesota, businessman Alex Kyyhkynen, was established in the summer of 1943. It seems that the founding of the society was inspired by Juho Rissanen's painting on Finnish pioneers in Minnesota, which he was asked to paint while on vacation in Minnesota. It was finished and presented to the Minnesota Historical Society with great ceremonies on October 16, 1944.[21] The MFAHS functioned and was supervised under the auspices of the Minnesota Historical Society and gained respectability in that way.

As an example of what happened in the localities in the Finnish American regions, we may examine the spreading of the MFAHS branches. It seems that more than twenty historical associations were founded in the state. Chaired by Alex Kyyhkynen, the original chapter was founded in Duluth, which remained the main seat of the MFAHS from 1943 until the present. Chapters were established in major Finnish settlements in rural and urban surroundings.[22] The greatest activity of founding the associations took place during the late 1940s and early 1950s. The reasons behind the founding of these associations may be varied. The activity may be due to the existence of a group of history-enthusiasts of Finnish extraction. Inspiration from the Delaware tercentenary could have been another factor. Additionally, a certain kind of Finnish unity and sense of community created by the Winter War as well as the extensive efforts to help Finland during and after the Second World War may have caused the desire to create historical associations as a cultural network.

In 1949, the MFAHS participated in the centennial celebrations of the declaration of Minnesota as a U.S. territory (Minnesota Centennial).[23] The governor of Minnesota gave a proclamation, declaring August 28, 1949, to be Finnish Day. The ceremonial speech by Alex Kyyhkynen referred to the 300 years of Finnish history in America and the signer of the Declaration of Independence in 1776, John Morton. Considering the great ideological splits in this ethnic group, it is important to note that the MFAHS was meant to be a forum for "all the Finnish Americans"; maybe even left radical Communists were involved.[24] Another strongly "Finnish" state was Michigan, with even a larger number of people of Finnish descent than Minnesota. In Michigan, the historical interest on the pioneer generation was rising about the same time as it was in Minnesota. The preparation of the state history book, however, took ten years longer.

Many organizational histories for churches, workers' societies, and cooperative associations were published after World War II. For example, the former editor of the *Raivaaja* (Pioneer), Elis Sulkanen, and his newspaper company published in 1951 an extensive history book of the Finnish labor movement in America.[25] Sulkanen was a former newspaperman and leftist who had been expelled from the Communist circles.

Statues were erected in many locations to commemorate the Finnish heritage of a certain community, and their total number may be about fifty. An example is found in Cokato, Minnesota, where the Pioneer Memorial was erected by the Cokato Finnish-American Historical Society on July 24, 1949. This statue states that the first Finnish settlers arrived to the location as early as 1865.[26] Another example may be mentioned from Hibbing, Minnesota, which was one of the largest mining centers in the Mesabi Iron Range. The Hibbing Cooperative Club appointed a committee in 1939, which started the campaign for the collection of historical records. An MFAHS chapter was established in 1947, and in 1949 it had 65 members. A massive eight-ton granite monument for the Finnish pioneers in the Hibbing area in 1892 was erected in 1957.[27]

Finlandia Foundation was established in 1953 in California as a new type of organization, whose aim was to offer philanthropic help for Finnish American endeavours. Its aim was also to be a kind of informal arm of Finnish foreign policy, "a friendship society of educated American Fennophiles," who could have a positive impact on the image of Finland in the country. According to professor Jon L. Saari, the politically neutral Finlandia Foundation also wanted to represent the Finnish American audience at large, not any specific sub-group. The Finlandia Foundation also wanted to address the decline in the number of Finnish American communities. Thus it continued the tradition that was born in the Help Finland efforts of the World War II period.[28] This kind of cooperation of various interest groups in the Finnish American community had been established around the 1938 Delaware celebrations, and also during the process of commemorating the heritage of Finnish immigrants in America as seen in the Minnesota Finnish American historical societies.

## New Ethnicity Discovered and Researched—1960s to the Present

An ethnic history boom in North America started from circa 1960 and still continues, although there have been many ups and downs. This interest has resulted in a number of new studies, and a whole generation of historians interested in migration and ethnic histories has emerged in North America as well as in Finland. Recent trends in historical studies such as multidisciplinary approaches and the analysis of the features of postmodern society have been reflected in historical writing as well. One typical feature throughout the decades has been the involvement of both academic and amateur historians.

These developments mirrored the turmoil in the American and Western societies. Especially in the 1960s new trends emerged in many countries: a growing interest in the history of ethnic groups in general and discussion on multiculturalism and its earlier versions such as cultural pluralism. This was all a part of a general ethnic history boom taking place in many European countries. The issues on the melting or nonmelting pots became quite heated, especially after significant studies such as Nathan Glazer and Daniel P. Moynihan's book *Beyond the Melting Pot* in 1970, which discussed issues in New York City,[29] as well as studies that investigated the past of ethnic groups such as South Slavs and many others.

A similar growing interest was seen among the writers interested in the history of Finns in America. It may be true that the interest in the Finnish American past flourished particularly strongly in relative terms when considering the numbers of Finnish Americans in the United States and Canada. These interesting histories are reflected in the contents of the following chapters of this volume.

The interest in the Finnish American past exploded in the 1960s, and it was also reflected in the academic community in Finland. As a whole, this was a period of the most productive historical writing on the Finns in North America as well as their exodus from Finland. It seems that the most extensive wave of research interest on Finnish Americans appeared especially during the 1970s and 1980s. Many groundbreaking research findings were published.

There were events that attracted special attention of a number of historians both in the United States and in Finland. The first one of these was the Bicentennial of the United States in 1976. The volume called *Old Friends—Strong Ties* came out in 1976.[30] It was a Finnish government-supported volume to honor the 200 years of independence of the United States, including official greetings from President Urho Kekkonen. A collaborative effort of Finnish and Finnish American researchers, cultural activists, and even some politicians who had an interest in history writing and enlarging archival collections at the time, the volume in turn involved rising scholars such as Reino Kero and Auvo Kostiainen. It was also interesting because it was a joint effort of Finnish and Finnish American historians.

The 1988 celebrations of the 350 years of Delaware colonial history provided another boost for research. Several books came out both in Sweden and in Finland on the topic, discussing the history of New Sweden in the seventeenth century. There was much more consensus on the role of the Finns in the colony now than there had been fifty years earlier in 1938, when it was debated who the actual settlers were, Swedes or Finns. The role of the Finns was quite widely recognized in 1988, although not unanimously.[31]

Major research projects were born, and large archival collections were created, with similar efforts in many countries. Large collections were created at the Immigration History Research Center (IHRC) in Minneapolis; at Suomi College Archives in Hancock, Michigan; and in Turku, both in the History

Department at the University of Turku and at the Institute of Migration. In Finland, another background factor was the large and acute emigration from Finland to Sweden, which raised interest even in the earlier migratory movements.[32]

Several notable historians became involved. John I. Kolehmainen and A. William Hoglund, both with Finnish ethnic roots, served as pathfinders, with a large number of publications starting from the state histories and organizational histories. Actually Kolehmainen started earlier with his dissertation in 1937, but his main studies were printed from the 1940s to the 1970s, while at the same time he served as a professor at Heidelberg College, in Tiffin, Ohio. He wrote state and organization histories and a large number of scholarly and semischolarly articles, with a bit of a romantic tone. He set, along with Hoglund, a kind of pattern for younger generations interested in history; both he and Hoglund collected large archives and libraries on Finnish American history and culture.[33] Kolehmainen also collaborated with historians in Turku. In 1960, Harry Rickard Doby published a sociological study on the rural community of Waino, Wisconsin, and its radicalized people. He analyzed social relations in the community and the lives of the villagers.[34] Apparently Doby was of Finnish American background.

Many historians of Finnish descent in the United States started their careers in the 1970s and the 1980s, continuing to the 1990s and even beyond that. Among them are the historian Varpu Lindström of Toronto; the geographer Arnold Alanen; the sociologist and historian Peter Kivisto; the cultural researcher Marianne Wargelin; the former labor activist and self-educated historian Carl Ross; the historian Paul George Hummasti; the geographer and historian Mika Roinila; the urban historian Melvin G. Holli; and many others. Especially the importance of the historian Michael G. Karni, the theologian and historian Douglas J. Ollila Jr., and the Estonian-born geographer Matti Kaups has to be recognized. They started the still continuing scholarly series of FinnForums at Duluth in 1974.[35]

In fact, there were signs of the rising interest in Finnish American heritage already earlier in the 1950s and 1960s. There had been historical associations formed and volumes on Minnesota and Michigan Finns compiled. Two publications produced in the United States date from the same time period, although they were printed a few years earlier by Ralph Jalkanen. He compiled a "social symposium" on the Finns in 1969[36] and *The Faith of the Finns* in 1972.[37] The social symposium reflected mostly the seventy-five years of Suomi Synod celebration, while articles included migration history by, for example, Reino Kero and Douglas Ollila Jr., but there were also contributions about Finnish Kalevala and musical heritage. On the other hand, *The Faith of the Finns* was a collection of essays on a wider scale about the history of the Finnish ethnic Lutheran Church in the United States.

In Finland, Anna-Leena Toivonen compiled the first academic thesis on emigration from southern Ostrobothnia.[38] She was followed by the University of Turku migration history project researchers, historians such as Reino Kero, Keijo Virtanen, Auvo Kostiainen, Hannu Heinilä, and Arja Pilli. Reino Kero's dissertation about the background and socioeconomic characteristics of emigrants in 1974 was the first achievement.[39] It was followed by Auvo Kostiainen (1978) on the left labor radicals,[40] Keijo Virtanen (1979) on the return of emigrants,[41] Arja Pilli (1982) on the Finnish press in Canada,[42] and Hannu Heinilä (2002)[43] on the cooperative movement among American Finns. Also at other Finnish universities, studies emerged on the topics of Finnish migration and settlements in North America. A different kind of study was prepared by Eija Kettunen-Hujanen, who wrote a collective biography of eastern Finnish emigrants to Canada, following their emigration and life in Canada.[44] A large number of theses and papers on Finnish American history and background were issued. In addition, a number of amateur historians participated in the writing. One of these was K-G. Olin, who wrote several volumes on the history of migration to North America and other continents.

Recent decades have witnessed many new developments in the field of historical studies connected with the initial rise of new ethnic history a few decades ago, which directed attention to groups not so frequently studied earlier, and to social and cultural history. Multidisciplinary approaches, in turn, came more to the focus in the 1990s, and now the developments of postmodern society are being featured in historical studies as well.[45]

Many basic features of the Finnish migration and immigrant lives in North America have been researched quite thoroughly. Perhaps the most thorough studies have been written on the departure of the immigrants in relation to their geographical, political, and socioeconomic background. When looking from a close range, it seems also that there is some tendency toward quite specialized research topics. Already five decades have elapsed since A. William Hoglund, in 1960, published the latest "complete history" in the English language of Finns in the United States establishing themselves in the new country, as well the founding of numerous societies and central features of their immigrant culture. Only few words were printed on the post–World War I decades.[46] In Finland, on the contrary, there have been successful attempts to accomplish a similar task: at the University of Turku, researchers Reino Kero, Auvo Kostiainen, Arja Pilli, and Keijo Virtanen published, in 1982-86, a three-volume book on the Finns in North America titled *Suomen siirtolaisuuden historia I–III (The History of Finnish Migration).*[47] It discussed many aspects of immigrant experiences in the United States and Canada. Reino Kero compiled two extensive volumes of the history of Finns in America, which were issued in Finnish by the Institute of Migration in Turku in its six-volume series of the Finnish migration history as a whole.[48] Kero also published a more popularized version of Finns in North America a few years earlier under the title *Suuren lännen suomalaiset* (The Finns in the Great West).[49] Women's history has also come of age, reflecting a phenomenon in humanistic studies in general. There is also a special reason to study the Finnish women in North America because they appear to have been exceptionally active in many kinds of societies—for example, in the labor circles.[50]

There are a number of large gaps, however. The post–World War II developments are scarcely studied from a historian's point of view. Ethnic culture of Finnish Americans must be reconsidered. New ethnicity of new organizations, ethnic publications, and networks should receive more attention. Immigrant generations and their differences, multiethnicity, races, and gender, as well as transnational issues, have been targets of some studies already. The role of the FinnFests and FinnForums in giving publicity and impetus for new research projects has been important.[51] In Canada, quite similar festivals have been also organized.

New research topics, as well as methodological solutions, have been presented. We have already witnessed the application of interdisciplinary methods for the study of landscape or ethnic culture. The interest in the destinies of the Finns in Delaware has given rise to the study of a number of interesting topics, especially about the legacy of this Swedish-Finnish colony. One of the major issues has been their influence on the log building architecture, which was claimed by cultural geographers Terry G. Jordan and Matti Kaups.[52] Increasing interest has also been directed to the descendants of the settlers, especially the role of John Morton and his life in general. New efforts are being made to find more information on the colonial settlers' roots in Finland and Sweden. The latest major effort in Finland is Outi-Kristiina Hännikäinen's recent dissertation in human geography on the Finnish Canadian community of New Finland in Saskatchewan.[53] In the United States, research on folklore, ethnology, and material culture and literature, for instance, becomes entangled with the interests of historical researchers.[54]

New research interest has been created again, and interest is directed, for example, to labor and radicalism issues, such as Gary Kaunonen's study on the Michigan Copper Country,[55] but also to identity questions more generally. Also, since Finnish Canadian history needs more research,[56] related interested has been growing in the history and culture of the Finns in Canada.[57] A long-lasting topic seems to be the "Red Exodus" of the North American Finns to the Soviet Union in the early 1930s, which has given birth to several historical studies and memoirs as well as documentary movies. This is apparently due to the collapse of the Soviet Union, better international movement possibilities of people, and new information accessed.[58]

Thus quite a few new studies are emerging, partly reinterpreting historical topics but also developing new viewpoints and ways of analysis. These include studies on transnationalism between the old and the new country or the study of immigrant heritage and immigrant cultures. Here we also face the problem of invented traditions, such as St. Urho's Day, which does not have any relevant patterns in Finland's history or heritage but was invented for having fun. On the other hand, there are actual cultural traditions such as *Laskiainen* (Shrovetide), Midsummer, Christmas, or other festivities based more clearly on Finnish heritage. New topics also deal with race and immigration policy, and whiteness studies have examined U.S. ethnic history from fresh viewpoints. Other major issues should include generation and identity studies. For example, the immigrant communities during the years following World War II and the Cold War need more study. Immigrants and their descendants faced many new problems, which may reflect something that Donna R. Gabaccia has called imagined ethnic nations, referring to the concepts of Benedict Anderson on the nationhood based on true or false images or desires.[59] Still another issue in Finnish American history deals with the attitude of the host government to the "nondesirable" elements inside various immigrant groups. Even this issue has been tackled by government officials again and again.

Finally, while dealing with a number of topics mentioned above, there may be difficulties in getting access to source materials because of closed archives. Another major obstacle may be the lack of linguistic skills among the interested history writers, which significantly reduces their possibilities to get involved in the study of this ethnic group. Those able to use Finnish-language sources are in a much better position to employ the abundant printed and unprinted source materials.

The historical study of the Finnish experience in North America has changed a lot during the years. Among the basic currents have been the nationalistic understanding of history and the emphasis of Finland's historical specialty and independence. The change in themes and methods reflects the developments in historical studies in general and the study of U.S. history in particular. Also, the backgrounds of the writers have been varied.

A number of amateur historians began with modest results; however, their participation has been important. The writing of history has been greatly influenced by the environment provided by American society, politics, and culture, which have affected the status of the immigrants and their identity.

**NOTES**

1. O. K. Kilpi, *Suomen siirtolaisuus ja 19. vuosisadan kansantalous. Taloustieteellisiä tutkimuksia XXII* (Helsinki: Sana, 1917).
2. Armas Järnefelt, *Suomalaiset Amerikassa* (Helsinki: Otava, 1898).
3. Sakari Pälsi, *Suuri, kaunis ja ruma maa: Kuvia ja kuvauksia Kanadan matkalta* (Helsinki: Otava, 1927).
4. U.S. Immigration Commission, *Reports of the Immigration Commission* (New York: Arno Press, 1970).
5. Clemens Niemi, *Americanization of the Finnish People in Houghton County, Michigan* (Duluth, Minn.: Finnish Daily, 1921), 43. Showing interest in linguistic aspects and apparent concern on the language skills of the youth, Niemi also issued a Finnish grammar in the English language, with later reprintings. Clemens Niemi, *A Finnish Grammar* (Hancock, Mich.: author, 1917). He may have been a second-generation immigrant; thus far no information on his contacts with church people has been found.
6. John Wargelin, *The Americanization of the Finns* (Hancock, Mich.: Finnish Lutheran Book Concern, 1924).
7. E. A. Louhi, *The Delaware Finns or the First Permanent Settlement in Pennsylvania, Delaware, West New Jersey and Eastern Part of Maryland* (New York: Humanity Press, 1925).
8. See Auvo Kostiainen, "On the Footsteps of the Delaware Finns and John Morton: An Interpretation of the Finnish-American History by Salomon Ilmonen," *Siirtolaisuus—Migration* 4 (1999): 8–15.
9. F. J. Syrjälä, *Historia-aiheita Ameriikan suomalaisesta työväenliikkeestä* (Fitchburg, Mass.: Suom. sos. kustannusyhtiö, 1925).
10. John Wuorinen, *The Finns on the Delaware 1638–1655: An Essay in American Colonial History* (New York: Columbia University Press, 1938).
11. John Syrjamaki, "Mesabi Communities: A Study of Their Development" (Ph.D. diss., Yale University, 1940).
12. Eugene van Cleef, *Finland—The Republic Farthest North: The Response of Its People to Its Geographic Environment* (Columbus: Ohio State University Press, 1929).
13. For historians' debates, see Mikko Ylikojola, *Delaware-siirtokunnan historian arviointi: Pro gradu-tutkielma* (Turku: Yleinen historia, Turun yliopisto, 2008); Max Engman, "The Tug of War Over 'Nya Sverige,' 1938" *Swedish American Historical Quarterly* 45 (1994): 67–117.
14. See especially Melvin G. Holli, *The Wizard of Washington: Emil Hurja, Franklin Roosevelt, and the Birth of Public Opinion Polling* (New York: Palgrave Macmillan, 2002).
15. Rafael Engelberg, *Suomi ja Amerikan suomalaiset: Keskinäinen yhteys ja sen rakentaminen* (Helsinki: Suomi-Seura, 1944).
16. Hans R. Wasastjerna, *History of the Finns in Minnesota*, ed. and trans. Toivo Rosvall (Duluth: Minnesota Finnish-American Historical Society, 1957), 283–93.
17. See Ylikojola, *Delaware-siirtokunnan historian arviointi*, 48–55.
18. Armas K. E. Holmio, *Michiganin suomalaisten historia* (Hancock, Mich.: Michiganin Suomalaisten Historia-Seura, 1967).
19. Katri Ekman, *A History of Finnish American Organizations in Greater New York 1891–1976: A Project of the Greater New York Finnish Bicentennial Planning Committee, Inc.*, ed., trans., and in part written by Katri Ekman, Corinne Olli, and John B. Olli (New York: Greater New York Finnish Bicentennial Planning Committee, 1976).
20. John I. Kolehmainen, *A History of the Finns in Ohio, Western Pennsylvania and West Virginia: From Lake Erie's Shores to the Mahoning and Monongahela Valleys* (Fairport Harbor, Ohio: Ohio Finnish-American Historical Society, 1977).

21. See Wasastjerna, *History,* 286–88.
22. Chapters founded were the following: 1944 Virginia; 1945 Cedar Valley (Salo); 1946 Cromwell, Palo (Townsend), Payla (Lake Vermillion), Zim; 1947 Alango, Ely, Hibbing, New York Mills, Sebeka; 1948 Nashwauk; 1949 Chisholm, Cokato, East Lake, Minneapolis, St. Paul; 1950 Jacobson; and in an unknown year Suomi.
23. See the history booklet *Minnesotan suomalaisten juhla-albumi Minnesotan valtion täyttäessä 100 vuotta,* ed. E. A. Pulli (Duluth: Minnesotan amerikkalais-suomalainen historiallinen seura, 1949); Tom Hiltunen, ed., *Finnish Pioneer Day: A Minnesota Territorial Centennial Celebration, St. Paul, Minnesota, August 21, 1949* (Duluth: Minnesota Finnish-American Historical Society, 1949).
24. Wasastjerna, *History,* 286–93.
25. Elis Sulkanen, *Amerikansuomalaisen työväenliikkeen historia* (Fitchburg, Mass.: Amerikan suomalainen kansanvallan liitto, 1951).
26. Wasastjerna, *History,* 108–9.
27. See Wasastjerna, *History,* 527–28.
28. Jon L. Saari, *Black Ties and Miners' Boots: Inventing Finnish-American Philanthropy—A History of Finlandia Foundation National 1953–2003* (Pasadena, Calif.: Finlandia Foundation National, 2010), 12–15.
29. Nathan Glazer and Daniel P. Moynihan, *Beyond the Melting Pot: The Negroes, Puerto Ricans, Jews, Italians, and Irish of New York City,* 2nd ed. (Cambridge, Mass.: MIT Press, 1976); for the rise of historiography, see Rudolph J. Vecoli, "European Americans: From Immigrants to Ethnics," in *The Reinterpretation of American History and Culture,* ed. W. H. Cartwright and R. L. Watson Jr. (Washington, D.C.: National Council for Social Studies, 1973), 81–112.
30. Vilho Niitemaa et al., eds., *Old Friends—Strong Ties* (Turku: Institute for Migration, 1976).
31. See Ylikojola, *Delaware-siirtokunnan historian arviointi,* 6–58.
32. Cf. Auvo Kostiainen, "Ulkosuomalaisia jäljittämässä. Siirtolaishistorian tutkimusta Turun yliopistossa," *Historiaa Auran rannoilla. Turkulaista historiantutkimusta ja historiantutkijoita.* With English Summary, ed. Auvo Kostiainen, *Turun historiallinen arkisto* 52 (1998): 133–35.
33. Kolehmainen and Hoglund donated their research materials to, for example, the University of Turku and the IHRC, University of Minnesota, where they are available for researchers.
34. Harry Rickard Doby, "A Study of Social Change and Social Disorganization in a Finnish Rural Community" (Ph.D. diss., University of California at Berkeley, 1960).
35. The first meeting in Duluth was not called FinnForum; that title was adopted after quite a few years.
36. Ralph J. Jalkanen, ed., *Finns in North America: A Social Symposium* (Hancock: Michigan State University Press for Suomi College, 1969).
37. Ralph J. Jalkanen, ed., *The Faith of the Finns: Historical Perspectives on the Finnish Lutheran Church in America* (East Lansing: Michigan State University Press, 1972).
38. Anna-Leena Toivonen, *Etelä-Pohjanmaan valtamerentakainen siirtolaisuus 1867–1939,* Historiallisia Tutkimuksia 66 (Seinäjoki: Suomen Historiallinen Seura, 1963).
39. Reino Kero, *Migration from Finland to North America in the Years between the United States Civil War and the First World War* (Turku: University of Turku, 1974).
40. Auvo Kostiainen, *The Forging of Finnish American Communism: A Study in Ethnic Radicalism, 1917–1924,* Annales Universitatis Turkuensis Ser. C 147 (Turku: University of Turku, 1978).
41. Keijo Virtanen, *Settlement or Return: Finnish Emigrants (1860–1930) in the International Overseas Return Migration Movement* (Helsinki: Suomen Historiallinen Seura, 1979).
42. Arja Pilli, *The Finnish-Language Press in Canada, 1901–1939: A Study in the History of Ethnic Journalism* (Helsinki: Suomalainen Tiedeakatemia, 1982).

43. Hannu Heinilä, *Osuustoimintaliikekasvatus USA:n keskilännessä 1917–1963* (Turku: Siirtolaisuusinstituutti, 2002).
44. Eija Kettunen-Hujanen, *Elämän pakkoraossa vai matkalla vaurauteen? Savosta, Pohjois-Karjalasta ja Kainuusta 1918–1930 muuttaneiden siirtolaisten sopeutuminen Kanadaan* (Helsinki: SKS, 2000).
45. Cf., for example, George H. Iggers, *Historiography in the Twentieth Century: From Scientific Objectivity to the Postmodern Challenge* (Middletown, Conn.: Wesleyan University Press, 2012), 101–17; Vecoli, "European Americans," 81–112.
46. A. William Hoglund, *Finnish Immigrants in America 1880–1920* (Madison: University of Wisconsin Press, 1960).
47. Reino Kero, Auvo Kostiainen, Arja Pilli, and Keijo Virtanen, *Suomen siirtolaisuuden historia I–III* (Turku: Turun yliopisto, Historian laitos, 1982–86).
48. Reino Kero, *Suomalaisina Pohjois-Amerikassa: Siirtolaiselämää Yhdysvalloissa ja Kanadassa*, Suomen siirtolaisuuden historia 2 (Turku: Siirtolaisuusinstituutti, 1997); Reino Kero, *Suureen länteen: Siirtolaisuus Suomesta Yhdysvaltoihin ja Kanadaan*, Suomen siirtolaisuuden historia 1 (Turku: Siirtolaisuusinstituutti, 1996).
49. Reino Kero, *Suuren lännen suomalaiset* (Helsinki: Otava, 1976).
50. Varpu Lindström, *Uhmattaret: Suomalaisten siirtolaisnaisten vaiheita Kanadassa 1890–1930* (Porvoo, Helsinki, and Juva: WSOY, 1991); a collection of interesting but overlapping articles is found in Carl Ross and K. Marianne Wargelin Brown, eds., *Women Who Dared: The History of Finnish American Women* (St. Paul: University of Minnesota, Immigration History Research Center, 1986).
51. Both of them, the FinnForum and FinnFest, are quite recent developments, established as a response to the need for historical analysis and information and for those interested in Finnish American culture as well as Finland. The FinnForums are more academic, with scholarly presentations, and have been held nine times at irregular intervals, starting in Duluth with the conference on the Finnish experience in the western Great Lakes region in 1974. The FinnFests date from the first festival in Minneapolis in 1983, while the FinnFest in San Diego in August 2011 was the twenty-eighth. The 1983 FinnFest created the basic paradigm for future FinnFests. Finnish food, arts and crafts, music, lectures, social events, and dances became the core elements of the festival. http://www.finnfestusa.org/about-us/history.html.
52. Terry G. Jordan and Matti E. Kaups, *The American Backwoods Frontier: An Ethnic and Ecological Interpretation* (Baltimore: Johns Hopkins University Press, 1989).
53. Outi-Kristiina Hännikäinen, *Identiteettien maisemat Saskatchewanin uudessa Suomessa—Uudisasutuksesta uusidentifikaatioon* (Turku: Siirtolaisuusinstituutti, 2010).
54. For example, Yvonne R. Lockwood, *Finnish American Rag Rugs: Art, Tradition, and Ethnic Continuity* (East Lansing: Michigan State University Press, 2009).
55. See especially Gary Kaunonen, *Challenge Accepted: A Finnish Immigrant Response to Industrial America in Michigan's Copper Country* (East Lansing: Michigan State University Press, 2010).
56. Research by Edward Laine was interrupted by his sudden death. His important study, "History of the Finnish Organization of Canada, 1911–2000," has not yet been published. See manuscript at the Institute of Migration, in Turku, Finland.
57. For example, the volume produced as the result of the FinnForum in Thunder Bay, Ontario, in 2010: Michael S. Beaulieu, Ronald N. Harpelle, and Jaimi Penney, eds., *Labouring Finns. Transnational Politics in Finland, Canada, and the United States* (Turku: Institute of Migration, 2011).
58. For example, Mayme Sevander, with Laurie Hertzel, *They Took My Father: Finnish Americans in Stalin's Russia* (Minneapolis: University of Minnesota Press, 2004).

59. Donna R. Gabaccia, *Immigration and American Diversity: A Social and Cultural History* (Malden, Mass.: Blackwell, 2002), 209–23; for imagination over immigrants' position in the United States, see also Orm Overland, *Immigrant Minds, American Identities: Making the United States Home, 1870–1930* (Urbana: University of Illinois Press, 2000).

PART 2

# Colonial Settlement of the Swedes and Finns

# The Delaware Colonists and Their Heritage

*Auvo Kostiainen*

In the mid-1600s, there existed the New Sweden colony, at the time when Finland was a part of the Swedish kingdom. Finns comprised a majority of the few hundred colonists who arrived to the Delaware River valley. The composition of the colony, however, has been a disputed topic and the target of nationalist writing in Sweden and in Finland; it has also bumped up against an interesting question of heritage: who were the settlers, and was the signer of the Declaration of Independence John Morton (in 1776) a descendant of Finnish colonists?

Nya Sverige (in Finnish, Uusi Ruotsi, and in English known as the New Sweden colony) was founded in 1637. The first ships arrived in 1638. Its founding was in accordance with the contemporary political aims of the Great Powers in Europe. It was hoped that the colony would help in maintaining and enlarging the power of the kingdom of Sweden. It was planned that fur trade and tobacco would be the main sources of richness from Delaware. The colony lasted for almost two decades, and it was taken over by the Dutch in 1655, who had in 1626 established Nieuw Amsterdam on the location of present-day New York City. The Dutch rule lasted until 1664, when the English took it over. New Sweden attracted fewer than a thousand colonists in twelve shiploads; however, more people arrived to the colony later. The colonists included government officials, soldiers, and clergy. The bulk of the population, however, comprised of settlers and farmers, most of whom were apparently of Finnish heritage.

The Swedish rule in the colony ended in less than twenty years. The colonial heritage, however, was recognized when much more extensive new migration began in the 1800s. Also, the nature of the ethnic base of the colony—Delaware Finns and Swedes—and its influence on the surrounding area has been debated for decades; the debate was especially heated before and during the tercentenary celebration of 1938.[1] Even in 2006 some discussion went on when the ancestry of the president of the United States, George W. Bush, was discussed.[2] There has been debate about the composition and ethnic background of the settlers, especially in Sweden and Finland. Major difficulties for this investigation are caused by the lack of adequate historical sources: original documentation of the settler population is scant. More specific information is available on the ship passengers to Delaware; there are also documents about their settler activities, land purchases, and other matters in the Delaware area.

## The Founding of the New Sweden Colony

A large number of people moved from Sweden to Finland and from Finland to Sweden after Finnish areas had become a part of the Swedish kingdom in the thirteenth and fourteenth centuries. Partly the changes were caused by the administrative orders from and activities initiated by the Swedish Crown. There was also a lot of migration caused by economic developments.

It is known that many of the immigrants to Delaware came from Forest Finn areas in Scandinavia—that is, Sweden and Norway, especially Värmland, Dalarna, and other provinces in central Sweden. There is the problem of sources, however, since not many documents have surfaced. It has been stated that the colonists were largely "burn beaters." The historical background is comprised of circa 13,000 "burn beaters," who came from Finland in the late 1500s and early 1600s to clear the forests of central Sweden and turn the wilderness into farming areas. They came mainly from central eastern Finland, from the province of Savo, but also from other regions such as the Ostrobothnian coastal area. The last-mentioned population consisted mainly of Finn Swedes.

During the 1600s, the policy of the Swedish Crown changed, and burn beating was no longer allowed. Instead, it was deemed suitable to send some of the former "burn beaters" to Delaware. It is also known that some of the settlers were actually deported or expelled to Delaware.[3] The twelve shiploads carried over the ocean some hundreds of settlers, administrators, clergy, and soldiers. The first ships, *Kalmar Nyckel* and *Fogel Grip,* landed on the Delaware coast in the spring of 1638. Some settlers arrived in the colony after the Dutch had taken over in 1655 and even later on. The total number of arrivals to the New Sweden colony was close to a thousand. Two of the twelve shiploads actually never arrived in Delaware; one ship was crushed in a heavy storm, and the second one was taken by mistake to Nieuw Amsterdam (New York). There are many estimates that at least half of all the newcomers were actually of Finnish extraction.[4] The population in New Sweden hardly ever exceeded 500 because some settlers returned to the home country, and others who were dissatisfied with the authorities escaped in order to settle elsewhere in North America.

The actual founder of the New Sweden colony was a Dutchman, Peter Minuit, who is also famous as the person who bought Manhattan Island for the Dutch from the local Indian population. The Dutch connection remained strong. The Dutch and the English were already present in the area, which became a Swedish colony. The Dutch considered the area to be theirs, and the Dutch West Indies Trading Company (GWIC) was instrumental in the Dutch colonization of North America. Actually the Dutch initially owned half of the New Sweden Trading Company, and its head was a Finnish nobleman, Klaus Fleming. This company was established according to the Dutch models, many ships arrived via Amsterdam, and the area in Delaware was in the immediate vicinity of other Dutch areas. The third governor of New Sweden was Johan Printz (1643–53). Before he left his home to travel to Delaware, he served as a garrison commander on the western coast of Finland, in the town of Vaasa. Apparently he recruited a number of people from this coastal region to become settlers in Delaware.

## Settler Families and Genealogies

Several studies have been written regarding the people who settled in Delaware. For example, a genealogist from Pennsylvania, Peter Stebbins Craig, has researched the families of the colonists and their descendants extensively.[5] A common problem thus far has been that scholars have found it very difficult to ascertain exactly what sorts of people were among the newcomers, particularly with regard to their ethnic background. As soon as they had settled in Delaware, their activities and family relationships are easier to follow. One of the explanations for the difficulty in examining the settlers' backgrounds is that many records that could reveal the their ancestry have been destroyed by fire or simply lost either in Swedish country churches or even earlier in Finland.

Swedish and Finnish historians have often disagreed about the importance of Finnish settlers and their descendants in the colonial history of Delaware. This debate was quite heated especially in the 1930s, but even later on a kind of competition has been going on between the two countries and their writers.[6] For example, the most important Swedish American historian of New Sweden, Amandus Johnson, rarely mentioned that there were Finnish-speaking settlers in the colony.[7] On the other hand, there have been Finnish American writers such as E. A. Louhi and Salomon Ilmonen who in turn have overemphasized the influence of the Finns in colonial Delaware.[8] Louhi was certainly not a modern and well-educated historian. His introductory section to his book on the Delaware Finns included many imaginary claims about the roots of the Finns in general, such as the Finns having been the ancestors of the Egyptian and Sumerian peoples and therefore pathfinders for ancient cultural achievements, and Finnish having been the first important language.[9] Essentially Louhi had uncritically reaffirmed these and other outlandish assertions from the ultraromantic Finnish historical writing of the seventeenth and eighteenth centuries.

When Louhi's book on the Delaware Finns was published in 1925, Amandus Johnson was very critical of it. Even in 2001 the Reverend Kim Eric Williams, one the leaders of the Swedish Colonial Society, disapproved of the recent reprinting of Louhi's book. Williams commented that no doubt Johnson had been offended when Louhi changed "allover" the words Sweden to Finland and Swedes to Finns, and otherwise copied information from Johnson's book. Williams was especially critical of Louhi's book because of its criticism of the Church of Sweden. Also, according to Williams, there were no grounds for the claim that families such as the Rambos, Kyns, and Holsteins were Finns.[10]

As mentioned earlier, the debate over Delaware and its heritage was a target of the "tug-of-war" between Finland and Sweden and was reflected in the debates among historians but also among civic societies and individuals in the United States. At the same time, many shorter commentaries appeared in the Finnish-language press and other publications such as calendars and novels, addressing the Finns' role in the history of the United States.

Also, the ongoing debate gained the attention of decision makers in the old countries of Finland and Sweden, which became evident in the composition of the very formal delegations sent overseas to celebrate the tercentenary in the Delaware and Philadelphia regions. Finally, the issue became a target of debate in U.S. government spheres and on Capitol Hill. While organization of the 1938 tercentenary celebrations progressed, historians such as John H. Wuorinen and Salomon Ilmonen participated in the organizing committees in leading roles. Interestingly, many rival groups in the Finnish American

FIGURE 1. While preparing for the Delaware Colony tercentenary celebrations in 1938, the famous Finnish sculptor Wäinö Aaltonen carved a large monument, which then was erected in Chester, Pennsylvania. (Source: IMT Photo collections, USA_0013)

community joined together in defending the Finns' role in North American history.[11] Finnish Americans were successful because now Finns were officially recognized by the U.S. Congress as a "founding nation" in addition to Sweden and a number of other nations.[12]

Probably the main issue of research has been exactly the one Williams mentioned: were the settlers ethnic Finns or Swedes? It seems that the problem of Swedish or Finnish heritage is important from several viewpoints. First, it reflects certainly nationalistic or even romantic views on the nations' pasts, and therefore the issue has been important for the self-respect of the Finns and Swedes in their own countries, but also for the immigrant generations in America. Second, the problem is important for understanding the role of ethnic groups and nationalities in America. Colonial America was made up of numerous ethnic groups from Europe and from America itself. Each group has left its marks on American heritage, culture, and society, and we have to study these features. Looking at the history from the present standpoint, we know that both Swedes and Finns were citizens of the kingdom of Sweden, but we also know that Finnish heritage was strongly held on to for decades and even centuries in the Forest Finn areas in Sweden. In New Sweden, the Finnish language gradually withered away, as did the Swedish language, as is reported in the diaries of Pehr Kalm from the mid-eighteenth century.[13] The heritage of the colonists was, however, present in the form of material buildings, and it affected the way of living and cultural habits, as generations of colonists' descendants lived in the area.

John H. Wuorinen was the first professional Finnish American historian to tackle the history the New Sweden, even though there had been amateur historians, such as Ilmonen, involved in this research earlier. Wuorinen based his study on Johnson's research, in which he found several inconsistencies and other shortcomings. Moreover, Wuorinen used colonial American documentary collections in order to support his main thesis that Finns played an important part in developing New Sweden, about half of whose inhabitants were ethnic Finns.

The colony was, of course, not very important when compared with many other colonies in North America. It had, however, great local importance, and Wuorinen also concluded that in the early 1700s 10 percent of the inhabitants in Pennsylvania, Delaware, Maryland, and New Jersey area were descendants of the New Sweden people.[14] John Wuorinen was also one of the leaders in the Delaware Finnish American Tercentenary Committee in charge of the 1938 celebrations. Despite his Finnish American connections, his views on American colonial history may be seen as quite objective and well documented.

Several New Sweden families have been important in the history of Delaware and adjacent colonies and in the American revolutionary era. The Swedish Colonial Society has a list of "qualified" families. This list is, of course, not complete, because it does not include information on all families, and to be included on the list you have to be able to prove genealogically that you are a descendant of a certain family.[15] There are forty-three families on the list, nine of which are listed as Finnish. The share of Finnish

**FIGURE 2.** Imagined meeting of Finnish settlers with American Indians in Delaware published during the tercentenary festivity period. Painting in *New Yorkin Uutiset*, June 21, 1938. (Source: IMT Photo collections, USA_4885)

families is apparently too small. Here we again confront the problem of inadequate sources, which are not detailed enough for any period before which Swedes and Finns departed for New Sweden. Among the largest families are the Mortons or Mårtensons or Marttinens. Mårtenssons, in Swedish, have been often referred to as the Marttinen (in the Finnish form) family from the Savo Province in Finland. A descendant of this family was John Morton, who signed the Declaration of Independence in 1776. The genealogically oriented book by K-G. Olin (2006) includes a long list of Morton/Marttinen/Mårtenssons, of whom many successive families are found. The genealogist Peter Stebbins Craig has also explained the genealogy of the earliest Mortons in America in his writings.[16]

Pehr Kalm (1716–79), then a professor of botany from the Academy of Åbo/Turku in Finland, traveled to Delaware in 1748–51; during this trip he also visited Niagara Falls. While in Delaware, he found some old church records in a Delaware Swedish church. Certain facts were found in the records on the immigrants to New Sweden. Kalm found that Mårtensson (often referred to as Martti Marttinen in Finnish form) was mentioned as having been born in Finland in Sweden.[17] This pointed to a person called Martti Marttinen, who had been born probably in the Savo region in east-central Finland and had moved to Swedish forests to clear new farmland with the techniques of burn beating.[18] He and his family came to Delaware in 1654 by the ship *Örnen* (Eagle). The old Martti Marttinen was the great-grandfather of John Morton. Morton was a member and Speaker of Pennsylvania's Provincial Assembly for nearly three decades. He served as high sheriff of Chester County (now Delaware County) and as a justice on the Pennsylvania Supreme Court.

There were a number of other families of Swedish and Finnish origin. For example, John Morton was married to Anna Justis, who actually was his second cousin and the great-grandchild of old Mårtensson. The family name was originally perhaps of Swedish or Finnish origin—Gustafsson or Juustinen, respectively. Furthermore, the debate continues about whether the large Rambo family was actually of Swedish or Finnish origin.

There were even quite detailed maps, based on facts and heritage, drawn of the Delaware Colony, showing the names and houses of the settlement. One detailed, widely circulated map, apparently based on Salomon Ilmonen's findings, was published in March 1938 in New York by the Finnish Book Concern and was created by the Suomi Art Studios. Ilmonen was at that time one of the best specialists on the history of John Morton as well as the history of the Delaware Colony, although he was not a historian by education but a Lutheran priest interested in migration history.[19] Ilmonen was an influential figure in the Finnish American preparations for the 1938 tercentenary celebrations.

DNA testing may offer a new way to study genealogical backgrounds and has been used in recent years for genealogical purposes. The studies are going on, but it is possible to compare the DNA of the descendants of the Morton or Marttinen family and other families that are recognized as the original settler families with the DNA heritage common in Finland and Sweden.[20]

### Interest in Finland

The interest in Delaware was born in Finland in the mid-1800s. However, more discussion was created after Salomon Ilmonen published some of his books, such as the history of Delaware Finns in 1916 and the short biography of John Morton in 1936, in Finnish and in English. Some of his other books on Finnish Americans were even printed in Finland. The Delaware tercentenary celebrations aroused enthusiasm in the new republic of Finland, whose citizens took pleasure in celebrating great Finnish historical figures and believed Morton to have been one of those figures. Finland even sent an official delegation to the celebrations, as did Sweden.[21]

The Finnish press, especially during the 1930s, published dozens of articles on the history of Delaware, and interest in this history did not cease after the tercentenary celebrations. For example, in 1956 the Finnish National Theater in Helsinki performed Simo Penttilä's play entitled *Delaware,* whose theme focused on the activities of Governor Prinz and his daughter in New Sweden. Of course, the Finnish settlers were portrayed as the righteous people who practically forced this unjust governor to return to Sweden. The best-known post–World War II actor in Finland, Tauno Palo, played the principal character, Governor Prinz. The generally laudatory reviews of this play may be found in the Suomi Seura newspaper clipping collection preserved at the Department of General History, University of Turku.

Among the Finnish American population, John Morton has the image of being an important Pennsylvania legislator and colonial officer who, for example, held the office of sheriff. However, generally he is not so well known for other reasons except because of the fact that he gave the decisive vote among the Pennsylvania delegates in favor of the independence of the United States in 1776. Thus far no major biographical study of him has been written, although Ilmonen's short "romantized" booklet as well as short biographical notes about him are available. Therefore, it is important to compile a full and competent biography of this descendant of the New Sweden colonists. His activities cannot be understood without the background given by the New Sweden colonists and their livelihood and social and cultural activities.[22]

## Living Heritage

Although the Delaware New Sweden colony was small and survived for less than two decades, it has attained considerable interest in America, Sweden, and Finland. As mentioned, interest in the Delaware settlement arose primarily from the early 1900s, and it was especially great during the preparations for the tercentenary celebrations of 1938. This interest culminated in the debate about the colonial history and its possible meaning for the contemporary world. Primarily it was a reflection and response of the Finnish Americans about their status in American society in general. Later on, at the time of the 350th celebration of the Delaware Colony in 1988, a new wave of interest in New Sweden history was seen, and a number of new studies were issued. However, at this time not so much debate was heard as fifty years earlier.[23]

The debate over the Delaware Colony mirrors the debate in American society at large. Naturally this debate has also some meaning for those persons who are interested in genealogical questions, which have become popular themes for present-day Americans, who show great interest in their ethnic roots. Founding fathers and genealogy are interesting topics, as well as the aforementioned interest in the multiethnic features of the United States starting in the 1960s and 1970s. At that time a popular television series called *Roots,* based on the novel *Roots: The Saga of an American Family* (1976) by Alex Haley, brought forward the historical experiences of African Americans and added to the general interest in family histories. As with other ethnic groups, the ancestry of the Finnish population in North America continues to be of great interest for many Americans, and this is how we may understand the importance of the question of Delaware colonial history. More impetus is presented by the significance of the nation's founders such as John Morton in the United States. Thus, even if the Delaware Colony was relatively small by size and lasted only a couple of decades, its heritage and importance are repeatedly addressed.

The importance of New Sweden is reflected in the history books and other written materials on Delaware's colonial past. For example, a lot of discussion arose in 1992 when two geographers, Terry Jordan and Matti E. Kaups, published their study on the cultural heritage the colonists brought with them to North America. Especially interesting was their thesis that the Delaware colonists had, in general, a great impact on the colonization of the American West, in which an essential role was played by the log cabin design, which the colonists brought with them to America. Jordan and Kaups claimed that this specific Swedish-Finnish building technique was used by the pioneers going farther into the continent, and even applied burn-beating agricultural methods.[24] These theses were developed further in, for example, an exhibition catalog that claimed even specific apple seeds or textile designs were imported by the colonial Finnish settlers.[25] The scholarly and semischolarly interests have produced the debate discussed above. Even in local histories we find reference to the Delaware colonists. For example, the history of the city of Fitchburg, Massachusetts, describes various ethnic groups in the city. It starts its discussion on the Fitchburg Finns with references to the Delaware history, and it claims the same thesis as Jordan and Kaups twenty years later: the Finns brought with them the convenient methods of felling trees and building log cabins. English pioneers adopted these methods and made them their own.[26]

## NOTES

1. Auvo Kostiainen, "Delaware as a Symbol of Finnish Immigration," in *Finnish Identity in America*, ed. Auvo Kostiainen, *Turku Historical Archives* 46 (1990): 49–70; Max Engman, "Dragkampen om Nya Sverige, 1938," *Historisk Tidskrift* no. 111 (1991): 186–225; Ylikojola, *Delaware-siirtokunnan*.

2. His distant forefather is claimed to be Måns Andersson, who came from Sillerud, Värmland, Sweden. In Finland, claims were presented that he actually was a Forest Finn from Värmland. See K-G. Olin, *Amerikafararna. Tillbaka till Nya Sverige* (Jakobstad: Olimex, 2006), 188–91.

3. Cf. Engman, "Dragkampen," 223–24; Reino Kero, "Finns in the New Sweden Colony," in Kostiainen, *Finnish Identity in America*, 4–5.

4. Kero, "Finns in the New Sweden Colony," 2.

5. For example, Peter Stebbins Craig, "Mårten Mårtensson and His Morton Family," *Swedish Colonial News* 1, no. 13 (1996).

6. Ylikojola, *Delaware-siirtokunnan*.

7. Amandus Johnson, *The Swedish Settlements on the Delaware: Their History and Relation to the Indians, Dutch and English 1638–1664* (New York: D. Appleton, 1911), 1–2.

8. E. A. Louhi, *The Delaware Finns or the First Permanent Settlement in Pennsylvania, Delaware, West New Jersey and Eastern Part of Maryland* (New York: Humanity Press, 1925); Salomon Ilmonen, *Amerikan ensimmäiset suomalaiset eli Delawaren siirtokunnan historia* (Hancock, Mich.: Suomalais-luteerilainen kustannusliike, 1916).

9. See Louhi, *Delaware Finns*.

10. Kim Eric Williams, "The Delaware Finns," *Swedish Colonial News* 2, no. 5 (2000): 16.

11. For historians' debates, see Ylikojola, *Delaware-siirtokunnan;* Max Engman, "The Tug of War Over 'Nya Sverige,' 1938." *Swedish American Historical Quarterly*. Vol. 45 (1994): 67–117.

12. It seems that Emil Hurja, a prominent Democratic counselor of Franklin Delano Roosevelt, played an important role in this process. Hurja was of Finnish ancestry and was well known for his

ability to develop polling systems for elections. See especially Melvin G. Holli, *The Wizard of Washington: Emil Hurja, Franklin Roosevelt, and the Birth of Public Opinion Polling* (New York: Palgrave Macmillan, 2002); Melvin G. Holli, "1938 Delaware Tercentenary: Establishing Finnish Presence at the 300th Anniversary Celebration," in Kostiainen, *Finnish Identity in America*, 33-48.

13. Fred Elfving and Georg Schauman, eds., *Pehr Kalms Resa till Norra Amerika* (Helsingfors: Svenska litteratursällskapet in Finland, 1929).

14. John H. Wuorinen, *The Finns on the Delaware 1638-1655: An Essay in American Colonial History*. New York: Columbia University Press, 1938.

15. For more information on the colonial "forefathers," see http://www.colonialswedes.org/Forefathers/FFPro.html.

16. Peter Stebbins Craig, "Mårten Mårtensson and His Morton Family," *Swedish Colonial News 1*, no. 13 (1996).

17. *Pehr Kalms resa I norra Amerika*, red. Fredr. Elfving and Georg Schauman. Helsingfors: Svenska litteratursällskapet i Finland, 1929): 219. In English, this death notice from Kalm's diary would read as follows: "May 31, 1706, the elderly Mårten Mårtenson at Amundsland, born in Finland in Sweden, and believed to be 100 years old."

18. This method of clearing woods is also called "slash and burn."

19. Auvo Kostiainen, "On the Footsteps of the Delaware Finns and John Morton: An Interpretation of the Finnish-American History by Salomon Ilmonen," *Siirtolaisuus—Migration* 26, no. 4 (1999): 8-15.

20. Auvo Kostiainen, "John Mortonin jäljillä," *Siirtolaisuus-Migration*, 37, no. 3 (2010): 3-7.

21. Ylikojola, *Delaware-siirtokunnan;* Engman, "Dragkampen."

22. Actually, the former ambassador of the United States in Finland, Marilyn Ware, is chairing a project for a biographical study of John Morton.

23. See Ylikojola, *Delaware-siirtokunnan.*

24. Terry G. Jordan and Matti E. Kaups, *The American Backwoods Frontier: An Ethnic and Ecological Interpretation* (Baltimore and London: Johns Hopkins University Press, 1989).

25. Olavi Koivukangas, *Delaware 350. Amerikansiirtolaisuuden alku. Näyttelyjulkaisu. Amerikaemigrationens början. Utställningskatalog. The Beginning of Finnish Migration to the New World. Exhibition Catalogue* (Turku: Institute of Migration, 1988), 36-43.

26. Doris Kirckpatrick, *Around the World in Fitchburg*, vol. 2 (Fitchburg, Mass.: Fitchburg Historical Society, 1975), 113.

PART 3

# Seamen, Masses, and Individual Migrants of the Nineteenth and Twentieth Centuries

# Migration from Finland to North America

*Reino Kero*

The mass emigration of Finns to the United States extended from the 1870s to the early 1920s, with a gross figure of about 389,000 Finns emigrating to North America, while every fifth person returned home. The 1920 federal census counted 150,000 persons born in Finland. The migrants were mainly peasants and laboring people from the countryside, with males clearly predominant. In the following pages, analysis is also presented on the minor migration wave of the post–World War II period, which is composed of different types of more educated migrants.

## How Did Emigration Begin?

As was true of other European countries, migration from Finland to North America began as a movement of sailors. The moment when this migration started cannot be determined precisely. In the first decades of the nineteenth century, Finnish sailors now and then deserted ships sailing in American coastal waters and remained in America, thus becoming immigrants. However, an appreciable increase in the number of sailors who migrated occurred at the time of the gold discoveries in California. This took place around 1850.

The emigration of sailors probably continued to be relatively common from the time of the California gold rush to World War I. It is perhaps typical of this emigration that a great portion of the émigrés left from towns—including such seafaring centers as Oulu, Raahe, Kokkola, and Turku.

After the end of the American Civil War, migration to the United States received a new tone. In addition to sailors, the "normal" population of rural districts in Finland became interested in emigrating. The year 1866 seems to mark rather clearly a turning point in Finland. It is the year when the first fairly large groups of emigrants left from the Tornio River valley and from the vicinity of Kokkola. By the beginning of the 1870s, emigration was already fairly extensive from these two areas and also from the vicinity of Kristiinankaupunki. Emigration from the interior parts of Oulu and Vaasa provinces also began to occur at the beginning of the 1870s.

At the beginning of the 1880s, emigration spread beyond Oulu and Vaasa provinces to the northern regions of Turku and Pori Province and to the Åland Islands. By the end of the decade, people from the coastal area between Turku and Pori began to emigrate, although emigration from this region was still comparatively small in the 1890s.

By the beginning of the 1890s, migration to America was occurring from all the provinces of Finland. However, with the exception of that from Vaasa and Oulu provinces, that from the northern regions of Turku and Pori Province, and that from the Åland Islands, emigration was rather sparse. Migration to America was an almost unknown phenomenon in many towns in Häme and Mikkeli provinces. Around the turn of the twentieth century, the phenomenon of emigration had spread, however, to all parts of Finland, but it remained rather sparse in the areas that it "conquered" last.

How did this migration to America begin? Some Finns had, no doubt, become familiar with this phenomenon by observing their relatives migrate to northern Norway, and some farther to North America. Those living in the Tornio River valley must have observed the lives of Finns who had migrated to the Swedish side of the river. In Swedish-speaking Ostrobothnia, trips to seek work in Sweden were undoubtedly also of significance. Also, sailors who had emigrated earlier must have spread information about the opportunities available in North America to the coastal regions of Finland. Additionally, in the eyes of the educated classes, America had become an ideal land where all things were better than in old Europe. This idea of America was attractive to many prospective emigrants.

### How Many Emigrants?

The official Finnish emigration statistics for Oulu and Vaasa provinces are from as early as the beginning of the 1880s, but they include information about the entire country only from 1893. For this reason, notions of immigration that took place before 1893 vary considerably. My estimates of the numbers of earlier emigrants (up to 1893) are based on passport lists, passenger lists of shipping companies, and information found in newspapers. These materials indicate that before 1870, perhaps several hundred persons emigrated. As mentioned earlier, large groups of Finnish sailors deserted their ships when they were sailing in American waters. These sailors, too, emigrated.

In the 1870s, there were probably about 3,000 emigrants; in the period 1880–86, about 18,000; and in 1887–92, about 40,000. All in all, perhaps about 61,000 emigrants left before 1893. The number of those leaving during 1893–1914 was about 270,000. Therefore, the number of emigrants leaving before World War I was something over 330,000. However, 7–8 percent of the persons included in this calculation, based on the names appearing in the passenger lists, traveled to America more than once. Thus, the number of persons taking part in the emigration before the First World War was smaller than 330,000. Quite likely it was a little over 300,000.[1] Emigrating from Finland to North America during World War I was exceptional, and in the 1920s the waves of emigrants were small compared to those before the war. About 60,000 Finns, however, emigrated in the 1920s. Thus the number of Finns taking part in the Great Migration to North America was more than 350,000. In the federal census statistics of 1920, there were 149,824 foreign-born Finns in the United States (85,287 or 56.9 percent, males, and 64,537 or 43.1 percent, females), 130,083 persons with both parents foreign born, and 15,423 persons with one parent foreign born, for a total of 295,330 Finns.[2] These numbers tell the figure that was enumerated in the census, which is not necessarily the ultimate exact number because not all Finns were found by enumerators.

**Table 1. The Number of Finnish Emigrants According to Official Statistics and Passenger Lists, 1893–1914**

| YEAR | OFFICIAL STATISTICS IN FINLAND | PASSENGER LISTS OF THE SHIPPING LINES | YEAR | OFFICIAL STATISTICS IN FINLAND | PASSENGER LISTS OF THE SHIPPING LINES |
|---|---|---|---|---|---|
| 1893 | 9,177 | 6,688 | 1905 | 17,427 | 18,754 |
| 1894 | 1,380 | 1,284 | 1906 | 17,517 | 17,556 |
| 1895 | 4,020 | 3,296 | 1907 | 16,296 | 16,930 |
| 1896 | 5,185 | 5,329 | 1908 | 5,812 | 6,433 |
| 1897 | 1,916 | 2,772 | 1909 | 19,144 | 21,009 |
| 1898 | 3,467 | 3,886 | 1910 | 19,007 | 20,285 |
| 1899 | 12,075 | 12,993 | 1911 | 9,372 | 10,251 |
| 1900 | 10,397 | 11,316 | 1912 | 10,724 | 11,795 |
| 1901 | 12,561 | 13,205 | 1913 | 20,057 | 21,855 |
| 1902 | 23,152 | 23,311 | 1914 | 6,474 | 5,925 |
| 1903 | 16,964 | 18,216 | | | |
| 1904 | 10,952 | 11,269 | *1893–1914* | *253,016* | *264,358* |

Source: Reino Kero, *Migration from Finland to North America in the Years between the United States Civil War and the First World War* (Turku: University of Turku, 1974), 36.

The Finnish population in North America is presented in Table 2 for the year 1930–31, including both first and second generations.[3]

If Finnish emigration is compared to emigration from other European countries, we can see that from the end of the 1890s, Finland was one of those European countries where emigration had a very great effect on population trends. In the 1870s, the 1880s, and the beginning of the 1890s, on the other hand, the number of Finnish emigrants was rather meager according to European standards, although it was strong in relation to the total population of Finland, about 3.5 million people. During the period 1820–1930, approximately 35 million people from Europe moved to the United States; among the greater sending countries were Germany, Ireland, and Italy. The reasons for emigrating were in general the same: economic pressure and hope of a better life in a new environment with new possibilities. Also political oppression and changes were in many countries a push factor, such as in Finland during the early years of the twentieth century.

### Emigration to America—An Ostrobothnian Phenomenon

Finnish emigration has commonly been viewed as a particularly Ostrobothnian phenomenon. This generalization can to a large extent be accepted. However, it should be kept in mind when examining the geographical distribution of Finnish emigration that the boundaries between areas of strong and weak emigration did follow provincial or regional borders. Thus, beyond the borders of Vaasa Province, emigration was also quite strong from some parts of Oulu Province, from northern Satakunta, from the vicinity of Rauma, from the Åland Islands, and from several communes along the coast and archipelago of Finland proper.

## Table 2. The Finnish Population in North America in the Early 1930s, Including Both First and Second Generations

| UNITED STATES, 1930 | PERSONS | % OF FINNISH POPULATION IN THE U.S. | UNITED STATES, 1930 | PERSONS | % OF FINNISH POPULATION IN THE U.S. |
|---|---|---|---|---|---|
| Michigan | 74,200 | 23.2 | North Dakota | 3,300 | 1.0 |
| Minnesota | 60,600 | 18.9 | South Dakota | 3,100 | 1.0 |
| New York | 27,200 | 8.5 | New Hampshire | 3,000 | 0.9 |
| Massachusetts | 26,900 | 8.4 | Connecticut | 3,000 | 0.9 |
| Washington | 22,000 | 6.9 | Maine | 2,900 | 0.9 |
| California | 16,400 | 5.1 | Idaho | 1,900 | 0.6 |
| Wisconsin | 14,600 | 4.6 | Wyoming | 1,400 | 0.4 |
| Ohio | 12,800 | 4.0 | Colorado | 1,300 | 0.4 |
| Oregon | 12,000 | 3.8 | Utah | 1,100 | 0.4 |
| Illinois | 9,600 | 3.0 | Vermont | 1,100 | 0.3 |
| Montana | 6,100 | 1.9 | Other states | 6,400 | 2.0 |
| New Jersey | 5,000 | 1.5 | | | |
| Pennsylvania | 4,600 | 1.4 | *Total United States* | *320,500* | *100.0* |

| CANADA, 1931 | PERSONS | % OF FINNISH POPULATION IN CANADA | CANADA, 1931 | PERSONS | % OF FINNISH POPULATION IN CANADA |
|---|---|---|---|---|---|
| Ontario | 27,100 | 62.3 | Saskatchewan | 2,300 | 5.3 |
| British Columbia | 6,600 | 15.0 | Manitoba | 1,000 | 2.3 |
| Alberta | 3,300 | 7.6 | Other provinces | 300 | 0.6 |
| Quebec | 3,000 | 6.8 | *Total Canada* | *43,600* | *100.0* |

Note: See Reino Kero, *Suureen länteen: Siirtolaisuus Suomesta Yhdysvaltoihin ja Kanadaan* (Turku: Siirtolaisuusinstituutti, 1996), 131; Reino Kero, *The Finns in North America: Destinations and Composition of Immigrant Societies in North America before World War I* (Turku: University of Turku, 1980); Jouni Korkiasaari, *Suomalaiset maailmalla: Suomen siirtolaisuus ja ulkosuomalaiset entisistä ajoista tähän päivään* (Turku: Siirtolaisuusinstituutti, 1989). The United States and Canada conducted a general census in 1930 and 1931 respectively.

## Table 3. The Number of Emigrants by the Provinces of Finland, 1870–1914

| PROVINCE | # OF EMIGRANTS | % OF TOTAL | PROVINCE | # OF EMIGRANTS | % OF TOTAL |
|---|---|---|---|---|---|
| Uusimaa | 13,179 | 4.4 | Kuopio | 9,896 | 3.3 |
| Turku and Pori | 43,753 | 14.5 | Vaasa | 158,408 | 52.3 |
| Häme | 8,795 | 2.9 | Oulu | 47,657 | 15.7 |
| Viipuri | 16,041 | 5.2 | | | |
| Mikkeli | 5,053 | 1.7 | *The whole country* | *302,782* | *100.0* |

Source: Kero, *Migration from Finland to North America*, 217–32.

**FIGURE 1.** The pioneer home built by Helmi and Klaus Ruotsalainen in Rock, Michigan, in 1914. This picture was sent to relatives as a postcard. (Source: America letter collections. s.a. 70. I, DGH)

Emigration from Finnish towns was generally stronger than from the surrounding countryside. However, an extremely large portion of the emigrants leaving from towns, perhaps as much as 70–80 percent, were people who had moved to these towns from the countryside and for whom the town in the homeland was only a temporary stopover on the trip to America.

Looking at the great migration from the whole of Europe, we may say that an economic situation existed, while a labor shortage, caused by America's rapid economic growth, prevailed on the American side of the North Atlantic. On the European side, economic growth was slower, and there existed an overabundant workforce. During this migration, labor reserves in Europe moved to the American side. Finnish emigration was a part of this phenomenon.

Several Finnish studies of emigration history discuss the question of why Finnish emigration was concentrated in Ostrobothnia. Instead, I have in my studies attempted to answer the question of how the situation arose in which emigration occurred much more frequently from a given area of Finland. This area was broader than just Ostrobothnia. I have called this area "Emigration Finland."

### Why to Countries Overseas?

I want to emphasize the following factors, all of which are rather well presented in the studies concerned with the problem of Ostrobothnian emigration. First, an extremely rapid growth in population occurred in Emigration Finland at the end of the nineteenth century. Second, not one important industrial center sprang up in Emigration Finland at the end of the nineteenth century. Third, a sort of division of labor seems to have developed between internal migration and emigration. People from Emigration Finland went to America, while those from the rest of Finland went to such industrial centers as Helsinki, Turku, Tampere, Viipuri, and St. Petersburg.

An important background factor of emigration, which affected the rest of Finland as well as Emigration Finland, is that at the end of the nineteenth and the beginning of the twentieth centuries, the mobility of the Finnish people was increasing and resulted in emigration. In other areas this increased mobility appeared as an acceleration of internal migration. The motives for emigration were mainly economic, but in less ordinary cases emigrants might base their leaving on almost any cause whatsoever.

### The Cycles of Emigration

Emigration was not evenly distributed between one month and another, one year and another, or one decade and another, but fluctuated greatly in its strength. At least three kinds of regular fluctuations can be distinguished: seasonal changes, changes depending on short-term economic cycles, and changes occurring in longer cycles of about twenty years.

In the 1870s and 1880s, Finnish emigration was generally at its strongest in the early summer, but later the peak of emigration during each year occurred in April. In very exceptional cases in the twentieth century, the peak of emigration occurred in December. In part, conditions of travel determined the monthly distribution of emigration. In the 1870s and the 1880s, winter navigation was still in its beginning stages, which forced emigrants to time their departure in the early summer. Later, the development of winter navigation made possible a more balanced distribution of emigration throughout the year. To some extent seasonal work in America and Finland probably also had an effect on the distribution of emigration.

The movement of short-term cycles discernible in the American economy shows very clearly in Finnish emigration. When a period of boom occurred in the American economy, Finnish migration to America increased immediately, while during American periods of bust, the Finnish migration became weaker. The rare exceptions to this pattern could be attributed to the results of American presidential elections, for example, or to labor strikes occurring in America.

Two long-term cycles can be distinguished in Finnish emigration: one extended from 1874 to 1893, and the other from 1894 to 1914. Contrary to that of other Nordic countries, Finnish emigration was appreciably more extensive in the latter than in the former of these cycles. This doubtlessly resulted in part from the rather late start of emigration from Finland, but its most important cause was probably the stagnation of population growth in Finland in the 1860s. Because of this, there were comparatively few people in Finland who were of suitable age for emigration in the 1880s, the greatest decade of emigration from Scandinavia. In addition to these two emigration cycles, there was also a third and smaller one after the Second World War. It was caused by differing background factors and composed of quite different types of emigrants. It will be discussed later in this chapter.

## Table 4. The Occupational-Social Composition of Finnish Emigration, 1893–1914

| OCCUPATION | # OF PERSONS | % OF TOTAL | OCCUPATION | # OF PERSONS | % OF TOTAL |
| --- | --- | --- | --- | --- | --- |
| Farmers | 13,433 | 5.3 | Cottagers | 67,915 | 26.8 |
| Farmers' children | 61,422 | 24.3 | Workers | 49,536 | 19.6 |
| Crofters (tenants) | 6,857 | 2.7 | Others | 29,219 | 11.5 |
| Crofters' children | 24,634 | 9.7 | *Total* | *253,016* | *100.0* |

Source: Kero, *Migration from Finland to North America*, 82.

### The Structure of Finnish Emigration

Immigrants from Finland did not have a homogenous background. Early immigrants—those of the 1870s—had a rather different social background from those immigrants who left Finland shortly before World War I. In addition, the political background of the early and late immigrant generations differed. Increasing numbers of late immigrants had been influenced by the developing Finnish labor movement. It should furthermore be noted that whereas immigrants during the 1890s and earlier were for the most part from Ostrobothnia, immigrants departing after 1900 included also sizable numbers from other parts of Finland, although the majority continued to come from Ostrobothnia. Almost 90 percent of Finnish emigrants left from rural districts. In addition, one must remember that a large portion of those leaving from towns were probably so-called stage emigrants. This group of emigrants had first moved from the countryside to the towns, and then after some time elapsed, they continued their journey to countries overseas.

Over half of the emigrants in the 1870s were farmers and their children. As the phenomenon of emigration developed, the proportion of especially farmers, but also clearly of their children, declined. Correspondingly, the proportions of cottagers and of the workers increased. This change in structure was probably in the first place the result of the fact that in the early stages of immigration, only farmers had sufficient means to purchase tickets for the trip. In the second place, it possibly resulted from the fact that emigration spread from Oulu and Vaasa provinces to the rest of Finland. This meant that the population base for emigration was different at the beginning of the twentieth century from what it was in the 1880s. Perhaps also of influence was the fact that as industrialization occurred, the occupational structure of Finland as a whole changed from a purely agricultural system to one that also included, to a certain degree, industrial trades.

The streams of emigrants originating in different parts of Finland differed to some extent from each other. Farmers appeared relatively frequently among emigrants from Oulu, Mikkeli, and Viipuri provinces. Crofters (*torpparit*) were numerous, particularly among emigrants from Turku and Pori Province, and cottagers were among those from Kuopio and Vaasa provinces. There were many workers and people in other occupational categories among the emigrants from Uusimaa Province.

Almost 65 percent of the emigrants leaving Finland during 1869–1914 were men. Compared to that of other Nordic countries, Finnish emigration was quite male-dominated. Especially in the opening phases of emigration, the proportion of men among the emigrants was greater than that of women. The largest

## Table 5. The Sex Composition of Finnish Emigration, 1869–1914

| YEAR | MEN | | WOMEN | | UNKNOWN SEX | | TOTAL |
|---|---|---|---|---|---|---|---|
| 1869–74 | 1,531 | 82.6% | 323 | 17.4% | — | | 100.0 % |
| 1875–79 | 721 | 71.5% | 287 | 28.4% | 1 | 0.1% | 100.0 % |
| 1880–84 | 9,604 | 73.7% | 3,117 | 23.9% | 318 | 2.4% | 100.0 % |
| 1885–89 | 16,879 | 75.6% | 5,280 | 23.7% | 164 | 0.7% | 100.0 % |
| 1890–94 | 14,132 | 67.2% | 6,845 | 32.6% | 46 | 0.2% | 100.0 % |
| 1895–99 | 15,607 | 58.5% | 11,056 | 41.5% | — | | 100.0 % |
| 1900–1904 | 47,184 | 63.7% | 26,842 | 36.3% | — | | 100.0 % |
| 1905–9 | 50,214 | 65.9% | 25,982 | 34.1% | — | | 100.0 % |
| 1910–14 | 39,487 | 60.2% | 26,147 | 39.8% | — | | 100.0 % |
| *1869–1914* | *195,359* | *64.7%* | *105,379* | *35.1%* | *529* | *0.2%* | *100.0 %* |

Source: Kero, *Migration from Finland to North America*, 91–2.

proportion of women occurred among emigrants leaving from Oulu Province, the smallest among those emigrating from Mikkeli Province.

There were almost as many women as men among emigrants from towns. There were also some rural areas, however, from which the emigration was fairly well balanced among the sexes. In particular, the coast and archipelago of Finland proper should be mentioned as such an area. The sex composition of a given area's emigration was especially affected by that area's population structure, by its job opportunities, by the attitudes toward emigration, and by internal migration. It was affected possibly also by the opportunities for work in the locality toward which the area's emigration was directed. On the other hand, the composition of emigrants leaving a given area might have determined the locality in America to which these people migrated.

The immigrant population in the area of its settlement was not so male dominated as the immigrant stream was, for it was more common among men than among women to return to the homeland. The structures of the societies formed by Finnish immigrants in different parts of North America varied greatly, probably because of the differences existing in work opportunities. While, on the one hand, men formed a definite majority of Finnish immigrants in the United States and Canada, on the other hand, migration from Finland to South Africa and Australia was still much more male dominated.

Finnish emigrants, as did emigrants in general, came from relatively young age groups from the beginning of emigration up to the First World War. However, as the phenomenon of emigration developed, the average age of those leaving became lower. In particular, the proportion among all emigrants of those under four years of age and fifteen-to-nineteen-year-olds grew over the years. Emigration of the very young was typical, especially in Vaasa Province, while emigration from Uusimaa and Viipuri provinces was to a certain extent composed of older age groups. Women who emigrated were on the average younger than men. Urban emigration differed from rural emigration: those under sixteen years and over twenty-five years composed a larger proportion of emigrants from towns than from the countryside.

Emigration itself fundamentally affected the distribution of emigrants' ages: in the area where emigration had been occurring for some time, emigrants would in time be composed principally of those just arriving at working age. Changes in the birth and death rates also undoubtedly had some influence. Thus the effect of the famine years of the 1860s was still distinctly evident in the age distribution of Finnish emigrants in 1905.

Researchers have studied what proportion of emigration from Nordic countries at different times was composed of the movement of entire families, and what proportion was composed of the movement of individuals. They have discovered that as the phenomenon of emigration developed, a definite shift occurred from family emigration to individual emigration. On the basis of available material, it seems probable that the same shift occurred in Finland.

While examining the different areas of Finland, we discover that emigration from Oulu and Viipuri provinces was distinctly an emigration of families. That from Turku and Pori, Häme, Kuopio, and Mikkeli provinces was definitely an emigration of individuals. Family emigration composed a larger proportion of urban than of rural emigration. Also family emigration was more common from the Finnish-speaking districts of Ostrobothnia than it was from the Swedish-speaking districts.

### The Destinations of Finnish Immigrants in America

The recruiting of immigrants is discussed in, for example, nineteenth-century newspapers as if it played an important role in the migration process. When one examines the recruiting attempts, however, it appears that the number of those actually recruited was very small. The earliest recruiting attempts were from the 1860s and 1870s. These may have had a significance to the extent that the few emigrants then recruited served as pathfinders for the people from northern Finland who later immigrated to northern Michigan. In addition to the United States, Canada, Australia, and Brazil also showed an interest in Finnish immigrants, but recruiting done on their behalf apparently produced very meager results.

When comparing the destinations of immigrants from different parts of Finland, it is possible to divide the rural areas of the country into several parts. In my studies, I have divided Finland into twenty-one areas. These divisions are, however, only tentative. The destination of emigration from certain towns, or groups of towns, remained unchanged for decades. In these cases, one is justified in referring to a very established emigration tradition. In most cases, these traditions, whether strong or weak, were terminated by World War I, which brought immigration from Finland to North America to a virtual standstill.

Immigrants from Vaasa Province constituted the bulk of Finnish settlers in most North American "Finn areas." There were, however, Finntowns and Finn areas where Vaasa Province's share was much smaller or bigger than its share of the total Finnish immigration to North America. It was especially large in Ohio, Illinois, and the Rocky Mountain and the Pacific states, as well as in Canada; near to the average in the Minnesota-Michigan area; and underrepresented in the eastern seaboard states.

The second and third important emigration provinces in Finland were Turku-Pori and Oulu, respectively. Turku-Pori's share was proportionally large in the eastern seaboard states, very near to average in the Minnesota-Michigan area and Canada, and underrepresented in the Illinois-Ohio area, as it was in the Rocky Mountain and Pacific states. Oulu's share was very large in the Pacific coast states, and near to the average in the eastern seaboard states, Minnesota-Michigan, and the Rocky Mountain states. Its share was very small in Ohio-Illinois and probably also in Canada.

**FIGURE 2.** Astoria, Oregon, became an important fishing and canning center for salmon. Union Fishermen's Co-Operative Packing Company was founded in 1896 by mainly Finnish, Swedish, Norwegian, and Icelandic fishermen as a result of a large strike. The company was located in the immediate neighborhood of Astoria's Finntown. The first Finns had come to Astoria in the 1850s from San Francisco. By 1905, Astoria's Finnish population numbered ca. 2,000, more than 18 percent of the town's population. The new packing buildings were erected in 1897, and the company expanded steadily. It was closed in 1975. Here is a postcard from Astoria to Finland in 1915. (Source: Postcard collections, DGH)

The importance of other provinces in emigration was much smaller than that of Vaasa, Oulu, and Turku-Pori. It should be mentioned, however, that the immigrants coming from Uusimaa were numerous especially in New York City. This was probably due to the influence of the growing Finnish capitol of Helsinki, where domestic immigrants may have had already some urban experiences.

The destinations of rural and urban immigrants were slightly different. The largest percentage of urban immigrants went to New York City, whereas an exceptionally large share of immigrants to Colorado and Montana came from the countryside. The differences were probably the result of the vocational differences of the two immigrant types.

Some differences are also apparent in the destinations of Finnish men and women. Of the states important for Finnish immigration, New York (mainly New York City) attracted, relatively speaking, most Finnish women. There were proportionally more men among immigrants destined for the Midwest and the mountain states. These differences were, above all, due to differences experienced by men and women in finding work.

Quite naturally, the American environment had an effect on the immigrants' religious and political views. Local differences in the behavior of immigrants can be explained by differences in their new environment. However, the departure area of different Finnish immigrant groups in North America varied to a great extent. On the basis of this, one is also justified in asking to what extent the Old Country origin of the immigrants explains why Michigan became such an important stronghold of the Suomi Synod, why the stronghold of the Laestadian Church was located in Michigan and Minnesota, why the Finnish Socialist Federation found such strong support among the Finns in New York and Massachusetts, and why the syndicalist Industrial Workers of the World (IWW) movement won so much support in Minnesota, Ontario, and the more western part of the United States.

### New Forms of Migration after the Second World War

The Second World War (1939–45) changed many patterns of migration in the whole world. New political boundaries were defined, and new international alliances were established, the most important of which was the drawing of the Iron Curtain in eastern Europe. There followed the period called the Cold War between the East and the West until the 1970s. That period finally closed in December 1991 when the Soviet Union was dissolved.

Europe was in great disorder after the Second World War ended, with millions of people displaced

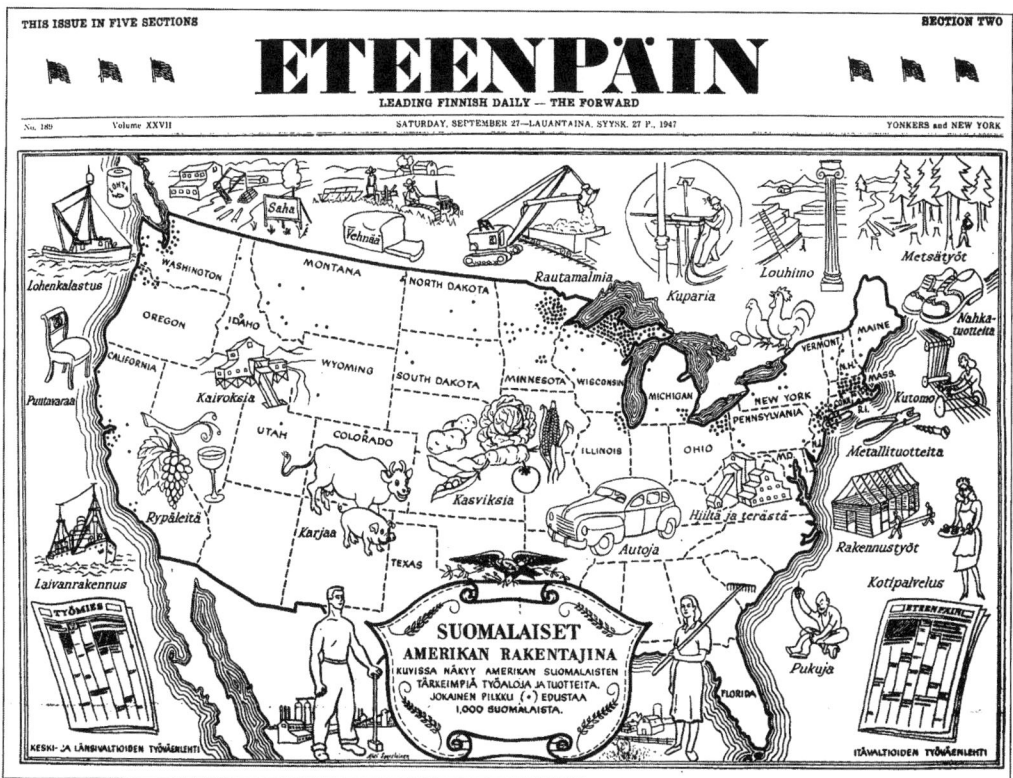

**FIGURE 3.** This map, published in 1947 by *Eteenpäin*, depicts the areas of settlement and the livelihood of the American Finns. (Source: IMT Photo collections)

## Table 6. Persons from Finland Obtaining Legal Permanent Resident Status, 1940–2011

| YEARS OF IMMIGRATION | # OF IMMIGRANTS | YEARS OF IMMIGRATION | # OF IMMIGRANTS | YEARS OF IMMIGRATION | # OF IMMIGRANTS |
|---|---|---|---|---|---|
| 1940–49 | 2,230 | 1970–79 | 2,829 | 2000–2009 | 3,970 |
| 1950–59 | 4,923 | 1980–89 | 2,569 | 2010–11 | 812 |
| 1960–69 | 4,310 | 1990–99 | 3,970 | Total | 25,613 |

Source: U.S. Department of Homeland Security, *Yearbook of Immigration Statistics: 2011* (Washington, D.C.: U.S. Department of Homeland Security, Office of Immigration Statistics, 2012).

and living in refugee camps. Several thousands of refugees found their way to North America. There was also a small number of migrants from Finland during the late 1940s, including a number of soldiers or political conservatives who were not secure of their future in Finland. As a consequence of the immigration laws of the 1920s, a few hundred Finnish migrants were allowed in the United States each year. These quotas existed until the liberalization of immigration in 1965. Therefore, new immigration remained small during those years. After the quota system was abolished, there was not so much interest any more in going to the United States; instead, there was a growing number of migrants to Finland's neighbor Sweden, which was fast expanding economically. Sweden became the most important target of labor migration, with more than 530,000 migrants in 1945-96, while in the same period the United States received a total of 16,000 immigrants. Even Canada had received a strong influx of Finns during the post–World War II decades, totaling 22,000 immigrants.

More exact information on Finnish immigration to the United States is available in the *Yearbook of Immigration Statistics 2011*. There it is reported that the total number of immigrants from Finland from 1940 to 2011 was 25,613, or an average of only 356 persons yearly.[4]

These immigrants received permanent resident status in the United States, and their country of last residence before that was Finland. Not included, therefore, are persons such as students or those with a working permit. In addition, information is not available on how many Finns returned to Finland or moved to other countries. We may estimate that net migration from Finland to the United States during the post–World War II decades may be around 20,000 persons.

An important feature of Finnish migration to the United States was the specific qualities of the incomers. During the early decades of the twentieth century, they were made overwhelmingly of laboring classes, while the postwar immigrants were more educated. Naturally, there were very interesting subgroups in the migrant population. To these belonged a couple of hundred political refugees who escaped from Finland when the future of the country after the Second World War looked most gloomy. Among them were several successful officers who gained their place in the U.S. military forces and participated in Finnish immigrant community activities. The most famous officers were Lauri Törni and Alpo Marttinen. Captain Törni (Larry Thorne) died in the Vietnam jungles in 1965, Colonel Alpo Marttinen after a successful career in the U.S. Army in 1975.[5]

It was also typical that the new immigrants found their way to cities and particularly to Florida, which had, along with California, become a major target for the aging Finnish immigrant population of the United States as well as that of Canada. In Florida, Finnish communities were created in Lake Worth, Lantana, and other locations, where Finnish communities and social and cultural life evolved in patterns quite similar to those of many other ethnic groups. The number of Finns in Florida in the year 2,000 totaled more than 26,000 persons.[6] In addition to Florida, similar development took place in California and even some other southern states on a much smaller scale. In the U.S. Census data in 1990, a total of more than 659,000 persons claim Finnish roots.

## NOTES

1. See appendices 1, 2, and 3. There is discrepancy between the numbers found in the official statistics and passenger lists. The main reason for this is the insecurity of information in both kinds of sources. Quite a few individuals skipped officials, others may use a pseudonym, there were misspellings, and so forth. Reino Kero, *Migration from Finland to North America in the Years between the United States Civil War and the First World War* (Turku: University of Turku, 1974), 12–13.

2. *The Fourteenth Census of the United States Taken in the Year 1920, II: Population 1920, General Report and Analytical Tables* (Washington, D.C.: Government Printing Office, 1922), 693, 897.

3. See Reino Kero, *Suureen länteen suomalaiset* (Helsinki: Otava, 1976), 131; Reino Kero, *The Finns in North America: Destinations and Composition of Immigrant Societies in North America before World War I* (Turku: University of Turku, 1980); Jouni Korkiasaari, *Suomalaiset maailmalla: Suomen siirtolaisuus ja ulkosuomalaiset entisistä ajoista tähän päivään* (Turku: Siirtolaisuusinstituutti, 1989).

4. U.S. Department of Homeland Security, *Yearbook of Immigration Statistics: 2011* (Washington, D.C.: U.S. Department of Homeland Security, Office of Immigration Statistics, 2012).

5. For a recent biography of Alpo Marttinen, see Pasi Tuunainen, *Marttinen: Kahden armeijan soturi* (Helsinki: Otava, 2012).

6. Ira M. Sheskin, "Florida's Planned Retirement Communities: Marketing Age, Religion, Ethnicity and Lifestyle," in *Engineering Earth: The Impacts of Mega Engineering Projects*, ed. Stanley D. Brunn (Dordrecht: Springer, 2011), 1839–41.

# Finnish Settlements in the United States: "Nesting Places" and Finntowns

*Arnold R. Alanen*

The broad pattern of enclaves that Finns established throughout the United States included typical Finnish buildings such as saunas, churches, halls, and cooperative stores. There were several periods of migration—the American colonial era, the Gold Rush era, but most important was the 1880-1924 mass migration movement. During the 1870s and the 1880s the incipient Finnish settlements were called "nesting places" (*pesäpaikat*) by some Finnish Americans, although non-Finns eventually began describing them as "Finntowns." Today, the term "Finntown" is commonly used to identify many former Finnish settlements, even if they were never called Finntowns in the past.

When compared to many other European groups, the approximately 300,000 Finns who settled in the United States from 1864 to 1914 represent a relatively small number of immigrants. After arriving in the New World, however, Finns often settled proximate to one another in villages, towns, and cities, where they developed localized businesses and institutions—cooperatives, public saunas, stores, taverns, shops, churches, halls, and so forth. These settlements have often been termed "Finntowns," as were some rural places that included a cluster of Finnish farmsteads with a nearby hall and/or church. Although it is difficult to determine when the term "Finntown" was first used, non-Finns may have employed the word as early as the 1880s or 1890s to identify settlements inhabited by immigrants who spoke a language that was totally unfamiliar to them. The word "Finntown" (sometimes written as "Finn Town") undoubtedly became more commonplace by the early twentieth century; today it is widely used to define Finnish immigrant communities of the past.

Finntowns notwithstanding, a much earlier term that Finnish immigrants heard or read when their New World settlements were described was *pesäpaikka* ("nesting place") or *pesäpaikat* ("nesting places"). In 1879, soon after Alexander Leinonen established his newspaper, *Amerikan Suomalainen Lehti* (Finnish American News), in Calumet, Michigan, the erudite editor and publisher included a section with the title "Information about Finnish Nesting Places in North America." Leinonen had previously visited several of these early communities, and he continued to do so during his sixteen-year-long tenure with the newspaper. But it was immigrant correspondents who provided most of the place-based information for *Amerikan Suomalainen Lehti*. These writers would send their comments and observations about Finnish American settlements (that is, nesting places) to Leinonen, who then published them in the newspaper. While Leinonen undoubtedly corrected some of the more noticeable spelling and grammatical errors, the published letters, often written in nineteenth-century vernacular Finnish, provide rich documentation and useful information about North America's earliest enclaves.[1]

The following account features the origins and characteristics of Finnish settlements—including both nesting places and Finntowns—in the United States through the 1920s. It then concludes with a brief discussion of the Finntown phenomenon in contemporary America. Since it is not possible to provide a complete overview of such an expansive topic in a single chapter, selected examples are used to represent the greater pattern.

While North America's first permanent Finnish settlements emerged during the mid-1860s when small groups of émigrés arrived in Minnesota and Michigan, limited numbers of Finns had departed for the New World at earlier points in time. Some Finns participated in colonization efforts undertaken by the Swedish Crown along the Delaware River valley during the seventeenth century; others were involved with Russian activities in Alaska from the 1790s to 1867; and Finnish seamen departed their ships at various American ports during the 1850s. Therefore, the following account also includes a brief overview of the few pre-1864 enclaves where Finnish émigrés settled, if only for a limited time. Since the most consistent sources of immigrant population numbers are found in the decennial censuses conducted by the U.S. government from 1790 onward, the discussion begins with an assessment of the qualities and shortcomings of these documents.

### The U.S. Census of Population: Counting and Locating Finnish Immigrants

The comprehensiveness and accuracy of censuses undertaken by the U.S. government since 1790 have improved over time, but any effort to determine the number and location of Finns residing in the United States prior to 1900 poses very significant problems. The first census that provides country-of-birth information is the 1850 tabulation; no Finns are listed in that count, but Finnish émigrés were grouped with Russians in the official census publications for the remainder of the nineteenth century: 1860, 1870, and 1880 (the original 1890 census forms no longer exist). Thus the only way to locate and count those respondents who identified Finland as their place of birth is to review the original manuscript schedules compiled by census enumerators. Until recently, this was a very laborious and time-consuming process since the diminutive Finnish immigrant population could only be located by viewing seemingly endless pages of census pages. Now, however, two commercially developed computer search programs offer rapid access to original census manuscript data. Primarily intended for genealogists, both programs are nevertheless very useful for scholars who engage in any facet of immigration history research.[2] Nevertheless, not all Finnish immigrants were counted by the enumerators, and Finns are generally underrepresented in all censuses conducted by the U.S. government.[3]

A notable change in census procedures occurred just prior to 1900 when representatives from several Finnish American organizations petitioned federal officials, requesting that Finns be listed separately in published census reports. After hearing arguments that Finland was not a province of Russia, that Finland was domestically independent, and that Finns and Russians represented "entirely different races," the officials agreed to list Finns as a separate group from 1900 onward. The directive, however, was not always followed everywhere. In 1910, one northeastern Minnesota enumerator still listed "Russia" as the country of birth for 240 Finns residing in three adjacent townships, and a similar occurrence took place in Brevort, Michigan, where all Finland Swedes were termed "Russian Swedes."[4]

Locating and counting the number of Finland Swedes in the United States is especially problematic, and virtually impossible to determine before 1910—the year that foreign-born respondents were asked to provide enumerators with their native language. While this information is very useful, an accurate count of Finland Swedes in 1910 and ensuing years is possible only by reviewing the original census manuscripts and searching for individuals who have "Finland-Swedish" included with their names. Again, this is a very laborious procedure, especially when considering large urban places. No easily accessible computer program exists for this task, although a Minnesota-based population research institution has recently pursued the language question by making a 1 percent sample of all foreign-born respondents listed in the 1910, 1920, and 1930 manuscript censuses. Because of the limited size of the Finland Swede population, the 1 percent sample underestimates their numbers in many states and localities, and its geographic accuracy is often questionable.[5]

### Serving Two Empires: Finns in New Sweden and Russian Alaska

Since several hundred Finns participated in the formation of the New Sweden colony in the Delaware River valley (1638–55), it is possible that some semblance of a Finntown briefly existed in this area of colonial America. Today, the most visible indications of a former Finnish presence are the place names, most notably Mullica, derived from the Finnish surname of farmer Eric Pålsson Mullika (in Finnish form, Mullikka). Mullica now identifies at least three geographic features and places in New Jersey—a river, a township, and a community (Mullica Hill). While there are no indications that Finnish language, Lutheranism, or sauna practices continued in the Delaware valley, some scholars have argued that Finns may have contributed to the development of America's log-building traditions and land-clearing techniques.

Two centuries after assisting in the formation of the Swedes' Delaware settlement, at least 575 Finland-born individuals, and perhaps as many as 1,200, spent some time in Russian Alaska, most notably the colonial capital of Sitka. They were laborers, seamen, carpenters, scientists, admirals, administrators, and Lutheran pastors. Finland Swedes, some of whom achieved success and notoriety within the Russian system (two served as governors), formed at least 70 percent of the entourage. Nineteenth-century maps of Sitka reveal the presence of several bathhouses, most of which were examples of the *banya* (a Russian steambath); nonetheless, it is almost certain that the Finnish sauna was also present in Sitka. The rain forest climate has removed most material evidence of Finnish activities, although the Russian Bishop's House still portrays the Finns' log-building skills. While a very small number of Finns remained in Sitka following the transfer of Alaska to the United States in 1867, most returned to their homeland. A few may have moved to Canada and others to California because of their familiarity with the former Russian outpost at Fort Ross. Alaska would not again emerge as a destination for Finnish immigrants until the late nineteenth and early twentieth centuries.[6]

### Finns in the United States Prior to the American Civil War

While 1864 marks the year when continuous Finnish immigration to the United States began, some Finns arrived sporadically during earlier decades of the nineteenth century. Very little is known about these early émigrés, although the unusual career of Charles Erik Engelbrekt Sjödahl, a Finland Swede who changed his name to Charles Linn in the United States, is relatively well documented. A sailor from Uusimaa Province, Linn moved to Montgomery, Alabama, where he established a mercantile business in 1838. After serving as a Confederate navy ship's captain during the Civil War, Linn returned to Montgomery and began recruiting Finnish workers to his commercial enterprise. The manuscript censuses identify Sweden as Linn's place of birth, but twenty of the people he recruited to Montgomery are listed as Finns. Linn financed the construction of a large bank in the nearby city of Birmingham in 1872, and some years before his death in 1884 the entrepreneurial immigrant organized the Linn Iron Works and the Birmingham Car and Foundry Company. Despite Linn's economic success, Alabama would never again serve as a destination for meaningful numbers of Finnish migrants.[7]

While the California gold rush of 1848 brought some Finnish fortune-seekers to America's Pacific coast, the largest group included several hundred sailors who departed ships blockaded in American ports during the Crimean War. Only 165 respondents (149 males, 16 females) identified Finland as their place of birth in the 1860 U.S. manuscript census, but it is certain that a fair number were never counted. Most were Finland Swedes: twenty-three had a surname of either Anderson, Johnson, Peterson, or Thompson, while a smaller group displayed other Swedish patronyms. The largest number had Anglicized their names, with the most popular being Brown, Wilson, and Smith.[8]

The 165 Finns were located in fourteen states, with almost half (80) in California. At least 32 of the Californians were gold miners, primarily in El Dorado (9) and Tuolumne (10) counties. The largest group (28) was concentrated in San Francisco, where most were mariners. If a Finntown existed in San Francisco at this time, it undoubtedly was centered at the inn or boardinghouse operated by thirty-year-old E. H. Inberg and his twenty-three-year-old wife, Mary. Both were born in Finland, along with eleven of the twenty men they accommodated in their facility. Also residing in the area was Finnish tavern keeper A. Johnson.[9]

Other port cities such as New York, Boston, Philadelphia, New Orleans, Pensacola, and Mobile had much smaller Finnish populations than did San Francisco. The few Finnish émigrés who lived outside these seven cities often blended into Swedish communities. The first Finn in Astoria, Oregon, for example, was a sailor, Charles Newman of Liminka, who arrived in 1859, one year after leaving his ship in New Orleans; by 1860 Newman had changed his name to Charley Brown—the only Finland-born person listed in the census for Astoria and Clatsop County.[10] Because Charley Brown and many other mid-nineteenth-century immigrants from Finland quickly adopted ubiquitous Americanized names, it is extremely difficult either to explore their origins or trace their subsequent paths in North America.

### Early Nesting Places and Finntowns, 1864–1880

No more than a few hundred Finns made their way to the United States during the latter half of the 1860s, but the decade is very important since it was at this time that Finnish-speaking immigrants established their first permanent settlements in North America. These enclaves emerged when Finnish immigrants arrived in rural Minnesota (1864) and Michigan's Copper Country (1865). Many came from either the Finnish or Swedish sides of the Tornio River, which had been designated as the border just after Finland became a grand duchy of the Russian Empire in 1809. Others departed from Arctic Norway. (Finns, called Kvens by the Norwegians, had been moving to northern Norway, or Ruija, since the 1600s.)

Many were followers of Lars Levi Laestadius, a pietistic Lutheran pastor who had an avid following in the Arctic region of the Nordic world.[11]

The first group, seventeen Finns (nine adults, eight children) from the Norwegian community of Vadsø (Vesisaari), made their way to the Mississippi River port of Red Wing, Minnesota, during the summer of 1864. Six of the adults were natives of northern Finland, and two originally came from the Swedish side of the border; all of the children were born in Norway. These Finns, along with some others who arrived during the latter 1860s, settled in the southern Minnesota county of Renville. In 1865, Peter Lahti became one of the first Finnish homesteaders to settle on the county's fertile prairies, where the small community of Franklin acted as the local service center. After Lahti and his son Carl acquired significant land holdings in the county, they paid for the transatlantic passage of other Finnish immigrants, who were accommodated in a grouping of buildings that included log cabins, bunkhouses, and a sauna. To repay their tickets, the recent arrivals were employed in the Lahtis' farming enterprises. The ensemble of buildings where the recent émigrés lived was called Finntown by non-Finns—undoubtedly one of the first times this term was employed in North America.[12]

In 1866, other immigrants established the nucleus for a Minnesota settlement that encompassed, until the 1880s, North America's largest contingent of rural Finns: Cokato (initially Mooers Prairie) in Wright County. Later that year and farther to the northwest, Minnesota's third Finnish settlement emerged in the Holmes City area of Douglas County. This settlement was entirely rural, and Holmes City itself never expanded beyond the size of a crossroads hamlet that initially focused on its Laestadian Lutheran church.[13]

When "America Fever" (*Amerikankuume*) spread to Finland proper during the 1870s, more émigrés made their way to Minnesota. Beginning in 1874 and continuing for several decades thereafter, many Finns who arrived in Minnesota settled in the New York Mills area of Otter Tail County, located in the west-central area of the state. According to the 1880 manuscript census, the 110 Finns who resided in Otter Tail formed Minnesota's largest Finnish community. New York Mills would soon emerge as the center for the most expansive Finnish farming district in North America, expanding to Sebeka, Menahga (Wadena County); and Wolf Lake or Susijärvi (Becker County). While most immigrants resided in rural settings, New York Mills was a Finntown in the truest sense of the word since it included houses, churches, halls, businesses, cooperatives, and the headquarters for a widely circulated newspaper, *Uusi Kotimaa* (New Homeland). In fact, Finnish-language newspapers would continue publication in New York Mills until 1980.[14]

Also in Minnesota was Minneapolis, which eventually embraced one of the nation's best-known metropolitan Finntowns. Finnish immigrants who moved on to Franklin, Cokato, Holmes City, New York Mills, and other rural areas of the Midwest during the nineteenth century often spent time in Minneapolis, where they earned money either for land purchases or making improvements to their farming operations. Minneapolis also attracted young single women who found work as servants and domestics in hotels, boardinghouses, and private residences. The first Finnish businesses—primarily grocery stores, tailor shops, and boardinghouses—developed along and close to Washington Avenue, one of the city's major roadways. When a Laestadian church was built several blocks to the south in 1900, the nucleus for an active and viable Minneapolis Finntown was established. The medieval axiom "city air makes one free" struck a chord with these Finns: some Laestadians even attended dances that occurred in Minneapolis.[15]

Elsewhere, other Finns started arriving in Michigan's Copper Country in 1865 when they accompanied larger numbers of Norwegians and Swedes who had been recruited to Hancock from the copper

# Number of Finnish Immigrants (by county)

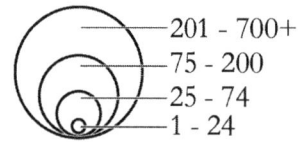
- 201 - 700+
- 75 - 200
- 25 - 74
- 1 - 24

## Counties and Associated Settlements with the Largest Finnish Populations, 1880

**California**
1 San Francisco: San Francisco
2 Mendocino
3 Placer

**Dakota Territory**
4 Billings

**Illinois**
5 Cook: Chicago

**Massachusetts**
6 Essex: Gloucester, Rockport
7 Suffolk: Boston

**Michigan**
8 Houghton: Calumet/Red Jacket, Hancock, Quincy, Franklin
9 Iosco: Oscoda
10 Keweenaw: Allouez
11 Marquette: Ishpeming, Negaunee, Republic
12 Newaygo: White Cloud

**Minnesota**
13 Carlton: Esko/Thomson Township
14 Douglas: Holmes City
15 Hennepin: Minneapolis
16 Otter Tail: New York Mills
17 Renville: Franklin
18 St. Louis: Midway Township, Duluth
19 Wright: Cokato, French Lake

**New York**
20 Kent: Brooklyn
21 New York: New York City

**Ohio**
22 Ashtabula: Ashtabula

**Oregon**
23 Clatsop: Astoria
24 Coos: Coos Bay, North Bend

**Pennsylvania**
25 Philadelphia: Philadelphia

**Utah**
26 Salt Lake: Bingham

**Washington**
27 Klickitat
28 Wahkiakum: Deep River

Note: Counties without settlement names had Finnish populations that were not concentrated in specific communities.

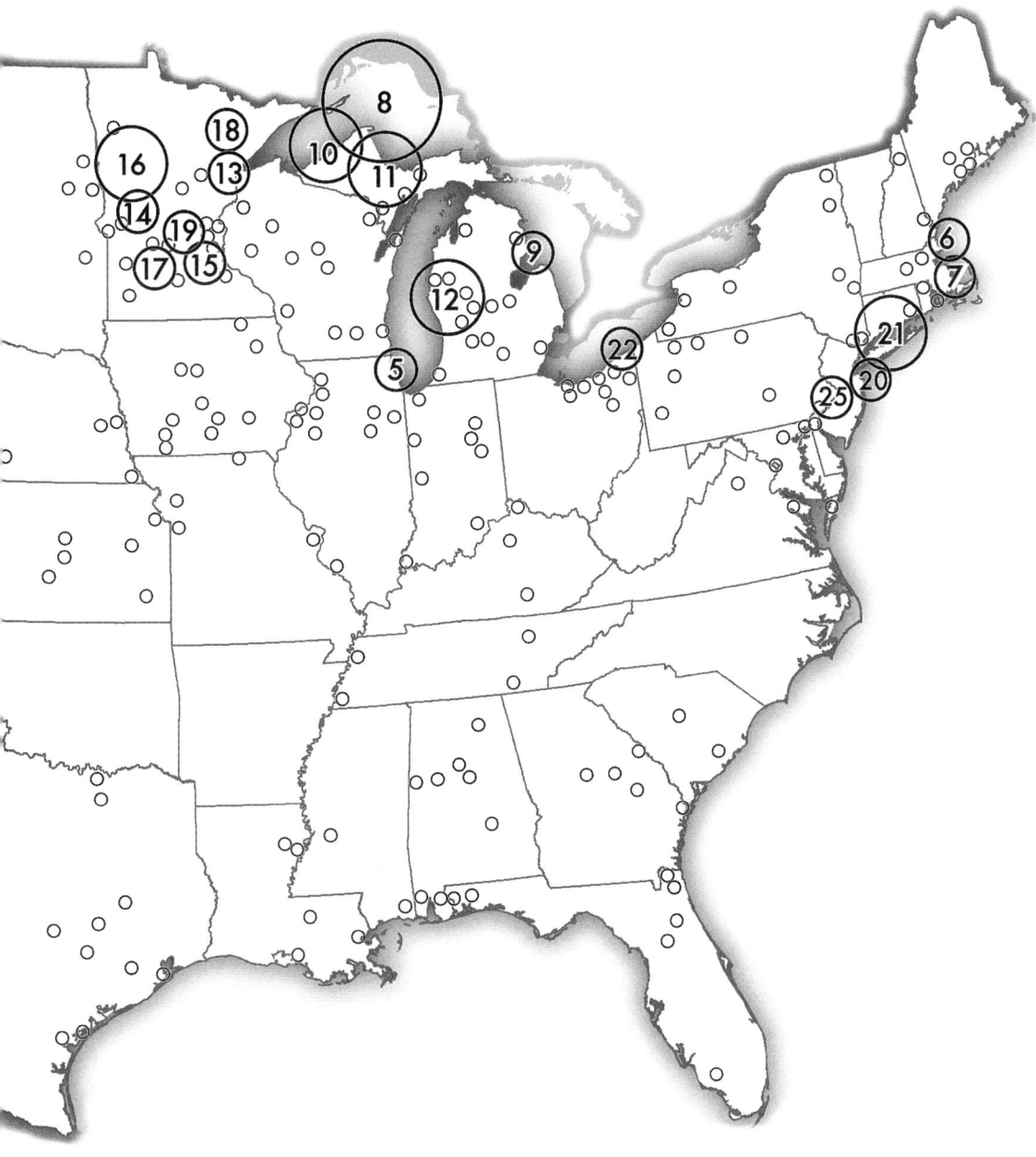

**FIGURE 1.** Finnish immigrants in the United States, 1880 (by county). Sources: U.S. manuscript census, 1880; *Amerikan Suomalainen Lehti* (Calumet, MI), 1879–80; Solomon Ilmonen, *Amerikan Suomalaisten historia ja elämäkertoja*, Vol. 2, 1923; *Newberry Library Atlas of Historical County Boundries*; and *Natural Earth Data*. Cartography by Margaret Raimann. Courtesy of Arnold Alanen.

mines at Alta and Kåfjord, Norway. The recruiter, Christian Tafte, a Norwegian immigrant employed by the Quincy Mining Company, was responsible for the departure of numerous Finnish recruits in 1865; at least fifty Finns resided in the Hancock area later that year, including the Norwegian Finns Peter and Mary Christopher and their three children. Peter Christopher carried a letter of recommendation written by a Cornish mining engineer at Kåfjord, which reportedly proved advantageous to all Finns who sought employment in the district. Some Finns were initially housed in Swedetown, a small residential district located next to the Quincy mine and originally intended for the Nordic immigrants recruited by Tafte. But when most of the first Swedes quickly departed the Copper County, some to join the Union army, this meant that the settlement actually served as a Finntown, even though the Swedetown name never changed.[16]

Those in the Copper Country, along with people in several other areas of Michigan, quickly saw the state become the most important destination for Finnish immigrants. By 1880, when census enumerators counted 3,400 Finns in the United States, 1,135 (one-third) were counted in Michigan; 745 resided in the Copper Country alone, where expanding mining activities provided steady employment opportunities. (The actual Copper Country count was larger than the census figure, perhaps two times, given that a significant number of Finns were born in either northern Sweden or Norway.) Calumet (originally called Red Jacket)—the headquarters for the Calumet and Hecla Mining Company, the largest and most influential of the Copper Country's industrial operations—soon became America's most important Finnish center and Finntown. It was here that North America's initial grouping of major Finnish businesses arose, most of them along Pine Street (Mäntykatu). The first general merchandise store was opened in 1875 by a Norwegian Finn, John Henrik Johnson, who later sold the firm to his compatriot, Johan Peter Noppa. Even more important were the cultural institutions that contributed to Calumet's emergence as a national center for the Finnish community. Of special note was Alexander Leinonen's before-mentioned *Amerikan Suomalainen Lehti,* published from 1879 to 1895. (Another newspaper, also called *Amerikan Suomalainen Lehti,* appeared in Hancock for one year in 1876, whereas *Sven Tuuva* was published during 1878 and 1879.) Calumet was especially important to the Laestadian Lutherans, who made the town their religious headquarters from the 1870s onward.[17]

Also in the Upper Peninsula of Michigan were iron ore mines that began drawing a small but steady flow of Finnish immigrants during the 1870s. The Marquette Iron Range, the first of three iron-ore mining districts that developed in Michigan, attracted Finnish workers as early as 1873, primarily to the cities of Ishpeming, Negaunee, and Republic; all eventually included significant concentrations of Finnish residents who organized numerous businesses and institutions that were concentrated in compact sections of each city. Negaunee included a small but viable community of Finland Swedes, several of whom began to arrive during the 1870s; their activities would eventually focus on Negaunee's large Österbottens Hall.[18]

Michigan's Lower Peninsula was an even more important destination for Finland Swedes. During the late 1860s, small groups settled in the west-central counties of Newyago (White Cloud), Mason (Ludington), and Kent (Grand Rapids), while other Finland Swedes were situated in the east-central county of Iosco (Oscoda and Tawas), located along Lake Huron. It appears, nonetheless, that a majority of outside observers identified any clustering of residences and businesses built by these Finland Swedes as Swedish enclaves.[19]

Small numbers of Finns also found their way to several other places in America throughout this

1864–80 period; some of these settlements would develop into Finntowns. San Francisco, where 40 percent (145 of 365) of the Golden State's Finns resided in 1880, maintained its role as the predominant Finnish settlement. During the 1870s, the nucleus for another Finntown was established 150 miles north of San Francisco in Mendocino County, where logging activities commenced along the Big River close to the Fort Bragg military outpost; after the garrison was abandoned in 1867, the town of Fort Bragg emerged as the center for local lumber mills and cattle ranches. Census enumerators counted ninety Finns in Mendocino County by 1880; eventually Fort Bragg's Finntown would include residences, three churches, two halls, hotels and boardinghouses, a cooperative store, and several private businesses. Small numbers of Finnish loggers and sawmill workers also settled much farther north of Fort Bragg in Humboldt County, where Eureka later became another important Finnish center. Both Fort Bragg and Eureka also attracted significant populations of Finland Swedes. Indeed, in 2013 Eureka was only one of two places in the United States—along with Dollar Bay, Michigan—that still maintained a hall associated with the Finland Swedes' once-thriving International Order of Runeberg. During the 1870s, another Finnish enclave emerged at Rocklin in Placer County, where most Finns worked as granite quarrymen.[20]

Oregon, by 1880, was home to 330 Finns. Charley Brown may have resided in Astoria already by 1860, but Oregon's initial Finnish communities were formed farther south along the Pacific coastline at Coos County (Coos Bay and North Bend), where a small group of immigrants landed in 1868; the county included ninety Finns by 1880. Astoria's permanent Finnish community was started by a group of fishermen during the early 1870s. Over the remainder of the decade, larger numbers of Finns arrived from both the Copper Country and Ashtabula, Ohio; almost 180 immigrant Finns were counted in the 1880 census of Astoria and Clatsop County. Salomon Ilmonen, however, claims that at least 300 Finns—many of them unmarried men from Kälviä—were actually residing in the "Helsinki of the West" at this time. Astoria's Finntown, later known as Uniontown, included numerous Finnish businesses that ranged from grocery stores, meat markets, bakeries, saloons, and restaurants to public saunas, boardinghouses, a cooperative fish cannery (organized with other immigrant groups), a cooperative store and dairy, one Congregational and three Lutheran churches, a workers' hall, and a temperance hall. A striking feature of Astoria's Finntown was its residential district, which developed along a steep embankment of the Columbia River valley.[21]

Agricultural settlements also developed in Oregon and the adjacent state of Washington. In northeastern Oregon and a great distance from the Pacific coast was Pendleton (Umatilla County), the state's primary Finnish farming community. The first Finn there was Elias Peltoperä (Johnson), who made his way to Pendleton in 1876, a decade after participating in the founding of Cokato's Finnish settlement. Once Peltoperä established his homestead in a remote area of the county, he encouraged other Finns to join him. Over the next two years at least five Finnish groups arrived from the Copper Country. Although several dozen Finns lived in rural Pendleton by 1880, the census only includes the names of two—probably because of the enumerator's failure to locate many Finns who resided in such an isolated setting. Because of northeastern Oregon's semiarid climate, the Finnish farmsteads of Pendleton were more widely dispersed than those in the Midwest; it is likely, therefore, that the settlement was not termed a Finntown, but as in many rural nineteenth-century Finnish American communities, the residents' common language and shared religious beliefs (Laestadian) contributed to considerable cohesiveness. Another enclave emerged at Brush Prairie, Washington (Clark County), termed the "Western Finns' oldest and most extensive agricultural area" by Ilmonen; elsewhere in southwestern Washington and just north of the Columbia River were the farming and logging settlements in the counties of Wahkiakum (Deep River), Pacific (Naselle), and Klickitat. Seattle's Finnish community, as well as several other settlements located along both sides of Puget Sound, emerged before 1880.[22]

The Rocky Mountain–Great Plains region also included a few Finnish settlements that date to the 1870s. Wyoming's first Finns arrived on the Union Pacific Railroad and began working in the coal-mining communities of Rock Springs (Sweetwater County) and Carbon (Hannah County); coal miners also made their way to Bingham, Utah (Salt Lake County). Billings County in western North Dakota included 45 temporary railroad workers in 1880, while a smaller contingent of Finns, most from the Copper Country, formed the nucleus for South Dakota's oldest Finnish settlement at Lake Norden–Poinsett (Hamlin County).[23]

When considering the eastern region of the United States, it is readily apparent that most early Finntowns, with just a few exceptions, were tied to activities other than agriculture. The Finns of Ashtabula, Ohio, who formed a foundation for their Finntown in 1874, worked on iron ore docks and in railroad shops; sixty Finns resided in Ashtabula by 1880. New England's first Finnish communities emerged in the Cape Ann area of Massachusetts: Gloucester, Rockport, and Lanesville. Here the Finns pursued fishing, although local granite quarries eventually provided even more employment opportunities. In 1878, Finns arrived in the textile-manufacturing and quarrying center of Fitchburg, Massachusetts, which soon became one of the most important Finnish centers in New England and the United States. The adjacent manufacturing city of Worcester also began serving as a major destination both for Finns and Finland Swedes throughout the 1870s.[24]

Finally, Boston, New York City, Philadelphia, and Chicago—major cities where Finns had resided since the 1850s—attracted larger numbers of immigrants from the 1870s onward. Some were clustered in a few neighborhoods, but they were hardly noticeable within such huge metropolitan settings. The one exception is the cooperative apartment complex that would be constructed from 1916 to 1927 in the New York City borough of Brooklyn by the Finnish Home Building Association. In fact, the entry for "Finntown" in the Finnish-language version of Wikipedia is almost exclusively devoted to a description of Brooklyn.[25]

### The Period of Large-Scale Immigration, 1881–1914

No more than 4,000 Finns immigrated to the United States between 1864 and 1880.[26] Despite their small numbers, these early émigrés managed to establish the nuclei for a relatively impressive number of Finnish settlements. Once Finnish immigration began to expand noticeably from the late 1880s to the onset of World War I, the existing enclaves grew, and new Finntowns were formed.

The census counted 62,640 foreign-born Finns in 1900, and 150,000 in 1920. Michigan's 1920 population of 30,100 Finns continued to lead the nation, but was followed closely by Minnesota (29,100); together, the two states accommodated almost 40 percent of America's Finns. Following Michigan and Minnesota were Massachusetts (14,570), New York (12,500), Washington (11,850), California (7,050), Wisconsin (6,750), Ohio (6,400), and Oregon. (6,050).

Within Michigan, the Upper Peninsula continued to attract most of the state's Finnish immigrants throughout the thirty-five-year period. During the 1880s, mining activities on the Menominee Iron Range drew Finns and Finland Swedes to Crystal Falls (Iron County) and Iron Mountain (Dickinson

**FIGURE 2.** Public saunas in towns and cities attracted both Finns and non-Finns. The Suomi Steam Baths served residents of Worcester, Massachusetts, until the 1960s. (Source: From the Collections of the Worcester Historical Museum, Worcester, Massachusetts)

County), while even larger numbers went to the Gogebic Iron Range, primarily the Gogebic County communities of Ironwood, Bessemer, and Wakefield. Many Finns also moved to the Upper Peninsula's rural farming districts—Pelkie, Tapiola, Toivola, Elo, Nisula, Liminga, Oskar, Chassel, Askel, Jacobsville, Eben, Bruce Crossing, Trout Creek, Aura, Covington, and other places in Houghton, Baraga, and Ontonagon counties. The eastern Upper Peninsula was characterized by such rural Finnish settlements as Trenary, Kiva, Chatham, and Eben (Alger County); Newberry (Luce County); Rudyard, Drummond Island, Rock (Delta County), and Sugar Island (Chippewa County). Kaleva (Manistee County), which attracted considerable attention when founded in 1900, was the best-known small Finntown in the Lower Peninsula, whereas the largest urban example emerged in Detroit, especially in and around the city's Woodrow Wilson neighborhood; the Motor City's Finntown grew noticeably when Copper Country Finns sought employment in automobile factories following a major mining strike in 1913–14.[27]

Minnesota experienced almost all of its late nineteenth- and early twentieth-century growth in Duluth and the northeastern region of the state. Duluth, in fact, became the most important center for

FIGURE 3. The Finntown that emerged along St. Croix Avenue in Duluth, Minnesota, by the early 1900s had one of the densest concentrations of Finns in the entire United States. (Source: *Amerikan albumi: kuvia Amerikan suomlaisten asuinpaikoilta* [Brooklyn, New York: Suomalainen Kansalliskirjakauppa, 1904], Arnold Alanen collections)

Finns residing throughout Minnesota and the Midwest, and was even dubbed the "Finnish capital of the United States" and the "Helsinki of America." During the 1870s, a token number of Finnish fishermen and workers had settled in Duluth, which Ilmonen described as "a little disorderly town." As more Finns arrived throughout the next decade, they initially made their way to St. Croix Avenue, a central district of Duluth that bordered the Lake Superior harbor; soon a Finntown with apartment buildings, boardinghouses, saunas, saloons, restaurants, and stores appeared. Finns would eventually disperse to other sections of Duluth and establish numerous institutions: churches, temperance and workers' societies, literary and debate clubs, theater groups, athletic and musical organizations, newspapers, a hospital, and the Finnish Work People's College (Työväen Opisto), one of only two Finnish higher educational institutions in North America. Some Finns, however, remained in the St. Croix Avenue neighborhood until urban renewal actions led to its removal during the 1960s. Another concentration of buildings was developed by Finland Swedes—residences, churches, taverns, a wholesale grocer, and a large construction company—in West Duluth.[28]

The greatest increase in Minnesota's Finnish population was fueled by the state's emerging iron ore industry, concentrated on the Vermilion, Mesabi, and Cuyuna iron ranges. Finns moved to the Vermilion in 1883, arriving first at Soudan and then Ely, but the Finns' primary magnet was the Mesabi, opened in 1892 as the world's largest iron ore producer. Virginia, Hibbing, Eveleth, Chisholm, Gilbert, Nashwauk,

Biwabik, and other Mesabi towns quickly became Finnish bastions; Ely was the foremost Finnish community on the Vermilion, while Crosby played a similar role on the Cuyuna. In fact, Finns were so prevalent throughout the Iron Range that they constituted the largest ethnic group in a mining district known for its many European immigrant groups. Overall, 10,500 Finland-born immigrants resided on the entire Iron Range by 1910. Finland Swedes also formed communities in Eveleth, Virginia, Chisholm, Hibbing, and Ely.[29]

The Finns of Minnesota pursued farming with an unmatched passion: 60 percent of Minnesota's Finnish immigrants were engaged in agriculture by 1920—the highest figure demonstrated by Finns anywhere in the nation. From the 1890s onward, most Finnish farms were found in northeastern Minnesota, where only one agricultural settlement had arisen during the 1870s—at Esko's Corner (now Esko), a notable Finntown. Northeastern Minnesota's Finnish farm totals jumped appreciably after 1907 when striking miners, termed "Finnish trouble makers" by mining company supervisors, were unable to secure work because of blacklisting. And "if a 'Finnish trouble maker' had money," Kero has written, "he bought a farm." Other land-hungry Finnish immigrants who arrived from urban areas, lumber camps, and directly from Finland developed even more farms. The many rural settlements included Kalevala, Kettle River, Cromwell (Carlton County); Lawler, Jacobson (Aitkin County); Suomi, Trout Lake (Itasca County); Floodwood, Embarrass, Makinen, Markham, Toivola, Palo, Alango, Brimson, Zim (St. Louis County); and Finland and Toimi (Lake County).[30]

Among the land sales schemes directed toward prospective Finnish agrarians was the one for

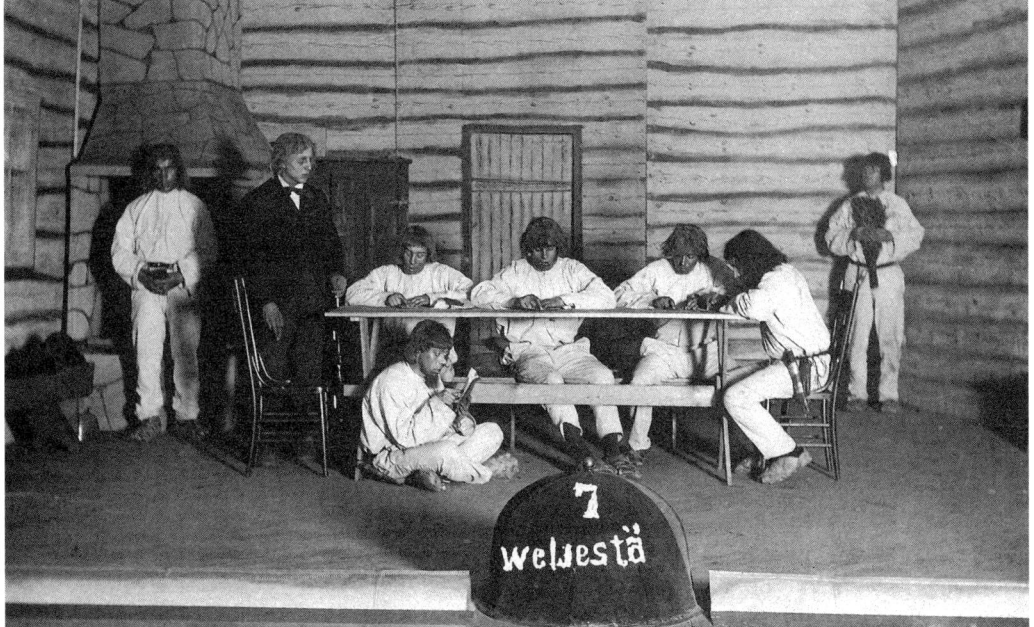

FIGURE 4. The halls located in Finntowns were known for their many programs, which included plays such as the classic Finnish play by Aleksis Kivi, *The Seven Brothers,* performed here in Nashwauk, Minnesota, ca. 1910s. (Source: Arnold Alanen collections)

**FIGURE 5.** Virtually every midwestern Finnish settlement included a cooperative store such as the Elanto organization in Nashwauk, Minnesota. Here a group of women associated with the Women's Cooperative Guild stand in front of the store in 1934. (Source: Arnold Alanen collections)

Nurmijärvi, located just outside of Finlayson in Pine County. Marketed by Finnish businessmen John Oldenberg and J. H. Jasberg for the St. Paul and Duluth Railroad, the men's 1894 advertisement asserted that Nurmijärvi's farmers would achieve immediate economic success because of railroads that led directly to Duluth in the north and Minneapolis–St. Paul in the south.[31]

Northern Wisconsin, situated between Michigan and Minnesota, also served as a destination for Finnish immigrants from the 1880s onward. Among the most important centers was the city of Superior, located adjacent to Duluth; two important landmarks in Superior's Finntown were the headquarters for the Finnish Central Cooperative Wholesale, and the office of *Työmies,* the radical newspaper that was read by Finns throughout the United States. As in Minnesota, agriculture proved important to Wisconsin's Finns, with the best-known settlement developing east of Superior in Oulu, once defined as the most densely populated township in the entire state. South of the Wisconsin border in Illinois were Waukegan and De Kalb; both included Finntowns similar to those found in other medium-sized cities.[32]

The first Finntowns that appeared in the western United States continued to accommodate Finns throughout the late nineteenth and early twentieth centuries, and additional enclaves emerged at several sites from 1881 to 1914. Among the most important was the Finntown in Berkeley, California, which developed after the 1906 San Francisco earthquake forced a number of Finns to flee the destroyed city. Berkeley's Finns formed a Finntown that would serve as a major bastion for progressive political ideas and activities that influenced the greater Finnish American community.[33]

Of the Finntowns that emerged in the mining towns and cities of the Rocky Mountain region, the one in Butte, Montana, serves as an iconic example. A significant movement of Finnish immigrants to Butte's silver mines did not occur until 1910, but they quickly formed a Finntown that at its peak had twelve saloons, six stores, eighteen boardinghouses, and three public saunas. Of great importance in Butte's history was the Finns' Industrial Workers of the World (IWW) hall, which served as a primary center for labor-oriented activities that occurred throughout the Silver Bow County mining district. All but a small area of the Finntown was erased during the 1950s when the Berkeley mine expanded. Eventually, the only remnant of the once-thriving Finntown would be the Helsinki Bar, which also included a public sauna for several years. (The bar remains, but is now called the Helsinki Yacht Club.) Elsewhere in Montana, the Finntown associated with the mining and agricultural service center of Red Lodge displayed a broader spectrum of institutional activity than did Butte. Red Lodge, for example, still has one of the oldest and most active Kaleva lodges in the United States.[34]

In New England, the Finns of Massachusetts expanded beyond Fitchburg, Worcester, and the Cape Ann district to form Finntowns in the manufacturing cities of Gardner, Westminster, Quincy, Pembroke, Maynard, and Lunenberg. Urban Finns also began leaving for New England's rural areas, where they established poultry farms and cranberry operations—from Canterbury, Connecticut, to Monson, Maine—on land abandoned by Yankee agrarians; the farming district also stretched westward to Spencer, New York. Although the Finns in these rural settlements were certainly more dispersed than in New England's towns and villages, saunas, churches, and halls defined all of them.[35]

**FIGURE 6.** The Helsinki Bar (2004), now the Helsinki Yacht Club, is the only remaining building in the former Finntown of Butte, Montana. (Source: Arnold Alanen collections)

## The 1920s to the Present: The Current Status of Finntowns

The large-scale immigration of Finns and Europeans to the United States ended abruptly following the outbreak of World War I in 1914, and new federal laws enacted during the early 1920s severely curtailed the admittance of migrants from throughout the world. Finns certainly moved within the United States after 1914, but few new Finntowns were established. Some Finns, however, did begin looking toward a region that had received only limited attention in the past: the American South. The first of the Finns' southern settlements developed at McKinnon, Georgia, where a cooperative farm was formed in 1922. Despite the Finns' best intentions, the cooperative effort did not thrive, and in 1966 the reforested land was sold to a paper-manufacturing company. The twenty or so families that still lived in McKinnon at the time of the sale were allowed to keep their individual lots; some of their descendants still own the properties today.[36]

Florida also attracted small numbers of Finns to a few early twentieth-century agricultural settlements, but the only one that maintained a Finnish presence over time was the colony at Astor (now New Port Richey). It was not until the years following the conclusion of World War II, however, that Florida became a major destination for Finns. During the mid to late 1940s, two new Finntowns emerged at Lake Worth and Lantana, whereas the one at New Port Richey expanded. When large numbers of retired Finns, most from the Midwest and New England, descended upon the three communities for the winter season, they immediately built halls to accommodate their social activities. Other institutions and numerous businesses followed, especially in Lantana and Lake Worth.[37] Today, all three halls still function, albeit not as actively as in the past, and some businesses continue to serve both Finnish- and non-Finnish-speaking patrons. The residents who constitute the Finnish community, however, are now dispersed throughout the metropolitan areas of West Palm Beach (Lantana and Lake Worth) and Tampa–St. Petersburg (New Port Richey).

If Florida's relatively young Finnish settlements have changed during recent years, then what can be said about the evolution and current status of the hundreds of Finntowns that formerly existed in several regions of the United States? It would be tempting to say that because of the passing of first- and second-generation Finns, and the abandonment or removal of buildings that once served different Finnish groups, the Finntown phenomenon no longer exists. Granted, the protection of a single or a few Finnish-sponsored buildings has been accomplished in some communities, but efforts to preserve larger sections of former Finntown environments have generally failed. In 1980, for example, officials in Virginia, Minnesota, which once included a significant Finntown, hired a professional consultant to develop a preservation plan for a six-block area that had seven major Finnish buildings: former halls, churches, cooperatives, and a large boardinghouse. The plan ultimately proved overly ambitious, and only a single building—the former Valon Tuote Temperance Hall—now represents the active cultural, social, and political life that once characterized Finnish life in this Iron Range city.[38]

It might be argued, on the other hand, that Hancock, Michigan, stands out as a contemporary version of an American Finntown, especially because the campus of Finlandia University is located at the center of the small city. Other buildings tied to former Finnish activities still remain in Hancock, but again, most are abandoned or utilized for different functions than in the past. Hancock notwithstanding, perhaps it is more useful to acknowledge that Finntowns, and most of America's ethnic communities formed decades or centuries ago, no longer need to be defined as places where spatially contiguous groupings of people and buildings exist. The FinnFest USA celebrations that have occurred throughout North America since 1982 demonstrate that Finnish American communities still function—even if their populations are dispersed over a wide area of a city or region. Nowhere has this been more evident than at Marquette, Hancock-Houghton, and Duluth, places where FinnFest programs have been extremely successful.

Finally, it may be argued that the vast Twin Cities metropolitan area of Minneapolis–St. Paul actually serves as America's largest contemporary Finntown. In 2000, the U.S. Census counted 37,130 people in the two cities and their suburbs who claimed at least some Finnish heritage; this is the greatest concentration of urban Finnish Americans in the nation. Much of the Twin Cities' Finnish-oriented activity is based at the University of Minnesota, which supports a visiting professorship in Finnish studies, a major Finnish American archive, Finnish-language instruction, and an annual program of Finnish music. Also of note are a number of large Laestadian/Apostolic Lutheran churches, located in several suburbs, which serve congregations with a combined membership of more than 6,000 people.[39]

It is difficult if not impossible to determine how America's Finntowns may be interpreted in the future. Certainly some buildings will be maintained, whether by government agencies, local organizations, or interested individuals; and publications, images, and archival collections will continue to provide further documentation. But will digitally generated "Virtual Finntowns" eventually allow people to re-create any number of experiences within the sanctuary of their own homes? It is quite likely the Finntowns of the past may eventually relive in ways that are beyond our comprehension today.

### NOTES

1. See the headlines "Tietoja Suomalaisten pesäpaikoilta Pohjois-Amerikassa," in *Amerikan Suomalainen Lehti* (Calumet, Mich.), especially 1879 and 1880.
2. The two programs are Heritage Quest and Ancestry.com; the latter is the most robust program and was used to gather data for this account.
3. Arnold R. Alanen, *Finns in Minnesota* (St. Paul: Minnesota Historical Society Press, 2012), 2.
4. Alanen, *Finns in Minnesota,* 2; A. William Hoglund, *Finnish Immigrants in America 1880–1920* (Madison: University of Wisconsin Press, 1960), 136; Mika Roinila, *Finland-Swedes in Michigan* (East Lansing: Michigan State University Press, 2012), 35; U.S. Census manuscripts, 1910.
5. The program, Integrated Public Use Microdata Series (IPUMS), is dedicated to the collection and distribution of U.S. census data. It is conducted by the Minnesota Population Center at the University of Minnesota.
6. Terry G. Jordan and Matti Kaups, *The American Backwoods Frontier: An Ethnic and Ecological Interpretation* (Baltimore: The Johns Hopkins University Press, 1989), 102–27, 135–78; Pirjo Varjola, *The Etholen Collection* (Helsinki: National Board of Antiquities, 1990), 12–68; Katherine Arndt and Richard Pierce, *A Construction History of Sitka, Alaska, as Documented in the Records of the Russian-American Company* (Sitka: Sitka National Historical Park, 2003); A. V. Grinev, *Kto est kto v istorii russkoy Ameriki: Entsiklopedicheskiy slovar-spravochnik* [Who's who in the history of Russian America] (Moscow: Academia, 2009); Maria Jarlsdotter Enckell, "In Search of a People Lost: The Finns in Russian America and Their Descendants," in *Over the Near Horizon: Proceedings of the 2010 International Conference on Russian America,* John Dusty Kidd, ed. (Sitka, Alaska: Sitka Historical Society, Inc., 2013).
7. Reino Kero, "Charles Linn: Amerikansuomalainen

'Self-Made Man' 1800 luvulta," *Suomen Silta*, no. 3 (1971): 7; Ernest J. Moyne, "Charles Linn, Finnish-Swedish Businessman, Banker, and Industrialist in Nineteenth-Century Alabama," *Swedish American Historical Quarterly* 28 (1977): 97–105; U.S. manuscript censuses, 1860, 1870.

8. Reino Kero, *Suureen länteen: Siirtolaisuus Suomesta Yhdysvaltoihin ja Kanadaan* (Turku: Siirtolaisuusinstituutti, 1996); U.S. manuscript census, 1860.

9. U.S. manuscript census, 1860.

10. Liisa Penner, "Finns in Astoria, Oregon," 1995, www.genealogia.fi/emi.art/article49e.htm; U.S. manuscript census, 1860.

11. Salomon Ilmonen, *Amerikan suomalaisten historia ja elämäkertoja II* (Jyväskylä: K. J. Gummerus Osakeyhtiön Kirjapaino, 1923); Kero, *Suureen länteen*; Alanen, *Finns in Minnesota*.

12. Ilmonen, *Amerikan suomalaisten historia II*; Alanen, *Finns in Minnesota*, 11–13; Hans R. Wasastjerna, ed., *History of the Finns of Minnesota*, Toivo Rosvall, trans. (Duluth: Minnesota Finnish-American Historical Society, 1957); Arnold R. Alanen, "In Search of the Pioneer Finnish Homesteader in America," *Finnish Americana* 4 (1981).

13. Alanen, *Finns in Minnesota*.

14. Alanen, *Finns in Minnesota*; U.S. manuscript census, 1880.

15. Akseli Järnefelt, *Suomalaiset Amerikassa* (Helsinki: Osakeyhtiö Weilin & Göös Aktiebolag, 1899); Ilmonen, *Amerikan suomalaisten historia II*; Alanen, *Finns in Minnesota*. The comment about Laestadians attending dances was made by William Toivonen of Minneapolis in an interview with the author on October 5, 2005.

16. Ilmonen, *Amerikan suomalaisten historiaa II*; Matti Kaups, "The Finns in the Copper and Iron Ore Mines of the Western Great Lakes Region, 1864–1905: Some Preliminary Observations," in *The Finnish Experience in the Western Great Lakes Region: New Perspectives*, ed. Michael G. Karni et al. (Turku: Institute for Migration, 1975); Armas K. E. Holmio, *History of the Finns in Michigan*, original 1967 Finnish-language volume translated by Ellen M. Ryynanen (Detroit: Wayne State University Press, 2001); Gary Kaunonen, *Finns in Michigan* (East Lansing: Michigan State University Press, 2009).

17. Kaups, "Finns in the Copper and Iron Ore Mines"; Holmio, *History of the Finns in Michigan*; Kaunonen, *Finns in Michigan*; U.S. manuscript census, 1880.

18. Holmio, *History of the Finns in Michigan*; Roinila, *Finland-Swedes in Michigan*; U.S. manuscript census, 1880.

19. Roinila, *Finland-Swedes in Michigan*; U.S. manuscript census, 1880.

20. Ilmonen, *Amerikan suomalaisten historiaa II*; Jerry P. Schofer, *Urban and Rural Finnish Communities in California, 1860–1960* (San Francisco: R and E Research Associates, 1975); International Order of Runeberg, "Lodges," www.orderofruneberg.org/lodges.html; U.S. manuscript census, 1880.

21. Ilmonen, *Amerikan suomalaisten historiaa II*; Paul G. Hummasti, "The Establishment of the Finnish Settlement in Astoria, Oregon: A Look at Community Development," *Finnish Americana* 1 (1978), 84–98; Paul G. Hummasti, "From Kälviä to Astoria: Finnish Families in Transition," in *Finns in North America: Proceedings of Finn Forum III, 5–8 September 1984*, ed. Michael G. Karni (Turku: Institute of Migration, 1988), 154–165; Marvin Swearingen, *The Pendelton Area Finns* (Portland, Ore.: Finnish American Historical Society of the West, 1971); U.S. manuscript census, 1880.

22. Ilmonen, *Amerikan suomalaisten historiaa II*; U.S. manuscript census, 1880.

23. Ilmonen, *Amerikan suomalaisten historiaa II*; Arnold R. Alanen, "Finns," in *Encyclopedia of the Great Plains*, ed. D. J. Wishart (Lincoln: University of Nebraska Press, 2004); U.S. manuscript census, 1880.

24. Ilmonen, *Amerikan suomalaisten historiaa II*;

Salomon Ilmonen, *Amerikan suomalaisten historiaa III: Yhdysvalloissa ja Canadassa olevat suomalaiset asutukset* (Hancock: Suomalais-Luteerilaisen Kustannusliikkeen Kirjapaino, 1926); Kolehmainen, *From Lake Erie's Shores;* U.S. manuscript census, 1880.

25. Vapaa tietosanakirja, "Finntown," http://fi.wikipedia.org/wiki/Finntown; U.S. manuscript census, 1880; Ekman, *History of Finnish American Organizations.*

26. Reino Kero, *Migration from Finland to North America in the Years between the United States Civil and the First World War* (Turku, Finland: University of Turku, 1974).

27. Michael Loukinen, "Second Generation Finnish-American Migration from the Northwoods to Detroit, 1920–1950," in *Finnish Diaspora II: United States. Papers of the Finn Forum Conference, Held in Toronto, Ontario, Canada, November 1–3, 1979,* ed. Michael G. Karni (Toronto: Multicultural History Society of Ontario, 1981), 107–26; Holmio, *History of the Finns in Michigan;* Kaunonen, *Finns in Michigan;* U.S. manuscript censuses, 1900, 1910, 1920.

28. Ilmonen, *Amerikan suomalaisten historia,* 222; M. E. Kaups, "Finns in Urban America: A View from Duluth," in Karni, *Finnish Diaspora II,* 63–86; Alanen, *Finns in Minnesota.*

29. Wasastjerna, *History;* Alanen, *Finns in Minnesota.*

30. Reino Kero, "Finnish Emigration to the United States," in *Scando-Americana: Papers on Scandinavian Emigration to the United States* (Oslo: American Institute, University of Oslo, 1980), 58; Alanen, *Finns in Minnesota.*

31. *Amerikan Suomalainen* (Hancock, Mich.), April 8, 1894; Alanen, *Finns in Minnesota.*

32. John I. Kolehmainen and George W. Hill, *Haven in the Woods: The Story of the Finns of Wisconsin* (Madison: State Historical Society of Wisconsin, 1951); Esa Arra, *The Finns in Illinois,* trans. Andrew I. Brask (De Kalb: Finnish-American Historical Society of Illinois, 1971); Arnold R. Alanen, "Back to the Land! Rural Finnish Settlement in Wisconsin," *Transactions,* Wisconsin Academy of Sciences, Arts and Letters 65 (1977): 180–203.

33. Thayer Watkins, "When West Berkeley Was Finntown," 1990s, www.sjsu.edu/faculty/watkins/finntown.htm; John Perala, *The Finns of Berkeley, California* (Portland, Ore.: Finnish-American Historical Society of the West, 1989).

34. National Park Service, "Butte-Anaconda Historic Landmark Nomination," 2006, www.nps.govinhl/designation/samples/mt/Butte-Anaconda.pdf; Leona Lampi, *At the Foot of the Beartooth Mountains: A History of the Finnish Community of Red Lodge, Montana* (Coeur d'Alene, Idaho: Bookage Press, 1998).

35. Liisa A. Liedes, ed., *The Finnish Imprint: A New England Experience* (Fitchburg, Mass.: New England Finnish American Bicentennial Committee, 1982); U.S. manuscript censuses, 1900, 1910, 1920.

36. Teuvo Peltoniemi, "Finnish Utopian Communities in North America," in Karni, *Finns in North America,* 127–41.

37. Keijo Virtanen, "The Migration of Finnish Americans to Florida after World War II," *Turun historiallinen arkisto* 31 (1976): 432–45; William R. Copeland, "Early Finnish-American Settlements in Florida," in Karni, *Finnish Diaspora II,* 127–41.

38. Kim F. Zarney, *Oldtown-Finntown: A Development Plan for a Pioneer Era Living Museum* (Medina, Ohio: TOWNSCAPE, 1980).

39. Alanen, *Finns in Minnesota.*

# Ambiguous Identity: Finnish Americans and the Race Question

*Peter Kivisto and Johanna Leinonen*

The debate on the racial identity of the Finns in the twentieth century reflected the "scientific discussion" in American society at large. In the following, both popular and literary definitions and the definitions that gained currency within the natural and social sciences in Europe and the United States in the nineteenth and early twentieth centuries are examined. In these depictions, Finns were linked not only to Mongolians but sometimes also to American Indians. These racial associations were a sensitive issue for Finns, although attempts to counter the negative stereotypes were more evident on the conservative "Church Finn" side of the ethnic community than from their "Red Finn" counterparts.

In 2007, Alex Ross, the music critic for the *New Yorker* magazine, published an appreciative article on the Finnish composer Jean Sibelius titled "Apparition in the Woods." Sibelius was one of the "regional" composers—along with Grieg, Dvořák, and Nielsen—who came from Europe's smaller nations. In one passage, Ross sought to indicate something of the remoteness of Sibelius's origins when he wrote, "Finns are strangers to the European family. Descendants of an errant Mongolian tribe, they speak a language unrelated to the Indo-European linguistic group." However, when that article reappeared as a chapter in Ross's *The Rest Is Noise: Listening to the Twentieth Century,* the passage was recast to read, "In a certain sense, Finns are strangers in the European family. Belonging to the Finno-Ugrian category, they speak a language largely unrelated to the Indo-European group."[1]

In this reworking of the passage, the idea that Finns stand apart from European culture is qualified twice, for now they are strangers only in "a certain sense," and the Finnish language is "largely unrelated" to the Indo-European languages, which implies that in some respects it is or at least might be related. Meanwhile, the "errant Mongolian tribe" has disappeared entirely. The reason that these editorial changes were made will not concern us here. Instead, we move back exactly one century earlier to a short-lived episode in a small mining community in northern Minnesota that has received attention in Finnish American historiography as well as in whiteness studies, particularly in David Roediger's *Working toward Whiteness.*[2]

On September 9, 1907, John Svan, a miner living and working in Eveleth, Minnesota, applied to become a naturalized citizen of the United States. Svan was born in Noormarkku, Finland, in 1874, and he had immigrated to the United States in 1900. He had applied for his "first papers" in 1904 and had every reason to assume that as the process proceeded, he would within a few years become a citizen of his new homeland. He—and indeed, the larger Finnish community—did not anticipate a challenge to his application based on the racial identity of Finnish immigrants. However, this is precisely what happened on January 8, 1908, when St. Paul District Attorney John C. Sweet held up Svan's application for citizenship on the grounds that, as the court papers he filed in the case put it, "being a Finn, he is Mongolian and not a 'white person' within the meaning of Sec. 2169, United States Rev. Stat., which provides that 'The provisions of this title shall apply to aliens being free white persons and to aliens of African nativity and to persons of African descent.'" Soon thereafter, the papers of fifteen additional Finns were also held up. All sixteen men had been active participants in the Finnish Socialist Federation and had been very involved in the 1907 Mesabi Iron Range strike, the first major labor action in that iron-mining region that would engage Finnish radicals. Estimates suggest that perhaps as many as 75 percent of the strikers were Finns, and perhaps not surprisingly the district attorney sought to draw an explicit linkage between race and political radicalism, contending that socialism constituted an "East Asian philosophy."[3]

If this argument had prevailed, Finns would have found themselves in a list of groups that had lost their own legal battles in the U.S. courts to become naturalized citizens, groups that included the Chinese, Burmese, Koreans, Hawaiians, Arabs, and East Indians. As such, they would have constituted the only European-origin group to be legally defined as nonwhite (and implicitly as nonblack). As it turned out, they ended up on another list, one that included Armenians and Syrians, consisting of those with uncertain racial identities whom the courts ultimately declared to be white.[4] This outcome was due to the decision of federal judge William A. Cant, the presiding judge in the U.S. District Court in Duluth, Minnesota. A mere two weeks after Sweet's legal action, Judge Cant threw out the case against the Finnish miners and declared them to be white. In his ruling, he contended that "if the Finns were originally Mongols, modifying influences have continued until they are now among the whitest people in Europe." Thus he concluded that John Svan was "without doubt a white person within the true intent and meaning of the law."[5] If the judge's logic was widely held, it meant that unlike the one-drop rule that defined black identity and the practice of hypodescent, nonblacks whose racial identities were of debatable provenance, like the Finns, could in fact over time become white by racial mixing.

The conclusion of the Svan case should be seen in light of the often contradictory and convoluted nature of racialist thought—both in the form of scientific racism and in public opinion. It appeared that in a relatively short time the judiciary came to appreciate the quandaries built into race theorizing, particularly as it pertained to articulating the boundaries of citizenship and the right to naturalization. Roediger summarized the situation well when he noted that despite the lengthy list of court cases involving non-Europeans, "the courts took special care not to raise the issue of the racial status of European new immigrants," for their experience with expert testimony had led judges to lose "their appetite for ethnology."[6]

We move in time once more, this time to 1957, which was exactly half a century after the Svan case. In that year, the Book Concern, the publishing wing of the Lutheran Suomi Synod, located in Hancock, Michigan, published *Finlandia: The Racial Composition, the Language, and a Brief History of the Finnish People*. The Knights of Kaleva (Kalevan Ritarit), the major Finnish American fraternal organization, had commissioned Saul Chalmer Olin to produce a book. More specifically, the primary purpose for contracting to have the book written was explained in the preface by the organization's secretary, Andrew I. Brask.

It was intended, he wrote, to convince readers that "Finland and her people are as Caucasian as any can be—anthropologically, geographically, historically, politically, and from the religious viewpoint."[7]

Olin was acutely aware of the fact that he wrote the book shortly after the publication of UNESCO's two statements on race that called into question the scientific basis for racial differences.[8] Although he conceded that "the term race is probably useless from the modern scientific standpoint," and was cognizant of the fact that a growing number of "anthropologists find it embarrassing to use the term 'race' due to recent ideologies of racial superiority," he nevertheless used the concept to offer a vigorous rebuttal of what the Knights of Kaleva clearly feared was the persistent belief that Finns are Mongolians.[9]

Despite the title's reference to history, the book focused most of its attention on physical anthropology, mustering evidence intended to prove definitively that Finns are different in significant ways from Mongolians. Olin made use of studies of the Cephalic Index, which particularly resonates with the Finnish case, as will be seen later on. He also discussed the "Mongolian spot," claiming that Mongolians are born with a mark at the base of their spines of varying size, though the spot disappears prior to the onset of puberty. Finns, he claims, have no such spot. In the case of the "Mongolian eyefold," Olin contends that while an extremely small number of Finns do have that eyefold, such is also true of other Europeans. He also turned to studies of average stature, concluding that whereas Finns are "moderately tall, Mongolians taken as a whole are very short of stature."[10]

These three episodes, occurring over the course of a century, are expressions of the fact that the racial identity of Finns was ambiguous from a very early point in their history in the United States up to the present. One thing is certain: they were not conclusively considered to be white on arrival. The court case is a reflection of the ways that an uncertain racial identity could be parlayed into a politicized agenda to deny citizenship rights to a particular group of immigrants, in this instance due to their radical political activities. The book commissioned by the Knights of Kaleva and published by the Suomi Synod offers testimony that a half-century later, certain segments of the ethnic community remained concerned about their place in the nation's racial formation. And most recently, Ross's article reflects the persistence of the view that Finns are somehow racially different, though what it means in the twenty-first century for both people of Finnish ancestry and others is by no means clear.

But as we shall see below, the racial identity of Finns was even more complicated, for another claim was sometimes asserted about the group that linked them, not to Mongolians, but to American Indians. This was an association that could be heard in the streets of mining towns in the Upper Peninsula of Michigan and the Iron Range of northern Minnesota where the Finnish immigrant population was heavily concentrated, and some of this thinking was captured in literary work of the era. In this regard, a distinction needs to be made between popular and literary definitions of Finnish racial identity, on the one hand, and the definitions that gained currency within both the natural and social sciences in the nineteenth and early twentieth centuries, on the other. As the following section indicates, the latter took shape in Europe before making its own migration across the Atlantic.

### The Science of Race in Europe and America

In her wide-ranging account of racialist thought over a vast expanse of time, Nell Irvin Painter reveals how racialist thinkers were devoted to addressing those groups that presented particular problems in attempts to locate them in one category or another, wrestling with the problems associated with boundary drawing.[11] Finns occupied precisely such a position. According to Aira Kemiläinen, they posed a problem for would-be classifiers for two primary reasons. First, Finnish, unlike most European languages, does not belong to the Indo-European family of languages. Second, Finland's geographical location in the remote northeastern corner of Europe enhanced the sense of Finnish isolation from the rest of Europe. As the world of Finno-Ugric peoples in Russia became increasingly familiar to outsiders, in particular ethnologists, by the end of the eighteenth century Finns were increasingly seen as having a close affinity to this group, who were typically characterized as engaging in "primitive" livelihoods, in stark contrast, for example, to the "more civilized" Magyars. The result was a perception that Finns stood in some sense outside of the European "family."[12] Moreover, it came to be assumed that understanding the origins, including the linguistic origins, of the Finnish people required looking eastward.

Early in the nineteenth century, in what would become the heyday of efforts to ground racial distinctions in science, Baron Georges de Cuvier located Finns as part of the Scythian or Tatar branch of the Caucasian race, which put them in a similar placement as the Turks—both conceived as borderland peoples located between the East and West.[13] But from the outset this conclusion was met by a counterposition that defined Finns as Mongolian, or some variant on that term. The hugely influential German naturalist Johann Friedrich Blumenbach, writing before Cuvier, was early in his career inclined to similarly locate the Finns as an offshoot of the Caucasian race, but over the course of time he changed his position and adapted what would become the most common position of race theorists during the nineteenth century, which is that Finns were actually Mongols. Initially, the Lapps most perplexed him because they in particular seemed to stand outside the Caucasian race. However, when he compared the skulls of a Finn, a Mongolian, and two Lapps (without apparent concern about his sample size), he concluded that they all resembled one another. When he published *De generic humani varietate native* in 1775, he produced the first race theory account of the Finns, locating them squarely in the Mongolian racial category. This conclusion more than any other proved to have a decisive impact on subsequent theorists as they arrived at a growing consensus that Finns were a racial Other standing outside the European family of races.[14]

Among the most widely read of the nineteenth-century race theorists was Arthur Comte de Gobineau. His four-volume work, *The Inequality of Human Races,* was published between 1853 and 1855.[15] Following what was becoming a fairly common pattern, Gobineau divided the races into a small number of categories: the white, black, and yellow races, essentially lumping the category red with the category yellow in contradistinction, for example, to the four-category typology of Swedish taxonomist Carl Linnaeus. Gobineau was unequivocal that the races were inherently unequal and that a distinct and unchanging hierarchy existed, with white clearly on the top, followed by yellow, with black located on the bottom. In his rendering, Finns constituted a branch of the yellow race, along with the Altaic, Mongol, and Tatar branches. The Finns were described as a primitive people, short in stature, with weak limbs and slanting eyes.[16]

The ideas of Gobineau and like-minded race theorists resonated with the ideas of their American counterparts. For instance, in his 1910 book, *Immigrant Races in North America,* Peter Roberts constructed a schema designed to capture the range of immigrants entering the United States during that time. In it, he divided the immigrants into four "stocks": Aryan, Semitic, Sinitic, and Sibiric. The last of these types, the Sibiric, were further divided into three groups: Japanese, Finnic, and Tataric. Roberts observed, "of this group [the Finnic] three peoples come to the United States—the Finns, the Esthonians

[sic] and the Magyars. They form a part of the great Asiatic race although found in Europe. The vast majority of the peoples of Asia are called Mongolians . . . or the yellow race, because of the color of their skin." Although Roberts noted that "the Finns of the Baltic Sea have been in contact with the Teutons and Slavs for centuries and are considered mixed, so that the pure Mongolian type is not found," he nevertheless regarded Finns as more Asiatic than Aryan, writing, "yet the straight hair, the yellow complexion, short nose, wide mouth, broad cheek bones and narrow slanting eyes of the Mongolian type are frequently seen among these Finns."[17]

While Roberts is a relatively little known figure in the history of race theory, Edward Alsworth Ross (1866–1951) was decidedly a major force to be reckoned with, and a complex one. A political progressive, he was also a eugenicist. An advocate for the labor movement, Ross was also a supporter of the anti-immigration movement. In 1914, he published *The Old World in the New: The Significance of Past and Present Immigration to the American People,* which purported to be a summary of the current state of scientific knowledge on race, but it also contained a clear political agenda insofar as Ross sought to lend his support to the movement to stem the tide of immigration.[18]

In one section of the book titled "The Lesser Immigrant Groups," he discussed a number of smaller immigrant groups in the United States, which in addition to the Finns included Magyars, the Portuguese, Greeks, and Levantines. The chapter opens with a stark warning about the threat that the new immigrants posed:

How few are aware that a third of Sicily, from which so many immigrants come, is chiefly Saracen stock, so that the heredity of the Bedouin tribes of Mohamet's time is to be blent [sic] with the heredity of our pioneering breed! Who reflects that, with Chinese and Japanese, Finns and Magyars, Bulgars and Turks, about half a million more or less Mongolian in blood have cast their lot with us and will leave their race stamp upon the American people of the future?[19]

The phrase "more or less Mongolian in blood" reflects Ross's awareness of the role that racial mixing has had with some of the groups he cited, particularly those residing in Europe. When it came to locating the Finns, he contended that they should be defined as members of the Finno-Tatar branch of the Mongolian race, this in spite of the fact that "since the dawn of history the western Finns have intermingled with the Swedes until their blondness and cast of countenance bespeak the Northern European."[20] Thus, although Ross notes the racial ambiguity of the Finns, he still confirmed the continuing impact of their racial roots in Asia on who they are and whether they are fit to become full members of American society.

The racial identities of the various immigrant groups from both eastern and southern Europe that arrived in the United States after the Civil War became increasingly salient by the end of the nineteenth century and spilling into the first two decades of the twentieth as the immigration restriction movement gained steam. The movement had achieved its first success with the passage of the Chinese Exclusion Act in 1882. The legislation came to be seen as a wedge, a beginning of a more encompassing legislative agenda that would stem the tide of all those groups deemed to be unlikely candidates for incorporation into the nation's mainstream. If other groups could be associated racially with the Chinese, they, too, could be seen as appropriate candidates for exclusion. As Erika Lee has pointed out, "the old Chinese exclusion rhetoric was one with which Americans were familiar . . . , and it served as a strong foundation from which to build new nativist arguments on the national level."[21]

Finns were not alone in being associated with Asians or Mongolians. For instance, Italians were depicted as the "Chinese of Europe," with the two groups occupying "an ambiguous, overlapping and intermediary position in the binary racial schema."[22] They were considered neither black nor white, but as in-between—yellow, olive, or swarthy. There was, however, a longer trail of race theory that had placed Finns outside the Caucasian race and into the Mongolian. That being said, there was also a counterargument that found Finns to be Caucasian or white. De Cuvier's argument advanced early in the nineteenth century persisted. For example, Harvard political economist William Z. Ripley argued that Finns were part of the Teutonic race, along with the various Scandinavian groups and the other peoples who occupied lands in the Baltic Sea region. This argument hinged on the notion of racial uplift due to racial intermixing. Ripley, it should be noted, was far from disputing the fundamental ideas associated with race theory. On the contrary, his influential book *The Races of Europe: A Sociological Study* advanced his own version of race theory, contending that Europe should be seen as composed of three major racial groups: the Teutonic, Mediterranean, and Alpine.[23] Like other race theorists, he viewed the races, both worldwide and within Europe, in terms of a hierarchy of racial superiority. He differed from figures like Ross only insofar as where he chose to locate some groups. This included the Finns, whom he spoke on behalf of, arguing "once for all, then, let us fully disabuse ourselves of the notion that there is anything ignoble in a Finnish ancestry."[24]

By the early twentieth century, the claims of those who emphasized the fact that Finns, whatever their origins, had experienced considerable race mixing that had succeeded in bringing them into the races of Europe had gained ground. Judge Cant's ruling was evidence of this assessment in the judicial arena. Four years after his ruling, the Dillingham Commission published its forty-one-volume report. The fifth volume in the collection, compiled and authored by Daniel Folkmar, was titled *Dictionary of Races or Peoples*. It constituted a distillation of the body of race theory that was intended to provide legislators with a clear sense of the racial composition of the immigrant population arriving in the United States at that time. In the report, Finns were still depicted as being connected to the Mongolian race. In this, they were not alone, for the author wrote that "the Mongolian race extends far into Europe, embracing not only the Lapps of Scandinavia, the Finns, Cossacks, and many other peoples of Russia, and the Turks of southern Europe, but even the Magyars of Hungary, the most advanced of all the Europeans of Mongolian origin."[25]

Assessing the physical appearance of the group, the report noted that not only Finns but "the entire Ugro-Finnic stock seems to have been, in origin lighter in color than most other Mongolians, perhaps as a result of their northern residence." But geography was not alone in shaping racial identity, for a long history of intermingling with Swedes had a sufficiently decisive impact on the physical characteristics of contemporary Finns—with their "prevailing blondness and European cast of countenance"—and the commission concluded that it was appropriate to locate Finns in the "Teutonic division" of races.[26] At least in terms of the scientific race theories, the Finns, in effect, had arrived.

### Finns in the Popular Imagination

The debates over the racial identity of Finns, however, were not solely confined to ascertaining whether they were Mongolian or Caucasian, for another racial association played a role as well: the connection between Finns and American Indians. The issue was captured succinctly in a passage of a work of fiction that just happened to have been published the same year as Alex Ross's book. We refer to novelist Jim

Harrison's *Returning to Earth,* set in Marquette, Michigan, and the surrounding environs of the Upper Peninsula. Donald, a construction worker who is part Chippewa and part Finnish, is dying of Lou Gehrig's disease. He is married to his high school sweetheart, Cynthia, who was born into a family founded by a mining and lumber baron. Donald's connection to the earth—to nature—and to a spirituality rooted in nature is such that he asked her and other family members to bury him in a spot across the border in Canada that he had earlier determined was his sacred resting place. In a section of the novel seen through the eyes of Cynthia, she reflects on an event from the 1960s: "I recalled in high school when the local Finns were angry because an anthropologist at the college had said that Finns were essentially northern European Indians. Clarence [Donald's father] and Donald thought the whole fuss quite funny with Donald being half and half."[27]

Generally, the connection was not posed in terms that explicitly equated Finns and American Indians. Rather, the relationship was predicated on an affinity based on both groups' rootedness in nature and in pre-Christian belief systems that reflected that rootedness and that typically included the shaman figure that has the power to heal and to control aspects of the natural world through spells and incantations. The idea that some Finns possessed magical powers circulated as early as the fifteenth century. The historian Marko Lamberg cites as one example the common belief that Finns sold "charmed knots" that could control the winds. This image of the Finn reached American audiences prior to the commencement of the mass migration of Finns, when Richard Dana's *Two Years before the Mast* appeared in 1840. In his memoir chronicling his sea voyages, Dana heard reports from his fellow sailors that Finns were considered by many at sea as witches possessing supernatural powers over the elements. Some seamen refused to sail on ships with Finns aboard. Dana wrote about a ship's cook who contended that he "had heard of ships ... beating up the Gulf of Finland against a head wind and having a ship heave in sight astern, overhaul, and pass them, with as fair a wind as could blow, and all studding-sails out, and find she was from Finland."[28]

A decade and a half after Dana's book appeared in print, Henry Wadsworth Longfellow published his epic poem *Song of Hiawatha,* which was largely derived from H. R. Schoolcraft's work on Ojibwa legends. Given its broad appeal over an extended period of time in American literary history, this work more than any other served to promote the view of the American Indian as the exotic Other. It is known that during the writing of the poem, Longfellow was not only aware of but was keenly interested in Elias Lönnrot's recently published *Kalevala,* which was based on the author's extended retrieval of the oral tradition of the peasants of Karelia in what is today eastern Finland and parts of bordering Russia. One affinity between Longfellow's Ojibwa and Lönnrot's Karelians is that both were depicted as primitives rooted in a nature-based sacro-magical worldview. In Lönnrot's work, for example, the Sampo is an important magic talisman that brings prosperity. These exotic Others, in short, were part of the natural world order of the primitive rather than the constructed world of modern civilizations.

It was not necessarily the case that those who viewed Finns as exotic found a parallel with American Indians. It was equally possible to treat Finns as exotic due to their presumed Asian character. This option was on display in an 1857 book by poet, literary critic, and translator Bayard Taylor titled *Northern Travel: Summer and Winter Pictures: Sweden, Denmark, and Lapland.* In departing Sweden and encountering Finns in Lapland, Taylor wrote,

> The blue eyes and fair hair, the lengthened oval of the face, and slim, straight form disappear. You see, instead, square faces, dark eyes, low foreheads, and something of an Oriental fire and warmth in the

movements. . . . The women wear handkerchiefs of some bright color bound over the forehead and under the chin, very similar to those worn by the Armenian women in Asia Minor. On first coming among them, the Finns impressed me as a less frank and open hearted, but more original and picturesque, race than the Swedes. It is exceedingly curious and interesting to find such a flavor of the Orient on the borders of the Frigid Zone.[29]

The romantic cast of these mid-nineteenth-century depictions of Finns as the premodern Other is evident in the choice of words found in Taylor's account. To describe them as "original and picturesque," offering to northern Europe the "flavor of the Orient," sets up a binary opposition, for "original" can be read as being untouched by the civilizational process that has transformed the vast majority of the peoples of Europe over the centuries. To describe Finns as Oriental is to state that they are in but not of the Occidental world. Finally, to view them as picturesque is to suggest that they are becoming subjects of the gaze of civilized modern people, the past living in the present, like museum artifacts. In this regard, the parallel between Finns and American Indians is obvious.

If the designation "primitive" at the hands of literary figures tended to carry with it a romantic cast and a consignment of Finns to being objects of curiosity, in other circumstances, to be viewed as primitive carried with it implications of danger, for the primitive savage could be perceived as a clear and present threat to the social order. Frans Joseph Syrjälä, the editor of the social democratic newspaper *Raivaaja*, published in Fitchburg, Massachusetts, described a scene of "summer nights [when] Finns danced bare-chested and bare-footed in the green turf of New England towns, attracting groups of townsfolk who regarded them as bands of gypsies, but fled in fright when the drunken brawls began." Syrjälä described what he considered to be a common attitude that many non-Finns harbored about Finns in the early twentieth century when he related an exchange between the editor of the local newspaper in nearby Gloucester, the *Gloucester Fisherman,* and a letter writer. The reader had posed the question, "Do those barbarians actually have human souls?" The editor's response was no doubt meant to be reassuring. He informed the reader that "Finns are truly people, though at the lowest stage of development."[30]

It is impossible to ascertain how many people wondered whether Finns were actually human, but there was evidence that the view that they were less civilized than native-born Americans and many other immigrant groups was a common opinion. Some of the earliest stereotypes of Finns in America were associated with their presumed propensity for heavy drinking, brawling, and knife-wielding (many working-class Finns carried a traditional knife called a *puukko*). As Edward Alsworth Ross put it, the "loaded" Finn is "a terrible fellow" because alcohol tends to "let loose in him fell and destructive impulses which had been held in the leash by moral ideas."[31] The emphasis here shifts from a concern about language, origins, or physiology to that of the character or personality of members of the group writ large. Finns came to be described in the popular imagination as phlegmatic, taciturn, inclined to melancholy, dominated by emotions, quick to anger, revengeful, unimaginative, and persistent (this last trait being clearly ambiguous insofar as it can have both positive and negative connotations, and from within the Finnish community was often seen positively in terms of what they call *sisu*).[32]

The negative stereotypes coalesced during the first two decades of the twentieth century, during the period when Finnish American political radicalism was at its zenith.[33] These stereotypes developed in a specific regional and temporal context. Finns were heavily concentrated in the mining and lumbering regions of the Upper Midwest, where over 50 percent of Finnish immigrants settled. The mining regions of northern Minnesota and the Upper Peninsula were also home to a significant number of American Indians, and conflict between them and European-origin settlers was a recent memory. On the other hand, few African Americans lived in the area, and thus the black-white racial divide that framed issues of race nationwide took form in a somewhat different manner than elsewhere. To put it simply, those two groups seen as most problematic in the region were perceived by many to be in-between people, neither black nor white: Finns and American Indians. Temporally, this was a period of significant labor conflict. Three major strikes occurred during this time period, the 1907 Mesabi Iron Range strike, the 1913 copper-mining strike in the Upper Peninsula, and a second strike on the Mesabi in 1916.

In his analysis of the discourses employed by local political and economic elites hostile to the strikers and to the significant presence of socialism in their midst, the labor historian Gerald Ronning contends that "anti-radicals emphasized the brutish, savage nature of the strikers, their childlike propensity for falling under the sway of the malevolent IWW, and cast the industrial struggle as a battle between the forces of civilization and savagery."[34] While radicals in general—particularly those aligned with the IWW—were accused of savagery, the charge fell especially hard on local Finns, for whom three explicit connections were made between them and American Indians. First, Finns were considered to be people of the forest, what Edward Alsworth Ross described as "lovers of wood and water."[35] This was a presumed preference that they were seen as sharing with American Indians. Related to this association, both engaged in forms of nature worship, replete with magical incantations, charms, and songs.[36] The ubiquitous sauna on Finnish homesteads was seen as the Finnish version of the American Indian smokehouse. Finally, Finns and Indians were seen as problem drinkers, with a tendency to drink to excess and to become violent when inebriated.[37] Given the problems with alcoholism within both communities, outsiders speculated about whether there were biological factors at play that inclined both groups to alcohol abuse. Such speculation served to reinforce the idea of a link between Finns and American Indians—whether or not in explicit racial terms, at least insofar as both were considered to be social problems.

At this particular moment in the history of labor conflict and the allegiance of a significant percentage of Finns to three forms of radicalism—socialism, Communism, and industrial unionism—antipathy toward Finns reached its peak. Ronning points out that Finns could be seen as "Reds" in three senses of the term. First, it was the color of miners as they emerged from the pits covered in hematite dust. Second, it was the color of political radicalism. And third, it was the color of racial discourse, a color that binds Finns and American Indians.[38]

### Finnish Sensitivity to Racial Labels

In a passage from Valto Eetu Kirri's 1945 novel, *Amerikan Vieras* (Stranger in America), the second-generation daughter of a Finnish immigrant pleads with her mother to speak English rather than Finnish when they are in public together. When asked to explain why, she tells her mother that she had been taught in school that Finns were Mongolians and that as a consequence she had become the object of ridicule by her classmates. She is clearly embarrassed by the immigrant generation, accusing them of being uncivilized and ignorant, while desperately seeking to assimilate and to gain the acceptance of the host society.[39]

This fictional character represented one response of Finns, particularly more acculturated second-generation ethnics, which was to distance themselves as much as possible from the Finnish community or to exit it entirely. However, those who remained committed to the ethnic group remained loyal to it while at the same time seeking to find a voice to articulate a more positive image of Finns in America. Such efforts commenced in earnest during the 1920s, just as immigration restrictions came into effect.

Attempts to counter the negative stereotypes were more evident on the conservative "Church Finn" side of the ethnic community than from their "Red Finn" counterparts. Leaders of the Suomi Synod and of fraternal organizations such as the Knights of Kaleva and Ladies of Kaleva assumed the role of claims-making on behalf of the Finnish American community writ large, seeking to find ways to facilitate acceptance by the mainstream society and incorporation into it. One major objective of such claims-making was to promote the idea that Finns were white and capable of Americanization because their cultural values actually dovetailed with those of American society. In one influential instance of attempting to address the race question, John Wargelin tackled it head on. Wargelin is important because he was the president of Suomi College, the only institution of higher education established by Finns, when he published *The Americanization of the Finns* (he would subsequently become the president of the Suomi Synod). In addressing the racial identity of Finns, Wargelin offered an account aimed at embracing commonly held notions of racial identity while subverting the pejorative implications of the classification. He concurred with the claim that Finns were part of the Finno-Ugric race, along with a number of other eastern European groups, which in turn was a division of the Ural-Altaic group. He went on to assert that among these groups, only the Finns, Hungarians, and Estonians had become "thoroughly civilized."[40]

That three decades after Wargelin published his book the Knights of Kaleva found it necessary to contract with S. C. Olin to make the case for Finns as white, and that the Suomi Synod publishing house was willing to produce such a book, is an indication of the long-term insecurity about racial identity felt by the leadership of the conservative side of the ethnic community. To what extent these views were shared by Finns more generally is difficult to discern, particularly as the era from the 1920s to the 1950s was characterized by the erosion of ethnic institutions combined with increased rates of intermarriage and other manifestations of assimilation. These changes suggest that, for many, it was likely that the issue was no longer germane. However, as late as the 1970s—shortly after the fictional Cynthia's account of Finns being depicted as European Indians—some Finnish Americans continued to be troubled by the possibility that many in the American mainstream harbored doubts about whether Finns were actually white. The historian Michael Karni, who played a major role in building the Finnish collection at the University of Minnesota's Immigration History Research Center, was asked to serve on an advisory committee of the Minneapolis public schools as the system initiated plans to introduce units of the history of the main ethnic groups of the Twin Cities into the curriculum. As one of the representatives of the Finnish contingent on the committee, he was surprised to learn that for some of the other Finnish members, "the first order of business was to include data which would prove that Finns are White."[41]

The position taken on the question of group racial identity on the part of the leadership of "Red Finn" organizations differed from that taken by their conservative counterparts. Whatever their private views on the matter, their public stance was simply to avoid the issue. This was understandable in terms of ideology, for however different reformist social democrats were from Communists and industrial unionists on matters of tactics and ultimate goals, they shared a view that class should supersede ethnic and racial identity and that the fostering of class consciousness among the working class could only succeed if other identities were seen to be of secondary importance.

This point was driven home in the case August Yokinen, a Communist who worked as a janitor at the Finnish Workers' Club in Harlem. His case has intrigued scholars for decades.[42] When three African American men were denied entrance to a dance at the club, Yokinen failed to come to their assistance and subsequently informed Communist officials that he did not disagree with those who refused to permit them to enter, claiming that he did not want to have to share a sauna with these men. This occurred at a moment in the history of the Communist Party when the "Negro question" agenda and, in particular, the party's Black Belt plan was being advanced and the recruitment of blacks was of paramount importance to the leadership. With this backdrop, Yokinen's actions were roundly condemned in a 1931 show trial in which he was accused and convicted of perpetrating "white chauvinism." He was expelled from the party, and a day later was visited by immigration officials who, determining that he had failed to apply for citizenship, proceeded to initiate deportation proceedings. Yokinen was ultimately deported to Finland, arriving at precisely that moment when the country was experiencing the height of influence of the fascist Lapua movement.[43] His fate is unknown. The bitter irony of this episode, given the persistent ambiguity about Finnish racial identity that has been chronicled in this essay, is that August Yokinen departed for Finland, at least in the eyes of the Communist Party and the U.S. government, a white man.

## NOTES

1. Alex Ross, "Apparition in the Woods: Rescuing Sibelius from Silence," *New Yorker,* July 9, 2007 52 and July 16, 2007; Alex Ross, *The Rest Is Noise: Listening to the Twentieth Century* (New York: Farrar, Straus and Giroux, 2007), 161.
2. David R. Roediger, *Working toward Whiteness—How America's Immigrants Became White: The Strange Journey from Ellis Island to the Suburbs* (New York: Basic Books, 2005), 61.
3. "Finlanders Are Not Mongolians," *Duluth News Tribune,* January 1908; "Ovatko Suomalaiset Mongooleja. Asia Ratkaistu Duluthissa," *Amerikan Suometar,* January 1908; Hans Wasastjerna, *History of the Finns in Minnesota* (Duluth, MN: Minnesota Finnish-American Historical Society, 1957), 477; Timo Riippa, "The Finns and Swede-Finns," in *They Chose Minnesota: A Survey of the State's Ethnic Groups,* ed. Judith Drenning Holmquist (St. Paul: Minnesota Historical Society Press, 1981), 298; Peter Kivisto, *Immigrant Socialists in the United States: The Case of Finns and the Left* (Rutherford, N.J.: Fairleigh Dickinson University Press, 1984), 128; K. Marianne Wargelin, "Contested Democracy," unpublished manuscript based on a paper presented at the conference Democratic Values, Past Present and Future: The Tenth North American Studies Conference, University of Tampere, Finland, May 18–21, 2005.
4. Stanford M. Lyman, "The Race Question and Liberalism: Casuistries in American Constitutional Law," *International Journal of Politics, Culture, and Society* 5, no. 2 (1991): 204, 206–8.
5. Wasastjerna, *History,* 477.
6. Roediger, *Working toward Whiteness,* 61–62.
7. Andrew I. Brask, "Special Introduction," in Saul Chalmer Olin, *Finlandia: The Racial Composition, the Language, and a Brief History of the Finnish People* (Hancock, MI: The Book Concern, 1957), vii.
8. UNESCO, *The Race Concept: Results of an Inquiry* (Paris: UNESCO, 1952).
9. Olin, *Finlandia,* 54, xi. Olin was an amateur scholar whose other books included *The Story of Fairport, Ohio. Official Souvenir Edition Commemorating Fairport's Sesquicentennial Celebration, 1796–1946* (Fairport Harbor, Ohio: Neal Printing, 1946); and *Sauna: The Way to Health. America's First Book about the Sauna: A Guide Book to Better Health* (New York Mills, Minn.: Health Factor Books, 1963).

10. Olin, *Finlandia*, 34–41.
11. Nell Irvin Painter, *The History of White People* (New York: W. W. Norton, 2010), 116, 220.
12. Aira Kemiläinen, "Johdanto," in *Mongoleja vai germaaneja? Rotuteorioiden suomalaiset*, ed. Aira Kemiläinen et al. (Helsinki: SHS, 1985), 12–13.
13. Niilo Kauppi, review of *Suomalaiset, outo Pohjolan kansa: Rotuteoriat ja kansallinen identiteetti* by Aira Kemiläinen, *American Historical Review* 101, no. 2 (1996): 510.
14. Jouko I. Kilpeläinen, "Rotuteoriat läntisistä suomalais-ugrilaisista kansoista Keski-Euroopan antropologiassa 1800-luvulla ja suomalaisten reaktiot niihin," in Kemiläinen et al., *Mongoleja vai germaaneja*, 165; Aira Kemiläinen, *Suomalaiset, outo Pohjolan kansa: Rotuteoriat ja kansallinen identiteetti* (Helsinki: SHS, 1993), 56–57.
15. Arthur Comte de Gobineau, *The Inequality of Human Races*, trans. Adrian Collins, introd. Oscar Levy (New York: H. Fertig, 1967). See Kemiläinen, *Suomalaiset*, 139.
16. Gobineau, *Inequality*, 142, 146.
17. Peter Roberts, *Immigrant Races in North America* (New York: YMCA Press, 1910), 9, 85–86.
18. Edward Alsworth Ross, *The Old World in the New: The Significance of Past and Present Immigration to the American People* (New York: Century, 1914), 168–69.
19. Ross, *Old World in the New*, 168–69.
20. Ross, *Old World in the New*, 169.
21. Erika Lee, *At America's Gates: Chinese Immigration during the Exclusion Era, 1882–1943* (Chapel Hill: University of North Carolina Press, 2003), 30, 36.
22. Donna R. Gabaccia, "The 'Yellow Peril' and the 'Chinese of Europe': Global Perspectives on Race and Labor, 1815–1930," in *Migration, Migration History, History: Old Paradigms and New Perspectives*, ed. Jan Lucassen and Leo Lucassen (Bern, N.Y.: P. Lang, 1999), 177–79.
23. William Z. Ripley, *The Races of Europe: A Sociological Study* (New York: W. Appleton, 1899), 205–6.
24. Ripley, *Races of Europe*, 365.
25. Daniel Folkmar, assisted by Elnora Folkmar, *Dictionary of Races or Peoples*, vol. 5 of *Reports of the Immigration Commission* (Washington, D.C.: Government Printing Office, 1911), 97.
26. Folkmar, *Dictionary*, 59.
27. Jim Harrison, *Returning to Earth* (New York: Grove, 2007), 241.
28. Richard Dana, *Two Years before the Mast: A Personal Narrative of Life at Sea* (New York: Harper, 1840), 31. Such imagery in American literature did not quickly disappear, as is attested in Jack London's *The Mutiny of the Elsinore* (New York: Macmillan, 1914), 275. In London's novel, published nearly three-quarters of a century after Dana's book, a Finnish carpenter on board a ship is depicted as a "warlock who played tricks with the winds and despitefully used poor sailormen."
29. Bayard Taylor, *Northern Travel: Summer and Winter Pictures: Sweden, Denmark, and Lapland* (New York: G. P. Putnam, 1857), 70.
30. Quoted in Carl Ross, *The Finn Factor in American Labor, Culture, and Society* (New York Mills, Minn.: Parta Printers, 1977), 19.
31. Ross, *Old World in the New*, 169–70.
32. John Wargelin, *The Americanization of the Finns* (Hancock, Mich.: The Book Concern, 1924), 36; A. William Hoglund, *Finnish Immigrants in America 1880–1920* (Madison: University of Wisconsin Press, 1960), 125.
33. Kivisto, *Immigrant Socialists*, 121–54.
34. Gerald Ronning, "Jackpine Savages: Discourses of Conquest in the 1916 Mesabi Iron Range Strike," *Labor History* 44, no. 3 (2003): 360.
35. Ross, *Old World in the New*, 169.
36. Marjorie Edgar, "Finnish Charms and Folk Songs in Minnesota," *Minnesota History* 17 (1936): 406–8, 410.
37. Ronning, "Jackpine Savages," 368–71.
38. Ronning, "Jackpine Savages," 376.
39. Valto Eetu Kirri, *Amerikan Vieras* (Helsinki: Smia, 1945), 241–42.
40. Wargelin, *Americanization of the Finns*, 27.

41. Michael G. Karni, "Yhteishyvä—Or, for the Common Good: Finnish Radicalism in the Western Great Lakes Region, 1900–1940" (Ph.D. diss., University of Minnesota, 1975), 148.

42. His Finnish name was actually Jokinen, but American press accounts consistently reported his name as Yokinen. An early account of the Yokinen case appeared in Irving Howe and Lewis Coser, *The American Communist Party: A Critical History* (New York: Praeger, 1962), 209–10. It is discussed in David John Ahola, *Finnish-Americans and International Communism: A Study of Finnish-American Communism from Bolshevization to the Demise of the Third International* (Lanham, Md.: University Press of America, 1981), 172–73; and Mark Naison, *Communists in Harlem during the Depression* (Urbana: University of Illinois Press, 1983), 47–51. For more recent recountings, see Matthew Frye Jacobson, *Whiteness of a Different Color: European Immigrants and the Alchemy of Race* (Cambridge, Mass.: Harvard University Press, 1988), 251–54; and Bryan D. Palmer, "Race and Revolution," *Labour/Travail* 54 (Fall 2004): 200–202.

43. Risto Alapuro, "What Is Western and What Is Eastern in Finland?" *Thesis Eleven* 77 (May 2004): 91.

PART 4
# Finnish Communities Organized

# Fighting for Temperance Ideas

*Paul George Hummasti*

Each immigrant group in America established its own organizations for a number of reasons. This can be partly explained as a means to maintain ethnic ties and family connections. Ethnic ties persisted for long periods and were even revitalized in immigrant communities. This may be partly seen as a kind of transnationalism that took on many forms. It was also practical to seek protection from working accidents, sickness, and other situations in which migrants were not able to support themselves properly.[1] The first Finnish ethnic organizations were actually temperance groups, responding to the problem of the immigrant population's abundant use of alcohol. They functioned in the same vein as many similar societies in Finland and North America. The heyday of temperance took place during the late 1800s and early 1900s, when it lost ground to other forms of social and cultural activity, and after the national Prohibition was repealed in 1933, temperance groups seemed to become unnecessary.

The growth of organizations was naturally tied to the growth of the immigrant population. The first notable organizations were established to promote the temperance movement and religious activities. In addition to these, the third major organizational and ideological group for Finnish Americans revolved around labor issues or the leftists. They in turn were split into three major subgroups: the socialists, the industrialists, and the Communists. Additionally, the influential cooperative movement was at certain periods closely related with the labor groups.

In his 1960 study of Finnish immigrants in America, A. William Hoglund noted the prevalence of drinking and drunkenness among them and the consequent importance of the temperance movement in their communities.[2] He rightly takes seriously the anxiety expressed by temperance advocates about the harm that excessive use of alcohol could do to these immigrants and their compatriots in the New World. Hoglund also properly interprets temperance organizations as immigrant societies, important to the socialization of Finns within their new country, and places these organizations solidly within their immigrant communities. Since his pioneering study, researchers have added many details to his portrait of the temperance movement among Finnish Americans, but his interpretation of its role within immigrant society remains basically unchanged. New interpretations since 1960 of the temperance movement in the United States and Finland, however, provide an opportunity both to assess further the role of temperance societies within immigrant communities and to place those societies more firmly in their national and international context.

As Hoglund suggests, a sincere desire to save their countrymen and women from the evil effects of alcohol clearly motivated the majority of people who joined temperance organizations, whether they were members of Finnish churches who saw that evil as a moral weakness or of socialist organizations who saw it as an important element in the capitalist exploitation of the working class. But for Finns, the temperance movement was more than simply a response to the impact of the overuse of alcohol. In both Finland and America, the temperance movement proliferated and reached its peak as Finns struggled with the shift from a primarily agricultural society to an industrial one. Supporters of the temperance movement saw themselves as the promoters of a "modern," more efficient approach to society and social problems, an approach that was different from the old, traditional responses of rural folk. In addition, the temperance movement also appealed especially to those in the middle class, who saw its programs as a way of controlling the increasingly worrisome stirring of the masses that threatened them from below. In America, the temperance movement also attracted those who were worried about how the reputation among Americans of Finns as drunken rabble-rousers might affect their own standing in their new communities. Some studies also indicate that, as the movement became more middle class, gender took on significant importance, as women grew more central to its activities. Finally, the Finnish temperance movement in America generated temperance societies that also served their members as immigrant institutions that helped them face the challenges of adapting to the New World. The Finnish American temperance movement, therefore, was a complex movement that played a complicated role within Finnish American communities.

### The Tradition of Alcohol Abuse

The concern that Finns and alcohol are a dangerous and damaging combination has existed for over a century and seems to have some basis in fact. Indeed, in the year 2005, during which Finns consumed an average of 10.5 liters of pure alcohol—more than any other Nordic people—alcohol became the leading cause of death among Finnish men and the second leading cause among women.[3] While reliable information on the amount of alcohol Finns drank is not available for the nineteenth century, the concern that they were drinking too much reaches back at least to 1834, when Elias Lönnrot founded the first Finnish temperance society in Kajaani.[4] Beginning in the 1870s, leading members of Finnish society became increasingly alarmed by the impact of alcohol on their country. No evidence exists that drinking actually increased in Finland at this time, but within a changing social and economic structure it seemed to become more dangerous. As Finland moved from an agricultural to an industrial society, alcohol became more noticeable as a problem when industrial workers concentrated their drinking in the evening hours after work, rather than spreading it throughout the day as was the practice among peasants in rural society. In addition, as industrialism diminished the importance of the village community, fears arose that corporate restraints on drunkenness and other evils were disappearing so that an individual's falling to the temptation of drink had became easier.[5]

Finnish immigrants to America left this changing society, particularly from areas where alcohol consumption was high,[6] and brought its drinking patterns, as well as the concerns about them, to the New World. Salomon Ilmonen, a Finnish American writer, pastor, and temperance advocate, had deep concerns about fellow Finns in America. He noted that after arriving in America, "otherwise decent young countrymen of ours under the influence of alcohol mistakenly allowed their vile natures to take control . . . and then braying could be heard that aroused terror, then the familiar *pohjalainen puukko* (northwestern Finnish knife) flashed through the air and crude curses increased the horror of the wretched situation."[7]

And he was not alone: in the late nineteenth and early twentieth centuries, Finns both in their homeland and in America had a reputation for drunkenness and for drunken brawling. Conditions in America also had an impact on the immigrants' use of alcohol, and in the early years of immigration, as Finns were establishing new communities around America, these conditions encouraged more drinking. The single young men who almost exclusively inhabited these communities had few outlets for entertainment and social life. In many cases, the only public space open to them was in saloons, where they could relax after work, meet with friends, and catch up on the latest news, including tips on new job opportunities.[8] Finns shared these activities with other American workers, immigrant or not, who frequented saloons and there created their own workers' cultures, making the late nineteenth century the golden age of the working-class tavern in the United States.[9] In addition, in the late nineteenth century, when Finnish immigrants began arriving in America in large numbers, drinking at the workplace—especially beer—was a common practice and one that Finns had experience with in the rural society of their homeland. Finnish dockworkers in Ashtabula, Ohio, indulged in this practice at least into the 1890s. Finally, the difficult and dangerous working conditions that most Finnish immigrants encountered in the mines and forests where they labored probably also drove some young men to drink.[10]

Thus Salomon Ilmonen was convinced that "even though Finns were acquainted with strong drink in their homeland, the evil of drink did not attain such power there as it did in the new conditions of America."[11] These new conditions included Finnish taverns that proliferated as soon as Finnish communities in America reached sufficient size. Since a demand clearly existed and since opening a tavern required little capital or skill, Finnish immigrants saw saloon-keeping as a promising business opportunity.[12] Already by 1891 nine Finnish saloons fronted the streets of Hancock, Michigan. Astoria, Oregon, had six Finnish saloons in 1898, and Eveleth, Minnesota, ten in 1902. According to one count, of 350 saloons in fifteen Minnesota mining towns in 1912, 60 were Finnish.[13] At one time, nearly 300 Finnish taverns offered alcoholic refreshment to Finns, and many taverns not owned by Finns had at least one Finnish-speaking employee.[14]

And Finnish immigrants did take advantage of the opportunities offered by these saloons. American employers in the upper Midwest saw Finns and Slovaks as particularly troublesome employees because of their frequent drunkenness.[15] A 1911 U.S. Census report on fifteen Minnesota towns indicated that these two groups most often ended up drunk in jail. A newspaper reporter in Newberry, Michigan, in a story on a drunken Finn arrested for fighting and carrying an illegal weapon, wondered whether the county jail was made only for Finns.[16] Finnish use of alcohol became such a problem that some state legislatures in the Midwest considered banning the sale of alcohol to Finns, as to American Indians. Even one of the most important leaders of the Finnish American temperance movement, Johan Wilhelm Lähde, had lifelong problems with alcoholism.[17] Perhaps, then, the words of one student of Finns in America, Hans Wasastjerna, are not much of an exaggeration: "In the saloons and in dark alleys Finnish knives used to flash, terrorizing whole communities. This restless life centered in the saloons, into which newcomers from Finland were so often drawn, threatened not only to destroy numerous promising young men but also threatened to brand the Finns as a whole."[18]

As the above indicates, Finnish immigrants, however much they actually drank, had a reputation among both Americans and Finns for drunkenness and rowdiness. Americans' descriptions of the Finnish immigrants in their midst tended to focus on drinking, fighting, and radicalism.[19] Upstanding members of Finnish American communities winced when they read stories in American newspapers, as the one in the *Wyoming Semi-Weekly Tribune* telling of a coroner's inquest clearing a sheriff of wrongdoing in the killing of Matt Maki: "Maki was a Finn and had been making a disturbance and brandishing a large knife. The officer attempted to arrest him and in the trouble Maki was shot and killed."[20] And as Juho Saari wrote in 1926, Finns twenty years earlier tended to see America as a land where people drank, lived dissolutely, rejected God, and acted like wild beasts.[21] Some, like the historian John Kolehmainen, argue that this reputation is an exaggeration, and, to a certain extent, this Finnish image of America may have resulted from attempts by Finnish authorities and Finnish employers to discourage emigration,[22] but clearly many truly believed with Akseli Järnefelt that habitual drunkenness among their countrymen and women in the New World was the most serious consequence of their misunderstanding and misusing of American "freedom."[23] The easy access to cheap alcohol and the attractions to young immigrants of the saloon, with its dances and fun and games,[24] led many to a dissolute life. Especially disconcerting to many Finns was that the tavern life attracted not only men but also women. Thus, as one said, "the tavern dances became dens of wretchedness, and constant fights over women arose among drunken men."[25] More alarming still, as a Finnish newspaper noted, saloons were places "where even the women were drunk."[26] A good indication of how sensitive Finns were to this reputation of overindulgence of alcohol was that a common charge leveled between rival groups in Finnish American communities, whether between different religious denominations or between church and socialist groups, was that the other's leaders encouraged drunkenness or were drunkards.[27]

### Against Alcohol with Good Templars

Excessive alcohol use by Finnish Americans, and the reputation that this engendered among both Americans and Finns, naturally worried many Finnish immigrants from the beginnings of Finnish settlement in the New World. An increasing number of people within these settlements became convinced that they had to do something to free their fellow Finns, especially the young, from the slavery to alcohol that they had fallen into when they came into contact with the free and unorganized conditions awaiting them in America.[28] In the early years of Finnish settlement in America, before Finns had gathered in numbers sufficient to found organizations of their own, people of this mind joined existing temperance societies founded by Swedish and Norwegian immigrants.[29] In 1883, for example, some Finns in Allouez, Michigan, joined the Norwegian society, Tornea.[30] It, as most of these Scandinavian societies, belonged to the Good Templars,[31] an American federation of temperance locals that had established a Scandinavian office in New York in 1882 to bring in members from Scandinavian immigrant groups.[32]

The Good Templars, like many American social organizations at that time, attempted to add spice to its members' lives through secrecy and ritual. Members recognized one another through secret passwords and handshakes, and their tightly closed meetings featured elaborate ceremonies conducted by officers with a variety of convoluted titles. Such ritualistic behavior, adapted from such middle-class organizations as the Freemasons, apparently appealed to Americans at the time, appearing even in working-class organizations like the Knights of Labor. Beyond the ceremony, the main purpose of the Good Templars was to assure temperance among its members, who had to take a pledge of abstinence from alcohol in order to join. Most of the business at the meetings consisted of the ferreting and punishing, usually by suspension or expulsion, of backsliders.[33]

Finnish members quickly grew dissatisfied with the Good Templar locals they had joined, partly because the elaborate ceremonies and secrecy apparently did not suit them.[34] A more important problem for the Finns, however, was language. While many Finnish immigrants in America at that time knew some Swedish and/or Norwegian, they naturally found themselves somewhat uncomfortable at meetings whose official language was not their mother tongue. Therefore, as soon as Finns found sufficient advocates of temperance among them to do so, they began to found their own locals of the Good Templars.[35] In 1884, Carl John Stenroos, who perhaps thus earns the title of the father of Finnish American temperance, founded the first strictly Finnish temperance society, Hyvä Toivo (Good Hope), in Ashtabula, Ohio.[36] The following year Finns founded the temperance society Pohjantähti (North Star) in Hancock, Michigan, followed quickly by several other societies in northern Michigan, including one at Calumet.[37] In 1886, Finns founded their first temperance society in Minnesota, Pohjan Leimu (Northern Flame) in Soudan, and then Toivon Tähti (Star of Hope) in Duluth and Kilpi (Shield) in New York Mills.[38] By 1887, nineteen Finnish temperance societies are known to have existed, of which fourteen were locals of the Good Templars.[39] But language continued to be a problem for the Finns: in the first place, correspondence with the national organization had to be in English, and many locals had difficulty finding someone sufficiently versed in that language to do this effectively.[40] Second, the rules of the Good Templars, which governed most of their societies, were published in only English and Swedish. When Onnen Aika (Time of Happiness) in Republic, Michigan, published a Finnish translation of these rules and when the Good Templars denied the society the right to do so, *Uusi Kotimaa* (New Homeland), a leading Finnish American newspaper in the Midwest, called for the founding of a national Finnish temperance society.[41]

### Finnish Immigrant Organizations for Finnish People

As Finnish Americans developed a temperance movement of their own, they had a strong Old World heritage to draw upon. While the alcohol problem had sparked discussion in Finland since the mid-nineteenth century, a real breakthrough for the temperance movement occurred during the 1870s, as people began to notice how fundamentally Finnish society was changing. In part, the movement grew out of religious revivals that swept through many parts of Finland in this century, as churches attempted to develop a method to combat sin—such as drinking alcohol—through individual personal conviction. In part, the temperance movement grew out of the Finnish independence group the Young Fennians, who saw reduction of drinking as a necessary step in constructing an effective, modern, independent state. In either case, temperance became part of a strategy for dealing with the change from the corporate society of the rural village to the individualistic society of an industrial nation. In its early years, the temperance movement in Finland drew those most personally affected by the changing society, and much of its membership in urban areas consisted of workers and artisans. In predominantly rural areas, like Pohjanmaa, temperance societies drew those whose lives were most upset by social and economic

FIGURE 1. Temperance society Lännen Ruusu (Western Rose) hall building and Finnish boardinghouse in Seattle, Washington. (Source: *Amerikan albumi* 1904, 129)

change—landless laborers and the sons and daughters of farmers. Thus many who emigrated to America had ties to this movement.[42] One student of Finnish temperance suggests that a disproportionate number of members of temperance societies in Pohjanmaa were among the emigrants to America, indicating perhaps that these societies were a first step of those who were actively trying to find a new place for themselves in a society in flux.[43] Important leaders of Finnish temperance societies, such as Pastor Karl Tolonen, Juho Jasberg, and Isaac Silberg, also emigrated to America and contributed their skills and knowledge to new societies there.[44]

In response to the call of *Uusi Kotimaa* for a separate Finnish temperance federation, five Finnish local temperance societies met in Republic, Michigan, in January 1888, declaring their intention to leave the Good Templars and to found their own organization because "it is clear to everybody that the temperance movement about Finns cannot achieve its purpose under the leadership of strangers."[45] The result was the Amerikan Suomalainen Kansallis-Raittius Weljeysseura, or the Finnish-American National Temperance Brotherhood.[46] The brotherhood held its first annual meeting at Hancock, Michigan, on June 23, 1888. It adapted a constitution based on that of the Good Templars. The new organization maintained the basic procedures of the Templars, including the central place of prayer in their meetings and even much of the ritual, which they gradually had become accustomed to and begun to appreciate as an effective means of providing structure; the insistence on secrecy and restricted membership were, however, eliminated.⁴⁷ Its basic function remained that of the Templars: helping its members maintain their pledge of abstinence and keeping watch for those who might slip.⁴⁸ At this first meeting also, the brotherhood prohibited its locals from sponsoring dances and organizing activities on Sundays.⁴⁹ The new organization proved a success, and within three years the brotherhood had a membership of about 1,500 people. Most members were workers who were ttered through thirty-nine local clubs—most of them in Michigan.⁵⁰ Between 1888 and 1902, a total of 161 locals joined the brotherhood.⁵¹

As indicated above, most of the members of the brotherhood in its early years were workers, and most of these were young men. Many of these looked for the temperance local to compensate for the social activities that they gave up in not joining their comrades in the saloon and thus were less than happy with the restrictive measures that religious-minded leaders, who saw dancing and frivolous activities on the Lord's Day as equally great a sin as drinking, had placed on locals of the brotherhood.⁵² This difference in attitude became a problem already during the brotherhood's first midsummer festival in 1888. The celebrants boarded a boat on Portage Lake, Michigan, to get to the site of the midsummer picnic. In a festive mood and with a band playing on deck, young people naturally began to dance. The horrified organizers of the event quickly set up chairs around the deck to put a stop to this spontaneous merrymaking.⁵³

More seriously, a conflict quickly developed within the brotherhood. At its second annual meeting at Ishpeming, Michigan, in 1889, representatives of the Calumet, Michigan, temperance local, Hyvä Toivo (Good Hope), challenged religious elements of the brotherhood's constitution: the ban on Sunday activities and the frequent use of prayer in meetings, particularly when new members were initiated. They argued that "especially because of the long drawn-out initiation ceremony with its Pharisee-like ritual many have stayed away from the temperance movement." They also believed that membership would rapidly grow if the brotherhood allowed activities on Sundays, given that the great majority of Finnish Americans were workers for whom that was the only free day. ⁵⁴ These arguments failed to sway a majority of the delegates, who left these portions of the constitution unchanged. This challenge did produce one important change however: in December 1889 the board of directors kicked Hyvä Toivo out of the brotherhood. In response, the Calumet local called together representatives of a like-minded local society on January 19, 1890, exactly two years after the founding of the brotherhood, to establish a competing federation, Raittiuden Ystävät (Friends of Temperance).⁵⁵ The constitution of the new organization differed little from that of the brotherhood, but gave more freedom to its locals to sponsor Sunday activities and games for youth.⁵⁶ It did not, however, remove prayer from the meetings of local societies.⁵⁷ Competition soon developed between the two organizations, both with the same goal and essentially the same approach to reaching that goal, but differing mainly on the place of social activities within their organizations. This difference diminished somewhat in 1893, when the brotherhood changed its constitution to allow locals to hold properly reverential activities on Sundays.⁵⁸

## Disputed Social and Leisure Activities

In these early conflicts over the social activities of the temperance movement, only the most radical of the more free-spirited organizations challenged the brotherhood's ban on dancing. Quickly, however, this became the most important issue to threaten the unity of the Finnish American temperance movement. Many locals saw dances as a powerful tool in attracting Finns, especially the young, to the temperance movement. Some got around the brotherhood's ban on dancing by allowing other organizations to sponsor dances in their halls, but the brotherhood in response changed its constitution to prohibit that also.[59] The majority in the brotherhood still believed, along with Pastor K. L. Tolonen, that "anyone who indulges in dancing is not yet totally temperate," and that "dancing does not prepare people for eternal life. Therefore it must be prohibited always and in every place. Dancing damages the cause of temperance."[60] But some groups within the temperance movement in Finland had approved of dancing already in 1887, and in 1893 several locals from across the country, including those in Lead, South Dakota; Fitchburg, Massachusetts; and Carbondale, Washington, left the brotherhood over this issue.[61] The annual meeting of the organization in Virginia, Minnesota, in 1896 saw a particularly bitter debate over this issue, which resulted in a larger number of locals leaving the brotherhood than ever before. In addition, in many Finnish American communities, temperance advocates who favored dancing established independent societies that often competed with the brotherhood local for members.[62] Soon dances became a common function at temperance societies around the country. A correspondent to a socialist newspaper mocked this change of direction in his report from Fairport Harbor, Ohio: "Dancing, which had been viewed as a terrible sin, now seems proper and a necessary weapon in the struggle against a great enemy of society. The Jesuit phrase 'the ends justify the means' seems to fit well here."[63]

The dispute over dancing points to an important characteristic of the Finnish American temperance movement: in addition to consisting of people genuinely dedicated to halting the use of alcohol among their countrymen and women, temperance societies were also immigrant institutions that served the needs of strangers in a strange land. Temperance societies offered not only a means by which Finnish Americans could work to reduce the impact of alcohol on their communities but also a public place to meet and enjoy social interaction. As with all other immigration institutions, temperance societies hosted a variety of social activities that, in many cases, quickly outstripped their original purpose in importance. Groups within the temperance locals formed clubs to promote these social activities. For example, Uljas Koitto (Brave Dawn), the temperance local in Quincy, Massachusetts, hosted a band; men's, women's, and mixed choirs; a sewing club; a social activities club; a children's club; and a drama society.[64] Not all locals were so active, but most sponsored at least some of these groups. The brotherhood encouraged such activity as a means of bringing in new members, and beginning with its 1897 meeting sponsored annual band and choir competitions for its locals.[65] In addition, most temperance societies maintained libraries, which provided their members reading material in Finnish, and many sponsored speakers' clubs to help members develop skills to spread their message, and athletic clubs.[66]

But such activities demanded public spaces, something not readily available to Finns as they settled into American communities. In fact, Valon Tuote (Product of Light), the temperance local in Virginia, Minnesota, had to hold its early meetings in a room above a tavern, for want of a better space.[67] This need convinced temperance leaders that they needed places of their own: many locals began raising money, and soon temperance halls sprouted in Finnish American communities throughout the country. Temperance locals built about twenty of these halls within three years of the founding of the brotherhood.[68] Temperance halls became centers of social life in Finnish American communities in the late nineteenth and early twentieth centuries, as Finns attempted to re-create there the communal lifestyle of Finnish country villages.[69]

Beyond providing opportunities for social interaction, Finnish American organizations attempted to re-create the atmosphere of Finnish rural society in American communities by developing a communal support network for individuals. Some local societies offered different mutual aid programs to their members, and the National Temperance Brotherhood, at its first annual meeting in 1889, decided to establish a fund to pay a funeral benefit of fifty dollars to the family of each deceased member.[70] In 1892, the brotherhood also began paying benefits to sick members.[71] With such aid, and with the rich opportunities for social activities, temperance societies offered many Finnish Americans a safe haven from which to face the challenges of life in a new world. Participation in these organizations also played an important role in the Americanization of Finns: the by-laws of the Temperance Brotherhood recognized that Finns who had not been acquainted with running organizations in their homeland needed to be taught how to conduct meetings and to administer the various activities of the organization,[72] thus advancing their skills in the participatory politics of American democratic society.

Largely because of the vibrant social opportunities provided in its halls, and also because of the competition between the two temperance federations—the National Temperance Brotherhood and the Friends of Temperance—the temperance movement succeeded among Finnish Americans. In the ten years following the founding of the first Finnish temperance society in Ashtabula in 1884, Finns had established about 150 local societies, of which 93 had joined the National Temperance Brotherhood and 23 the Friends of Temperance, while 34 had remained independent. Not all of these survived long, but in 1895 the National Temperance Brotherhood consisted of 104 locals with a total membership of 3,720 people. In addition, seventeen locals with combined membership of 612 people belonged to the Friends of Temperance, while nineteen independent local societies had a membership of 670 people.[73] Two years later, in 1897, Finnish temperance societies in the East Coast states, wanting more direct control over their affairs, established a third federation among Finns, the Idän Suomalainen Raittius Yhdistys Amerikassa (Eastern Finnish Temperance League in America).[74]

Also in that year an important element within the immigrant group—Swedish-speaking Finns—began to establish locals of their own. Within three years they had founded about thirty societies, of which twenty-two joined the National Temperance Brotherhood.[75] In 1902, these organizations created their own central organization, the Svensk-Finska Nykerhetsförbundet av Amerika (Swedish-Finnish Temperance League of America).[76] The split of the Swedish locals from the brotherhood was friendly, however, and the two central organizations closely cooperated.[77] In the meantime, temperance continued to gain support among Finnish Americans, and by 1900 they had founded about 200 local temperance societies, of which about 150 with a combined membership of 6,550 members survived. Of these, about half belonged to the National Temperance Brotherhood and half to the other federations.[78] In some communities, a substantial portion of the Finnish population joined the temperance movement. In 1903, for example, the Valon Tuote society in Virginia, Minnesota, had 372 members, which was about 40 percent of the adult Finnish population of the town.[79] And when a prohibition law went to voters in Oregon in 1914, Finns in Astoria voted eight to one in support of it.[80] The high point of Finnish temperance activity in America was apparently 1908, when 245 local societies with an average membership of fifty-three existed. Of these, 108 belonged to the National Temperance Brotherhood and 53 to the Swedish federation. The total membership of these societies was about 13,000 people.[81] In that year, Finnish American temperance supporters attempted to unite within a single central federation to be known as the Amerikan Suomalainen Raittiusliitto (American Finnish Temperance League), but the attempt failed.[82]

## Ideological Battlegrounds

Such success, of course, did not come without controversy and conflict. Within the temperance movement itself, the most serious conflict raged around the question, already considered, of how large a role social activities, including dancing, should play within local societies. As these activities became more common, opponents redoubled their efforts against them, arguing that they drew the wrong kind of people into the locals, those who preferred light-minded entertainment instead of serious endeavors, to advance the cause.[83] Other issues also led to disagreements among temperance advocates. The original leaders of Finnish temperance in America had envisioned a primarily inward-looking movement whose main function would be to help members resist the temptations of alcohol. Soon, many members of the societies began to see this focus as too restrictive. A group known as the "progressives" arose within the movement and challenged the leadership to broaden the scope of activities to reach beyond members by emphasizing the creation of more literature and the sponsoring of more lectures and classes to spread the temperance message to others in the community. They also pushed the leadership to more active participation with the American temperance movement, particularly in working for prohibition laws.[84]

In addition to managing internal relationships, Finnish American temperance societies, as central institutions in almost all Finnish communities in the New World, also had to deal with other people within those communities, especially with the two dominant groups among Finns in America, the religious "Church Finns" and the socialist "Red Finns." Because the early Finnish American temperance movement tended to base its approach on the religious outlook that drinking was an individual moral weakness, or sin, its relationships with Finnish churches in America were at first very close. As a minister in Conneaut, Ohio, noted, membership in his Lutheran congregation and the temperance local were virtually the same.[85] In some communities, such as Virginia, Minnesota, where the temperance local was established first, the church used the temperance hall for services while building its own structure.[86] But tension also existed between these two groups. Religious leaders, especially ministers, were concerned that temperance societies, however noble their cause, would compete with the church for the attention and energy of Finns in the community. The concern grew after more "frivolous" Finns joined the temperance societies and moved them toward Sunday activities, which directly conflicted with church functions and toward "sinful" activities such as card playing and dancing.[87]

With the Red Finns, as with the Church Finns, the temperance movement had an ambiguous relationship. As already noted, most members of Finnish temperance societies were workers, and many of these became involved in the socialist movement in the early twentieth century. As an organized group, Finnish American socialists supported temperance: at its 1906 national convention, the Suomalainen Sosialisti Järjestö (Finnish Socialist Federation) endorsed this statement: "Understanding that the vice and sale of alcohol are a foundation post of bourgeois social and economic organization and of the middle class that benefits from it, which is in opposition to the interests and endeavors of the working class, and asserting temperance as our ideal, we demand an uncompromising national prohibition law regarding alcohol, except for industrial and medical purposes."[88] Thus temperance locals in many communities provided a middle ground, where Church Finns and Red Finns could work together toward a common goal and play together at social activities. Religious leaders of the temperance movement, of course, grew increasingly uncomfortable with the socialist presence within their organizations,[89] and, especially as more Finnish workers became serious about socialism, in many communities the uneasy alliance between the two groups in the temperance locals broke into open conflict.

This conflict resulted mainly from the generally widening gap—based partly on class—between Church Finns and Red Finns in the early twentieth century, but also rested specifically on different approaches to the problem of alcohol. Unlike religious Finns, who saw drinking as an individual moral weakness, socialists, as the above quotation indicates, believed it was a social problem brought on by the capitalist economic structure. They argued that blaming individuals for their drinking played into the hands of the capitalist authorities, as did the tendency of middle-class leaders of the temperance movement, concerned about the general reputation of Finns in America, to downplay the extent of alcoholism among Finnish Americans.[90] In many communities, the socialist local built its own hall and began to compete directly with the temperance society as the social center for Finns. In other places, especially in the West, socialists used their presence within the temperance local to attempt to wrest control of the organization, and of its hall, from its founding members.[91] In Aurora, Minnesota, for example, socialists gained majority control of the Länsi Toivo (Western Hope) temperance society and sold its hall to a socialist organization.[92] Such bitter conflicts generally ended any cooperation between the two groups, and, as the socialists concentrated on advancing their political agenda, the Finnish American temperance movement became increasingly middle class.

This trend in the Finnish American temperance movement indicates that it shared much with both its American and Finnish counterparts. In both the United States and Finland, the movement had started out with broad support within the working class, then become increasingly middle class in membership. In the United States, this change had occurred about half a century before it did among Finnish Americans,[93] who fit more closely to the pattern of the Finnish movement, where workers left the temperance movement in large numbers after the general strike of 1905, when they began to devote their energies more to strictly working-class activities.[94] Finnish Americans also shared the complex of motivations behind the temperance movements in America and Finland. In all three cases, people joined and worked for the temperance movement because they genuinely feared the damaging impact of alcohol on themselves and their neighbors. But the movement really took off both in America and in Finland as their economies were in the midst of the transformation from agricultural to industrial, which clearly also sparked further interest in temperance, whether because people believed that the dislocations produced by the massive change would increase the temptation to drink or that "modern" society demanded a more systematic ordering of personal life than required in country villages.[95] In addition, particularly as the temperance movement became more middle class, some saw temperance as a way to control the "masses," who were no longer restrained by the corporate customs of village societies.[96] Certainly American employers sought to use temperance to maintain a more effective, more malleable workforce, and some employers of Finnish labor provided aid, including gifts of land upon which to build temperance halls, to Finnish American temperance societies.[97] The Finnish American middle class, especially because they recognized that the transformation from agricultural to industrial society was jarring for recent Finnish immigrants and also because of their concern that their reputation among Americans would suffer if Finnish workers in America continued to overindulge in alcohol, also supported temperance as means of social control.[98]

## Prohibition and Its Aftermath

Despite close parallels to the American temperance movement, Finnish Americans for the most part worked in isolation within their own communities, indeed within their own societies. Nonetheless, they recognized that to succeed they needed to work to change conditions in their new homeland, America, and they cooperated on a limited scale with American organizations such as the Anti-Saloon League and the Prohibition Party, especially to achieve legal prohibition of the sale and use of alcohol.[99] This is particularly true when they were able to work on the community level, in states that had local-option laws allowing limited jurisdictions to pass prohibition laws. In Oregon, for example, Finns in Astoria voted the ward of the city in which they lived dry in 1904.[100] Of course, Finnish Americans supported the attempt to make prohibition national and rejoiced when the Nineteenth Amendment passed in 1919.

Prohibition in the United States marked the success of the temperance movement, but naturally led to a decline in the membership of prohibition societies. For Finnish Americans, this coincided with another important transformation—the end of mass migration from Finland coming with the First World War and the establishment of quotas for immigrants by the U.S. government. The immigrant generation was growing older, and home and family increasingly replaced common social activities at the center of their lives.[101] The younger generation in Finnish American communities was no longer immigrant, but the American-born children of immigrants who were culturally and linguistically assimilated and thus less attracted to separate immigrant activities. Finnish American temperance societies lost members, therefore, not only because many no longer saw the need for temperance activities in a country where the sale of alcohol was illegal but also because they were less likely to draw people to their halls with social functions.[102]

This decline in membership and activity in temperance societies opened the question of the use of the temperance halls, often impressive structures that had become the center of social activity in Finnish American communities. In Astoria, Oregon, by 1922 the temperance society had declined to a membership of ten, but still owned the Suomi (Finn) Hall, the only major social space for Finns in the town. In order to keep control of this valuable asset, those ten refused to allow new members to join the local, until the angered Finnish community of the town joined together and forced them to open up membership in 1924, which temporarily revived the dying society.[103] In 1934, the dwindling temperance local sold Suomi Hall to the local of the Finnish Brotherhood, a fraternal organizational among Finns on the West Coast.[104]

But Prohibition did not end drinking in the United States, so the need for temperance activities continued, for Finns as well as others. Emphasis now shifted to enforcing Prohibition laws. For Finnish Americans, the issue also became a generational one. Many Finnish parents saw the Americanization of their children not as a natural process but as a sign of moral decline. Instead of participating in Finnish American activities, young people were drinking and frequenting dancehalls that "smelled like saunas used for malting barley," while young women were painting their lips and nails bright red.[105] For older Finnish Americans, temperance became a way of saving their children. For some, this meant providing a good example, by insisting that adults refrain from drinking. As a member of the Finnish Kaleva Brotherhood, a mutual aid organization on the West Coast, worried: "Now that it is against the law of the land (to sell alcohol), our meeting places have in a fashion become taverns, loitering places for drunks. . . . What can parents expect of their children who come along to places like this?"[106] For others, this meant taking active steps to keep alcohol from the younger generation.

Such attempts to help their children sometimes drew together the bitter enemies within Finnish American communities, the Church Finns and the Red Finns. For example, in Astoria, Oregon, in 1925, members from the two sides joined together to attack the problem of drunken teenagers roaming the streets of Uniontown—the Finnish section of town—in the middle of the night. Concerned Finns called a meeting of all parents for the evening of May 29, with the statement: "At present it appears that young people have disintegrated culturally, causing sorrow for their parents and pain for the young themselves. It is a well-known secret that many young Finns even here act in a shameful manner. And it looks like our youth as a whole are sliding downward." At the meeting, Finns of all political and religious persuasions selected a committee to ask Astoria authorities to enforce Prohibition laws more energetically and decided to hold monthly discussion sessions on how to raise teenagers.[107]

Of course, with the repeal of Prohibition in 1933, a broader reason for a more active temperance movement emerged, but by this time Finnish American temperance societies appealed primarily to an aging group of first-generation immigrants. Thus the decline in activity initiated by Prohibition continued. By 1945, only twenty local Finnish temperance societies existed in the United States, and since the new wave of post–World War II Finnish immigrants tended to turn to organizations like Alcoholics Anonymous (AA) to deal with problems of drink, these societies gradually died with the old generation of immigrants. In 1963, seventeen Finnish temperance locals remained. In 1972, the national organization held its last summer festival, and by the 1980s apparently only one local—Sovittaja (Conciliator) of Worcester, Massachusetts—was still active.[108]

But in their heyday, Finnish American temperance societies were a vibrant part of a larger movement that flourished both in America and in Finland in the late nineteenth and early twentieth centuries. Like these broader movements, the Finnish American temperance movement was complex in both motivation and membership. It thrived primarily because so many of its members were so genuinely concerned with the problem of alcohol use among Finns and with the reputation of Finnish Americans as drunk, knife-wielding troublemakers and because it served an essential social function for immigrants trying to come to terms with their new land. But also like the broader movements in the United States and Finland, it was not only about ending drunkenness and social activities. It was also an important instrument in the halting attempts of Finns in the United States to define modern society and their place in it. In addition, it was a reflection of basic divisions—class and gender—in human society as one group—in this case, the middle class (or business owners) and women—to reform workers into something that was perceived as more proper. The movement also caught the enthusiasm of this era of reform: the sense that real improvement was possible, even likely. The cheery names they gave their societies—Hyvä Toivo, Pohjan Leimu, Onnen Aika, Uljas Koitto, Sovittaja—demonstrate the optimism with which they approached their task.

### NOTES

1. See, for example, Donna Gabaccia, *Immigration and American Diversity: A Social and Cultural History* (Malden, Mass.: Blackwell, 2002); and John E. Bodnar, *The Transplanted: A History of Immigrants in Urban America* (Bloomington: Indiana University Press, 1985).

2. A. William Hoglund, *Finnish Immigrants in America 1880-1920* (Madison: University of Wisconsin Press, 1960).
3. "Alcohol Now Finland's Top Killer," BBC News, http://news.bbc.co.uk/1/hi/world/europe/6106570.stm.
4. Irma Sulkunen, *History of the Finnish Temperance Movement: Temperance as a Civic Religion* (Lewiston, N.Y.: Edwin Mellen Press, 1990), 2.
5. Sulkunen, *History*, 6-7.
6. Reino Kero, *Suomalaisina Pohjois-Amerikassa: siirtolaiselämää Yhdysvalloissa ja Kanadassa*. (Turku: Siirtolaisuusinstituutti, 1997), 51-52.
7. S. Ilmonen, *Historiallisia kuvauksia juoppoudesta ja raittiudesta* (Calumet, Mich.: n.p., n.d.), 3.
8. S. Ilmonen, "Amerikan suomalaisen raittiusliikkeen historia. Edellinen osa," in *Juhlajulkaisu Suomalaisen Kansallis-Raittius-Veljeysseuran 25-vuotisen toiminnan muistoksi*, ed. S. K. R.-Veljeysseura (Ishpeming, Mich.: S. K. R.-Veljeysseura, 1912), 12.
9. Perry R. Duis, *The Saloon Public Drinking in Chicago and Boston, 1880-1920* (Urbana: University of Illinois Press, 1983); Jack S. Blocker Jr., *American Temperance Movements: Cycles of Reform* (Boston: Twayne, 1989), 120-22.
10. Michael G. Karni, "Finnish Temperance and Its Clash with Emerging Socialism in Minnesota," in *Finnish Diaspora II: United States, Papers of the Finn Forum Conference, Held in Toronto, Ontario, Canada, November 1-3, 1979* ed. Michael G. Karni (Toronto: Multicultural History Society of Ontario, 1981), 166.
11. Ilmonen, "Amerikan suomalaisen raittiusliikkeen," 12.
12. Sakari Sariola, *Amerikan kultalaan* (Helsinki: Tammi, 1982), 52.
13. John I. Kolehmainen, *The Finns in America: A Students' Guide to Localized History* (New York: Teacher's College Press, 1968), 20.
14. Kero, *Suomalaisina Pohjois-Amerikassa*, 52.
15. Sariola, *Amerikan kultalaan*, 40-1.
16. Hoglund, *Finnish Immigrants*, 88-89.
17. Timo Riippa, "Toimittaja Lähde: Finnish Immigrant Newspaperman, Temperance Advocate and Minister," *Finnish Americana* 3 (1980): 30-40.
18. Hans R. Wasastjerna, *History of the Finns in Minnesota*, ed. and trans. Toivo Rosvall (Duluth: Minnesota Finnish-American Historical Society, 1957), 359.
19. Hoglund, *Finnish Immigrants*, 125.
20. *Wyoming Semi-Weekly Tribune*, March 8, 1904, 1.
21. Juho Saari, *Mitä Amerikan suomalaisista kotimaassa Suomessa, ajatellaan. 20:nen vuoden Muisto-Julkaisu, 1906-1926* (Monessen, Pa.: Monessen ja Monongahelan Jokilaakson Suomalaisten Loukkaus-Sairaus-ja Hautausapurengas, n.d.), 29-30.
22. Sariola, *Amerikan kultalaan*, 40.
23. Hoglund, *Finnish Immigrants*, 11-12.
24. Kero, *Suomalaisina Pohjois-Amerikassa*, 51.
25. Ilmonen, "Amerikan suomalaisen raittiusliikkeen," 12-13.
26. Sakari Sariola, *The Finnish Temperance Movement in the Great Lakes Area of the Midwest* (N.p: Federal Legal Publications, 1985), 292.
27. Hoglund, *Finnish Immigrants*, 102-3.
28. Ilmonen, "Amerikan suomalaisen raittiusliikkeen," 5.
29. Carl Ross, *The Finn Factor in American Labor, Culture and Society* (New York Mills, Minn.: Parta Printers, 1977), 23; Hoglund, *Finnish Immigrants*, 43.
30. Karni, "Finnish Temperance," 164.
31. Kolehmainen, *Finns in America*, 20.
32. Sariola, *Amerikan kultalaan*, 56.
33. Blocker, *American Temperance*.
34. Sariola, *Amerikan kultalaan*, 56.
35. Wasastjerna, *History*, 360.
36. Hoglund, *Finnish Immigrants*, 43; Sariola, *Amerikan kultalaan*, 46-47.
37. Kero, *Suomalaisina Pohjois-Amerikassa*, 55; Ross, *Finn Factor*, 23.
38. Karni, "Finnish Temperance," 163.
39. Kero, *Suomalaisina Pohjois-Amerikassa*, 55.

40. Ilmonen, "Amerikan suomalaisen raittiusliikkeen," 35.
41. Kero, *Suomalaisina Pohjois-Amerikassa*, 55; Ross, *Finn Factor*, 23.
42. Sulkunen, *History*, 2–5, 173–74, 180–82.
43. Sulkunen, *History*, 182.
44. Hoglund, *Finnish Immigrants*, 49.
45. Ilmonen, "Amerikan suomalaisen raittiusliikkeen," 37.
46. Wasastjerna, *History*, 360; Hoglund, *Finnish Immigrants*, 43; Karni, "Finnish Temperance," 165.
47. Ilmonen, "Amerikan suomalaisen raittiusliikkeen," 35.
48. Kero, *Suomalaisina Pohjois-Amerikassa*, 56; Wasastjerna, *History*, 360; Karni, "Finnish Temperance," 165.
49. Sariola, *Amerikan kultalaan*, 60.
50. Ross, *Finn Factor*, 23.
51. Karni, "Finnish Temperance," 166.
52. Sariola, *Amerikan kultalaan*, 49–50.
53. Ilmonen, "Amerikan suomalaisen raittiusliikkeen," 44.
54. Ilmonen, "Amerikan suomalaisen raittiusliikkeen," 54.
55. Ilmonen, "Amerikan suomalaisen raittiusliikkeen," 55.
56. Sariola, *Amerikan kultalaan*, 61; Wasastjerna, *History*, 361.
57. Ilmonen, "Amerikan suomalaisen raittiusliikkeen," 55.
58. Ilmonen, "Amerikan suomalaisen raittiusliikkeen," 68.
59. Ilmonen, "Amerikan suomalaisen raittiusliikkeen," 70.
60. Ilmonen, "Amerikan suomalaisen raittiusliikkeen," 75.
61. Ilmonen, "Amerikan suomalaisen raittiusliikkeen," 70–71.
62. Ilmonen, "Amerikan suomalaisen raittiusliikkeen," 90–95.
63. *Raivaaja*, February 14, 1914, 5.
64. Kero, *Suomalaisina Pohjois-Amerikassa*, 61.
65. Ilmonen, "Amerikan suomalaisen raittiusliikkeen," 106.
66. Kero, *Suomalaisina Pohjois-Amerikassa*, 61; Wasastjerna, *History*, 363; Hoglund, *Finnish Immigrants*, 97.
67. Ilmonen, "Amerikan suomalaisen raittiusliikkeen," 86.
68. Ilmonen, "Amerikan suomalaisen raittiusliikkeen," 50.
69. Kero, *Suomalaisina Pohjois-Amerikassa*, 57; Ross, *Finn Factor*, 24–25.
70. Sariola, *Amerikan kultalaan*, 58.
71. Ilmonen, "Amerikan suomalaisen raittiusliikkeen," 64.
72. *Käsikirja: Perustuslaki, siwulait, paikallis-yhdistysten säännöt. Järjestys- ja työ-ohjeet, lasten raittiusosaston säännöt, sairastus-apuyhdistyksen säännöt*, 7th ed. (Hancock, Mich.: Amerikan Suomalainen Kansallis-Raittius Weljeysseura, 1906), 6–7.
73. Ilmonen, "Amerikan suomalaisen raittiusliikkeen," 79–80.
74. Ilmonen, "Amerikan suomalaisen raittiusliikkeen," 107.
75. Ilmonen, "Amerikan suomalaisen raittiusliikkeen," 108.
76. Wasastjerna, *History*, 362.
77. Kero, *Suomalaisina Pohjois-Amerikassa*, 59–60.
78. Ross, *Finn Factor*, 26; Hoglund, *Finnish Immigrants*, 43–44.
79. Kero, *Suomalaisina Pohjois-Amerikassa*, 60.
80. *Morning Astorian*, November 6, 8, 1914.
81. Kero, *Suomalaisina Pohjois-Amerikassa*, 60.
82. Kero, *Suomalaisina Pohjois-Amerikassa*, 65.
83. Ilmonen, "Amerikan suomalaisen raittiusliikkeen," 139–140.
84. Ilmonen, "Amerikan suomalaisen raittiusliikkeen," 130.
85. K. H. Mannerkorpi, "Conneautin suomal. Ew.-luth. Seurakunnan historia 20-wuotisajalta 1895–1915," *Paimen-sanomia* 27 (July 12, 1915): 539.
86. Ilmonen, "Amerikan suomalaisen raittiusliikkeen," 86.

87. Sariola, *Amerikan kultalaan*, 50.
88. *Pöytäkirja Amerikan Suomalaisten Socialistiosastojen Edustajakokouksesta, Hibbingissä, Minn., Elokuun 1–7 päivänä 1906* (Hancock, Mich.: n.p., 1907), 78.
89. Ilmonen, "Amerikan suomalaisen raittiusliikkeen," 137.
90. Sariola, *Amerikan kultalaan*, 283, 286.
91. Kero, *Suomalaisina Pohjois-Amerikassa*, 63.
92. Sariola, *Amerikan kultalaan*, 128–29.
93. Blocker, *American Temperance*, 22.
94. Sulkunen, *History of the Finnish Temperance Movement*, 153.
95. Sulkunen, *History of the Finnish Temperance Movement*, 4–5; Blocker, *American Temperance*, 36, 93; Karni, "Finnish Temperance," 165.
96. Blocker, *American Temperance*, xii; cf. Sulkunen, *History of the Finnish Temperance Movement*, 22–23.
97. Hoglund, *Finnish Immigrants*, 37–38.
98. Sariola, *Finnish Temperance Movement*, 291; Kero, *Suomalaisina Pohjois-Amerikassa*, 54.
99. Kero, *Suomalaisina Pohjois-Amerikassa*, 65.
100. *Astoria Budget*, November 9, 1904, 2.
101. Kolehmainen, *Finns in America*, 21; cf. Auvo Kostiainen, "Amerikansuomalainen raittiusliike: taistelu viinan kauhistusta vastaan," in Auvo Kostiainen and Arja Pilli, *Suomen siirtolaisuuden historia osa II. Aatteellinen toiminta* (Turku: Turun yliopiston historian laitos, 1983), 76–80.
102. Kero, *Suomalaisina Pohjois-Amerikassa*, 64.
103. *Toveri*, February 3, 1922, 4; May 7, 1924, 4.
104. N. R. Hannula, *An Album of Finnish Halls* (San Louis Obisbo: Finn Heritage, 1991), 8.
105. *Toveri*, October 7, 1926; *Veljeysviesti*, September 1929, 15–16; *Amerikan Suometar*, January 11 and 18, 1936.
106. *Veljeysviesti*, September 1929, 10–11.
107. *Toveri*, May 28, June 1 and 9, 1925.
108. Kero, *Suomalaisina Pohjois-Amerikassa*, 256–58.

# Religious Activities of the Finns: An Examination of Finnish Religious Life in Industrialized North America

*Gary Kaunonen*

After the long and arduous trip across the Atlantic, Finnish immigrants were now living in America, a secular country. This was quite the transition from living in Finland, where ecclesiastical doctrine and legislation dominated cultural, economic, and social life. While immigration from Finland to America was a transition from a Lutheran religious state to a secular nation, the secularism of America was perhaps mostly illusory. Nominally, America was indeed a secular country. However, while this secularism was officially a right guaranteed by the U.S. Constitution's First Amendment, industrial America in the Gilded Age equated laissez-faire capitalism squarely with the Protestant work ethic. In areas where Finns immigrated to in large numbers—eastern U.S. granite quarries and factories, midwestern U.S. mines, the industrial forests and sawmill towns of the Pacific Northwest, and southern Canadian forests, mines, and mills—corporate paternalism, or industrial welfare programs, combined with the social pressure of Protestant mores to reinforce the institutionalized regimenting of economic system *and* individual soul. This was a powerful combination of religion and economics.

First defined by sociologist Max Weber in 1904, the Protestant work ethic attempted to trace the roots of capitalism in northwestern Europe. In his celebrated work *The Protestant Ethic and the Spirit of Capitalism,* Weber concludes that the individualism of Protestant reform movements, especially Calvinism, encouraged people to work outside of the church—in the secular world—while developing an entrepreneurial spirit that reinforced free, unrestricted trade and individual wealth accumulation. In short, a strong work ethic in the secular world was a service to God, and in Weber's view this theory explained the hearty embrace and dramatic rise of capitalism in northwestern Europe during the Reformation.

While Weber's explanation of the Protestant work ethic was socioeconomic, the American labor historian Herbert Gutman studied the way culture affected the lives of America's working class. Particularly in *Work, Culture, and Society,* Gutman relocated Weber's analysis of the intersections between economy and religion in the formation of capitalism in northwestern Europe and transferred the Protestant work ethic's cultural dimensions to America. Gutman opined that religious institutions acted on members of America's working class by creating "a conformist, 'culture-bound' Christianity that warmly embraced the rising industrialist, drained the aspiring rich of conscience, and confused or pacified the poor."[1] For Gutman, the religious life of America's working class cannot be understood unless in the proper economic, cultural, and social frameworks: "Unless one first studies the varieties of working-class community life, the social and economic structure that gave them shape, their voluntary associations (including churches), connections to the larger community, and particular shared values, one is likely to be confused about the relationship between worker, institutional religion, and religious beliefs and sentiments."[2]

The Protestant work ethic had a profound impact on Finns in North America not because Finns came imbued with this ethic from Finland or its state church (Weber argued that Lutheranism placed too much emphasis on the divine spirit and the soul to espouse a true Protestant work ethic), but rather because men who expected, promoted, and practiced aspects of such an American Protestant work ethic administered the industries in which the Finnish immigrant working class labored. This was only part of the story, however, as American capitalists needed a conduit to reach the Finnish immigrant working class and quickly identified a religious institution as the prime means of culturally translating the expectations of an Americanized Protestant work ethic into a newly arriving immigrant population. This institution was the Suomi Synod, or Finland Synod, which was attempting to define itself as the official extension of Finland's state church in America, but lacked a sponsor such as the "state" in Finland to legitimize and subsidize religious authority in the New World.

Thus two powerful forces, one trying to transmit American capitalist ideals and the other looking for a benefactor in America, joined in shaping the religious landscape for Finns in America. Evidence for this assertion comes from two sources, written by pastors in the Suomi Synod. As part of the Suomi Synod's early bargain with American capitalism, it accepted donations of land and money from copper mining companies, many headed by managers who could trace their lineage to northwestern Europe or Calvinism, in its home base known as the Copper Country. As mining companies bartered land and money for a faithful transmission of the American Protestant ethic to Finnish immigrants, Rev. Arthur Puotinen wrote that "in securing property and donations from the companies, church leaders among Finns and other immigrant groups also broke ground for future criticism by labor leaders, who saw clergymen as beholden by such benevolence to support the company position in labor disputes."[3] The acceptance of a capitalist-centric view of America also led Suomi Synod leaders and press offerings to dismiss ideology, organizations, and political parties that challenged or resisted the power of American industry. In his 1924 examination of the process of Americanization on Finns, Rev. John Wargelin of the Suomi Synod wrote of socialism, a movement in which many immigrant Finns joined, that "*we do not attempt to find justification for it, for in our opinion it cannot be justified.*"[4]

For many Finns in America, therefore, "religion" wrapped around the acceptance of or resistance to an industrially sanctioned lifestyle, which was heartily imbued with ideas of an institutionalized, American Protestant work *and* lifestyle ethic. This certainly does not dismiss the place of religious piety, spirituality, or good intent in any church. Rather, the analysis contained in this chapter seeks to contextualize the cultural, economic, and social forces that were acting upon the religion of Finns in America. The transition for Finnish immigrants' religious life in America was not so much a transition of religious practice; after all, most Finns remained Lutherans in America. Rather, the transition was from centers of power and hegemony—from state control of religion in agricultural Finland to capitalist control and influence of religion in a heavily industrialized America.

This contextual framework, a decidedly materialist and secular perspective, will be the scholarly lens this chapter uses to view religion. It is not, however, a familiar or theologically comprehensive perspective. In reviewing this materialist approach, the Finnish theological historian Rev. Juha Meriläinen, lecturer in the Department of Church History, University of Helsinki, wrote that the limitations of such a perspective on the study of religion in Finnish North America included:

> Some things that are explained as authority conflicts or differences between structural models are also, or even more so, questions of different theological positions and ways of interpreting the social order . . . for example, the Suomi Synod, which did try to carry the heritage and the authority of the Lutheran state church in the United States, was led mostly by theologians that had roots either in Pietistic movement ("Herännäiset") or in the school of "biblical realism" ("Beckiläiset"), or often in both. These theological emphases sometimes explain the statements or actions of the Suomi Synod better than power or class.[5]

Though a materialist and secular perspective of Finnish immigrant religious life in America has definite shortcomings in regards to theology, this type of analysis regarding the Finnish religious experience in America provides an opportunity to explore a new perspective on the history of Finnish immigrant religious life in America. The hegemony of the Suomi Synod, an organization that sided with American industry, has dominated the narrative and study of religion in Finnish North America. Additionally, most of these narratives are celebratory of the synod, and, more specifically, of the men who served the synod. Pastors, synod board members, and prominent lay members of the church get much attention, with little reflection on context, power relationships, or class. In this vein, the Finnish Lutheran Book Concern published a number of the leading histories of Finns in America that center on religion, and most of these published synod histories were written by pastors in service to the synod. This chapter looks outside the walls of such a framework and analyzes the religious activity of Finnish immigrants and Finnish Americans using a "bottom-up" approach that seeks to examine the religious experience of North American Finns in the context of class, industrial setting, power relationships, and resistance.

### Pagan, Catholic, and Orthodox "Finland"

Finland was, of course, not always a Lutheran stronghold. Stepping back historically before the country of Finland existed, before the religious upheaval of the Protestant Reformation, and even before Catholicism dominated most of western European life, there was a time of paganism in Finland. Whether the ties are noticed or not, Finland's pre-Christian era had, and continues to have, a significant effect on the population of Finnish nationals and the Finns who immigrated to America. As the anthropologist Matti T. Salo wrote: "Many of the songs which every Finnish schoolchild learns from the Kalevala as examples of early Finnish aesthetic expression were in reality sacred ritual texts and myths, whose performance made the well-being of the (ancient) people possible."[6]

In America, homesick and lonely Finnish immigrants named social organizations, fraternal lodges, and rural hamlets after mythical characters from the Kalevala or other otherworldly phenomena. The Sampo Temperance Society, the Knights and Ladies of Kaleva, and the settlement of Tapiola, Michigan, can trace their etiologies to pre-Christian Finnish tribal religion.

Little is known about pagan Finland, but what is known comes mostly from language. As the ancient Finno-Ugric tribes made their way in to the borders of what would become present-day Finland, a rich spiritual belief system followed. Largely a shamanistic culture, the ancient Finns derived religious thought from interactions with the natural world, and this reverence for the natural world included a sharp distinction between the known and unknown. The home was controllable, while innumerable spirits and powers existed in the unknown forests, skies, and waters. All of this acted on the tribe and individual to create a cycle of life that articulated ways to explain creation, birth, illness, and ultimately death. This was a world of spirits, of black and white shades of good and evil, and of mystery, which was lovingly and painstakingly preserved through oral tradition.[7]

Better understood are Catholic and Orthodox Finland. Early forms of Christianity would find Finland by the thirteenth century, but more time was needed to make the complete transition from pagan to Christian society in most of Finland proper. The land that would become known as modern-day Finland happened to be a dividing line between the two most powerful forces in pre-Reformation Christianity: the Roman Catholic, or Western, Church and the Orthodox, or Eastern, Church. Contemporary Finland has its economic, political, and religious roots buried in this division. Turku (Swedish name Åbo) became the first diocese in Finland, and thus the center of the Catholic hierarchy in Finnish-speaking sections of the Swedish Empire. This bureaucratic move ensured that when Sweden's monarchy joined the Reformation, most of Finland did as well. There was, however, a stronghold of Orthodox power in Finland, and this minority remained true to the faith. Even today Finland recognizes two state churches: the Lutheran, with approximately 90 percent of Finnish parishioners, and the Orthodox, with roughly 3 percent of Finland's religious population.[8]

### Swedish Rule, the Reformation, and Russification

By the fourteenth century, much of present-day Finland came under the rule of the Swedish Empire. The Swedish and Russian monarchies seemed to use Finland as a continual sparring ground, but from roughly the fourteenth century until 1809, much of Finland was a part of the Swedish monarchy. During this time, the Swedish Crown underwent the change from a Catholic kingdom to a Protestant sovereignty. By the 1520s, elements of the Protestant Reformation had spread to Sweden from nearby Germany, and by 1652 Sweden had become a Lutheran empire. This transformation had great significance for Finns because the bureaucracy of the Swedish kingdom was now a Lutheran theosophy.[9]

Sweden lost possession of Finland during the Napoleonic Wars. Russia seized upon Sweden's preoccupation with the wars, annexing Finland in 1809, and Finland remained a possession of the czar until 1917. For the most part, Russian imperialism did not impinge on Finnish religious life, which remained grounded in Swedish Lutheranism. The official language of bureaucracy remained Swedish, and the Lutheran Church remained at the forefront of cultural, political, and religious life. However, especially during the time of intensive czarist Russification programs, the power of the Lutheran state church and Russian cultural repression in Finland came under scrutiny. Social reformers such as Johan Snellman, Minna Canth, Arvid Järnefelt, Matti Kurikka, and A. B. Mäkelä brought to public consciousness secular ideas. These ideas slowly took root in the collective Finnish identity, and in 1889 a Dissenter's Bill passed in Finland's legislative body, allowing people to affiliate with other denominations. However, it was not until 1923 that people in Finland gained full religious liberty. This emancipation occasioned the rise of numerous official, semiofficial, and independent religious organizations, as well as revival movements, such as the Laestadian movement.[10]

Revival movements in Finland were especially influential in the religious outlooks of Finnish immigrants in America. In his article "The Influence of the Revival Movements of Finland on the Finnish Lutheran Churches in America," Walter J. Kukkonen writes that there were four such revival movements in Finland dating back to the early nineteenth century. Of these four movements, three had an especially significant impact on Finnish religious life in North America. Two of the three movements, the Awakenist and Evangelical movements, centered in the southern half of Finland, while the Laestadian movement swept northern parts of Finland.[11]

These revival movements created important alternatives that challenged mainstream religious doctrine in the middle of the nineteenth century, but according to Kukkonen, the era of immigration and the changes in Finnish society and religious life from 1870 to 1910 had an important impact on keeping the Finnish state church intact as one governing body:

> Compared to the middle decades of the nineteenth century, the years from 1870 to 1910, the era of emigration, saw an entirely new situation in Finland. The cultural revolution was producing an upper class in Finnish society with a secular outlook, bent on ordering life with little or no reference to religion or the church. The vacuum created in the church's life, as well as the vacancies in the clergy roll, were filled by the lower classes, largely rural people, many of whom were adherents of revival movements.[12]

While the revival movements were at various times reinventing the official state church of Finland via dissent and protest, and as the state church came under increasing fire from secular social reform; Finland's religious population (and general population) began to decrease due to increasing emigration. Thus, the upstart revival movements that once sought to reinvent Finland's official church were now attempting to renew interest in religion through the very same state church in the rapidly changing and decreasing Finnish population.[13]

### Finns, Industrial America, and Religion

Finnish immigrants took this collective sociocultural and religious baggage to America. For many immigrants, the bulk of whom came prior to 1923's liberalization of religion, the state church and its authority were a despised institution. Remembrances of the home country included a highly bureaucratic religious-state, oppression of national identity under the Swedish and Russian empires, and a growing resistance movement to all the aforementioned. While Finns arriving in America seemed to share a predisposition toward cultural sameness, this was not, of course, the reality. By the late nineteenth and early twentieth centuries, the Finnish immigrant community was dynamic and somewhat disassociated, but to outsiders Finns seemed to exist as a monolithic social entity. Finnish immigrants tended to live in the same areas with other Finns, get involved in the same laboring occupations as other Finns, and join similar civic, political, and cultural organizations. Underlying the same point of origin and the appearance of ethnic unity was a quickly evolving resistance to forms of Finnish authority in America. As Finns streamed into the American industrial setting, a sense of class struggle and antagonism followed in many immigrants.

As a case sample of immigration patterns to industrial areas in the examination of Finns and religion in America, this chapter turns to one of the most significant "nesting places" for Finns in America:

Houghton County in Michigan's Upper Peninsula. This region beckoned many immigrant Finns to the promise of "America." Beginning in the early 1860s, Finnish immigrants began to settle in Houghton County. These early immigrants paved the road into the Copper Country, a bastion of mining wealth, for future waves of Finnish immigrants. Clemens Niemi, an early Finnish American geographer, wrote that it was not until about 1861 that the actual immigration from Finland begun. At this time, it was told, a group of Finns from Sweden and Norway, where they had been engaged in mining and fishing, arrived in Houghton County. These pathfinders originated from northern Finland and were followed by friends and relatives.[14]

As later numbers of Finnish immigrants arrived in Houghton County, many found work in Lake Superior copper mines. The first Finnish immigrants to arrive in Houghton County in the 1860s were familiar with mining from work in northern Norway in the Finnmark region. As Finnish immigrants began to arrive from Finland proper, the level of skill and knowledge in the extractive industries dramatically decreased. The Finnish immigrants swarming into the Copper Country industry were a blank slate when it came to mining. Many were receptive to agriculture, but had no land to farm or had to clear large tracts of acreage to begin farming.[15] Finnish immigrants found that if they were to make a living in Houghton County, it would first have to be as unskilled labor in area copper mines before saving money to begin a life of farming.

Finnish immigrants flooded Houghton County copper mines and, accordingly, Houghton County's urban areas. According to the thirteenth census of the United States conducted in 1910, foreign-born Finns comprised 11,536 of Houghton County's 88,098 residents. The mass immigration of Finnish immigrant workers into Houghton County precipitated a change in the workforce, especially at larger mining companies such as Calumet and Hecla, the Quincy, and the Copper Range mines. In the early days of the Copper Country mining boom, Cornish, Irish, and Germans comprised most of the area's mining workforce, but by the mid-1880s this changed as Finns, Italians, and eastern Europeans began to take unskilled jobs in area mines.[16]

Most of the general population of Finnish newcomers to North America, practiced Lutheranism, as did Houghton County's Finnish immigrants. However, once unleashed on an outwardly secular America, the rather unified Lutheranism of Finland began to disintegrate. Finns in America contorted religious practices into new perspectives, including abstaining from religion altogether. Noticing the erosion of state-sanctioned power, the Suomi Synod began to devise ways of bringing members into a type of American flock that resembled the institutionalized state church of Finland. There was, however, a mitigating factor in America: while the synod attempted to act as the official church of the Finns in America, it simply was not. The synod had to find ways to re-create the power of a centralized Lutheran church in America. Two important aspects of re-creating the Finnish state church in America were economics, or the money to fund religious activities and buildings; and the development of a trained clergy. The problem of training a clergy in America was addressed when the synod established a theological seminary named the Suomi Opisto, or the Finland College, in Hancock, Michigan. This endeavor, like much of the synod's operation, needed funding, and the search for a powerful benefactor began and ended with American industry. The synod needed to find a benefactor in America to underwrite its status in the Finnish immigrant community. This benefactor became American industrial capitalism. Big American companies, especially in isolated industrial areas, provided money for the procurement of land and the building of facilities. In exchange, the synod often took the side

**FIGURE 1.** Finnish Lutheran church in Savo, South Dakota. The original church built in the late 1800s, was destroyed by a tornado and rebuilt in 1922. In the churchyard is the Savo Monument for Finnish pioneers, erected in 1960. (Source: IMT Photo collections, USA_0479)

of the company in labor disputes, and retained a clergy that advocated and preached the tenets of the Protestant work ethic.

While the absolute hegemony of the Finnish state church was gone in America, a new type of religious hierarchy in the synod, backed by American capital, set about reestablishing and nurturing the role of religion in industrial communities in which Finnish immigrants tended to first work and settle. The Suomi Synod adopted and perpetuated ideals of the American Protestant work ethic, and evidence for this perspective is given by former synod president and pastor John Wargelin: "In our judgment it is not only our privilege but our duty to see that the democratic principles and Christian ideals, on which the foundation of this nation (United States) was based, are perpetuated in our national life."[17]

In *Americanization of the Finns,* Wargelin acknowledged the separation of church and state in America, but does so begrudgingly and does little to place the Suomi Synod as anything but a companion to the Protestant work ethic and American capitalism. In doing so, the book extolled the dominant place of the Suomi Synod in Finnish immigrant life. This perspective often brought the synod into direct conflict with other religious and secular organizations in the Finnish immigrant community and with newly arrived immigrants expecting to find freedom in America. Therefore, the sometimes figurative and once-in-a-while literal battle for the hearts and minds of Finnish immigrants was on in America.

Therefore, the religious life of Finns in America can be characterized by the rise and fall of power relationships not at the state level, as with a state-sanctioned church, but rather at the regional and local level. The reorganization of the religious power structure in America had far-reaching consequences. The ideals of secularism were lost in sometimes metaphorically, and sometimes literally, walled-off industrial communities. In these compounds of the Protestant work ethic, the Suomi Synod flourished as it unflinchingly guarded a Finnish-styled Protestant morality in America.

It should not be assumed that the Suomi Synod was the only Finnish church in America to accept money from American industry, and the power of congregations to raise money to support the synod's economic, religious, and social goals must not be overlooked. Additionally, it is possible, even likely in some areas, that other churches accepted donations from industrial benefactors. However, the Suomi Synod received seed and supplemental money from American industry and in exchange bought into, almost lock, stock, and barrel, the amplification of American iterations of the Protestant work ethic. This is in stark contrast to other Finnish immigrant religious bodies that supported organized labor or antimaterialistic doctrines that may have been antithetical to American forms of laissez-faire capitalism. Early, the Suomi Synod positioned itself to be in direct conflict with other Finnish immigrant religious organizations and working-class groups that did not tow the proverbial "company line."

With a source of patronage identified and engaged, the Suomi Synod and its clergy in America had a definite base of power and began establishing a top-down hierarchy that consolidated power in the Finnish immigrant community between the synod's ministerium and consistory at church and seminary headquarters in Hancock. Synod pastor and critical social historian Douglas Ollila Jr. wrote that the synod was "a traditionalist, conservative element in the immigrant population, and (was) inclined to favor a paternalistic church and clergy."[18] This top-down framework turned some immigrant Finns away from the church because many emigrated from Finland to escape the power, practices, and bureaucracy of an all-powerful centralized church. This authoritarianism was the primary reason for the establishment of the upstart Laestadian, Apostolic, National, Congregationalist, Methodist, Baptist, and independent Finnish churches that functioned in America autonomous of the synod. While the synod certainly remained the grandest force in soul saving for American Finns, challenges to this authority came from many directions, including secular movements, and from a bevy of other religious institutions. The tenets of Martin Luther and the Reformation were still the guiding religious principles in America, but the somewhat unified Lutheranism of Finland was a genie that could not be put back into the American bottle, and as such, Finnish Lutheranism split into several competing factions in the United States and Canada.[19]

### The Early Finnish Religious Community in America

Some of the first Finns to settle in America on a permanent basis did so on a heavily industrialized perch atop Quincy Hill, in Houghton County, Michigan. The hill was named after the Quincy Mining Company, and the company did all it could to nurture and support fledgling organizations that gave workers a wholesome pastime that was conducive to reinforcing a compliant workforce. The first small congregation of Finns in North America occurred in this industrial setting at a place of worship that consisted of Swedish, Norwegian, and Finnish parishioners. The Scandinavian Evangelical Lutheran Church, or known to its members as the Norske, Quaener, og Svenske,[20] organized as a multiethnic congregation.

Norwegian pastors administered to the multiethnic flock, and interpreters relayed the sermons in Finnish to the "Quaeners" within the congregation. While this multiethnic setup worked for some time, a split in the overall ethnic harmony was in the offing. A forbearer of this split was perhaps inherent in how the various ethnic parishioners referred to the church by name. The Finns and Swedes referred to the church as the Scandinavian Lutheran Church, but the Norwegians referred to it as the Norwegian congregation.[21]

Not only was the small congregation of Scandinavians on Quincy Hill multiethnic, it was also multi-denominational within the realm of Lutheranism, at least within the congregation's Finnish population. Included in the Quincy Hill flock were Finnish Lutherans who identified with the national Lutheran Church in Finland, as well as Laestadians who identified with the Lutheran revival movement of Lars Levi Laestadius. While the Laestadians in Finland chose to remain within the state church of Finland, once in America the inclination to split from a perceived wayward church took hold.

## The Laestadians

A botanist from Pajala in northern Sweden, Lars Levi Laestadius founded the Laestadian branch of Lutheranism as a sort of nonmaterialistic movement in the northern areas of Scandinavia, Finland, and Russia peopled largely by Sámi inhabitants. Laestadianism included strict abstinence from perceived trappings in the material world, including dancing, gambling, and alcohol. Alcohol was an especially reviled transgression, and the title of Laestadius's pastoral thesis completed in 1843 signifies his disgust with alcohol: "Crapula Mundi" or "The World's Hangover."[22] Among other facets of Laestadian practice are customary sermons by laypersons, communal or public confession of sins, and worship in unblemished, austere churches.[23]

The Laestadian contingency of the Quincy Hill congregation soon became distressed with the doctrinal teachings and alleged materialism of Norwegian minister Pastor H. Roernaes. For his part, Roernaes had little patience for the pious religious scrutiny of the church's Laestadian members. This antimaterialism highlighted the Laestadians' grievances with Roernaes's ministry, as Armas K. E. Holmio has commented: "All finery in dress was considered sinful. This idea was carried so far as to deny even plain straw hats to women and neckties and watch chains to men. At funerals the hearse and floral wreaths were forbidden. Altar paintings, pulpits and church bells were condemned as devices used by Satan against Christianity."[24]

In 1872, unable to get along with the Laestadians, Roernaes upped the stakes and refused to give them some of the basic sacramental rights. This act pushed the Laestadians away from other Lutherans, including their fellow countrypersons who remained in the Scandinavian Lutheran Church for a time, leading to a rift that exists to the present day. Once on their own, the Laestadians formed their own congregation, which also began cleaving and reconciling and again splitting.[25] From these early splits, many more splits occurred intradenominationally and continue to occur as of 2004 with the splitting of the Grace Apostles from their parent church.[26] Not coincidentally, there is no "center" for the Laestadian or Apostolic movement. Branches, and even individual congregations sometimes, have a sort of independent and moveable congregational structure, and often the churches with the largest number of parishioners become geographic centers for Laestadian and Apostolic governance. Historically (and currently), Calumet, Michigan, was home to large populations of competing Laestadian congregations.

**FIGURE 2.** This historic photograph from inside the Old Apostolic Church on Calumet's Pine Street shows the sad effects of the Italian Hall tragedy during the 1913-14 Michigan Copper Strike. Finns who died in Italian Hall, many of whom seemingly had ties to the Apostolic faith, were given a collective funeral in the Old Apostolic Church and then buried in Lake View Cemetery. (Source: Gary Kaunonen collections, from *Pelto ja Koti*, December 1913)

These two branches published two influential but competing newspapers, *Valvoja* and *Opas*, which nurtured the movement in America well into the post–World War II era.

Laestadians are often seen as conservative on many social issues, but many Laestadians were involved as strikers in the 1913-14 Michigan Copper Country strike. Sadly, this disclosure comes from the fact that many of the Finns who died in the Italian Hall disaster in Calumet were likely involved with the Laestadian movement. An examination of the names of those who died in the hall reveals that many of the surnames originated in the northern parts of Finland. Adding to this familial connection, services for many of the dead Finnish persons from Italian Hall came at the Old Apostolic Lutheran Church on Pine Street in Calumet.[27]

Other branches of Laestadianism were sympathetic to the labor and leftist political movements in the Finnish American population. This identification with radical politics set the stage for one of the most noted splits in a single congregation between the so-called Big Meeting and Heideman groups. In the 1920s, the Laestadian movement in the western United States was in flux. Into this turmoil came

Antti V. Itänen, who preached in the Heideman tradition. Itänen came into conflict with Berkeley, California, pastor B. G. Färdig over doctrinal issues as related to the New Awakening, but also because Itänen was a subscriber to *Toveri* (Comrade), a Finnish-language, Communist-themed newspaper. Because of Itänen's reading habits, his followers split with Färdig's flock, and Itänen and followers formed a new church.[28]

In another interesting aspect of Laestadianism, a formal study is not available, but an article or chapter in the Laestadian history of America should be written on the interweaving of Finnish Sámi immigrants and Native Americans. As part of this cultural study, the place of the Laestadian Church's naturalistic, revivalist movement and disdain for alcohol must be noted. In regions such as Minnesota's Iron Ranges and Michigan's Copper Country, the marriage of Finns with the "first Americans" created a unique and often overlooked culture. Known to some with a pejorative connotation and to others in loving terms, "Finndians" represented the happenstance meeting of prehistoric cultures, Finnish Sámi immigrants, and the Ojibwa of the northern Great Lakes region.

The two cultures, that of the nomadic close-to-the-land Sámi and the similar naturally reverent Native Americans, may have provided for an instant cultural connection upon meeting in areas of the United States and Canada. Perhaps aiding in this cultural connection was the importance of the religious practices of the Laestadian Sámi: respect for the natural world, antimaterialism, the disapproval of formal institutionalized schooling for religious leadership, and perhaps most important, the birch tree. Additionally, many of the social injustices and problems faced by the Sámi in Finland and Scandinavia were the same tribulations faced by Native Americans in the United States and Canada. These included the battle with alcohol dependency and the struggle to retain ownership of cultural ways in the face of cultural repression by dominant governmental bureaucracies.

Despite a rather turbulent organizational history, the Laestadian movement in America has been very influential in the Finnish American religious community. Michigan, Minnesota, the Pacific Northwest, and New Ipswich, New Hampshire, have been especially influential in the development of the Apostolic and Laestadian Lutheran churches in America. Because of their intense fractioning, in the early to mid-1970s there were at least five Apostolic or Laestadian branches functioning in places such as Michigan's Upper Peninsula. While they fractioned frequently, their importance to maintaining Finnish ethnic heritage in America cannot be understated. In many instances, Apostolic and Laestadian congregations have been torchbearers for Finnish culture and language, in large part because of their piety and reverence for Laestadius's ecclesiastical legacy in northern Finland. Armas K. E. Holmio, a Synod pastor and historian remarked, "The strength of their national and religious spirit . . . is seen in the fact that when other leading Finnish churches merged with American churches in the early 1960s, the Laestadian churches remained independent and retained their (ethnic) identity."[29]

## Suomi Synod

The next Lutheran body to split from the Scandinavian church in America was the Suomi Synod. As mentioned, the synod attempted to maintain direct ties with the national Lutheran Church in Finland. In 1886, the synod's first organizational meeting was held in Minneapolis, Minnesota, when J. K. Nikander, J. J. Hoikka, William Williamson, and Karl Bergstadius met with J. Eisteinsen of the Norwegian Hague Synod to plan a governing body for Finnish Lutherans in America. Another interesting figure, J.

W. Eloheimo, came from Finland later and added a curious dimension to the fledgling movement of Synodians in America. The efforts to establish a board to serve the religious polity sputtered for some time until December 17, 1889, when Eloheimo, Nikander, and Kaarlo Tolonen, a pastor from Ishpeming, met in Hancock to form a consistory, a sort of executive committee.[30]

In March 1890, the Suomi Synod became an official organization, and Hancock became the synod's headquarters. From the start, the synod and its delegates were a traditionalist and conservative element in the immigrant population.[31] The synod's first constitution was very authoritarian. A clause ferreted out by reviewer Ino Ekman stated that the church could seize property of the individual congregations by force if necessary. The early days were beset with administrative problems, but Nikander acted as the moderate to Hoikka and Eloheimo, guiding the synod through tough times. Perhaps the most bizarre turn of events was when Eloheimo, then pastor of the Ironwood, Michigan, flock, declared himself the sovereign to usher in the Second Coming of Jesus Christ. Without doubt, the proclamation turned some heads, as Ollila wrote:

> Strange stirrings were fomenting in his (Eloheimo's) mind and before long he engaged in paroxysms of mystical rapture in the form of special revelation. Before long, a bizarre document written in English and titled "Proclamation of the Universal Kingdom during the Chiliad to Come." Its apocalyptic character was not so unusual; it was rather the fact that both the angel Michael and Jesus Christ revealed to humble minister William Elohim that he had been chosen by God to usher in the universal kingdom before the second coming of Christ. . . . Elohim was not only given sovereign power in life and death in the theocracy, but he was also to build a kingdom of peace and love where there were no taxes and where men worked an eight-hour day.[32]

It did not take the judicious folks at synod headquarters long to put two and two together and presuppose that William Elohim was Eloheimo. His declaration, the synod noticed, elevated Eloheimo to places where mortal men were not to go. Not long after Eloheimo anointed himself the sovereign of the Second Coming, he soon "resigned" from his position as leader of Ironwood's church. However, the parishioners in Ironwood called for his return, as many were laborers who likely saw Eloheimo's vision of no taxes and an eight-hour day as a bit of heaven on earth.[33]

The synod consistory rejected this plea, even after Eloheimo made an emotional speech at the 1892 church convention, in which he implored the synod's members to publicly confess their transgressions against *him*. The synod rejected his readmission to the ministerium. The ensuing rancor over the Ironwood congregation's meltdown forced the synod to rethink its constitution. The synod's new constitution was friendlier toward individual congregations, but much of the power remained in the hands of consistory, and a new clause added that "the provisions for an unchangeable constitution were omitted in the new constitution."[34]

At the turn of the twentieth century, despite the synod's problems, it amassed 6,210 members, and that number rose to 15,413 (tallies include men, women, and children) by 1918, though Ollila writes that these numbers are likely inflated. Publication of the newspaper *Amerikan Suometar* (American Finn) by the closely associated Finnish Lutheran Book Concern printing company further heralded the synod's message in this early stage of the synod's development. The synod also added a theological seminary designed to train pastors for Finnish-language service in the New World and later added commercial courses to the seminary's theological curriculum. With the added secular classes, in 1896 Suomi College

**FIGURE 3.** Pastor M. J. Kuusi with his confirmation school students, early 1900s. (Source: IMT Photo collections, USA_1024)

was founded in Hancock, and became a symbol of growth and prosperity for the synod's religious mission. Acting in unison with Suomi College and the Finnish Lutheran Book Concern, the Suomi Synod became a formidable purveyor of soul saving in America.[35]

For some time a major grievance against the Suomi Synod was that it overlooked the economic and cultural conditions of many of its potential parishioners. This ecclesiastical negligence for the plight of the working class (with the exception of a few synod pastors such as William Rautanen) opened the door for other religious and secular organizations to administer to the cultural, economic, and spiritual needs of Michigan's Finns. As Ollila wrote: "One of the Synod's limitations was her rigid definition of herself as an authentic offshoot of the Church of Finland. Once she imposed that image upon herself, she found it impossible to be very tolerant of viewpoints other than her own. Industrial workers were naturally alienated and fellowship with others became impossible. She was very often suspicious of the fine cultural efforts of the Kaleva lodges and Nikander even argued that clergymen should not involve themselves in temperance societies."[36] Nikander's pious nature reflected the synod's rather inflexible dogma, and he became a sort of lightning rod for the church's authoritarianism. While Nikander certainly seemed the pious individual, he was, as Ollila contends, a mitigating force against totalitarianism in the church. This did not, however, spare him from the wrath of the emerging labor and congregationally based religious movements.

**FIGURE 4.** Satirical cartoon published by the labor and socialist newspaper *Työmies* (ca. 1907) depicting members of the Suomi Synod clergy and laity enticing the working class with carrot and stick. A large ogre-like figure, representing capitalism, seems to be directing the work of the synod members. The pastor is likely Juha K. Nikander, while the layperson is probably J. H. Jasberg, a prominent Finnish immigrant businessperson and member of the synod board at that time. The cartoon's title is "The Holy Trinity of Our Day." (Source: Gary Kaunonen collections)

Despite the Suomi Synod's problems relating to specific sections of the Finnish immigrant population, it did grow greatly within the Finnish immigrant religious community, especially in Michigan. The synod enjoyed great prosperity as an organization well into the post–World War II years, but as discussion of merging with North American Lutheran organizations began because of the transition from the synod's identification as a Finnish immigrant institution to a Finnish *American* organization with English-speaking clergy, dissention began to build in the ranks.

As questions of ethnicity and Americanization began to filter into the synod's congregations, it sought to administer to and control the geographic margins from Hancock. Bitter feelings ensued, as was the case with a synod congregation in the Aberdeen-Naselle area of Washington State. In this all-important debate over affiliation, which occurred in the years 1948 and 1949, the synod comes off as a careful yet totalitarian entity. When Rev. O. Kaarto, of the Aberdeen-Naselle area, refused to join or support a synod mandate to affiliate with the multiethnic United Lutheran Churches (ULC), the synod came down rigidly on Kaarto and his followers. The synod sent representatives from Hancock to Seattle to quell what could have become the "Seattle Split." There was to be no debate regarding affiliation, and dissention in the ranks was not tolerated in the synod's hierarchy.[37]

The Suomi Synod's merger with American Lutheran churches was a significant event in Finnish religious history in America. The merger and conversion to American Lutheranism began slowly but nonetheless grew intensely in the years after World War II. As John I. Kolehmainen wrote regarding the reasons for the merger in his study of the Finns in Ohio, Pennsylvania, and West Virginia, language and American-born clergy were major factors in the movement of the synod toward Americanization:

> The increasing use of English in Sunday and summer schools and confirmation classes, as new generations of American-born children appeared on the scene; introduction of English-language services, initially perhaps once monthly, but in time tending toward a totally different situation, that is one Finnish service a month . . . dropping from church titles all references to their Finnish origins. . . . Facilitating, indeed compelling these changes were not only the American-born generations but an American-born clergy, articulate and aggressive, which was eager to assimilate with larger American groupings.[38]

The merger with American Lutheran bodies proved difficult to many in the synod who wished to hold on to a strictly Finnish religious heritage, but the process toward American transformation of the synod had firmly taken hold of the church. This time of merger was also a time of reflection. Dwindling numbers in church pews occasioned ventures to seek reconciliation with the Laestadian/Apostolic and National churches. None of these reconciliations ever materialized, but the motive for compromise signified a new era of progressive nature in the synod. In light of declining membership numbers, which had dipped to 20,000 or so adult members by the early 1960s, the synod as a body voted to join the recently constituted Lutheran Church of America in 1961. Not all was lost, however, for those wishing to maintain the ethnic connection to religion. In 1962, a Suomi conference was established within the Lutheran Church of America and came to represent the historical importance of the synod to North American Lutheranism. [39]

### The Kansalliskirkko and the Lähetyskirkko Congregational Churches

Congregational churches, or denominations driven by local control of ecclesiastical concerns, were a direct repudiation of the Suomi Synod's power in North America. In working-class terms, these churches could be described as organizations that were responsive to the "rank and file." These churches, one maintaining Lutheran affiliation and the other independent of Finnish Lutheranism, offered an absolute refutation to the power of the state church in Finland. Finnish North American congregational churches were a unique and wholly American institution, which was created and crafted by new people in a new land.

The Kansalliskirkko, or National Church, has an interesting history that begins with a former synod pastor. J. W. Eloheimo, the previously introduced "religious sovereign," was a busy man and is the reason for the last major partition of the affiliated Finnish Lutheran churches in America. In 1890, and before his aforementioned visions, Eloheimo was the pastor of a synod church in Calumet, Michigan. When a number of parishioners in the Calumet church opposed joining the fledgling Suomi Synod, Eloheimo excommunicated 500 members of the congregation. Shortly after this, the synod transferred Eloheimo to Ironwood, Michigan, but the 500 excommunicated members of the Calumet church began to foment the formation of a new congregationally based church. The idea was well received by a number of Finnish Lutheran congregations across America, and at a meeting held in Rock Springs, Wyoming, a band of fifty-five congregations voted through representatives to form a loose federation of churches known as the Kansalliskirkko, or National Church. The National Church was a direct response to the hegemony and power vested by the Suomi Synod in its consistory and pastors and thus away from individual people and congregations. Simply, the National Church was a congregationally controlled church. It was very much a populist *American* institution.[40]

During its early years, the National Church was a loose affiliation of independent churches, but in an amazing set of coincidences, Eloheimo became president of the National Church in 1898 when the rather independent congregations elected to federate more intensely to form the Finnish National Evangelical Lutheran Church in America. Unlike the synod, the National Church did not seek an affiliation with the Lutheran state church in Finland and early on supported affiliation with organized labor. As Ollila writes about the National Church, "most immigrants heaped scorn into the Synod's lap, and they chose to create their own democratic lay-centered institutions."[41] The irony in Eloheimo's presidency of a congregationally controlled church was that in the synod, he was a rather authoritarian figure in favor of centralization, and the National Church was likely home to around 500 people whom he had excommunicated from the synod in 1890. Eloheimo, almost predictably, grew disinterested in the National Church because of doctrinal differences and left to administer independent congregations in Wyoming around 1900. This very colorful character in the history of Finnish North American religion died "out west" in 1913.[42]

Identifying the need for a bridge between the Finnish immigrant working class and religion, the National Church sought to make inroads with the labor and socialist movement of American Finns. In doing so, members of the National Church worked to establish a school that would challenge the authority and doctrine of Suomi College in Hancock. As synod pastor Douglas Ollila Jr. writes in his history of the endeavor to create a folk school affiliated with the National Church, many in the immigrant community saw the synod and Suomi College as "not only the representative social structure and repressive old order of the motherland, but (Suomi College) was perceived as elitist since the academy's classical curriculum stressed Latin, Greek, and the other traditionalist subjects which were the marks of the educated upper classes in Finland."[43]

With the mission of establishing an academy for Finnish working-class immigrants in America, the National Church joined with burgeoning elements of the Finnish immigrant labor movement in America to found a school. The combination of stakeholders for the educational endeavor might seem like an odd-couple marriage, but at least two of the clergy in the National Church were acknowledged socialists, and many of the church's parishioners were working-class members of the Finnish immigrant labor and socialist movements.[44]

In 1903, at a meeting of the church in Ely, Minnesota, the Folk School was established. The academic design of the school was secular in nature, and the curriculum mainly centered on the basic 3Rs (reading, (w)riting, and (a)rithmetic. The original location selected for the school was Minneapolis, but within weeks of opening, the school moved to Smithville, Minnesota, just outside of Duluth proper. In Smithville, numerous problems plagued the school's operation. Rancor and fighting ensued over the curriculum and philosophical nature of the school. Church-affiliated members advocated establishing religion as a part of the school's curriculum, while socialists who were drifting toward Marxist materialism wanted nothing to do with religion.[45]

The result of this collision of philosophies resulted in the socialists wrestling away the school from the National Church. In a rather shrewd set of economic moves, especially for antithetical Marxists, the socialists bought out the capital stock of the school in April 1907. The school retained a rather neutral affiliation until the summer of 1907 with the outbreak of the Mesabi miners' strike. At this time the socialists moved to rebrand the institution as a strictly working-class institution affiliated directly with radical elements of the socialist and labor movements. To highlight this radical turn, the school became known as Työväen Opisto, or Work People's College, thus losing all affiliation with the People's Church.[46]

Through the years Ironwood, Michigan, became the home base of the National Church, perhaps because of the publication of *Auttaja* (Helper), a newspaper dedicated to church activities, events, and doctrine. Much like the Suomi Synod, the National Church moved to merge with an American body. The impending merger was due to a lack of trained Finnish-language pastors and a shrinking ethnic language congregation (in 1948 membership in Michigan was 2,205, but by 1960 membership had dropped to 1,386). Acknowledging these deficits, the National Church approached the Missouri Synod of Evangelical Lutheran churches in 1923 looking to merge. The president of the Missouri Synod attended the meetings at which the merger came into discussion, but no association was in the offing due to a single sticking point: women's right to speak and vote in church affairs. The National Church allowed the practice, but the Missouri Synod did not, and the merger fell through. A later merger did however occur, but not until 1964.[47]

The Finnish Congregational Church in America has an interesting history, one that is similar to the National Church, and perhaps rightfully so as both groups were congregationally driven organizations. The first Finnish Congregational church to organize in America did so in Ashtabula Harbor, Ohio, in 1891. After Finnish immigrants in that Great Lakes port community could find no effective religious instruction from synod pastors who visited the community sparingly, an American pastor in the Ashtabula Harbor Congregational Church wrote for help. Two seminary students arrived from Chicago and served the community for a short while until a pastor who renounced Lutheranism in Sweden and completed evangelical training in Finland was called to lead a Congregational church in Ashtabula Harbor. This pastor, Frans Karl Lehtinen, was the first Finnish person to be ordained by the Congregational Church in America.[48]

The Finnish Congregational churches seemed to grow at a rather stymied pace, but nonetheless did grow over the years. Finnish Congregationalism seems to have been most strong in the New England region and southerly midwestern sections of the United States. Congregational churches in South Thomaston, Maine, and Fitchburg, Massachusetts, are noted in the historical record. As Kolehmainen notes in his history of Ohio, Pennsylvania, and West Virginia, Finns from the original Ashtabula Harbor congregation spread the Congregationalist message to Fairport, Burton, Warren, and Conneaut, Ohio, and then into Pennsylvania. However, the population of the church did not likely ever surpass 1,000 members. The Congregationalists also appear to have had a strong interest in the publishing trade. A number of Congregational ministers served as editors for newspapers and periodicals, and, as Auvo Kostiainen writes, the Lähetyskirkko (Congregational Church) has been the publisher of seventeen different periodicals.[49]

## Baptists and Methodists

The number of Finnish immigrant congregants in Protestant but non-Lutheran churches was much smaller than Lutheran denominations. As discussed previously, the Finnish Lutheran and Finnish Orthodox churches were the only legal churches in Finland until 1923, so the practice of the Baptist, Congregationalist, and Methodist faiths in Finland was difficult at best. This assertion is elucidated by 1929 statistics regarding religious practice in Finland. In 1929, there were 5,313 Baptists and 2,091 Methodists in Finland, out of a population of 3,526,359 people.[50]

Once in America, a nominally secular nation, non-Lutheran denominations became a viable religious alternative for Finns, and as John I. Kolehmainen writes in his bibliographic history of Finns in America:

> Conditions of religious freedom prevailing in America stimulated the appearance of non-Lutheran movements. In a number of Finnish settlements there arose churches and communicants bearing a non-Lutheran label, if not always a distinctly non-Lutheran outlook; among them were the Finnish Baptists, Congregationalists, Methodists, Pentecostalists, Unitarians. . . . The emergence of non-Lutheran bodies, while giving variety and color to the immigrant religious scene, engendered a series of highly controversial issues as to the ethics of missionary activity among a people traditionally Lutheran and the compatibility of non-Lutheranism with a "true Finnish spirit."[51]

Though Kolehmainen suggests that many Finns found these non-Lutheran denominations in America, it appears that leaders of many of these movements came from Finland or had some type of religious training in Finland.[52]

Supporting this speculation, seemingly many Finnish immigrants joined the Baptist denomination from interactions with Finland's Swedish minority prior to emigration. In more recent cases, Finnish Americans joined the Baptist flock from dealings with Swedish neighbors in America, or with Finland-Swedes who immigrated to America. Most Finnish Baptist churches in America occur in urban locations with large Finland-Swede populations such as Duluth, Minnesota; Felch, Michigan; Chicago; and Seattle. While there seemed to be a small, nascent Baptist movement in Finland, especially in areas populated by Finland's Swedes, perhaps most Finnish Baptists in the New World came to the movement while in America. From current research, it appears as if most Baptist congregations began after the turn of the twentieth century, but before 1910, and many had lost their Finnish inflection by the 1950s. The spreading of the Baptist message can be attributed almost entirely to missionary work conducted in America.[53]

The first Finnish Methodist congregation in the United States commenced work in Carlton County, Minnesota, in 1891. A man by the name of John Michaelson, a sailor by trade, converted to Methodism while in America and went about doing informal missionary work among Finns in the Midwest. Michaelson settled on a farm outside of Moose Lake, Minnesota, and established a congregation among the rocky boulders, scrub spruce, and small fields of the area. By the turn of the century, a Methodist minister from Finland moved to Moose Lake, and the enduring establishment of the Methodist church in that community was complete. The small congregation suffered greatly when the Great Fire of 1918 swept through northeastern Minnesota.[54]

From these meager beginnings, mission work began in Duluth and later reached the Finnish immigrant population of Minnesota's Mesabi Iron Range by the early 1900s. Congregations also developed in Michigan's copper and iron mining towns, which were all heavily influenced by the political economy of mining companies. There also seems to have been a network between congregations in Minnesota and Michigan as ministers traveled often between the two states.[55] In Clemens Niemi's study of Finns in Houghton County, Michigan, he identified a Methodist congregation in the county with 187 congregants and one minister, but never relates the location. This church also administered to one Sunday school that had ten teachers and seventy-five students. Most Finnish Methodist congregations seem to have been absorbed into the English congregations at an earlier date than Finnish Lutheran organizations.[56]

The rural Finnish Methodist congregation in Moose Lake was a bit of an anomaly because Methodism seemed to exist, in most part, as a significant Protestant denomination in mining communities. Methodism was the denomination of Cornish miners and managers, and Finnish ethnic iterations of Methodism likely did well to increase the social standing of congregants in the iron and copper mining regions of Minnesota and Michigan.

Established in the 1850s in London, England, the Salvation Army was an outgrowth of the Methodist Church that provided material and spiritual help to those in need. The group began functioning in Finland as early as 1889, and the Salvation Army followed Finnish immigrants to America at the turn of the century. The Salvation Army movement was somewhat suppressed in Finland, and similar reaction to the Salvation Army existed from the Suomi Synod in America, so when Finns came to America one of the only viable options to engaging in Salvation Army activity was to join Swedish or Scandinavian branches of the movement. Beginning in the late nineteenth and early twentieth centuries, and being most vibrant in the eastern United States, the Finnish Corps of the Salvation Army also came to be associated with the Finnish Congregational Church. Army work in Massachusetts, New York, New Jersey, and Ohio hit an apex in the 1920s, while attempts to create a functioning Finnish Corps in the Midwest during the early 1900s sputtered in areas of Minnesota's Mesabi Iron Range and Michigan's copper-mining capital, Calumet. The number of active corps never rose higher than six, but attempts to establish a Finnish Corps is an interesting footnote in the religious history of Finns in the United States.[57]

### Other Facets of Religion—Assimilation and Finnish American Catholics

It may have taken more than 400 years, but Finns would again find Catholicism. This time, however, it was on another continent and thousands of miles away from Finland as second- and third-generation Finnish Americans in the United States. Additionally, this time Catholicism came not through the Swedish Crown but through the process of assimilation into American society. This amalgam, the "Finnish American Catholic," was the result of Finns in America marrying into working-class Catholic ethnic groups, often in locations of heavy industry such as the Minnesota iron ranges, Michigan mining regions, Portland fisheries, Detroit auto factories, New York shipping docks, and Chicago meat-packing plants.

Assimilation had many facets—social, cultural, religious, and, of course, familial. Perhaps more than any other circumstance or institution, marriage assimilated many Finns into North American society. As second- and third-generation Finnish Americans encountered non-Finns in school, at work, and in social situations, inevitably the discovery of the opposite sex negated such "trivial things" as culture, ethnicity, and religion. When a blue-eyed "Finn" boy met a beautiful black-haired Italian girl, or when a blonde, taciturn Finnish American girl met a brash Irish-Catholic boy, the lure of love knew not an ethnic boundary. An excellent example of this form of assimilation is recorded in a 1972 oral history interview with Irish Canadian James O'Meara, who was living in Detroit. O'Meara was visiting a local Detroit dance hall when he met a stunning young woman by the name of Lydia Saukko. Thinking Saukko was maybe a Polish name due to the funny pronunciation, O'Meara contemplated that he was becoming romantically interested in a fellow Catholic. He would soon find that Saukko was Finnish (and likely Lutheran), but as O'Meara remembers, "Of course it didn't make a difference whether she was Eskimo, Polish or what, but it was hard to believe and that was the first time I had met a Finn." James and Lydia married in 1928, and this type of union repeated itself often in Finnish American working-class environs creating a rather common new religious dynamic—Finn-Catholics.[58]

### Thoughts on the Finnish Canadian Religious Experience

Though Canada and the United States are connected by the longest unrestricted national boundary in the world, the Finnish immigrant religious experience in Canada was much different from that in the United States. Two basic characteristics come to define a sense of disparity and distinction in the religious practices of Finns in Canada: the first and perhaps most significant difference centers on the role of socialism, industrial unionism, and Communism in the everyday lives of Finnish immigrants in Canada and later Finnish Canadians. In a critique of Rev. Yrjö Raivio's *Kanadan Suomalaisten Historia* (History of Canada's Finns), the Finnish Canadian social historian Varpu Lindstrom-Best elucidates the ongoing tension between the Finnish Canadian "Left" and religion: "From the beginning, the sponsors and authors have been unable to divorce this project from the sectarian strife among the Finns in Canada and have, therefore, emphasized the achievements of nationalistic, conservative institutions such as the Lutheran Church at the expense of the history of the Finnish Canadian labor movement. Because of this, the product is more propaganda than scientific history writing."[59]

The rather weak position of the Suomi Synod in Canada was even acknowledged by synod pastors, with one writing: "It would appear that the immigrant Finn (in Canada) no longer cares for those things that formerly had been dearest and holiest. . . . The God-denying tenants of the Communism have had freedom for too many years and have poisoned young minds."[60] From the 1910s through the 1930s, interest in radical politics and unions detached many Finnish Canadians from religious perspectives. Port Arthur (currently a part of Thunder Bay) seemed especially significant in the fouling of religious inroads in Canada, but as Ahti Tolvanen wrote in his history of Finns in Port Arthur: "There is evidence, however, that large numbers of Finns, perhaps most, never considered the two institutions to be mutually exclusive."[61]

Perhaps because of the synod's rigid inflexibility on the question of radical and even progressive politics, it never gained a real foothold in Canada. Missionary attempts were made, but these religious sojourns into Canada never found the success of the synod's control in the United States. Instead, the National Church did rather well in amassing a following in Canada, as did other Finnish religious organizations. Laestadian congregations dot the Finnish Canadian religious landscape, having an especially significant population in Saskatchewan. A number of Finnish Baptist churches organized in Canada, with one locating just outside of Thunder Bay in Intola, Ontario. A Finnish Pentecostal congregation organized in the Thunder Bay area as well. All of this varied religious activity mirrored that of America with one large exception: the Suomi Synod was denied a dominant place among Canadian Finns.[62]

The second difference in Finnish Canadian and Finnish American religious activity is the prominence of later immigration periods of Canadian Finns. While the United States had given quotas to

Finnish immigrants, the gates stayed mostly wide open in the land of butter tarts, maple leaves, and beavers, with an exception occurring during Canada's years of economic depression in the 1930s. There have been three periods of heightened immigration to Canada by Finns: the first lasted from the early 1900s until 1921, which somewhat mirrored the time of heightened Finnish immigration to the United States. A second period of intense immigration to Canada occurred between 1921 and 1931, when the United States had enforced immigration quotas. A third period of immigration ran from the early 1950s to the close of that decade. Generally, the United States did not experience much in the way of Finnish immigration in the second or third periods of Canadian immigrant intake.[63] This factor had a significant effect on religious practices in Canada.

As previously discussed in this section, religious and secular organizations other than the Suomi Synod found an equal footing in Canada. The power exercised by the synod over Finnish immigrants in the industrial United States did not translate well in Finnish Canadian immigrant society regardless of temporal period. This power was downright resisted by the first wave Finnish immigrants to Canada in the early twentieth century, and by the time many of the second- and third-wave Finnish immigrants had made it to Canada, the religious power of the Finnish state church had dissipated. A large number of Finns immigrating to Canada came after the 1923 religious liberty laws, and these immigrants had little sense of, or time for, the traditions of the highly authoritarian Finnish state church. Therefore, an institution like the Suomi Synod, which came to define many aspects of the Finnish religious experience in the United States, had difficulty gaining a place of dominance in Canada because of specific patters of immigration that were unique to Canadian Finnish immigrants.

## Conclusion

The history of the Finnish religious experience in North America is most certainly a study in relations of power, class, and industry. Because of the Suomi Synod's insistence on placing itself as the unofficially ordained companion to the Finnish National Church in America, it alienated many Finnish immigrants from religion as practiced in the Old Country. As A. William Hoglund wrote of the synod's mission in the New World: "Being favored by the state church of Finland, the Suomi Synod assumed that it had a special prerogative to guide the immigrant religious life. Although lacking any formal control over the Synod, the state church hoped that such favoritism would strengthen it in the competition with other religious groups."[64]

As part of what essentially became a power grab in America, the Suomi Synod hitched its proverbial wagon to the fates and fortunes of American industry, and ultimately this association hastened the process of Americanization in the synod. Entering into an alliance with American capitalism as a conduit for the Protestant work ethic to Finnish immigrants, the synod attempted to replicate its perceived place as the representative force of the Finnish state church in America. This enduring obedience to ideals of the Protestant work ethic—and its acceptance, advocacy, and complacency toward American laissez-faire capitalism—disenfranchised many in the Finnish immigrant population. In many instances, the synod's overlooking of the material conditions of Finnish immigrants in America occasioned the vacuum for competing religious and secular movements to have great influence on Finnish immigrants. This created a diverse and vibrant religious community in Finnish North America that defined itself by *resistance* to authoritarian forms of religious and industrial hierarchy and patronage.

## NOTES

Some research and writing from this chapter comes from my previous work, *The Finns in Michigan* (East Lansing: Michigan State University Press, 2009) and *Challenge Accepted: A Finnish Immigrant Response to Industrial America in Michigan's Copper Country* (East Lansing: Michigan State University Press, 2010).

1. Herbert G. Gutman, *Work, Culture, & Society in Industrializing America: Essays in American Working-Class and Social History* (New York: Vintage Books, 1976), 82.
2. Gutman, *Work, Culture, & Society*, 83.
3. Arthur Puotinen, "Early Labor Organizations in the Copper Country," in *For the Common Good: Finnish Immigrants and the Radical Response to Industrial America*, ed. Michael G. Karni and Douglas J. Ollila Jr. (Superior, Wis.: Työmies Society, 1977), 119–66.
4. John Wargelin, *Americanization of the Finns* (Hancock, Mich.: Finnish Lutheran Book Concern, 1924), 173.
5. Rev. Juha Merilainen to Gary Kaunonen, "Correspondence," October 17, 2012.
6. Matti T. Salo, "The Pre-Christian Religion of the Finns," in *The Faith of the Finns: Historical Perspectives on the Finnish Lutheran Church in America*, ed. Ralph J. Jalkanen (East Lansing: Michigan State University Press, 1972), 5.
7. Salo, "Pre-Christian Religion of the Finns," 1–12.
8. Salo, "Pre-Christian Religion of the Finns," 15–17; Mikko Juva, "The Finnish Evangelical Lutheran Church," in Jalkanen, *Faith of the Finns*, 19–20.
9. Salo, "Pre-Christian Religion of the Finns," 17; Juva, "Finnish Evangelical Lutheran Church," 20.
10. Juva, "Finnish Evangelical Lutheran Church," 20–21; Harry Siitonen, "Free Thought and Secularism in the Finnish Diaspora," FinnFest 2008, University of Minnesota at Duluth, July 24, 2008, http://www.finnlabor.net; Juha Seppo, "The Freedom of Religion and Conscience in Finland," *Journal of Church and State* 40, no. 4 (1998): 847–72.
11. Walter J. Kukkonen, "The Influence of the Revival Movements of Finland on the Finnish Lutheran Churches in America," in Jalkanen, *Faith of the Finns*, 80–93.
12. Kukkonen, " Influence of the Revival Movements," 93.
13. Kukkonen, "Influence of the Revival Movements," 93.
14. Clemens Niemi, *Americanization of the Finnish People in Houghton County, Michigan* (Duluth, Minn.: Finnish Daily Publishing, 1920).
15. Niemi, *Americanization of the Finnish People*, 6–8.
16. Charles K. Hyde, *Historic American Engineering Report: Quincy Mining Company* (Washington, D.C.: Department of the Interior, 1978), 196–200.
17. Wargelin, *Americanization of the Finns*, 107.
18. Douglas Ollila Jr., "The Suomi Synod: 1890–1920," in Jalkanen, *Faith of the Finns*, 158–59.
19. Kansalliskirkko or Evankelisluterilainen kansalliskirkko should be translated as Evangelical Lutheran National Church, not People's Church. In Finnish form, People's Church should be *kansan kirkko*, which refers to the church by lay members. "National Church" refers to the ethnic or national base.
20. Norwegian, Kven—an ethnic Finnish group in northern Norway—and Swedish.
21. Scandinavian Evangelical Lutheran Church Records, Finnish American Churches Box B-3, Manuscripts Collection, Finnish American Historical Archive, Finlandia University, Hancock, Michigan; Armas K. E. Holmio, *History of the Finns in Michigan*, trans. Ellen M. Ryynanen (Detroit: Wayne State University Press, 2001), 173–75.
22. Aila Foltz and Miriam Yliniemi, eds., *A Godly Heritage: Historical View of Laestadian Revival and Development of the Apostolic Lutheran Church in America* (Frazee, Minn.: self-published, 2005),

20–21.
23. Foltz and Yliniemi, *Godly Heritage;* Uuras Saarnivaara, *The History of the Laestadian or Apostolic-Lutheran Movement in America* (Ironwood, Mich.: National Publishing, 1947).
24. Holmio, *History of the Finns in Michigan,* 175.
25. Holmio, *History of the Finns in Michigan,* 175.
26. Foltz and Yliniemi, *Godly Heritage,* 195–208.
27. Larry Molloy, *Italian Hall: The Witnesses Speak* (Hubbell, Mich.: Great Lakes GeoScience, 2004), 144–45; Dave Engel and Gerry Mantel, *Calumet: Copper Country Metropolis* (Rudolf, Wis.: River City Memoirs, 2002), photograph of the inside of the church, 211; Pirjo Mikkonen and Sirkka Paikkala, *Sukunimet* (Helsinki: Otava, 1992); Larry D. Lankton, *From Cradle to Grave: Life, Work, and Death at Lake Superior Copper Mines* (New York: Oxford University Press, 1991), 238.
28. Saarnivaara, *History of the Laestadian,* 60–61.
29. Foltz and Yliniemi, *Godly Heritage,* 195–208; Holmio, *History of the Finns in Michigan,* 181–83.
30. Ollila, "Suomi Synod," 158–60.
31. Ollila, "Suomi Synod," 158–60.
32. Ollila, "Suomi Synod," 162.
33. Ollila, "Suomi Synod," 162.
34. Ollila, "Suomi Synod," 162–63.
35. Holmio, *History of the Finns in Michigan,* 202–4, 395; Ollila, "Suomi Synod," 165–69.
36. Ollila, "Suomi Synod," 168.
37. Rev. Edward Isaac Collection, "Letters to Aberdeen-Naselle, Washington, 1948–49," Suomi Synod Collection, FAHA.
38. John I. Kolehmainen, *A History of the Finns in Ohio, Western Pennsylvania and West Virginia: From Lake Erie's Shore to the Mahoning and Monongahela Valleys* (Fairport Harbor, Ohio: Finnish-American Historical Society, 1977), 174.
39. E. Olaf Rankinen, "Suomi Synod: Maturation and Americanization of the Church (1921–1962)," in Jalkanen, *Faith of the Finns,* 186–88.
40. Ollila, "Suomi Synod," 161–64; Douglas Ollila Jr., "The Suomi Synod in Perspective" in *The Finns in North America,* (Hancock, Mich.: Suomi College, 1969), 191–94.
41. Douglas J. Ollila Jr., "The Work Peoples' College: Immigrant Education for Adjustment and Solidarity," in Karni and Ollila, *For the Common Good,* 90.
42. Ollila, "Suomi Synod in Perspective," 192–93; Holmio, *History of the Finns in Michigan,* 208–9.
43. Ollila, "Work Peoples' College," 90.
44. Ollila, "Work Peoples' College," 87–97.
45. Ollila, "Work Peoples' College," 87–97.
46. Ollila, "Work Peoples' College," 97–100.
47. Holmio, *History of the Finns in Michigan,* 212–14.
48. Kolehmainen, *History of the Finns,* 129–33.
49. Kolehmainen, *History of the Finns,* 129–33; Finnish Heritage House, "Tervetuloa . . . Welcome to . . . ," http://www.finnheritage.org; Auvo Kostiainen, "Features of Finnish American Publishing," Genealogical Society of Finland, http://www.genealogia.fi/emi/art/main6e.htm.
50. Ralph Henry Smith, "A Sociological Survey of the Finnish Settlement of New York Mills, Minnesota and Its Adjacent Territories, Revised" (master's thesis, University of California, 1933) (Minneapolis: Snellington Publishers, 2005), 39.
51. John I. Kolehmainen, *Finns in America: A Student's Guide to Localized History* (New York: Teacher's College Press, 1968), 37.
52. Genealogical Society of Finland, *Articles and Books about the United States-Local History,* http://www.genealogia.fi/emi/art/main6e.htm.
53. Genealogical Society of Finland, "Baptist Church Articles," *Articles and Books about the United States-Local History.*
54. Elin J. Pitkanen, "The First Finnish Methodist Congregation in United States," *Articles and Books about the United States-Local History.*
55. Pitkanen, "First Finnish Methodist Congregation"; Allan Pitkanen, "Ellen Durchman Pitkanen' Diary of Her Migration Voyage to United States, October 9–28, 1911," *Finnish Americana* 3 (1980): 53.
56. Pitkanen, "First Finnish Methodist Congregation"; Niemi, *Americanization of the Finnish People.*

57. Mika Roinila, "A Forgotten Outreach: The Finnish Salvation Army in North America," *Journal of Finnish Studies* 11, no. 1 (August 2007): 32–40.
58. James O'Meara, interview by Arthur Puotinen, July 13, 1972, FAHA.
59. Varpu Lindstrom-Best, "Book Reviews," in *Finnish Americana* 3 (1980): 76–77.
60. Raymond W. Wargelin, "Finnish Lutherans in Canada," in Jalkanen, *Faith of the Finns,* 131.
61. Ahti Tolvanen, *Finntown. A Perspective on Urban Integration: Port Arthur Finns in the Inter-War Period: 1918-1939* (Helsinki: Yliopistopaino, 1985), 11–17.
62. Tolvanen, *Finntown,* 11–17; Laestadian Lutheran Church, "Our History," http://www.llchurch.org/our-history.cfm.
63. Tauri Aaltio, "A Survey of Emigration from Finland to the United States and Canada," in Jalkanen, *Finns in North America,* 68–69.
64. A. William Hoglund, "Breaking with Religious Tradition: Finnish Immigrant Workers and the Church, 1890-1915," in Karni and Ollila, *For the Common Good,* 30.

# Politics of the Left and the Right

*Auvo Kostiainen*

The abundant Finnish American political activities were a response to the labor conditions, resulting in strikes and demonstrations. The activities were mostly concentrated in rival ideological groups: the first orientations were those of European-type socialists or social democrats, which suffered several ideological splits and lost supporters to syndicalism or industrial unionism as well as to Communism. A lot of debate took place on the role of social and cultural activities in labor circles, called "hall socialism" ("hall" meaning meeting place), which attracted political and nonpolitical people to events and various circles of activity. A number of persons—for example, Gus Hall—rose to radical party leadership positions. The conservatives had their own political groups, which were not as visible as those of the left-wingers.

In addition to temperance and religious groups, the third major organizational and ideological group for Finnish Americans revolved around labor issues. There are three groups that are relevant for the discussion of labor issues: the socialists, the industrialists, and the Communists. Additionally, the influential cooperative movement was at certain periods closely related with the labor groups. This was especially the case in the major areas of Finnish population settlement. The temperance and religious groups did not have direct political affiliations; however, some conclusions may be drawn about their direct or indirect political inclinations. The labor groups, on the other hand, were by their very nature involved in political activities. There remained, however, several problems having to do with their political affiliations as well as possibilities to get involved. These included, for example, the linguistic abilities of the workers and the possibility to participate in left party activities that were available.

The activities of various workers' groups and associations have drawn the attention of quite a few non-Finns and quite often even that of the local, state, or federal officials, as well as employers. In those instances, they have evaluated the labor activities in a negative or a positive way. As discussed below, the ideological stand and active political participation of many Finnish American laborers confronted frequently the perceptions of the leading circles in the society. On the other hand, it will come out that there were many positive results from the associational life, various subgroup activities, and many things that were products of the laboring Finnish Americans—for example, the eagerness to find out the facts of American society and to interpret its form and contents.

## The Finnish Socialist Federation

Reino Kero has found that many of the active members of the Finnish American labor movement came from southern Finland, which was the industrialized part of the country at the time of emigration.[1] The strong links of the socialist group in the United States with Finland were essentially the result of the migration of key socialist organizers, editors, and other activists from the movement in Finland. There was also an exodus of socialist organizers as a result of pressure from the czarist regime. Later on, in the 1920s and 1930s, in turn, the Finnish Communists in the United States were in active contact with Finnish Communist leaders in exile in Soviet Russia after the Civil War of 1918. The industrialists or syndicalists, however, represented a more American version of the labor movement.

Several labor groups in the United States had strong Finnish participation. The reason for their activism is usually explained with reference to their literary skills and political activism that had been inherited from Finland. Finns became the major ethnic force in three of the movements outlined above. In 1913, the socialists had close to 13,000 members from the Finnish American community in 260 locals, while in the syndicalist-oriented Industrial Workers of the World (IWW), the number of Finnish Americans peaked in 1920 at close to 10,000. The Communists contributed the majority of the membership (around 6,000) to the Workers Party of America. Actually half of the Workers Party membership in the mid-1920s was comprised of ethnic Finns.

In 1890, the first Finnish American workmen's association, named Imatra, was formed in Brooklyn, New York. It was based on bourgeois reformism, quite similar to the so-called Wrightism in the Finnish labor movement—that is, employers cooperated with the workers, and stress was put on the improvement of educational opportunities among the working people. Imatra's purpose was thus the promotion of higher aspirations and mutual aid among Finnish American workers. Many of the early leaders of the Finnish American labor movement had previously participated in the labor movement in Finland, such as F. J. Syrjälä, Mooses Hahl, and A. F. Tanner. Under Tanner's leadership, the socialist local Myrsky (Storm) was formed in 1899 in Rockport, Massachusetts. This was the first Finnish socialist local to join the Socialist Party of America. After this, socialist locals were formed all over the country in accordance with the advice of Tanner and his disciple, Martin Hendrickson. Additional "agitating forces" entering the United States during the early 1900s included Taavi Tainio, A. B. Mäkelä, Alex Halonen, Vihtori Kosonen, Santeri Nuorteva, and Matti Kurikka. In the early stages of the development of the Finnish American labor movement, these active socialists from Finland played a very important role. But especially after the strike waves of 1906 and 1907 in the Midwest, the Finnish American labor movement viewed the American system of politics and economy with antipathy. At the same time, the leadership of this movement fell more and more into the hands of men who had not participated actively in the labor movement in Finland, but whose experiences of working life were inherited from confrontations between employees and employers in the United States.

The desire to improve working conditions appears to have been one of the most important factors leading Finns to join the labor movement in large numbers. At the same time, workmen's associations were often the only form of social activity outside the church and temperance groups, which sometimes had intertwining desires and activities, and this attracted Finnish Americans more and more into workmen's associations. Finnish immigrants, however, were often first exposed to socialist ideas in temperance societies. Many officers of the workers' societies and socialist locals learned their organizational

**FIGURE 1.** Workers' demonstration in Mohawk, Michigan, in 1913. (Source: IMT Photo collections, USA_2975)

skills in these groups. With the spread of socialist ideas, many of the temperance societies fell more and more firmly under the domination of the church. In other societies, however, the supporters of labor ideology gained a majority, and temperance societies of this kind slowly turned into workmen's associations.

Matti Kurikka arrived in America around this time. In Finland, he had been one of the labor movement's most conspicuous figures with utopian and theosophist leanings. After a spell in Australia, he arrived in British Columbia, Canada, in 1900. Under his leadership, a utopian colony, called Sointula (Harmony), which was based on socialist principles, was formed in Malcolm Island, British Columbia. People were persuaded to go there to escape the "clutches of capitalism and the rapacious class struggle."[2]

Kurikka's communal enterprise, however, caused the first factional dispute in the Finnish American labor movement. Many Finnish American supporters of pragmatic socialism, members of the so-called reformist political school, had gone to Sointula dazzled by the images of utopian society painted by Kurikka. They soon, however, returned disenchanted with the colony and the serious dissension that broke out there. In this first conflict over policy among Finnish American socialists, the antagonists were the advocates of utopian socialism and the champions of pragmatic action.

The years preceding 1903 may be considered to be the period of awakening in the Finnish American labor movement. "Apostles of socialism" traveled around the country, many workmen's associations were formed, and their activity was lively. The first workmen's association on a national scale, Amerikan Suomalainen Työväenliitto Imatra, or the Finnish American Labor League Imatra, was formed in 1903 in Gardner, Massachusetts. The organization's bylaws, as did those of the Imatra associations, stressed temperate and decent living habits. The locals were advised to assist the league's members in finding work and other matters. The league's membership was mainly concentrated in the eastern and midwestern sections of the United States, and, at its height, thirty-two local associations belonged to it. One of Imatra's main purposes was also the preservation of the Finnish American labor movement on an ethnic basis. Each association bore the name Imatra and was differentiated by number.

From the beginning, there were many followers of international socialism among the associations belonging to the league. At the same time as Imatra, another workmen's central organization was formed in the midwestern states: Amerikan Suomalainen Työväenliitto, or the Finnish American Labor League. It held its first convention in August 1904 in Duluth, Minnesota. The most important question discussed there was whether the organization should join the Socialist Party of America. The opponents of such a move still, however, carried the day. Organizational disputes continued for years, and competing factions were born. The activity of the newly formed state organizations began to concentrate mainly on the holding of festivals, the arrangement of appearances for speakers and lecturers, and the distribution of informational literature. The regional dispersion later hampered greatly the operations of the state organizations, and the next step was to be the creation of a common organization for the entire country.

The actual organizational process started with the establishment of "conservative" workers' societies at the turn of the twentieth century, especially in Massachusetts and New York. The atmosphere was more radical in the Midwest and the West, where radical labor organizations, such as the Western Federation of Miners, gained a foothold. Strikes were frequent, for example, on the Minnesota Mesabi Iron Range, where the labor force confronted the interests of the employers.[3]

In about 1905 and 1906, at the time of the great general strike and the Viapori rebellion in Finland,[4] many city and industrial workers who had already belonged to labor organizations in their homeland arrived from Finland. Many of them later became leaders of the Finnish American labor movement. Among these men were A. B. Mäkelä, Taavi Tainio, and John Viita (Wiita). The general strike and the Viapori mutiny had aroused great enthusiasm among the workers by offering examples of the methods available to them in carrying on their struggle. At the very time, Finnish American socialists met at Hibbing, Minnesota, in August 1906 to form a central organization for the Finnish socialist locals. The Viapori mutiny was a topic of heated discussion. On the other hand, there were difficulties in cooperating with the American labor parties. For example, linguistic difficulties caused all kinds of problems in the management of party matters. There existed a desire to create a unifying agency for the scattered Finnish inhabitants of the country.

The convention in 1906 held in Hibbing, in the middle of the Mesabi Iron Range, established Suomalainen Sosialistijärjestö, or the Finnish Socialist Federation, which was the first foreign-language federation to join the Socialist Party of America. The federation selected its own secretary-translator, who set up his office at the party headquarters in Chicago. There the secretary-translator could act as a link between the party and the Finnish Socialist Federation. The arrangement was found to be so successful that other ethnic groups likewise soon placed their own secretary-translators in the Socialist Party's headquarters. The executive arm of the Finnish Socialist Federation was its central committee. For practical operations, the country was divided into three "agitation districts": the Eastern, Western, and Central districts. *Työmies* (Worker), founded in 1903, and *Raivaaja* (Pioneer), founded in 1905, were approved as party newspapers.

**FIGURE 2.** Group of mine workers, many Finnish immigrants, in Belt, Montana, ca. 1904. Finns flocked to industrial regions in America looking for work. In many instances jobs were plentiful, but pay was low, and on-the-job danger was high, especially in dark and damp mines. (Source: Gary Kaunonen, *Amerikan Albumi*, 1904)

At the very first meeting of the Finnish Socialist Federation, and repeatedly later, the question of the stand to be taken toward the Industrial Workers of the World (IWW) arose. At first, the IWW had been in close contact with the Socialist Party of America. The IWW was formed in 1905 to coordinate the activities of different organizations in the trade union movement. The IWW soon changed, however, into a near anarchistic syndicalist oppositionist movement, the slogans of which were "Direct Action," "Sabotage," and "General Strike." The IWW's main objective was to bring the factories and, at the same time, society as a whole under the control of the workers.

At the Hibbing convention, there were also many IWW adherents who demanded the breaking off of relations with all the old trade unions. The largest of these was the American Federation of Labor (AFL). The majority of delegates, however, opposed the adoption of a hostile position to trade unions, and in the end, after long debates, a compromise resolution was accepted. It demanded the ending of cooperation with everything "bourgeoisie" and the supporting of a trade union movement that was based on class struggle and that upheld the work of socialist education.

### The IWW and the Breakup of the Finnish Socialist Federation

From 1906 to 1914, the Finnish Socialist Federation—and the Finnish American labor movement in general—flourished as never before or after. At no later time did any Finnish single labor organization in the United States attain comparable membership. Ten years later, in the early 1920s, the combined number of supporters of Finnish American socialism, Communism, and the IWW, however, exceeded the Finnish Socialist Federation's membership in 1913. The regional support of the Finnish Socialist Federation in the United States followed the geographical division of the Finnish population. For example, in 1911 the largest number of registered members was in the area of the Central district, 5,733 members in ninety-seven locals. There were 4,046 members in fifty-six locals in the Eastern district, and 3,888 members in fifty-four locals in the Western district.[5]

On the average, counting the whole country, circa 5 percent of the Finnish population were members of socialist locals. Numerically, most of the Finnish Socialist Federation members lived in Minnesota (2,824), Massachusetts (1,928), Michigan (1,478), Washington (1,062), Montana (681), and New York (650). Comparing the number of socialists with the total Finnish population in each area, the highest percentages are generally found in the western states. In Nevada, 26.2 percent of the Finnish population belonged to socialist locals; in Wyoming, 27.8 percent; in Arizona, 14.8 percent; and in Idaho, 12.8 percent. In the midwestern states, there were proportionally the most socialists, with 19.1 percent in Illinois, 17.1 percent in Indiana, 6.4 percent in Minnesota, and 5.5 percent in Wisconsin. The Quincy, Massachusetts, Finnish socialist local had the largest membership, 470 persons; the New York City local had 344; Duluth, 231; Fitchburg's Saima, 222; and Chicago's Socialist Local No. 1, 217.[6]

The activity in the locals took many forms. Various committees were set up to perform specific tasks: agitation committees, women's work committees, and so on. Special committees were also formed to collect money for local members in financial straits, for the promotion of election propaganda, and so forth. The agitation committee took care of ideological activity and education, Finnish Socialist Federation hired lecturers to travel around the country to speak at the different locals on topics of the day and, at the same time, to spread the ideals of socialism. Courses were often arranged in which a series of lectures were held on selected topics. Especially popular were also the so-called debating sessions, at which two speakers would introduce the proposition at length and then proceed with briefer arguments, after which the audience could take an active part in the debate.

In 1912, a total of sixty-three Finnish socialist locals owned a meeting hall (in American Finnish or Finglish, a *haali*) or some other building. Social events, lectures, political meetings, as well as other possible activities were centered in the halls—if the local did not own a building, one was rented. For practical purposes, there was activity in the halls every night of the week. In 1912, Finnish American socialist locals sponsored the following subsidiary organizations: 106 dramatic clubs, 83 agitation committees, 12 women's associations, 22 glee clubs, 28 bands, 89 sewing circles, and 53 athletic clubs.[7] Many locals had libraries and reading rooms, which received newspapers from Finland. The variety of activities is reflected in the fact that the socialist locals arranged English-language courses as well as Sunday and summer schools for children. At the beginning of the twentieth century, the ideals of the cooperative movement began to spread among Finnish Americans, but it was not until the 1920s that it really began to flourish.

Finnish American women were active participants in the socialist groups. While looking at, for example, the various activities described above, women were visible in the formation of women's associations as well as sewing circles. This type of tradition was carried on in most Finnish American labor groups, even after the ideological splits discussed below. Various reports of the women's associations and sewing circles show that these meetings had an important task to do—first, to educate immigrant

**FIGURE 3.** Finnish IWW supporters' summer festival on *Saima* Farm in Fitchburg, Massachusetts, 1920s. (Source: IMT, photo collections, USA_1668b)

women but also to form a basis of network in various professions, such as housemaids, servants, factory workers, or housewives. In 1911, there were 13,667 listed members in the Finnish Socialist Federation, while 3,790 (27.7 percent) were females and 9,379 (72.3 percent) were males. There were twelve agitation committees for women, with 131 members; ninety-one sewing circles included 1,359 members. Additionally, women certainly participated in many other groups, such as drama or gymnastics.[8]

The actual leadership seems to have been mostly in the hands of males, even reflecting the composition of Finnish immigration, which especially in the early phases was male dominated. However, the share of women in the immigrant population grew to about 40 percent at the turn of the twentieth century (see appendix 6). But there were separate activities and publications for women, and quite a few important female leaders. Among the active women were agitators and editors, such as Ida Pasanen, Selma Jokela McKone, and Helmi Mattson in the United States, and Sanna Kannasto (Kallio) in Canada. Finnish women are mentioned as an activist group showing the model to organize immigrant women as well as to demonstrate. However, it is important to note the participating rank-and-file members, not only visible leaders or agitators.[9] This conception is based on the important share of women participating in labor activities. On the other hand, the pattern of activity reflects not only the rise of socialism in Finland and its strong female leaders but also the rise of the women's rights movement in Finland. This was reflected in the general voting rights for males and females adopted in Finland in 1906, among the first countries in the world to do so. Also, patterns of activity were gained from the American continent, where female organizers and agitators such as Mother Jones (Mary Harris Jones) appeared in the mining or textile strikes in the East as well as Elizabeth Gurley Flynn in the Mesabi strikes of early the 1900s for the IWW or Communists, probably spreading enthusiasm among a number of Finnish immigrant women.

Because of the variety of the activities that centered in the halls, the charge has been made that Finnish American socialism was "hall socialism." By this is meant that socialism, as an ideal, remained secondary, and the main thing for Finnish American socialists was social activity, gymnastics, cooperative enterprise, theater, and so on. The important share of social functions in the halls cannot be ignored. The activity, however, can hardly be dismissed as mere "hall socialism" because there was also considerable participation in the activities of the parent party, and the effort was made to spread socialism among not only Finns but also other ethnic groups.

Newspapers, periodicals, novels, and book printing were very important for the Finnish American labor movement as a means of not only keeping in contact but also spreading socialist ideals or agitation work. Around the turn of the twentieth century, there were many short-lived attempts at establishing newspapers sympathetic to the labor movement. Indeed, in January 1900 A. F. Tanner founded the first socialist newspaper for Finnish Americans, *Amerikan Työmies* (American Worker). Another paper, *Amerikan Suomalainen Työmies* (Finnish American Worker), began to be published in Worcester, Massachusetts, in 1903, moving to Hancock, Michigan, as *Työmies* and later to Superior, Wisconsin, which became the real leftist stronghold for the Finns for decades. A lot of local leftist activities circulated around the *Työmies* Society, which published the newspaper. After 1950, the paper was called *Työmies-Eteenpäin* (Worker-Forward) when the paper merged with the New York *Eteenpäin*. Another strong Finnish American socialist newspaper was *Raivaaja,* established in 1905 in Fitchburg, Massachusetts. A third important Finnish American socialist daily was *Toveri* (Comrade), which was published on the West Coast, in Astoria, Oregon, from 1907 to 1931. The circulation of these Finnish-language newspapers was quite extensive: *Työmies* in Hancock, Michigan, had a circulation of 12,000; *Raivaaja* in Fitchburg, Massachusetts, 6,000; *Toveri* in Astoria, Oregon, 4,000. Newspaper companies also did a lot of publishing.

A noteworthy role was also played by Työväen Opisto, or the Work People's College, in the development of the Finnish Socialist Federation. The original institution was founded in 1903 as a religious school by Kansalliskirkko, or the National Church organization, in Minneapolis. It was named Suomalainen Kansanopisto ja Teologinen Seminaari, or the Finnish People's College and Theological Seminary. The next year it moved to Smithville, a suburb of Duluth. In 1907, the National Church lost control of the college, which was captured by the socialists and renamed Työväen Opisto.[10] As a workers' college, it was quite a rare phenomenon in the country. The institution managed quite well economically, too, and it was officially made the educational seat of the Finnish Socialist Federation. The curriculum of the college became centered on ideological problems of socialism as well as on practical subjects such as English and economics. In fact, the training of the federation's functionaries played a central role in the life of the college. In the radicalized Midwest area, the left radical ideas gained increasing support, and the Work People's College started to advance the IWW thinking. In 1914, the Finnish Socialist Federation no longer controlled the Work People's College, and it became the institution for the IWW.

Between the years 1906 and 1914, Finnish American socialists took part in many strikes, which left a clear mark not only on the development of the Finnish Socialist Federation but also on the position

**FIGURE 4.** The Työmies Kustannusyhtiö—or Työmies Publishing Company—building in the 1910s was a center of many activities in the Midwest. (Source: IMT Photo collections, original in the publication *Työmies kymmenvuotias*)

of Finnish American socialists in American society. The Finns had played a leading part in the strike in the Mesabi area, in northern Minnesota, in 1907. Also in 1912–13, there were major strike movements in the United States; in particular, the eight-month strike in the Copper Country in Michigan received attention. Many Finns actively participated in that strike. The conflict between strikers and management became so serious that the federal government had to send in troops to calm down the situation. It was preserved in the folklore with the tragedy at the Italian Hall, where more than seventy adults and children were killed during the 1913 Christmas party and the ensuing panic.[11]

These and many other labor disputes in which Finns played a prominent role had the general effect of giving the Finnish Americans a "Red" reputation, which was preserved even for decades. Some employers placed all Finns on their blacklist, and this forced many Finns to take up farming. In some areas, the churchgoing Finns organized protest movements to reestablish the reputation of Finns as good workers. Among them were the so-called Judas resolution movements. This activity continued during the World War I period with the establishing of the Lincoln Loyalty League, to be discussed below.[12]

During the course of the strikes, the IWW demanded swift changes and "direct action" rather than

**FIGURE 5**. Photo sent to Finland explains that here was a lumberers' cabin in Minnesota in the 1910s, in which Amanda and Erland Mattila had a diner for the men. (Source: America letters, Satakunta/IKA/LVIII, DGH)

dabbling in politics, which was the main concern of the Socialist Party's program. No wonder the IWW drew more and more supporters from the ranks of unskilled immigrant labor. Among Finnish Americans, industrial unionism gained a foothold especially in the midwestern and western states. Disagreements between the advocates and opponents of political action led finally, in 1914, to the breakup of the Finnish Socialist Federation. Of the 12,500 members, 3,000 quit or were expelled. The largest proportion of expulsions was carried out in Minnesota.

Membership loss and disputes over tactics and ideology followed. A schism appeared as a result of the Russian October Revolution of 1917 and the newly born Communist movement. The revolution carried out by the Bolsheviks was solidly approved by Finnish American workers; however, the question arose whether the methods used by the Bolsheviks could be applied in the United States. Feelings became more heated later when the Moscow-based Communist International began to play a leading role in the international labor movement. Moreover, disagreements were intense over the situation following the Civil War in Finland in the spring of 1918, as well as the issue of the establishment of the Communist Party of Finland by the refugees from Finland in Soviet Russia. During the late 1910s, the IWW movement experienced its heyday, with thousands of Finnish Americans becoming its supporters. Many Finns were active in organizing and calling for demonstrations. Their leadership position is not very clear due to the organizational structure of the IWW. It is also well known that the Wobblies, as members of the IWW were called, had a vivid subculture of their own, which among the Finns was seen as the survival of "hall activities" with theater, singing, and various clubs.[13] It is not possible to arrive at an exact count, for the Finns did not form a separate language group officially within the IWW fold but were all members of the same organization. Conceivably, the number of Finns belonging to the IWW was somewhere between 5,000 and 10,000.

Finns appear to have been a somewhat deviant group within the IWW. Their activity continued in nearly the same style as in connection with the Socialist Party. They still had their own "halls," in which they held social functions, staged plays, arranged dances, and so on. To maintain contact among themselves, the Finns organized their own regional associations. The activities of the Finnish American Wobblies centered to a fairly large extent around two institutions, the journal *Industrialisti* and the Work People's College. After the 1914 split, the Finnish Americans supporting the IWW founded their own newspaper, named *Sosialisti* (Socialist), and began to publish in Duluth. It was not long until publication had to be discontinued, but the paper made a comeback under the name of *Teollisuustyöläinen* (Industrial Worker). In 1915, the name was changed to *Industrialisti*. Its circulation apparently peaked in the early 1920s, probably exceeding even 10,000, which reveals the approximate number of Finnish American IWW supporters. The circulation of the paper, as well as the support of the IWW among the Finnish Americans, was centered in the Midwest, particularly in Minnesota and Upper Michigan, along with the West Coast. Also the IWW supporters living in Canada were diligent readers of *Industrialisti,* which was an important source of information for them.

Finnish American members of the IWW were active in many ways to spread information on the IWW activities. Their publishing was concentrated in Duluth, at the Worker's Socialist Publishing Company. The Work People's College continued to operate in Duluth, but its student enrollment was steadily declining. While it became officially an IWW institution, quite a few English-speaking students began to be admitted, too. The school continued to serve as an IWW seat of learning until World War II, and in 1941 it ceased to function as an educational institution.[14]

From the beginning of the 1930s, support of the IWW steadily dwindled among the Finnish American population. Even before that, at the beginning of the preceding decade, a sizable break in the ranks had occurred, when many Finnish syndicalists moved over to the Communist camp—for instance, during the so-called Rowan rupture, when Communist elements attempted to take over the IWW. At the end of the 1920s, the Great Depression hit the United States, and increasing unemployment forced many of the jobless to wander around the country in search of work. The Wobblies' ties to their organization were weakened and in certain cases broken entirely. Another reason for the dwindling of the IWW's influence was the emergence of a new generation. The immigrants who had come over from Finland were getting old, and the younger generation did not feel the same interest in the common activities of their elders but preferred to seek their contacts among Americanized contemporaries. The same phenomenon is to be observed in all the organized activities of the Finnish Americans—in church just as surely as among the Wobblies, socialists, and Communists.

Since World War II, Finnish American members of the IWW concentrated more and more on supporting the *Industrialisti,* and like other newspapers of Finnish American labor organization, it played a central role for this specific part of the immigrant population for information services, social activities, and also ideological support of the IWW. Very few new immigrants became IWW supporters and the responsibility of running the paper rested mainly on the shoulders of the old-time immigrants. A new center of IWW activity among the Finnish Americans, in addition to Duluth, developed in Florida, where

FIGURE 6. Photo sent to Finland, ca. 1920, describing a dangerous woodcutting machine. It is explained that their boss, Valtteri Arvola, used to wake up lumber workers in the morning shouting, "Hey boys, wake up and see how you will die!" (*Hei pojat nouskaas ylös katsomaan henkenne lähtöä!*) (Source: Photo collections, DGH)

the retiring Wobblies established a meeting hall. The *Industrialisti* had pockets of support in other parts of the country as well.

The importance of the IWW Finns has to be considered. First, they were active in organizational work and supported several strikes during the first two decades of the twentieth century. Some of them were active in organizing and leading local strikes. Second, they kept alive a lot of "hall activities," offering the framework for the social, cultural, and political life and debates. This point of view is related also to the publishing of the *Industrialisti* newspaper, as well as several other journals, calendars, and works of fiction by the publishing company York in Duluth. Third, Työväen Opisto was an important educational tool for Finns in the IWW, but it also served the larger nationwide IWW movement.

The social democratic wing of the Finnish American labor movement, on the other hand, emphasized the special conditions prevailing in the United States. The Finns in the Socialist Party were badly split, and particularly Finns in the midwestern and western region were strongly adopting the left-wingers' ideas, pushing toward the Communist camp. The matter of seceding from the Socialist Party of America was put to the vote among the members of the Finnish Socialist Federation. After a fierce propaganda campaign, the voting ended with over 60 percent of the membership in favor of remaining in the party. The situation in the Finnish Socialist Federation did not calm down, however, for a long time, and at the convention held at the end of 1920, the advocates of secession from the party gained the upper hand. The federation decided to declare itself an independent organization unaffiliated to any party, but each of the Socialist Party locals was empowered to make its own decision in the matter.

The supporters of the independent organization had no intention of merging the Finnish Socialist Federation—at least, not immediately—with the Communist Party but only aimed to follow developments in a "spirit sympathetic to the Communists." In reality, however, the organization's declaration of independence marked the beginning of the Finnish American Communist movement. In line with the resolution passed, therefore, each local decided for itself whether to belong to the Socialist Party or to stay with the now independent federation. After disputes that in many cases reached a violent pitch, some 180 socialist locals finally joined the independent organization. About 60 locals remained under the wing of the Socialist Party. Nearly 30 locals split, with the result that in their communities two rival factions formed. Of the 7,000 or so members belonging to the independent organization, the majority were from the midwestern states, while those 3,000 members staying in the Socialist Party of America lived in the eastern states, especially Massachusetts.

The Communist parties referred to were soon forced underground because of the persecution to which radicals were subjected by the authorities. Few Finns were members of these underground parties. Finns had always demanded obedience to the law and democratic procedure, and when the Worker's Party of America, a legal Communist party, was founded at the end of the year 1921, the independent Finnish Socialist Federation joined it. The Finnish American working-class movement was thus divided into three main groups: the "IWWs," or supporters of syndicalist ideas; the socialists; and the Communists. In addition, there were a few independent labor associations that had not joined any of the major organizations. These divisions remained quite stable later on.

With the breakup of the Finnish Socialist Federation, the majority of its members threw in their lot with the Communists, while the minority stayed in the Socialist Party. These socialists formed a new Finnish Federation within the fold of the party. Support of the organization came mostly from those in the eastern states, where in the 1920s and 1930s it had from 3,000 to 4,000 members. The main Finnish American stronghold of socialism was the state of Massachusetts, especially the town of Fitchburg, where the newspaper *Raivaaja* was published and a variety of activities were centered, such as a workers' bank, a cooperative store, and hall activities in general.

Yhdysvaltain Sosialistipuolueen Suomalainen Järjestö, or the Finnish Federation of the Socialist Party of the United States, continued along established lines: essentially, it held functions in the meeting halls, essentially in the tradition of "hall socialism." As in the case of the Wobblies and *Industrialisti,* the activities of the Finnish American socialists largely centered on the support given to their own newspaper, the *Raivaaja*. The Finnish American socialists gave the American Socialist Party their loyal backing and participated in its election campaigns. They were also active participants in a number of labor strikes. In the mid-1930s, Finns left the parent party after new factional strife within the Socialist Party. According to Elis Sulkanen, the editor of the *Raivaaja,* Finns looked for the appearance of a "truly influential political working-class party"; they did not want to be a part of a quarrelsome nonsignificant group.[15] For the maintenance of social and cultural activity, in 1940 Amerikan

Suomalaisen Kansanvallan Liitto, or the Finnish American Democratic League, was formed. This was a liberal social democratic movement. The biggest problem was the dwindling support, owing to the toll taken by age. The young Finnish American socialist-minded youngsters joined English-language organizations. Perhaps the most important field in which the Finnish American socialists have been active since the 1920s was the cooperative movement, which carried a specified, desirable progressive label.

### The Communists

The third Finnish American leftist group, which attracted quite a lot of attention from the rest of the Finnish American community as well as the non-Finns, was the Communists. After the ideological and organizational split, they kept the name of their organization, the Finnish Socialist Federation, from 1919 to 1921. Officially, they joined the public Communist Party, the Workers' Party of America, at the beginning of 1922. In 1924, the Finnish Socialist Federation took on the name Workers Partyn Suomalainen järjestö, or the Finnish Federation of the Workers' Party of America. This was followed by the active period of the Finnish American Communists. The party ideology was vigorously propagandized, and Finns became the largest national group in the Workers' Party by far, for in 1924 the party had 7,099 Finnish members, or 40.8 percent of the total membership.

However, Finnish American Communists soon found themselves at heated odds with the parent party, since the Communist International, or Comintern of Moscow, decided that the world Communist movement had to be reorganized through so-called Bolshevization. It was ruled that the former organizations based on nationality had to be eliminated, and instead international and workplace cells must be introduced. It was not very easy to persuade Finnish American Communists to accept new organizational structures, since many wanted to keep the language-based organization. The chief reason for this was probably the difficulty Finns had with the English language, but also the established, conventional way of dealing with hall activities. Because of the Finns' stubbornness, the Comintern sent Yrjö Sirola, a former Red leader of the Finnish Civil War and teacher at the Duluth Work People's College, from Moscow to settle the differences between the Finnish Americans and the Workers' Party. Probably because of Sirola, the opposition yielded, and the Finnish organization ceased to function.

However, not all Finnish American Communists joined the new organization; only fewer than 2,000 members did. Because of the decreasing membership, the Communist leadership took measures to create a new Finnish mass organization. The result was the formation of Yhdysvaltain Suomalainen Työvänjärjestö (STJ), or the Finnish Workers Federation of the United States, in which control was given through the Finnish American party headquarters to the leaders of the Workers' Party and further to the Comintern.

However, many Finnish American Communists were disappointed because of the continuing interference of the Comintern and the Workers' Party in the internal affairs of the organization, and another Finnish American ideological battle ensued. In 1928–30, a large number of leaders and ordinary rank-and-file members were expelled from the Finnish Workers' Federation and also the party. The critical opposition was concentrated especially in New York and the town of Superior, Wisconsin, in the Midwest. The newspaper *Työmies* was published in Superior, sticking fast to the Comintern line in its staunch advocacy of international Communism. The Finnish Workers' Federation leaders were accused of dictatorial measures. It was claimed that the rank-and-file members of the federation wanted to preserve the Finnish character of the organization, whereas the leadership favored pursuing the international line. Help from Moscow was needed again. This time, it was the turn of Kullervo Manner and Otto Ville Kuusinen's second wife, Aino Kuusinen. Manner operated mainly in Canada, but Aino Kuusinen concentrated her attention in the United States between 1930 and 1933. Under the pseudonym A. Morton, she established a strong position within the Finnish Workers' Federation, and she was able to carry out a number of changes within the organization. The spread of the opposition's support was kept under control.

Hence, during the 1930s many factors contributed to the downfall of the Communist movement. Party schisms were important, as was the rupture in the cooperative movement. Many members of the Finnish Workers' Federation stepped away from the political field to concentrate their efforts more on purely cooperative activities. Another important factor was the so-called Karelia fever that raged in Finnish American circles in the early 1930s. Soviet Karelia was in sore need of skilled workmen, such as construction workers and men with experience in various jobs in the woodworking industry. Since at the same time the entire Western world was undergoing a severe economic depression, it is no wonder that many Finnish American Communists were overcome by "Karelia fever." After selling all their possessions, they left with their families to return to the old continent to build a "real socialist state." In the early 1930s, at least 6,000 Finns left the United States and Canada for Soviet Karelia, and as a result many workers' associations ceased to function altogether.

The growth of the Finnish American Communist movement was actually cut short at this point. A more important factor in halting development than the organizational disputes or the emigration to Soviet Karelia was, however, the same as in the case of the socialists and the Wobblies: the aging of people. Also, the Immigration Act of 1924 imposed tight restrictions on immigration to the United States, and the number of arrivals from Finland was limited yearly only to a few hundred. The younger generation did not join the Communist organization in greater numbers; they became Americanized and either stayed outside the labor movement or joined the American movements proper.

In 1941, the International Workers Order (IWO) was established in the United States, and many Finnish American Communists joined. Operating in association with the IWO, they gained better connections than before with the American labor movement. When, in the late 1940s, repressive actions against radicals again started and in the 1950s culminated in the McCarthy hearings, the IWO had to disband. Then, the political activity of Finnish American Communists was increasingly integrated with the American party. Still, up to the 1950s, several men of Finnish origin held leading positions in the American Communist movement. The best known, perhaps, of these men was Gus Hall (Arvo Gustav Halberg), a second-generation Finnish American from northern Minnesota. He was the Communist Party candidate for U.S. president in the 1972, 1976, 1980, and 1984 elections, the last two times with black civil rights proponent and university teacher Angela Davis.

As in the case of the socialists and the members of the IWW, the activity of the Finnish Communists in the United States since the heyday of the labor movement was limited largely to upholding the cultural interests of the Finnish American community. For this purpose, newspapers, periodicals, and other publications were most important. *Työmies-Eteenpäin* (Worker-Forward) and *Naisten Viiri* (Women's Banner) continued to be published in Superior until the 1970s. On the other hand, "hall activities" have also been continuous: theater plays were performed, summer festivals were held, and various kinds of cooperative projects have been undertaken.

The influence of their newspapers on the Finnish American community was also ideological, since they endeavored to propagate class ideology stubbornly, holding faithfully to the party line. But it is just as true of the Communists, the socialists, and IWW adherents that their newspapers were increasingly vehicles of communication within the Finnish American community, until the closing of the papers, which varied somewhat in different parts of the country: the Communist *Työmies-Eteenpäin* closed in 2000 and turned into the *Finnish American Reporter,* which continues on a monthly basis in Hancock, Michigan, and without radical inclinations. The *Industrialisti* closed in 1975 after being edited from Florida in the local IWW community by Jack Ujanen, while the socialist-liberal *Raivaaja* was turned into a web publication in May 2009. The lifecycle of the papers mirrored that of the immigrant generation proper and a part of their descendants.

## Leadership Question

The leadership of the left politically oriented groups was not in the hands of Finnish Americans in the socialist, syndicalist, or Communist groups, with the important exception of Communists such as John Wiita and Gus Hall. There was leadership, of course, on the lower levels of organizations. Even socialist-minded Finnish Americans were able to be elected in minor locations in the Midwest.

John Wiita was a farmer's son from rural southern Ostrobothnia of Finland, a strongly religious region. His destiny was to become a worker and radical leftist group leader in America. Wiita gained various working experiences and educated himself. He achieved the status of a leading member of the American Communist Party in the 1920s. He, however, quit party politics during the Second World War, starting the new career of a real estate dealer.[16] On the other hand, the leadership position of Gus Hall is quite exceptional in American society. At the moment, a detailed biographical study on him is under preparation.[17] When looking at his career, it is obvious that he inherited from his home and radical ethnic Finnish neighborhood the pattern of political participation. Hall got involved in labor issues as a youngster in the Communist youth ranks, and he was increasingly drawn into political organization work. In the 1930s, he worked in the lumber camps. In 1931, he spent a couple of years in Lenin school in Moscow. After returning to the United States, Hall became an important organizer of steelworkers in Ohio. Following World War II, he experienced the anti-Communist atmosphere after rising to the leadership of the Communist Party. In 1948, Hall and eleven other Communist leaders were indicted under the Smith Act for conspiracy to teach and advocate the overthrow of the U.S. government by force and violence. Hall spent eight years in Leavenworth Federal Penitentiary. Later Hall gained fame while serving as a presidential candidate for the United States in the 1970s and 1980s. He was a strong supporter of the Soviet Union until its collapse.

As for trade union activity among Finnish Americans, the information for the period since the 1920s is not very accurate because the organizations involved were simply American, with scarcely any differentiation of foreign-language groups. On the whole, however, the Finnish American role in the trade-union movement has been noteworthy, for Finns fall into the ranks of organized labor in American society. Finns have done a lot of work by promoting the organization of the workers and, in particular, by taking part in the build up the Congress of Industrial Organizations (CIO).[18] Worthy of mention, furthermore, is the participation of Finnish Americans in the development of the Farmer-Labor parties. The role played by Finns has been especially significant in the ranks of the Democratic Farmer-Labor Party in the midwestern states. Apparently, however, they gained no leadership positions.

These important cases show that the left Finnish Americans had access to political careers. However, the fact is that in the various labor groups in which Finnish Americans participated, their influence was more limited to local level. At that level, we may even find collaboration crossing the linguistic and ethnic as well as ideological boundaries in times of societal tension. For example, Arnold Alanen has paid attention to the various language groups of the united front in the Iron Range elections in 1907, or in nonradicals joining in a common effort to win a mayor's position for the Socialist Party in Hibbing, Minnesota.[19] This kind of cooperation in elections probably was not very common for Finnish Americans, although the socialist ideology in general called for international solidarity.

### Non-left Political Activities

Set apart from the labor and left groups were various groupings representing more conservative ideologies. If we look at the Finns in North America, we may find that Judy Erola, from Ontario, Canada, made the most impressive political career in the Liberal Party. She became a member of the Canadian government in the early 1980s as the minister of state for mines, minister of state for social development, minister responsible for the status of women, and minister of consumer and corporate affairs.

However, she appears to be an important exceptional political figure with a Finnish background. It was more customary that non-left political issues gained support mainly through the party organizations offered by the Democratic Party or the Republican Party in the United States. However, it seems that the Republicans had most of the votes of the Finnish immigrant population. An explanation for this may be, according to Reino Kero, that economically prosperous periods in United States history were identified with Republican Party rule, while often the more depressed economic periods were identified with Democratic Party rule. However, during the Great Depression, the Democrats received massive support from Finnish Americans.[20]

In the United States and Canada, quite a few Finnish immigrants or their descendants have gained positions in local politics. It is impossible to find out exactly the political influence on the local level, unless we consider certain locations at certain critical times, or unless we look at the ethnic background of local officeholders. Locally interesting interethnic confrontations occurred, for example, at the time when strike waves took place in the midwestern mining areas in the early 1900s. Certain non-left groups of Finns issued statements called by the left Finns as "Judas resolutions" urging "proper behavior," as mentioned earlier. It seems that a number of Suomi Synod priests were quite active in these circles.[21] During World War I, those on the left objected to the participation of the United States in the war. On the other hand, the Lincoln Loyalty League was organized in 1917, with the aim to convince Finnish Americans about the "real" nature of the Finnish American population, who were said to be good citizens, instead of troublemakers. Its prominent leaders included the lawyer Oscar J. Larson and businessman J. E. Jasberg.[22]

Thus there were only a few political Finnish American leaders in the United States who yielded real political power. Primarily this fact was the result of the relatively small number of Finnish Americans in the country. Thus far, the sole representative of Finnish origin in the U.S. Congress is Oscar J. Larson

(1871–1957), who represented Minnesota during the 1910s. He also actively worked to help Finland by organizing food donations and other material help in the early 1900s. Yet in several state assemblies, there seems to have been at least a dozen state representatives. Among them were John Saari in Minnesota, and A. A. Anderson and G. A. Hellberg in Oregon. One governor of Finnish background served in the Midwest, a Finn-Swede named Elmer Anderson. A Republican, he served as the governor of Minnesota in from 1951 to 1955, and was elected five times as the vice-governor. The high-ranking representatives came mostly from the Midwest, a stronghold of Finnish American ethnic population. If we analyze the lower levels of the political decision-making hierarchy, we find scores of elected town mayors, sheriffs, and other local leaders with Finnish backgrounds.[23]

Emil Hurja (1892–1953) was another important figure whose career was very different from that of Gus Hall. A second-generation Finn from Upper Michigan who became a journalist, Hurja became interested in politics and political analysis; he especially wanted to develop systems of predicting election results. In the 1920s, he acquired a position in the Democratic Party organization and offered his services for electoral predictions. His offers were finally accepted, and he had great success in the 1932–36 elections. As a result, he became a member in the party leadership circles. He even appeared on the cover of *Time* magazine as the "Crystal Gazer from Crystal Falls." However, during the late 1930s Hurja's predictions were not so successful; he was dissatisfied and finally quit the Democrats and offered his services to the Republican Party. His offer was accepted, and he worked for the Republicans until his death, being influential during the 1952 Eisenhower election.[24] Otherwise, Hurja was an active lobbyist for the great tercentenary celebrations of the Delaware Colony in 1938. At the time, he wanted to get the Finns recognized as the "founding nation" of the United States. This aim was actually fulfilled, and Hurja's role was apparently of great importance in this development.

### Citizenship Question

Naturalization and citizenship were important issues for the various ethnic groups in the United States and Canada. It seems that they were offered some vague information already before migration, during the trip, as well as at the arrival to the new country, and especially after having settled in the new country. These issues were most important if they wanted to participate in the political and societal activities of the host society, such as elections, or compete for political positions. However, since the immigrants did not have much formal education, and most of that generation belonged to the working class, elections were not of immediate importance for a large majority of the immigrant population for many years. On the other hand, many migrants planned to stay abroad for only a few years, and they did not need excessively to ponder about the citizenship.

However, for the majority of the immigrants from Finland, coming to America proved to be a more or less permanent move, so they needed to think over the matter of citizenship. After they arrived in the United States or Canada, they found information about it on many occasions and at many forums. Most of these issues were discussed in the ethnic press and other publications. For example, calendar books were frequently read by immigrants, and they included quite detailed information on the process and requirements of becoming a citizen, which may vary somewhat depending on the state in which they were living. In a 1910 calendar, there was information on the process of how to become a citizen of the United States, according to the law for naturalization from September 27, 1906. It was explained that one needed to live for five years in the country before becoming a citizen. The process description included two phases: first, the "first papers" or intention for adult immigrants, and later the final paper application. Included were various costs of the procedure and information about the fact that the application should be directed to a court of law. Accordingly, a person needed to show ability in English as well the fact that he or she was not an anarchist or a polygamist. Information was also available on voting rights. For example, in a number of states immigrants could vote if they had the first papers for naturalization.[25] The naturalization issues were considered by the local authorities as well as Finnish immigrant communities. However, it seems that there were quite a few persons who never made the final citizenship application, but remained Finnish citizens. Of course, there must have been quite a few cases in which citizenship was denied for one reason or another, but their number is not known. A case was presented by John Swan and other Finnish Americans who applied for citizenship in Duluth in 1908, but who were denied by the court because of the Mongol issue; this decision was later overturned.[26]

About 70–75 percent of Finnish immigrants remained permanently in America. Those who stayed in the United States were soon faced with the question of naturalization in order to establish their position in the new society and in order to vote. However, there is some contradictory information on the willingness of the Finnish Americans to become citizens. For example, when comparing foreign-born citizens in 1910, we find that 45.6 percent of all foreign-born adult males were citizens, while 30.6 percent of all Finnish immigrants were naturalized. In 1920, the percentages were 47.8 and 39.2, respectively.[27] Thus during the ten-year period the number of naturalized Finns had grown notably, but they were still less active in seeking citizenship than foreign-born males in general. The percentage of Finnish citizens may be the result of their more recent arrival to the country and the fact that the medium age of Finns must have been higher than the immigrant population in general.

Certainly, ignorance of the English language was an important barrier to citizenship and assimilation. Because Finnish differs totally from English and other Germanic languages, Finnish immigrants faced abnormally great difficulties in acquiring the necessary skills in English. It also seems that the rank-and-file immigrant ultimately knew quite little about the naturalization process and the requirements connected with it, even if many publications in Finnish or English were available. The confusion on the naturalization processes and citizenship problems became evident, for instance, in the World War I years when hundreds, perhaps thousands, of immigrants went to Canada to avoid military service in the U.S. Army, among them many Finnish American radicals. A great number of radicals and aliens were arrested because they were ignorant of the duties involved with military service or did not want to join the army.[28]

There is some contradictory information of the citizenship question, revealed in various studies on the willingness of Finnish Americans to become naturalized in the United States. According to the reports of the Immigration Commission of 1910, Finns were quite active in becoming naturalized. For example, the report states that 65.7 percent of foreign-born male Finns twenty-one years of age or over at the time of coming to the United States were fully naturalized after ten or more years in the country. The respective number for all immigrants was 56.9 percent. Finns also appear to be close to the top among the new immigrant nationalities in seeking citizenship.[29] The Immigration Commission statistics show high willingness of Finnish Americans to become citizens. It may be that the immigrants of the late 1800s applied for citizenship relatively soon, while those who were a part of the Finnish mass immigration in the early twentieth century waited longer to apply for citizenship. Perhaps there were among the earlier immigrants a larger share of those who wanted to settle permanently in the country.

For those willing to become naturalized, federal and state programs offered courses that taught the necessary skills. But the immigrants themselves also actively worked toward this goal. John Wargelin says that Finns in general were "very anxious" to become naturalized, particularly during World War I, when they founded and actively participated in organizations working toward this goal.[30] Wargelin's opinions were given at the time when pressure for "loyal America" increased and radicals were sought after.

When we examine the Finnish American workers' organizations, we find that the question of naturalization was raised for the first time at the 1909 convention of the Finnish Socialist Federation. At that time a general resolution was adopted that each Finnish socialist branch should form a naturalization committee to help persons willing to become naturalized. The resolution grew out of a discussion based on the proposal by A. Pekkola, who demanded that each member of the Finnish Socialist Federation should become a citizen in order to go to the polls.[31] Interestingly enough, the Communists also pushed for naturalization. While in 1906, 11.2 percent of the members of the Finnish Socialist Federation were U.S. citizens, in the Communist-minded Finnish Socialist Federation in 1923, the percentage was as high as 36.1 percent.[32] It is probable that the fast growth in the willingness of the radicals to become naturalized was largely the result of World War I, when the pressure against radical and alien elements was growing in intensity. Antagonism against these groups culminated in the famous "Red raids" under Attorney General A. Mitchell Palmer, when thousands of radicals were arrested and many of them deported from the United States. This and the drive for restrictions on immigration embodied in the laws of the early 1920s further pushed radical Finns toward naturalization.

As hardly no new blood was entering immigrant communities, contacts with American society increased with the growing second generation of Finnish Americans. This happened in the great majority of Finnish American communities, from the far left to the far right. A study has been conducted on the timing of the naturalization of the Finnish immigrants, based on the returned questionnaires. The answers given by 517 immigrants show that naturalization did not take place in a great hurry, although A. William Hoglund has argued that, for example, Finnish American socialists tried to become naturalized as early as possible in order to be able to go to the polls.[33] In the study, it was found out that about 25 percent of the immigrants were naturalized within ten years of their arrival in the United States. Within twenty years, 55.7 percent were naturalized, while 26.3 percent were naturalized after more than twenty years of residence in the country, a total of 35 out of 517 people (6.8 percent) were not. In this sample, there was not an important difference between the Finns who were participating in labor activities or were part of the churchgoing group. In addition, the "labor Finns" of the sample were found to be even a bit slower in naturalizing.[34]

The delays in naturalization may of course be due to many factors. One factor may be result from the idea of many an immigrant to return home after only a few years in America. One could not normally apply for naturalization until he or she had lived in the country for five years. In the sample, after more than forty years in the country many were still Finnish citizens. Probably some of them had a kind of emotional attachment to their home country and decided never to become citizens of other countries. There were also language problems that made it difficult to become naturalized; quite a number of older immigrants had lived for decades in ethnic communities where English was not "necessary." In addition, when we consider Finnish American radicals, they were perhaps persons so strongly opposed to the American capitalistic system that they never wanted to become citizens. This attitude is reflected by the mass movement of Finnish American radicals to the Soviet Union in the late 1920s and particularly in the early 1930s, when they wanted to leave the "rotten capitalistic world" and build a new labor republic in the Soviet Union.

Finnish participation in the IWW diminished clearly in the 1920s with the fading importance of the movement. Douglas J. Ollila Jr. states that the syndicalist Finns Americanized very rapidly because the IWW was a completely American organization. The core of Finns in the IWW were foreign-born, as was the case for the supporters of the Socialist Party of America. Social democrats preserved most of the tradition of hall socialism when they stayed out of political parties and directed their attention more to their ethnic institutions. Both of these groups preserved many ethnic functions. In the 1940s, Finnish American Communists became integrated into the American Communist Party, although some degree of ethnic functions still persisted thereafter.[35]

The socialist- and Communist-dominated cooperative movement had a very strong foothold among Finnish Americans, and Americanization also proceeded rapidly. From the beginning the cooperative movement emphasized contacts with international and American cooperative movements. From the 1920s, the use of English became more common, and particularly after World War II Americanization proceeded swiftly. Finnish American cooperative stores gradually merged with the other American stores.[36] The conservative side was not necessarily well organized. By its very nature, for example, the aforementioned Lincoln Loyalty League pushed Americanization and citizenship. In Canada, there were also similar types of Finnish Canadian groups.[37]

On the other hand, there was a special group, which is still active, named Kalevan ritarit ja naiset, or the Knights and Ladies of Kaleva. It was conceived according to the national epic of Finland, the *Kalevala*. Founded in 1898, it gradually gained supporters around the Finnish settlements. It was a national romantic organization that drew on ideologies of "sacred Finnishness" or the heroes and heroines of the *Kalevala*. It was also strongly influenced by American Freemasons and their rituals. It wished to advance "Finnish" values, ideals, and history. Although originally a secret fraternity, it slowly opened more doors, and turned into something of a Finnish cultural organization. Its total membership reached 3,000–4,000 in the 1930s, with approximately sixty to seventy male and female chapters.[38] At the same time as these knights and ladies have appreciated the Finnish traditions and culture, they also have shown appreciation of American society and values.

### Conclusion: Special Ethnic Features

The international labor movement in its various forms exercised a strong effect on Finnish Americans and their willingness to become Americanized. As was pointed out earlier, internationalism was one of the central themes in their minds from the beginning of the organized labor movement. It led them to join American radical organizations, and it made the Communist-minded Finnish Americans obey orders from the Communist International. Consequently, radical workers' organizations clearly pushed their members toward Americanization and assimilation. Behind this kind of behavior lay two ways of thinking: immigrant workers should be able to take advantage of the economic opportunities offered by America, and at the same time they should become eligible to go to the polls, which would be the way to influence and change the future course of American society. On the other hand, the human desires of individuals in many cases slowed down the Americanization process. For example, the inability to learn

English, contacts with and longing for the Old Country, or dislike of the American capitalist system often became the final obstacle to naturalization. It is difficult, however, to examine these factors in detail.

But how do the facts that have been presented in the discussion above actually fit in with the general theory of American ethnicity and immigrant culture? Traditionally, American history writing stressed the concept of the American melting pot, but since the 1960s cultural pluralism has gained more and more supporters. When we look at the history of Finnish American laborers and their organizations and culture, we cannot agree completely with assimilation or cultural pluralist theorists. This special group of immigrant workers pursued Americanization and assimilation notably because of their own will and ideology when preparing for the future socialistic America. But their positive attitude toward assimilation was also affected by coercive Americanization: U.S. immigration policy, the quest for loyalty, and the attitudes of the mass media and the education system. Additional pressure was exerted by employment policy, which dealt with the immigrant workers unfavorably.[39]

What has been discussed in the preceding pages gives more information on the Americanization of immigrant workers. However, it should be pointed out that the left labor Finnish Americans ultimately made only a part of a minor immigrant population group. Accordingly, the experiences of these Finns certainly differed from those of a major ethnic minority group such as, for example, Italian, Polish, or Jewish Americans, the mere numbers of whom made their societal and cultural life quite different. The radical Finns were unusually active participants in the political labor circles, even though they used to stress the importance of ethnic social activities in addition to political participation. The social gatherings and functions made it easy for them to get acquainted with and used to various political acts, protests, as well as ideologies; therefore the "hall socialism" was a helpful means of left politics.

The political aspects of Finnish immigrant community discussed above are complex. Certain features, however, are visible. First, because of the relatively small number of the Finns in North America, their impact has been in general terms very limited. Only a small number of individuals have gained public recognition or importance, and their impact has been limited to certain geographical areas, where Finns have concentrated. Finns have, of course, gradually become naturalized, and therefore eligible for various positions in society. The time it took for naturalization has been surprisingly long, but may be explained by cultural and linguistic factors as well as by a lack of information.

Second, we have to recognize the share of the Finns in the labor and left radical circles. Since these circles have not been part of the mainstream of the United States or Canada, Finnish participation has been a somewhat exceptional activity, and its roots and forms have been targets of much debate. At the same time, as other groups of Finnish American immigrants have dissociated themselves completely from the labor movement, the divisions between the various factions within the movement have been sharp and clear. On the other hand, the so-called bourgeois groups in the Finnish American immigrant community have by no means put on any united front but have been at least as disunited as the Finnish American workers ranks: the temperance movement broke up in its time into different groups, and the same thing happened to the churchgoing people. The Finnish American labor movement has been characterized by divisiveness brought about mainly by disputes of both an ideological and personal nature.

The political labor movement is an area where Finnish Americans have truly called attention to themselves. In this field of activity, they made an impact on society at large by agitating for improvements in the general condition of the working class, working for social reforms, and so on. Although the Finnish American labor movement has always been accused of isolationism, the very fact of its joining the international labor movement and American labor parties indicates that its objective has not been only social and cultural activity within the circle of its own membership. Compared with certain church groups, for example, the Finnish American labor movement has shown a marked tendency to cooperate with other American groups.

### NOTES

1. Reino Kero, "The Social Origin of the Left-Wing Radicals and 'Church Finns' among Finnish Immigrants in North America," *Publications of the Institute of General History, University of Turku, Finland* 7 (1975): 55–62.
2. For Kurikka's biographical information, see, for example, Kalevi Kalemaa, *Matti Kurikka: Legenda jo eläessään.*
3. See Arnold R. Alanen, "Early Labor Strife on Minnesota's Mining Frontier, 1882–1906," *Minnesota History* 52, no. 7 (1991): 246–63.
4. Viapori (officially called Suomenlinna; in Swedish, Sveaborg) rebellion erupted in the summer of 1906. It was an unsuccessful military rebellion in the large fortress in Helsinki. The mutineers attempted to bring the fortress under their control, but the rebellion was defeated four days later. The events were inspired by the revolutionary unrest in Russia.
5. See *Suomalaisten sosialistiosastojen ja työväenyhdistysten viidennen eli suomalaisen sosialistijärjestön kolmannen edustajakokouksen Pöytäkirja 1–5, 7–10 p. kesäkuuta, 1912,* ed. Aku Rissanen (Fitchburg, Mass.: S. S. Järjestön toimeenpaneva komitea, n.d.), 29–53 (hereafter cited as *FSF Proceedings 1912*)
6. *FSF Proceedings 1912,* 55.
7. "Report of the Finnish Translator-Secretary to the Socialist Party National Convention 1912," in *National Convention of the Socialist Party Held at Indianapolis, Ind. May 12th to 18th, 1912,* ed. John Spargo (Chicago: n.p., n.d.), 237–39.
8. *FSF Proceedings 1912,* 54.
9. Cf. Carl Ross and K. Marianne Wargelin, eds., *Women Who Dared: The History of Finnish American Women* (St. Paul: University of Minnesota Immigration History Research Center, 1986); Gary Kaunonen, *Challenge Accepted: A Finnish Immigrant Response to Industrial America in Michigan's Copper Country* (East Lansing: Michigan State University Press, 2010), 37–44. In *FSF Proceedings 1912,* there is a lengthy statement signed by Elina Aaltio, representing the voices of the Work People's College female students. It discusses the need to organize female workers especially in the trades of servants and maids, who are severely underpaid and have harsh work conditions. *FSF Proceedings 1912,* 54, 78–82.
10. For curriculum and teaching, see Keijo Virtanen's chapter in this volume; cf. Auvo Kostiainen, "Work People's College: An American Immigrant Institution," *Scandinavian Journal of History* 5, nos. 1–4 (1980): 295–99.
11. See, for example, Kaunonen, *Challenge Accepted,* 150–68.
12. There is reference to biblical terms: Judas betrayed Jesus, and in this case it was claimed that a number of Finns betrayed Finnish Americans.
13. Matti Huhta (1880–1940) was born in Finland and became a well-known singer, poet, and songwriter for the IWW. See Franklin Rosemont, ed., *Juice Is Stranger than Friction: Selected Writings of T-Bone Slim* (Chicago: Charles H. Kerr, 1992).
14. The school building was sold in 1953, and the last board meeting was held in 1962. They also had a long-lasting periodical *Tie Vapauteen* (Road to Freedom), as well as special Christmas issues under the name *Industrialistin Joulu* (The Industrialist's Christmas). The Work People's College had a periodical of the student body, *Ahjo* (Forge).

15. Cf. Elis Sulkanen, *Amerikan suomalaisen työväenliikkeen historia* (Fitchburg, Mass.: Amerikan suomalainen kansanvallan liitto, 1951), esp. 253–54.
16. The IHRC in Minneapolis holds Wiita's personal papers.
17. Tuomas Savonen is presently working on a biographical study of Gus Hall.
18. The Congress of Industrial Organizations (CIO) was a federation of unions that organized workers in industrial unions in the United States and Canada from 1935 to 1955. Because of the suspicions over Communism, it fell into trouble with the government representatives. The CIO merged with the American Federation of Labor to form the AFL-CIO in 1955.
19. Alanen, "Early Labor Strife," 262.
20. Reino Kero, *Suomalaisina Pohjois-Amerikassa: Siirtolaiselämää Yhdysvalloissa ja Kanadassa* (Turku: Siirtolaisuusinstituutti, 1997), 68–69.
21. See Auvo Kostiainen, "Suomalaiset siirtolaiset ja politiikka," in Auvo Kostiainen and Arja Pilli, *Suomen siirtolaisuuden historia. Osa 2. Aatteellinen toiminta* (Turku: Turun yliopiston historian laitos, 1983), 90–91, 103.
22. Kostiainen, "Suomalaiset siirtolaiset," 91.
23. Kostiainen, "Suomalaiset siirtolaiset," 123–25.
24. For example, Melvin G. Holli, *The Wizard of Washington: Emil Hurja, Franklin Roosevelt, and the Birth of Public Opinion Polling* (New York: Palgrave Macmillan, 2002), 81–118.
25. See the information section in *Kalenteri Amerikassa asuville suomalaisille vuodelle 1910*.
26. See the chapter in this volume by Peter Kivisto and Johanna Leinonen.
27. Cf. A. William Hoglund, *Finnish Immigrants in America 1880–1920* (Madison: University of Wisconsin Press, 1960), 112–14.
28. See, for example, Douglas J. Ollila, Jr., "Defects in the Melting Pot. Finnish Immigrants and the Loyalty Issue, 1917–1921," *Turun Historiallinen Arkisto* 31 (1976), 398–99.
29. *Reports of the Immigration Commission*, Abstracts of Reports of the Immigration Commission 1970 (New York: Arno, 1970), 485–87.
30. John Wargelin, *Americanization of the Finns* (Hancock, Mich.: The Finnish Lutheran Book Concern, 1924), 171.
31. *Kolmannen Amerikan Suomalaisen Sosialistijärjestön Edustajakokouksen Pöytäkirja. Kokous pidetty Hancockissa, Mich. 23–30 pvä elok. 1909*, ed. F. J. Syrjälä (Fitchburg, Mass.: n.p., n.d.), 247.
32. *FSF Proceedings 1912*, 12; cf. Auvo Kostiainen, *The Forging of Finnish American Communism. A Study in Ethnic Radicalism, 1917–1924* (Turku: University of Turku, 1978), 147.
33. Hoglund, *Finnish Immigrants*, 113–14.
34. Auvo Kostiainen, "For or against Americanization? The Case of the Immigrant Finns," in *American Labor and Immigration History, 1877–1920s: Recent European Research*, ed. Dirk Hoerder (Urbana: https://volter.linneanet.fi/cgi-bin/Pwebrecon.cgi?v1=1&ti=1,1&Search%5FArg=hoerder&Search%5FCode=NAME%5F&CNT=50&PID=zNAuhIBj6HpLeYcZZIFlEiq8kpz4&SEQ=20100315142607&SID=1University of Illinois Press, 1983), 259–75. There were 58 persons or 11.2 percent of respondents who did not answer to this kind of question at all.
35. Cf. Ollila, "Defects," 411; Sulkanen, *Amerikan suomalaisen*, 254.
36. Arnold Alanen, "The Development and Distribution of Finnish Consumers' Cooperatives in Michigan, Minnesota and Wisconsin, 1903–1973," in *The Finnish Experience in the Western Great Lakes Region. New Perspectives*, ed. Michael G. Karni et al. (Turku: Institute of Migration, 1975), 103–30.
37. See Yrjö Raivio, *Kanadan suomalaisten historia* (Copper Cliff and Sudbury, Ont.: Canadan suomalainen historiaseura, 1979) 1–2.
38. Auvo Kostiainen, "Amerikkalainen Kalevan ritarikunta," in Kostiainen and Pilli, *Suomen siirtolaisuuden historia*, 164–80.

39. Recent decades show new trends in historical study, with emphasis on, for example, legal issues and reconsideration of the meaning and importance of the race question. See, for example, Diane C. Vecchio, "Immigrant and Ethnic History in the United States Survey," *History Teacher* 37, no. 4 (2004): 494–500; David R. Roediger, *How Race Survived U.S. History: From Settlement and Slavery to the Obama Phenomenon* (New York: Verso, 2008).

# "Sooner or Later You're a Cooperator": The Finnish American Cooperative Movement

*Hannu Heinilä*

The formation of the cooperative stores is a landmark of the Finnish immigrant history, with national importance. They were strongest and most active in the Midwest, although Finnish communities both on the East and West Coasts were also known for their cooperatives. The Finnish American masterpiece was the Central Cooperative Wholesale (CCW) and its educational department. By training cooperative activists, store managers, and bookkeepers, among others, it gave an excellent example to all cooperative communities in America. A political schism ended in the creation of two rival central organizations, one strongly leftist and the other a liberal-type central cooperative.

The cooperative movement has been one of the most visible forms of cooperation among the Finnish immigrants in the United States. Membership in a co-op meant safety for the tens of thousands of immigrants arriving in the new country, the same way as religious activity and the workers' movement did. For many, the membership was part of everyday life, but it may have had much more significance than the daily visit to the store that was possibly the only one in the region. The movement was strongest in the northern parts of the Midwest, although immigrants were familiar with cooperatives everywhere they formed ethnic communities. The largest were the dozens of Finnish communities formed around mining, forestry, and farming in the northern parts of Minnesota, Wisconsin, and Michigan.[1]

When studying the phases of cooperatives in the history of the United States, one cannot avoid stating the fact that no other group of immigrants had more influence on the development of the American cooperatives than the Finns. Many immigrant Finns had some experience with cooperative stores from the Old Country, where they had rooted after the British model. The first cooperatives were founded in Finland primarily during the 1890s, but the actual rise of the cooperatives took place during the first and second decades of the twentieth century. In 1919, there were already more than 500 cooperative stores in Finland, serving both countryside and urban dwellers, such as the working class. Nonetheless, Finns did not bring the cooperatives to the United States, nor did they necessarily have a strong influence on the structure of local economies with their business. In some places, however, the influence could be strong. Finns, especially, managed to form a large network of cooperatives; the best known of them emerged in the northern parts of Michigan, Minnesota, and Wisconsin.[2]

Finns worked hard to establish consumers' cooperatives and have left their mark in their way of operating. This is the opinion of many active co-op members; the same opinions are confirmed by researchers. Basically, producers' cooperatives have been and are established occupational groups so as to marshal their productive forces within a more efficient and profitable framework. Since the membership consists only of individuals belonging to that particular group, the major concerns of the organization generally are limited to those involving the group itself. Consumers's cooperation, on the other hand, is a wider-ranging concept that goes beyond such limited objectives by recognizing that everyone is a consumer and, theoretically at least, a potential cooperator.

To keep people active in the cooperatives and to increase their number, various types of activities were needed, ranging from those for small children to adults, and this created whole co-op families. All these activities organized with the leadership or assistance of the CCW can be referred to as cooperative education or extension. For a long time, there was also a link with the political side of the issue. For many years, Finns sought to expand even beyond these dimensions by making cooperation an instrument of the working-class struggle. Even though most Finnish cooperatives were intended to alleviate very real problems in retail distribution activity at the local level, the movement eventually was engulfed by forces and events occurring within the national and international arenas of political and economic activity. This concern with the broader issues of the socioeconomic spectrum undoubtedly contributed to the visibility of the Finnish cooperative movement, but it also led to severe divisions within the ranks of the cooperators themselves. These divisions, in turn, contributed to some of the most deep-rooted internal strife the Finnish American community had ever experienced.[3]

## The Early Stages of Finnish American Cooperative Activities

The year 1903 is generally considered as the beginning of Finnish consumers' cooperatives in North America, even though several cooperative ventures had already been started earlier in different parts of the new homeland. In this context, it was too early to talk about entrepreneurship, but that type of activity had started in Calumet, Michigan, around 1878 in the form of a mutual fire insurance cooperative. Soon similar activities were initiated in other "Finn centers" as well, such as in Monessen, Pennsylvania; Ashtabula, Ohio; and Hancock, Michigan. In these places, the initial cooperation of Finns, in addition to fire insurance activity, gave birth to mutual benefit and insurance cooperatives to help out distressed co-op members, whether it was sickness, accident, or death that had caused financial difficulties. Started in 1890, the Imatra Society in New York's Brooklyn sought from the very beginning not only mental but also financial security for its members. The oldest Finnish co-op dairy is probably that in New York Mills, Minnesota, established in 1901.[4]

Furthermore, if not quite traditional, boardinghouses can, however, be considered as some kind of early form of cooperation. Boardinghouses accommodated young men who had just arrived in the country by providing them with accommodations and food in exchange for money. As a similar attempt in the cooperative direction, there is also the utopia experiment of Matti Kurikka in Malcolm Island, British Columbia, in Canada to be considered.

The growth of Finnish American cooperation into a movement concerning fairly large groups of people and gradually into a genuine business took place from the first decade of the twentieth century onward. The causes for the birth of the consumers' cooperatives—as one might guess—were clearly due to circumstances. By operating together, it was easier to adapt to the financial insecurity that was a constant presence among the unskilled immigrants who had just arrived in the country. At any place that had a lot of Finnish immigrants—as in Astoria, Oregon; Waukegan, Illinois; Ashtabula, Ohio; and many other "Finn" places—the first-generation immigrants began to set up consumers' cooperatives. They usually did not have any, or even at best very little, experience in or practical knowledge about entrepreneurship.

When in 1903 thirteen rural families put their savings together in Menahga, Minnesota, and raised a mere $170 to start up a co-op store (The Cooperative Sampo of Menahga), nobody, of course, could predict that at that moment a foundation was laid down for a business that seventy years later reached a revenue of almost $2 million. After this, in the years 1904–7, stores—or, better to say, shopping sites—were set up in Brantwood and Clifford, Wisconsin, and also in Biwabik, Minnesota, and Republic, Michigan. By 1913, more than ten co-op stores or shopping sites had been started by Finnish immigrants in three midwestern states.[5]

In 1906, "roads were still bad and communication poor," began a history of the Farmer's Industrial Association of Clifford, Wisconsin, "so it was impossible for farmers to trade at farther points." The isolation of the farmers made them dependent on the "excessive prices" of the local storekeeper. In Clifford, sixteen Finnish farmers chipped in $10 each to create an economic alternative. Similar conditions led to the founding of the Brantwood Supply Company in New York. The Finnish homesteaders around Brantwood survived chiefly by cutting and selling the timber on their land. Local merchants had set up a deal whereby they agreed to market the homesteaders' lumber while at the same time sell the farmers necessary supplies on credit. Accounts were to be settled once a year.

To their surprise, the Finns around Brentwood often discovered during the annual accounting that their timber had been sold at a less than previously agreed upon price and that somehow it always turned out that they owed money to their local middleman. They decided the only solution was to establish their own cooperative. So began the Finnish cooperative movement. A strike by copper miners in Michigan in 1913–14 and another strike on the Mesabi in 1917 led to the formation of still more co-ops. In all, by 1917 sixty-five co-ops had sprung up in the three-state region of northern Minnesota, Wisconsin, and Michigan.[6]

Many rural cooperatives had been born because of the strong need to get products at a more reasonable price since the local storekeeper was able to freely dictate the prices. Finns realized that the lowering of prices could be achieved through a store of their own. On the labor movement side, the advocates of cooperation appealed to the workers by explaining that a cooperative is a very practical solution to some of the central issues over which the workers had to fight against the capitalists. It is clear that the founding of the Finnish Socialist Federation in Hibbing, Minnesota, in 1906 had its effects on the cooperative activity by dividing it in two directions. However, it is quite obvious that many rural cooperative stores were born because of the simple need to have a village store where it was possible to do one's daily shopping. Thus the political goals were not crucial, but normal everyday needs were.

The position of the labor magazines was quite crucial during the first decade of the Finnish American cooperative activity. With their assistance, the cooperative ideology could be spread effectively. When large strikes were experienced in the Finn regions at the start of the twentieth century, an idea of a workers' own co-op store easily gained popularity. With many workers, the situation could get to a point where a private storekeeper would not do business with a broke customer who was on strike, at least not solely on credit for too long. Immediately as a consequence of the large mining strikes of 1907, new cooperatives were born in the Virginia area of Minnesota as well as a little later in the Mesabi area. The cooperatives in these areas functioned as catalysts of a sort for the birth of many other cooperatives, especially in the Finn areas of Minnesota. This occurred during the middle of the 1910s in the cities as well as in the countryside. All in all, more than ten new cooperatives were born in these areas within a few years. The struggles between the workers and the employers in Michigan's mining areas, and the Copper Country strike in particular, also resulted in the birth of many new cooperatives by the end of 1917.[7]

While in the beginning of the 1910s there was still relatively little cooperative activity, already before the middle of the decade new cooperatives abounded. The development in Wisconsin, where there hardly were similar industrial actions, was clearly slower in pace. In 1913, only Brantwood and Clifford had a labor co-op store; by 1917, there were already six more stores. According to calculations made by Arnold Alanen, about sixty-five Finn-led cooperatives were born in the areas of these three states between 1903 and 1917.[8] From these trends, one can clearly detect the connection between labor's political activity and the birth of the cooperatives.

As noted, cooperative activity was found in Finn centers around the continent. The Finnish immigrants on the west coast of Oregon set up cooperatives, for example, in Berkley and Rocklin. Elsewhere significant cooperative enterprises were found in Ashtabula Harbor, Ohio, which had the Finnish Co-op Grocery Company, with a membership of several hundreds, and Sampo Co-op. Association in Monessen, Pennsylvania. However, in addition to the northern Midwest states, the large Finn centers of the East Coast were the best breeding ground for the cooperative activity.[9]

The majority of the co-op stores and other co-op-based enterprises on the East Coast were founded in the Finn regions of Massachusetts. The Workers' Co-operative Company in Gardner, which was the largest single cooperative, consisted of almost 500 members already in its early years. By the mid-1910s, a workers' credit institution and savings bank, Workers Credit Union, had been founded as a new significant form of business, the first by Finns in the United States. The decision for the foundation of the bank had been made in the 1914 representative meeting of the eastern district of the Finnish Socialist Federation, and in May 1914 it began its operations as a mutual savings deposit and credit cooperative. Even though numerous new co-ops had been born, they were nonetheless too small to properly function on their own. Therefore already early on it was understood that better operative prospects could be achieved through joining together Finnish forces. The first meeting concerning the merging of the Finnish cooperatives of Massachusetts was held in 1911, and the following year United Co-operative Company was founded.[10]

Cooperation is not just business, and the Finnish cooperative activities on the East Coast also saw cooperative education as a necessity. To carry out this job, a cooperative union of the Finns on the East Coast was founded. In addition to education and advisory work, a matter of merging together different co-ops soon became a part of the union's activities. Even though it was the task of the union to supervise and coordinate the practical side of things of the different cooperatives, such as carrying out joint acquisitions, its real purpose all along was educative work. The union hired visiting speakers and lecturers, and published and distributed cooperative literature and other literary material. The activities were thus quite similar to that of the Central Cooperative's education department in the Midwest. There was, however, rather little collaboration between the midwestern and eastern co-op activists.

The United Co-operative Society was eventually founded in the summer of 1919 in Boston. In the founding meeting, there were co-op representatives from Fitchburg, Maynard, Gardner, Worcester, Norwood, Peabody, and Quincy. A known socialist and cooperative opinion-maker, Vilho Boman was elected head of the society. Even though joining co-ops together was not a small and simple matter, in November 1919 the business got started. Soon fourteen shopping sites and four milk stores were part of the cooperative, as well as four cafeterias and two bakeries. At the same time, the membership rose to about 2,500 persons. As stated earlier, the largest of the single cooperatives was the Workers' Co-operative Company in Gardner. In the early stage of the cooperative, the enthusiasm had been so high that the important registration had been completely forgotten. It was not until one and a half years after the cooperative had started that it was legalized. This happened on July 25, 1908. In the beginning, the store was situated in the back side of a building, in the basement, but soon it became possible to move to the most handsome building in the village, the Rome building. Soon they got new premises at the Workers Building, a Finnish labor society hall built on Ash Street, where the business continued for years. In 1918, the cooperative opened a branch store at 229 Pine Street, and it seemed to be doing well. Furthermore, in September of the same year a deal was made to create a co-op cafeteria in a labor hall, which also ran successfully. It seemed that the difficulties that had been experienced ten years earlier were long gone, and the growth of cooperation still seemed to be getting stronger. Most of the early difficulties can be put down to incompetence and inexperience. Occasionally there might have also been dishonesty involved. The most problematic aspect, however, in almost all cooperatives was selling on credit.[11]

A history of the Turva Co-operative Store Company gives a good example of the early difficulties of the co-op stores. The store was founded as early as 1905 in Quincy, Massachusetts. In the beginning, the store depended on the enthusiasm of a few people who had arrived from Finland and had been involved in cooperative activity. It was not driven by the labor movement at first, but rather it was born out of a bourgeois and a Finnish national sentiment. From the beginning, the Turva Co-operative Store operated on an idealistic basis, as often occurred in these ventures, which meant a "nonexistently" small capital of about $300. This was not enough to purchase even decent equipment. Goods were taken for sale on credit, and efforts to pay for them were made as best as one could. At the same time, a considerable amount of goods were sold on credit to the customers, and therefore the sales debt added up to several thousand dollars within the first few years. The store's management and the board were put in a very awkward situation. Before long many co-op people who had been genuinely involved started to doubt the chances of success after sacrificing their mental as well as financial resources for the store. At the same time, it gave a boost to those who opposed the whole idea of cooperation.[12] Gradually over the next years the boards put the co-op's matters in order. This became possible only after they started educating the long-term employees to become storekeepers.

All in all, the individual cooperatives had fought for their existence almost from the beginning. Merging together to create a bigger whole brought to some extent more credibility and a wider financial base, but it did not solve the problems per se. Telling examples are the Finnish cooperatives in Worcester, Massachusetts. The Finnish workers started a cafeteria co-op in 1917, in addition to the grocery store and a milk store that had been set up earlier. A little later, they started one more grocery store, a second milk store, and a bakery. The last two were functioning stores bought from private entrepreneurs. The grocery store and the bakery had the most difficulties in the early years. After joining the United Co-op

Society, from 1919 onward the initial losses were thousands of dollars per year. Even though the cafeteria and the milk store were profitable from the start, the store management had to consider the reasons for the losses. The managing of the store was found to be the biggest reason. In other words, often one did not know how to act according to business economy principles. Goods might end up lying in stock when they should have been sold on time. The business supervision was also not up to standards, which might lead to incompetence or, in some cases, dishonesty. Since the revenue was also relatively small, even the minor neglects that seemed insignificant ate up profits.[13]

In big cities such as Worcester, managing the small branches was difficult because of distances. Compared to now, it was considerably harder to move about and to move goods. Therefore one was not able in practice to utilize the advantage of being a large consortium, in this case the United Co-op Society. Also the nature of a big city had the effect that a loyal membership base could not be created to the extent that would have been necessary. Stores, especially the grocery store and the bakery, had to cope as strictly businesses, which required that they aspire to satisfy the needs of all customers and not only the co-op members. It was estimated that in the beginning of the 1920s, at least half of the Worcester stores' customers were non-Finnish.[14]

The reality was also that even not all Finnish workers cared about their "own" cooperative. The political struggles cast a shadow over the cooperative activity as they did with almost all cooperation among the Finnish immigrants.

One of the best examples in terms of real co-op stores has been the Settlers Cooperative in Bruce Crossing, Michigan. The first store was opened for business in May 1917 with the help of the Hancock Co-op Store and its general manager, John Nummivuori. On March 1919, the independent co-op store was incorporated under the name Settlers Cooperative Trading Company, and from that point on the co-op progressed slowly. For example, in 1921 consumer goods prices fell drastically from their World War I inflated values. At the same time, consumer purchasing power decreased just as sharply. Wholesale houses that had sold the co-op goods on credit now demanded immediate payment through their central organization. That time period was perhaps the most difficult in the Settlers history. It barely avoided total bankruptcy by the hard work of its board of directors and active co-op members. Many cooperatives faced the same overwhelming problems and were forced to end business.[15]

From 1922 to 1930, the store operations were very successful, with sales increasing each year. The substantial amount of net savings was distributed to the patrons according to their purchases. Thus one of the cooperatives' original ideas had come true. The early 1930s, however, were very difficult. The Great Depression was not the only reason for the difficulties. At the same time the aforementioned disagreement and split aggravated conditions. Nonetheless, from 1933 the sales again showed increases year after year, originally because of governmental action in improving the economic situation. There have been years showing a decrease in the sales, but overall sales have increased steadily, reaching the $1 million milestone in 1969.[16]

Bruce Crossing has not been the only location for Settlers co-op activities. There have been stores in Paynesville, Trout Creek, Mass City, and Ewen. Since the early 1950s, the membership grew to over 1,000, and that large membership gave possibilities to be involved with nearby cooperatives other than Settlers itself. For example, Ontonagon Valley Cooperative Creamery Association, Cooperative Oil Association, and Rural Electric Cooperative were partly organized and operated by Settlers members.[17]

## Heart of the Movement: The Central Cooperative Exchange

The idea of forming a central cooperative for local cooperatives was discussed for some years mostly through a magazine called *Pelto ja Koti* (Farm and Home). In August 1917, the magazine published an invitation to a meeting where a central cooperative was to be created. One example of how people were attracted to join the cooperative is: "Let's collect our shopping in the same bag, let's make a *jappari*[18] of our store together, through which we will buy on behalf of all the stores the goods, that each store needs to buy." On the last day of August 1917, the Finnish cooperative men who had come to the first meeting decided, unanimously, to form a central cooperative and a bakery called the Central Cooperative Exchange (CCE). In Finnish, it was named Keskusosuuskunta. The town of Superior, Wisconsin, became the central place for the CCE.[19] The name remained unchanged until 1931, when it was renamed the Central Cooperative Wholesale (CCW).

The connection between the cooperative and the labor movements was very evident; the rules were written so clearly that there was no misunderstanding about the interrelation of the two movements. Most of the fundamental work for the cooperation between cooperatives and the socialists was done by the magazine *Työmies*, which supported cooperative ideas from its start in 1903. The task of the CCE and its educational department was to spread the idea of the consumers' cooperative movement among

FIGURE 1. The Central Cooperative Exchange (CCE) (or Central Cooperative Wholesale [CCW]) and other cooperatives showed how communist ideological symbols were used in advertising, which was typical of the American capitalist economy, and mingled with class-oriented cooperatives in the 1920s and 1930s. The Red Star, as well as the hammer and sickle were used as trading brands for coffee, vegetables, corn flakes, engine oil, and other products. Also, other brands were developed, such as White Star, Blue Star, and Yellow Star. (Source: The Co-operative Pyramid Builder, May 1931. Journal collections, DGH)

**FIGURE 2.** Central Cooperative Wholesale's Red Star "flour girls" in 1926. The women wear flour sacks with the words "Coperator's Best Flour" printed on the front. The flour was produced by the Central Cooperative Wholesale mill. (Source: CCW Records, photo collections, IHRC)

all Finns. Noteworthy is that the leaders of the CCE represented the left wing of the American Socialist Party, which ultimately turned into the Communist Workers Party of America. Among the left-wing leaders of the Finnish Socialist Federation were George Halonen, Severi Alanne, and Elis Sulkanen, who were also leaders of the CCE. Even other central figures in the CCE became members of the Communist Party, such as Eskel Rönn, Matti Tenhunen, and Oscar Corgan. The leadership of the CCE entered into heavy political struggle, which lasted throughout the 1920s.[20]

The Communist Party tried desperately to get a stronger hold of the CCE and, by doing this, of the whole Finnish American cooperative movement. In fact, the party wanted the whole movement under strict control, which caused an extremely tough struggle. The toughest struggles took place in 1930 when the annual meeting of the CCE brought the final solution. The political fight ended with a victory for the moderates, which made it possible to transform the CCE from a political actor into a cooperative educational body with business operations. The CCW would suffer for a long time from the label of being a Communist—or at least leftist—society, although orientation toward the traditionally neutral cooperative movement was the target.

The task of the CCW's educational department was very central in the promotion of the cooperative movement. It organized educational activities, published cooperative magazines, and sponsored and printed cooperative literature, cooperative material for education, and many types of leaflets and pamphlets throughout the decades. V. S. Alanne, Yrjö (George) Halonen, Eskel Rönn, and others served as leaders of the educational department. Alanne and Halonen were also productive writers. Their main inspiration was the traditional idea of the cooperative movement, and they were much less interested in the political—especially the radical issues early in the 1920s. H. V. Nurmi introduced his simple but efficient bookkeeping system to cooperative societies, which, until then, often had existed on nothing more than faith alone. Educational efforts were increased and credit sales discouraged. Also, as more of the older societies began to join the CCE, other cooperatives were started on new soil. In many cases, the CCE recommended developing branch outlets. It was argued that such an approach reduced the possibility of duplicating serious errors, increased the total purchasing power of societies, and centralized management and bookkeeping operations.[21]

There was a strong will to get rid of the "Red" label, changing the old hammer-and-sickle sign that was used on the co-op goods to the neutral cooperative label. After this the main attention was drawn to the Rochdalean consumer's cooperative ideas developed in England. It must be acknowledged that the activities continued to have some characteristics of the labor movement for years—for example, the name of the paper continued to be *Työväen Osuustoimintalehti* (Workers' Co-operative News)—but political neutrality was soon adopted as the main theme of the operations. At the same time, the American cooperatives accepted the Finnish American cooperative movement, and it even served as a good example to follow. Also, the Cooperative League of the United States of America (CLUSA) started to allow Finnish-born cooperative activists on their staff. The Americanization process of the cooperatives was no longer slowed down by political factors.[22]

Whereas the local cooperatives were, early on, almost completely Finnish, people of non-Finnish origin began to come along from the 1920s onward. This was the result of the fact that the cooperative movement was spreading more widely, for the movement was better known than earlier. In many places where the cooperatives started to function well, people of "other languages" came to be their customers.

### The Americanization Becomes Stronger

Guild activity was without a doubt one of the most important factors to guide and speed up the process of Americanization. In some places, the women's guild may have been the last fortress of Finnish identity, but generally speaking—especially among the young—the guild activities were organized in English from the very beginning.

The dominant position of the Finnish language became less strong, but not so suddenly and quickly. A major factor in this is the fact that from the very first annual meeting onward, the language of the guild meetings was English. The same future orientation was evident in magazines, and articles for children and youth in the cooperative magazines were written in English and took gradually more space than did the pages in Finnish. In 1930, for the first time, the CCW employed as a sign of the new times a fieldworker who did not understand any Finnish.[23] A few years later, connections to the non-Finnish-speaking cooperatives had become more and more common. In addition, strong signs of

**FIGURE 3.** A photo from ca. 1927 inside the modern-looking Cloquet, Minnesota, cooperative store. Manager Peter Kokkonen is fourth from the left. (Source: Photo copy owned by Hannu Heinilä)

Americanization were the connections established with the surrounding schools in the mid-1930s, and cooperatives had become well acknowledged even by the federal government. The CCW had its own important role; also important was the investment in cooperative education in the midwestern schools.

There is no doubt that the cooperative work of Finnish Americans has partly contributed to the fact that today the universities of Wisconsin and Minnesota have an strong position in the research and development of the cooperatives. The CCW had started the cooperation with these universities in the 1930s. While cooperation in the beginning meant mostly helping the universities with some lectures, the development reversed from the late 1940s onward. Now the CCW needed professional assistance in its growing difficulties with business management and marketing. During the following decennium, the development of the CCW business management was based on cooperation with these universities to a great extent.[24]

### From Accounting to Languages

Educational activities started by the CCE have been pioneering projects even when we think about the United States as a whole, for there had been no such activities among the cooperatives before this. While this first developed in the 1920s, the cooperative courses had become quite established already during Alanne's leadership. Course development was occasionally discussed, although political passions were so strong that other matters tended to be neglected. The recurring question was how long the cooperative courses should take. Although the courses were extended to be eight weeks long, it appeared difficult to put this into practice. At some stage even the thought of setting up a special cooperative school together with the Northern States Cooperative League came up.[25]

In the mid-1930s, when the CCW activities became stronger after the most difficult political and economic years had passed, the Educational Department had again a central role in many ways in developing the Finnish American cooperative activities. The number of applications rose to its maximum in the years 1936 to 1938. In 1938, there were no fewer than ninety-five applications. As to the number of participants, the course was not the largest one, for the educational department had to limit the number of participants to thirty-five mostly because of the lack of lodging space. The number of participants in autumn 1919 was, for these practical reasons, not exceeded at this time or later.[26]

Taking into consideration how short the courses were, the number of subjects and the hours spent on them did not vary much in the years that passed. When comparing the course programs of the end of the 1920s, mostly, to those of the end of the 1930s, the similarity of the courses can be seen. The central role of accounting became stronger year after year, whereas the number of subjects taught increased only by one when, in the mid-1930s, a ninth subject called "Economics and Society" was added. The course contents remained rather unchanged after this until the end of the 1930s. Through the 1920s, the course template included also courses with a strong political message, even though major parts of the courses were oriented toward purely practical cooperative skills, such as courses titled Administration of the Cooperatives, Cooperative Store Management, Business Mathematics, and Accounting. However, the course History of the Labor Movement then was one of the basics for every participant.[27]

### The CCW Is No Longer Needed

The late 1930s were the most prosperous years in CCW history with nearly 120 local member stores, approximately 40,000 members, and annual revenues of nearly 4 million dollars. Even if those numbers grew later on (in early 1960s the CCW had approximately 240 local member co-ops and annual revenues reached 20 million dollars), the best operational years were far behind. The developments after World War I and World War II and in the 1950s made it more difficult for the CCW to operate. There was no sudden change, however, but this was the result of a long process. The question why this happened is not difficult to answer: the operating environment and changes in it meant that there was no other choice, although efforts were taken more than once to maintain and even strengthen the position of the CCW in the changing circumstances. Making the position stronger was a completely unrealistic target, and they did not even manage to maintain the existing position of the CCW. The central issue in the changing circumstances was the generation shift taking place in the immigrant society. Second, the cooperatives were threatened by another factor; the society based on agriculture was changing rapidly. In many areas, the change had become striking after World War II.[28]

Issues of merging together had been discussed for a long time, but considering the multifold character of the issue—such as emotional reasons—the process needed a long time to mature. On some occasions, these types of thoughts emerged in the 1930s, but they came out more seriously in the mid-1940s. In fact, in 1944, at the annual meetings of the CCW, Midland Cooperative Wholesale, and Farmers' Union Central Exchange, all three societies discussed how they could work together as closely as possible. At the meetings, merging into one central cooperative was found to be a sensible target, for all three of them were operating in the midwestern area with similar aims and partly overlapping organizations. The idea was kept alive in the following years, although resolving such principal questions was not possible in the abnormal circumstances. In any case, the boards of these cooperatives and their staff and operational management held numerous meetings about this issue.[29]

In general, it was very well understood that overlapping operations would become more harmful with the extending business and especially if planning together was not practiced more successfully. On the other hand, working together started quite well in practice through joint business operations. This can be seen in businesses specializing in joint acquisition and financing.

The supermarket had started in the United States in the beginning of the 1930s on the East Coast, and the "help yourself idea" soon became a success. Large facilities were divided into departments full of goods, and the clients soon became used to choosing the products they wanted. The counters were at the other end of the lines, and this made the clients move on their own to the point of payment. This included, naturally, massive advertising in local papers and unheard-of low pricing. What was also new were longer shopping trips. Especially on the weekends, curious clients could drive up to fifty miles to wander around the new kind of shopping site and to do their shopping for less money. After first astonishment, the quickest private shopping store-chains were able to meet the new challenge. The CCW, too, should have been alerted when new ways of shopping began to spread in the Midwest.[30]

However, it was only in the second half of the 1950s that the first supermarkets opened their doors, and this was absolutely too late. At this stage the CCW business group could not even be saved by growing local cooperation or by setting up new shopping centers. In December 1962, the long-prepared proposal for joining together the CCW and the Midland Cooperative Wholesale was ready to be presented to the bodies of both societies. Although both groups were skeptical, the plans to merge into one organization were accepted. Finally, all the thirteen local meetings of the CCW accepted the merger, and in the morning of the second meeting day, on March 19, 1963, the annual meeting unanimously confirmed this decision.[31]

After the first years, in order to make the commercial side strong enough and in order to react more swiftly to changing circumstances, the CCW and its member societies should have directed their operations to the centers with growing populations. Functioning as a rather closed ethnic society had been the will of the members, however, and the central target of the operations had never been to create as big and successful a business as possible.

Ideas of successful business operations were brought up once in a while in the plans of some leading figures, but the CCW was primarily established to serve societies of Finnish origin in the large northern area of the Midwest. In this task it sometimes succeeded even very well, and for its functions in the educational and advisory roles, so important for the business, the CCW is remembered as a good model for many other American cooperative societies. Small village stores were transformed into a large economic and idealistic body, and some remains of its functioning can even today be found in the northern areas of Michigan, Minnesota, and Wisconsin.

## NOTES

1. Hannu Heinilä, *Osuustoiminta liikekasvatus USA:n keskilännessä 1917-1963* (Turku: Siirtolaisuusinstituutti, 2002), 11.
2. Arnold Alanen, "The Development and Distribution of Finnish Consumers' Cooperatives in Michigan, Minnesota and Wisconsin, 1903-1973," in *The Finnish Experience in the Western Great Lakes Region: New Perspectives*, ed. Michael G. Karni et al. (Turku: Institute for Migration, 1975), 103-4.
3. Heinilä, *Osuustoiminta liikekasvatus*, 47, 208.
4. Heinilä, *Osuustoiminta liikekasvatus*, 30.
5. Alanen, "Development," 110-11; Cy O'Neil, *Origins and Legacies: The History of a Cooperative Movement* (Minneapolis: Scoop Collective, 1977), 7.
6. O'Neil, *Origins and Legacies*, 7-8.
7. Alanen, "Development," 112; Elis Sulkanen, *Amerikan suomalaisen työväenliikkeen historia* (Fitchburg, Mass.: Amerikan suomalainen kansanvallan liitto, 1951), 284; O'Neil, *Origins and Legacies*, 7-9.
8. Alanen, "Development," 112.
9. Heinilä, *Osuustoiminta liikekasvatus*, 34.
10. *Miljoona-osuuskunta: United Co-operative Societyn Juhlajulkaisu* (Boston: United Co-operative Society, 1921), 3.
11. *Miljoona-osuuskunta*, 4, 11-12.
12. *Miljoona-osuuskunta*, 12.
13. *Miljoona-osuuskunta*, 15-16.
14. *Miljoona-osuuskunta*, 16.
15. *75 Years 1917-1992* (Bruce Crossing, Mich.: Settlers Cooperative, 1992), 2.
16. *75 Years*, 7, 17.
17. *75 Years*, 9-10.
18. The word "*jappari*" is a very rare expression. Probably it points to someone who is buying something, since there is the slang word in Finnish "*joppari*."
19. *Pelto ja Koti*, August 1, 1917; Sulkanen, *Amerikan suomalaisen työväenliikkeen;* O'Neil, *Origins and Legacies*, 7-11.
20. *Pelto ja Koti* 24 (1920): 1; Michael G. Karni, "Yhteishyvä—or For the Common Good: Finnish Radicalism in the Western Great Lakes Region, 1900-1940" (Ph.D. diss., University of Minnesota, 1978), 138; see also Timo Riippa, Inventory to the Records of Central Cooperative Wholesale at the IHRC, 1992, 3.
21. *Co-operative Pyramid Builder* 3 (January 1928): 2; Alanen, "Development," 115.
22. O'Neil, *Origins and Legacies*, 28-29; Heinilä, *Osuustoiminta liikekasvatus*, 47-49, 336.
23. Heinilä, *Osuustoiminta liikekasvatus*, 209.
24. *Pöytäkirja. Liikkeenhoitokomitean kokous, February 28, 1936; The Cooperative League Year Book 1936*, 41; Heinilä, *Osuustoiminta liikekasvatus*, 209.
25. *Pöytäkirja. Keskusosuuskunnan vuosikokous, March 21-22, 1920. Keskusosuuskunnan vuosikirja 1920*, 16-17; "Osuustoimintakurssit v. 1920," *Pelto ja Koti* 24 (1920): 1, 15-16.
26. *Pöytäkirja. Keskusosuuskunnan toimeenpaneva komitea, September 24, 1936;* see also V. S. Alanne, *A Story of Cooperative Training. Central Cooperative Wholesale* (Superior, Wis.: Central Cooperative Wholesale, 1951), 4.
27. *Pöytäkirja. Keskusosuuskunnan toimeenpaneva komitea December 15, 1925;* Alanne, *Story of Cooperative Training*, 4.
28. *Cooperative Builder*, January 5, 1961.
29. *Pöytäkirja. Keskusosuuskunnan johtokunta, April 21, 1947; Pöytäkirja. Keskusosuuskunnan vuosikokous, April 2-23, 1947; Pöytäkirja. Keskusosuuskunnan toimeenpaneva komitea, October 11, 1948*.
30. O'Neil, *Origins and Legacies*, 43-44.
31. *Pöytäkirja. Keskusosuuskunnan vuosikokous, March 18-19, 1963* (Superior, Wis.: CCW, 1963).

PART 5
# The Multitude of Cultural Life

# Finnish Identity in Immigrant Culture

*Keijo Virtanen*

The many-sided and rich cultural pursuits and interests such as arts, theater, music, schooling, and sports played a central role in the process of Finnish immigrant adaptation to the new society in the United States and Canada. A close look at the development of such pursuits, and at variations in the levels of activity, can help us to interpret the process whereby immigrants, and their descendants, became integrated and adapted to their new life circumstances. At the same time, it also casts light upon the persistence and preservation of Finnishness in this new context.

Some of the earliest cultural activities were initiated by the temperance societies, which from the 1880s onward had begun to build "halls" (Finnish American *haali*) as meeting places. These rapidly gave rise to enthusiastic collaboration, in diverse forms, aimed at raising the educational and cultural level of the members in general.[1] Almost from the very beginning the activities of the temperance societies included choral groups, sports and gymnastics clubs, musical bands, and amateur dramatic societies.[2]

The labor organizations practiced analogous cultural activities, from the beginning of the twentieth century, aimed at activating the membership. One example: in 1912, the Finnish Socialist Federation (Yhdysvaltain Suomalainen Sosialistijärjestö) had some 200 sections, which in turn included the following groups: 107 dramatic societies, 91 sewing circles, 53 gymnastics clubs, 23 choral societies, and 126 literary clubs.[3] Other organizations were similar: the cultural activities of the Knights and Ladies of Kaleva were designed specifically to preserve the Finnish national culture and to maintain its prestige.[4] In the case of Swedish-speaking Finnish immigrants, cultural activities were channeled in particular through the Runebergorden (Order of Runeberg); founded in 1920, it united the earlier temperance societies and mutual support groups under a single umbrella.[5] These examples illustrate that immigrant culture was closely connected with organizational activities. The Finnish American labor movement even developed its own annual calendar of festivals. For the Communists, for instance, the summers of the 1920s culminated in a summer festival, with a highly diversified program: among other offerings, it included speeches, musical performances (both choral and orchestral), sports, athletic and gymnastic events, *tableaux vivants,* dramatic performances, and dancing. Fall events included celebrations of the

Russian Revolution, along with Christmas. The spring season began immediately after Christmas, with New Year celebrations; more important, however, were events honoring Lenin's life and work and those commemorating the Finnish "class struggle," that is, the Civil War of 1918. The month of March saw International Women's Day; this was followed by May Day, the international labor movement's day of celebration, which in the case of Finnish immigrants was combined with "*vappu,*" the traditional Finnish spring holiday celebrated on the first of May. This was the culmination of the spring calendar. Along with these "fixed" events there were also numerous "moveable" ones, such as events celebrated by various individual sections; thus there was enough cultural activity to keep those responsible for organizing it busy for the whole year.[6]

The organizations tried to recruit as many members as possible to take part in these cultural activities. The level of participation in fact depended crucially on the success with which a given organization operated in its principal domain. Women often played a major role in organizing festivals and celebrations—for instance, in the labor movement. At its highest, the proportion of women among the membership in the Organization of Finnish Socialists was 40 percent; in the church congregations and temperance societies, too, a considerable proportion of members were women.[7] On the other hand, it has been suggested that despite their steadily growing numbers, the influence of women in the Organization of Finnish Socialists was actually declining. During the first decade of the twentieth century, women were regularly elected, for instance, to boards of directors, entertainment committees, and building committees. Gradually, however, they began to be relegated to miscellaneous tasks involved in the organizing of a festival, such as catering. Their participation in actual decision-making powers was thus distrusted. The most common form of women's activity in the local socialist sections was in fact the sewing society, whose chief responsibility was fund-raising—for example, for a library or even for the organization's own building.[8]

A particularly important role was played in the cultural pursuits of the Finnish American immigrant community, and in immigrants' leisure activities more generally, by amateur dramatic groups, music, and sports. In the following, I focus on the development of these three areas, along with a fourth, which will in fact be dealt with next: the cornerstone of all cultural activity, that is, education—in other words, the immigrant community's own independent schools and other educational activities.

Naturally other areas of cultural and artistic endeavor, in particular architecture and painting, have played their part in shaping the Finnish American immigrant identity, and in creating and maintaining connections between the immigrants and the home country. When Eliel Saarinen was awarded Second Prize in the architectural competition organized by the *Chicago Tribune* in 1922, this was undeniably significant for Finnish American self-respect—particularly since Saarinen then settled permanently in the United States. In the mid-1920s, the noted Finnish artist Akseli Gallen-Kallela was active for some time in the Chicago area and spread an awareness of Finnish art among Americans. The same was true of certain other Finnish artists, and there were also artists among the immigrant community itself whose names would be worth mentioning.[9] Here, however, our focus is on the cultural life of the Finnish American immigrant community from the point of view of the so-called ordinary immigrant—for instance, in terms of individual participation; thus I pay less attention to the artistic elite and its "great men," who here are relegated to the periphery.

As a whole, we still need a lot of new research on the cultural activities of the Finnish immigrants—such as Yvonne R. Lockwood's recent treatment on art tradition and ethnic continuity among the

Finns.[10] In my text, in addition to the research literature in hand, I use newspapers and periodicals as well as records of societies and other contemporary material.

## Education and Schools

In terms of levels of literacy, Finns were not a typical immigrant group. A majority had attended school in Finland. In 1871, there were 108 elementary schools in Finland; in 1891 the number was almost 900, and in 1901 about 1,900, for a total population of some 2.5 million. According to U.S. statistics, only 2 percent of Finnish immigrants over the age of fifteen who arrived in the country between July 1899 and June 1910 were illiterate; at the same time, the average level of illiteracy among newly arrived immigrants in general was 26 percent.[11]

Along with the official American school system, Finnish immigrants aspired from the earliest stages of immigration to maintain their own schools and educational activities. As early as 1873, an elementary school teacher from Kemi in Finland, David Castrén, arrived in the town of Calumet, Michigan, leading to the establishment of a Finnish-language elementary school. The town council, however, soon intervened in the matter, since the school was unable to teach English classes to the same extent as in the regular school system. The children had to transfer to the American school. After that, classes taught in Finnish were held on Saturdays and Sundays, and during the summer vacation.[12]

In the late 1880s, the temperance movement became for many years the central force in maintaining Finnish American cultural activities, including education. The goals of almost every temperance society included the achievement of its own reading room and library, according to Eija Lehtinen.[13] At almost the same time, from 1905 onward, temperance schools began to be established for children; these were usually held on Saturday afternoons to make sure they did not interfere with the Sunday school activities of the Finnish congregations. In the early enthusiasm of the movement, attempts were even made—at least in Minnesota and Michigan—to establish actual temperance societies for children, the so-called Bands of Hope. The children's slogan—"Tremble King Alcohol, we shall grow big"—nevertheless grew silent in a few years due to a lack of teachers and group counselors.[14]

Some temperance societies were bold enough to establish so-called weekly schools, which taught regular school subjects along with temperance principles. One such school was established as early as 1900 in the town of Republic, Michigan, by the members of the Onnen Aika (Time of Happiness) Temperance Society; its member hired a teacher, Lyyti Kasurinen, then a student at Suomi College.[15] Many other temperance societies also looked to the college in seeking teachers, but there were far too few students to fill all the need.

Thus schools for children established on a national basis and emerging from the temperance movement died off relatively quickly. Almost all such endeavors were plagued by a lack of teachers, and in fact the energy and enthusiasm with which such attempts had started did not last long. In addition, the Finnish Evangelical Lutheran Church of America (known as the Suomi Synod) saw them as competing with its own Sunday schools and systematically opposed all educational institutions maintained by the temperance societies.[16]

The tradition of Finnish American Sunday schools goes back as far as the establishment of congregations themselves. According to Salomon Ilmonen, a congregation and a Sunday school would start up together. Ilmonen places the first Finnish American Sunday school at Hancock, Michigan, in the winter of 1871. The work of the school was chiefly focused on teaching Finnish-language skills, along with religion, to the children of immigrants. According to the—admittedly not particularly reliable—figures collected by Ilmonen, in 1902 the Suomi Synod had eighty Sunday schools, with 360 teachers and 3,000 pupils. By 1920, there were 200 schools, with 1,567 teachers and more than 10,000 pupils. If figures were available for other denominations, Ilmonen estimated that these numbers would be doubled. In 1910, a separate body was established, the Finnish Evangelical Lutheran Sunday School Association, to coordinate the activities of the schools. The influence of the association extended within the Suomi Synod chiefly to Michigan, Minnesota, and the western states; by the mid-1920s, the participants were prepared to begin negotiations to disband it.[17]

From the perspective of maintaining and preserving the Finnish national culture and language among immigrants and their descendants, however, the Sunday schools played a highly significant role. They also helped to prepare the children of immigrants for entrance into the schools and colleges of the new country, at the same time breaking the ground for other educational institutions maintained by the immigrant community itself.

The most important of these was the Suomi-Opisto (Suomi College; now known as Finlandia University). After the establishment of the Suomi Synod in 1890, a resolution was passed at the very first meeting as to the need for a college (that is, an upper secondary school) of one's own, on the one hand to train clergy for the church, and, on the other, to provide general education for young people within the immigrant community. The ceremonial inauguration of Suomi-Opisto took place in Hancock on September 8, 1896. Its regulations stipulated that the college was intended primarily for Finnish students of both sexes. The college was divided into a three-year preparatory division, a four-year upper secondary school, and a theological seminary. The curriculum included diverse subjects ranging from religion and history to mathematics, the natural sciences, and the arts and humanities. From 1906 onward, there was increased emphasis on the teaching of English so as to bring the college more closely into line with American schools.[18]

The college aimed at preparing its students not only for the church but also for secular life, as demonstrated by the establishment in 1906 of a commercial division.[19] In 1923, a junior college was added, with a curriculum corresponding more or less to the first two years of a four-year college. Soon afterward came a music division. These various additions and expansions ensured that the college was able, even after the First World War, to maintain its prewar enrollment of over 100 students, the level it had had from 1907 onward; during the first year of the college, in 1896–97, there had been 25 students.[20]

Maintaining such a diverse curriculum necessitated considerable financial activity to ensure funding for the school. Suomi College competed for students with the Work People's College (Työväen Opisto), established by the Finnish Socialist Federation and intended for young people within the labor movement. Suomi College did not in fact appeal even to all religious or nonsocialist circles among the immigrant community; it was long seen as serving just one denomination, the Suomi Synod. From the 1920s onward, the question of language became increasingly topical; in the early years of the college, the students had mostly been born in Finland, but gradually the second generation, children born in the United States to immigrant parents, began to dominate—especially since immigration from Finland had come more or less to a standstill. Thus the college began, via its students, a natural process of integration into mainstream American society. Since in addition one of its aims was to prepare students for entrance into American schools and colleges, its ultimate Americanization was inevitable; this process nevertheless gave rise to considerable disputes and factions within college circles.

According to Ralph J. Jalkanen, up to the 1960s the college was nevertheless characteristically a Finnish school, if only because a majority of the students were of Finnish origin, even if the significance of Finnish culture and society in the curriculum was gradually declining.[21] The Suomi Synod ceased to exist as an independent denomination in 1962, at the same time bringing about the final step in the transformation of Suomi-Opisto into an American college. In 2000, it was renamed Finlandia University.

The long history of the college, reaching back as it does to the end of the nineteenth century, has nevertheless meant that the school has played a central role in Finnish American education. It ensured for immigrants and their descendants a good starting position in postprimary education, and in that sense has played a significant role in Finnish American cultural history.

In 1898, the Suomi Synod faced another central denomination within the immigrant community, the Finnish American Evangelical Lutheran National Church (Amerikan Suomalainen Evankelis-Lutherilainen Kansalliskirkko).[22] The existence of two different denominations, with parallel goals and operating within the same area, was a sign of some degree of disagreement. The National Church was seen as appealing more forcefully to ordinary people than the synod; it was more sociable—in fact, it was closer to the American Social Gospel movement.[23] From the very first years of the National Church there was talk of establishing a school of its own, on the model of Suomi College. The purpose would be similarly dual: to provide general education and training for young people from Finnish American families and to train clergy for the needs of the church. In distinction from Suomi College, there would be less emphasis on the classics and other "demanding" subjects and more on fulfilling the needs of the surrounding society.[24]

At the fifth annual meeting of the National Church, held in Ely, Minnesota, in 1903, a resolution was passed to initiate college classes that same fall. The connection with the church was defined as loose; this was to be highly significant for the future development of the school. It was to be "under the supervision and care of a board of directors, independent of any church; but the theological seminary was to be supervised by the Church."[25] Thus the Finnish People's College and Theological Seminary (Suomalainen Kansanopisto ja Teologinen Seminaari) was ready to open, at first in Minneapolis, with nine students; a year later the college moved to Smithville, a suburb of Duluth in Minnesota. In the spring semester of that year, there were already thirty-six students.[26]

The People's College, however, rapidly began to radicalize and was taken over by the Finnish American socialists. Why did this happen? There are various views and interpretations. Historians with a religious background consider that the socialists illegally took over a school that—in the view of these writers—belonged to the National Church.[27] This is also the view of Salomon Ilmonen, who agrees that the National Church was the true owner of the college. In 1905, according to him, the socialists saw an opportunity to gain control of the college; they bought shares (which, at a dollar a share, were very cheap), enabling them to vote in the meetings of the school's support organization. By 1905—that is, only two years after its founding—the socialists, according to Ilmonen, had taken control of the college.[28]

Writers with a left-wing background, on the other hand, view the shift as natural: the students demanded inclusion in the curriculum of subjects relevant to modern society, such as social studies and science, and teachers who would be competent to teach such subjects. According to Auvo Kostiainen,

**FIGURE 1.** The students of the Work People's College, Duluth, Minnesota, in 1926–27. (Source: IMT Photo collections. USA_2332)

the stockholding system underlying the financial organization of the school was a central factor explaining why the college was so quickly radicalized. On the other hand, the socialists may have been the only ones interested in the college and willing to acquire shares in it.[29]

In the summer of 1908, the records speak for the first time of the Työväen Opisto (Work People's College or Workers' College).[30] The curriculum had changed already the previous year, in 1907–8, showing a clear shift toward greater integration into society. One newly introduced subject was the theory of evolution, approached specifically from a materialistic perspective. The position of the social sciences, including economics, was strengthened. The most important subject, however, was English, which was seen as the key opening the way to the surrounding world. That year, only one student out of the total of seventy-one was considered to be a nonsocialist.[31] At this point, those members of the National Church who still owned shares in the college now sold them, having witnessed its complete takeover by the socialists. The new bylaws, enacted in 1908, stated the following:[32] "The name of the association is the Workers' College, and its purpose is to maintain and direct the institution. Education will be provided for working people's children and for women and men: in addition to elementary education, instruction will also be offered in business and technical subjects, social studies and economics, the natural sciences and other general sciences and arts, to prepare students for higher educational institutions and universities."

The Workers' College now belonged to the Finnish Socialist Federation. Its enrollment was at its highest in 1913–14, with 157 students. The proportion of women generally never exceeded 20 percent of the total number. Most of the students were young adults, between twenty and thirty years old, and a majority had a working-class background: they included lumber and construction workers, miners, and household servants and their children. One problem was that by no means all the students were able to spend the whole academic year on their studies; many of them had to work at intervals in between studying.[33]

The decade of the 1910s can be seen as the peak time of the college. The college produced numerous socialist leaders and journalists who later contributed to the Finnish labor movement in the United States and Canada. For some members of the immigrant community, it also served as an alternative to the church-oriented Suomi College. There was, however, one crisis still ahead: in 1914 the college became an open supporter of syndicalist ideas and the Industrial Workers of the World (IWW). It was now the turn of the Finnish Socialist Federation to step aside, as the National Church had done some ten years earlier. At the same time, this meant a split in the Finnish labor movement, between the socialists and the syndicalist IWW (popularly known as the Wobblies).[34]

This ideological shift did not entail any major changes in the curriculum. English language maintained its position as the most important subject. Teaching took place on three levels, due to the wide variation in the students' educational backgrounds. The most significant change, both concretely and intellectually, took place in the context of the First World War. During the war, any movement or ideology that tended to divide the society was in difficulty in the United States, and the same atmosphere persisted into the 1920s. Ethnic groups were targeted in this respect, with the end result that in the 1920s, national and ethnic quotas were introduced to restrict immigration. The Russian Revolution of 1917 brought a new split in the Finnish American labor movement, with the rise of the Finnish American Communists. This was a blow for both the IWW and the Workers' College. During the 1920s and 1930s, operating conditions were poor, and enrollment continued to decline, with only a few dozen students enrolled each year. In 1941, the Workers' College came to the end of its lifespan and closed down.[35]

Thus the Workers' College did not survive the crisis of the interwar period. In this respect, it was unlike Suomi College, which can be seen as its model. For both schools, this was a very difficult time, due to the almost complete end of new immigration and thus the loss of the schools' traditional student recruitment pool. Suomi College succeeded in merging more or less naturally with the mainstream American educational system and in moderating its traditional image as associated with the church (the Suomi Synod). The Workers' College would in principle have had the same possibility, but it was unable to do so; the main reason for this was probably the breakdown of the Finnish American labor movement during the 1920s into three competing subgroups—the socialists, the syndicalists, and the Communists.

Both schools were an expression of the immigrants' desire to obtain an education paralleling that offered by the official American educational system. Many of the graduates of ethnic schools and colleges entered ordinary American universities. According to Salomon Ilmonen, for several years during the 1920s the student body at the University of Michigan at Ann Arbor included some 100 Finns, and there were also Finnish students at other universities.[36] Some of the students who had attended or graduated from the Workers' College returned to Finland, and during the 1920s and 1930s a few of these were elected to the Finnish Parliament as representatives of the Social-Democratic Party.[37]

Such independent educational activity on the part of the Finnish American community—ranging from Sunday schools and summer schools to the two colleges described above—served as a resource and an inspiration for other intellectual activities within the community. Such activities were very lively, regardless of ideological orientation. All in all, this contributed to the maintenance of an immigrant identity and the durability of the immigrant community, while at the same time creating a pathway to the social reality that would inevitably face the children and grandchildren of Finnish American immigrants.

### Theater and Drama

Immigrant theater in both the United States and Canada served a variety of functions, which in turn were related to their seamless connections with organizational activities. So-called independent theaters were a rarity in the Finnish American community, although a few of them did arise, in particular in remote farming areas. The Finnish dramatic society in Tapiola, Michigan, for instance, was known in the nearby villages; its activities had nothing to do with the labor movement, the temperance groups, or any other organization.[38] Any information as to such "art for art's sake" activities, however, is both scanty and unsystematic, and is derived chiefly from individual recollection. More information, in terms of source materials and even systematic research, is available for dramatic activities connected with various organizations. The most complete sources are those available in connection with the labor organizations, nor is there any reason to doubt that dramatic activities were most lively in these groups. It should nevertheless be stressed that these circumstances, with regard to source materials and research, may unduly foreground the role of the workers' theaters compared to other groups.

The models for all immigrant theaters had been imported from Finland. Particularly at the start of the century the repertoire derived from the home country, if only because no "native" immigrant plays had yet been written. During the entire era of Finnish American theater—the peak period of which occurred during the 1920s and 1930s, although the latter decade already showed a clear decline—close connections were maintained with Finland.[39] This included the commissioning of plays; only 6 percent

**FIGURE 2.** Finnish Americans loved stage performances, which varied from classics to folk culture and ideology. Here Simson and Delila are shown on the Saima theater in Fitchburg, Massachusetts, in 1926. (Source: Photo collections, DGH)

of the plays presented within the labor movement groups had been written by Finnish American immigrants, Timo Riippa writes.[40] Immigrants had brought the vigorous Finnish tradition of amateur theater to America at the turn of the century, and it rapidly achieved a significant role in Finnish American leisure pursuits and activities.

During its entire lifetime, the Finnish American immigrant theater remained an amateur activity, in the sense that the actors were not paid for their work. Particularly the largest groups, however, aimed at a quasi-professional standard. This was made possible by the hiring for these theaters of professional, paid directors, whose role was central to the flourishing of dramatic activity. Only the largest theaters, however, had such directors.[41]

It was the director who chose the plays to be performed, although the final say, especially in groups associated with the workers' movement, remained with the board. The director also assigned roles to individual actors as he or she thought best. This, not surprisingly, was a source of constant friction; the actors considered that they knew best which roles were right for them and which were not.[42] The distinction between the paid director and the unpaid amateur actors led to other problems as well; the actors' attitude toward learning a part, for instance, was often poor. Female actors might be more interested in the costumes than in the part itself, and if they disliked the costumes they might reject the part altogether.[43]

The director, on the other hand, sometimes forgot that the actors were not professionals and would demand too much of them, leading to frequent clashes between the two sides. During the peak years of Finnish American theater, good professional directors were nevertheless sorely needed; the demand was higher than the supply. In particular during the early years, before the First World War, many directors had received their training in Finland; these included Felix Hyrske from Turku and Ella Haanpää from Helsinki, both of whom played a central role in the Finnish American immigrant theater over several decades.[44]

Elis Sulkanen has drawn up a list of 115 Finnish American theater directors. While the list is not exhaustive,[45] it does show that considerable energy as well as money was spent on finding a suitable director. The theater was serious work.

The Finnish American immigrant theater served a number of functions. From the point of view of the organization with which it was connected, the theater was important for fund-raising. The drama clubs developed into the most important form of activities at the "halls" built and maintained by the workers' organizations; since they were also highly profitable, constant attention was devoted to these groups and their quality. The profits derived from their performances were channeled into the construction of many new halls, which at their best were true cultural centers, as in the case of the Socialist Opera House in Virginia, Minnesota. This was a three-story building: the ground floor held a restaurant and meeting room, kitchen, dressing rooms, and boiler room; the second floor housed the auditorium and stage; and the third floor contained rehearsal spaces and the manager's office.[46]

Clearing the halls of debt required various forms of activity, and the drama club was often the most important. Even a cautious estimate places the number of Finnish American drama groups during the peak period at several hundred. In the local branches of the Finnish Socialist Federation, the drama group was usually the most important local unit, with a higher membership than the others.[47] In the late 1920s, the newspaper *Työmies* (Worker) wrote that Finnish American immigrant theater might not have arisen at all if not for the great need for money.[48]

As an example of the economic importance of the drama clubs, we can look more closely at the balance sheet for 1918 of the workers' theater of Gardner, Massachusetts. Income for the year totaled $2,217; this was used to pay the director, to advertise in the local newspapers ($170), and to pay for the performance rights for plays and roles ($18). Thirty dollars was spent on makeup, $25 went to the band, and another $25 went for published plays. When the $63 spent on stage costumes and props and the $5 spent on paper for copying scripts are both added, total expenses amounted to $1,357. The net profit was thus some $800. The level of profit naturally varied from one year to the next, according to the state of the national economy, among other factors; on the whole, however, up to the late 1920s the dramatic societies did very well, as reflected in the annual reports and in the accounts rendered by the drama clubs to their branch organizations.[49]

According to Eero Boman, one of the most prominent directors in the Finnish American immigrant theater, fund-raising was by far the most important functions of the theater.[50] On the other hand, every effort was made to keep ticket prices low, so that everyone who wanted to see the play would be able to do so.[51] Here we see the other central function of the theater: the theater was an important form of entertainment, a significant part of social activity within the Finnish American community. Going to the theater often involved the whole family, and following the performance there was dancing. From the point of view of the individual immigrant, the central function of the theater was in its entertainment value; he or she was not interested in the amount of profit it generated for the organization or branch.

FIGURE 3. This building, named the Socialist Opera, was owned by the local Finnish socialist club in Virginia, Minnesota, and provided the stage for numerous classic and ideological performances. (Source: IMT Photo collections, USA_0437)

Over the years, a close relationship arose between the actors and their audience, of a kind that was not possible in the professional, institutional theater.

According to the Finnish American actor, director, and scriptwriter Lauri Lemberg, who was prominent in the immigrant theater for decades, very few members of the Finnish American community were actually interested in the ideas of the temperance movement or in socialist teachings; cultural activities as such were far more important than the ideologies to which they were connected. John Wiita, an activist in the Finnish Socialist Federation, calculated that only some 20 percent of branch membership were involved in socialist activity for political and ideological reasons; the other 80 percent were motivated by cultural interests and other leisure activities.[52]

The didactic, propagandistic function of the theater was nevertheless seen as important, especially within the labor movement. This was the third principal function, along with fund-raising and entertainment, and we shall return to it below in connection with the historical development of various Finnish American immigrant organizations. A fourth function can be seen in terms of aesthetic value. Assuming that for the background organization the main objectives were fund-raising and the education of the membership, while for the audience it was above all theater as entertainment, for the actors and the director artistic values also took on increasing importance over the years: they wanted to produce the best possible theater, and with increasing experience they also believed they could do so.

The Finnish American theater was very much a matter of the first immigrant generation, those who had themselves come from Finland. It is therefore not surprising that after the peak years, here as in other organizational activities, interest in the theater fell in the early decades of the twentieth century.

The high point, as already noted, was in the 1920s. The new Immigration Act of 1924 radically reduced immigration to the United States by the introduction of quotas for various ethnic and national groups, and similar restrictions were imposed in Canada beginning in 1930; thus the Finnish American immigrant community failed to receive the new blood from Finland that would have been crucial for the dramatic societies. The second generation did not share the same interest in Finnish-language cultural activities but rapidly became Americanized. Taking into account the impact of the worldwide economic depression beginning in 1929, which diverted people's attention to acute issues of basic livelihood, it is clear that the golden age of theater—in terms of both plays and performance—was over by the beginning of the 1930s. The first three decades of the century were nevertheless so productive that we may well call the theater the "favorite child" of Finnish American immigrant culture, as Reino Kero writes.[53]

The Finnish American theater had its roots, somewhat before the turn of the century, in the temperance movement. The older and more conservative of the central temperance organizations, the American Finnish People's Temperance Brotherhood (Amerikan Suomalaisen Kansallis-Raittius-Weljeysseura), frowned upon dancing, acting, and card-playing; plays were considered to promulgate murder, theft, adultery, and other vices. In particular, younger people, however, wanted greater freedom, and the Finnish American temperance movement split apart in 1890, with the founding of the more liberal Finnish Association of the Friends of Temperance in America (Raittiuden Ystäväin Liitto). The Finnish American theater had its origins in this organization. The first group was founded before the turn of the century: in 1895 an amateur dramatic group was established in Maynard, Massachusetts, in connection with the local Finnish temperance society, Alku (Beginning), and two years later the same occurred with the temperance society Sovittaja (Reconciler, Peacemaker) in Worcester, Massachusetts.[54]

The repertoire of the dramatic clubs ranged from historical dramas to comedy, from popular folk plays to tragedy. In general, the clubs would put on anything they thought would appeal to their audience. Classics included Aleksis Kivi's *Nummisuutarit* (Heath Cobblers) and Ludvig Holberg's play from 1722, *Jeppe Niilonpoika* (Jeppe of the Hill, or The Transformed Peasant; Norwegian original *Jeppe på Bjerget eller den forvandlede Bonde*). Plays with a temperance theme were naturally favored. Most popular of all, however, were more or less contemporary Finnish comedies, such as *Olenko minä tullut haaremiin* (I've Joined a Harem!) by Yrjö Soini (pen name Agapetus); *Syntipukki* (The Scapegoat), likewise by Agapetus; and *Naimahulluja* (Wedding Madness) by Taavi Vilho Ylönen (pen name Taavetti Sylvesteri).[55]

Starting at the turn of the twentieth century, the workers' organizations gradually began to take over the temperance societies and replace them in Finnish American organizational activities. Nevertheless, particularly on the East Coast, the dramatic societies remained relatively active and vigorous until the 1920s. When an attempt was made in the 1920s to revive and reinvigorate the temperance movement, those involved tried to appeal to the "good old days," referring in particular to the lively theatrical activities of past years.[56] But even this appeal to nostalgia was insufficient to revive the declining ideology of temperance, which in any case was made irrelevant by Prohibition in both the United States and Finland.

Modest theater activity was also carried out by other organizations connected with maintaining Finnish American identity, such as the Knights and Ladies of Kaleva, but these activities were hampered by the quasi-secretive character of these organizations. Only few of the lodges possessed the spaces needed for dramatic performance. What plays were performed were such as to promote "Finnishness," in particular classic Finnish plays by Aleksis Kivi and Zachris (Sakari) Topelius.[57]

The United Finnish Kaleva Brothers and Sisters (Yhdistyneet Kalevan Veljet ja Sisaret), a charitable organization based on the West Coast, was more involved in theater activities than the Knights and Ladies of Kaleva, which operated on the East Coast and especially in the Midwest. Timo Riippa refers in particular to the dramatic societies of Seattle, Washington, and Astoria, Oregon, which in the 1920s were actually prosperous enough to hire a professional director.

From 1917 onward, there was yet a third focus for Finnish American theater, along with the temperance and workers' organizations: this was the cooperative movement, whose theater activities continued into the 1930s. The dramatic society in Superior, Wisconsin, produced its own plays both in Finnish and in English, with a focus in the plots on themes related to the cooperative movement. Plays in Finnish included, for instance, *Nurkanperän Osuuskaupan vuosikokous* (The Annual Meeting of the Nurkanperä Cooperative) and *Liittyykö Mäenpään isäntä Osuuskauppaan* (Will Farmer Maenpaa Join the Cooperative); English-language productions included the musical comedy *A Gala Day in a Cooperative Store*.[58]

Little is known about the theater activities of Swedish-speaking Finnish American immigrants. The Swedish-language Order of Runeberg seems to have offered a program at its festivities very similar to that of the Finnish-language organizations: speeches, music and singing, *tableaux vivants,* dialogues, and plays. At the gala held in San Francisco in 1935, the play *Österbottningarna* was presented before a large audience.[59]

As already noted, the greatest amount of source material and research is available for the theaters organized by the labor movement. This was in any case the most visible part of Finnish American theater, whether in terms of level of activity or of artistic significance. Already in the home country the amateur theater was an important form of activity in the workers' associations, and during the early decades of the twentieth century many of those prominent in the workers' theater in Finland crossed the Atlantic and became an active force in the Finnish American immigrant theater.[60] According to Taru Sundstén, the Finnish American workers' theater was most active in immigrant areas on the East Coast, in New England and New York State. But activity was vigorous elsewhere, too, up to the 1920s; the number of dramatic societies and their activities were naturally commensurate with the size of the local branch of the socialist federation.[61]

One indication of the activity of the socialist stage was the establishment in 1918 of the Theater Alliance (Näyttämöliitto); its purpose was to find and acquire plays that would be both ideologically and artistically suitable, in order to make it easier for the socialist dramatic societies to find good material. When a new production was being planned, one problem was always finding a suitable play. This took time and trouble, and cooperation was therefore desirable. The alliance also planned to maintain close connections with the home country, so as to be able to acquire plays directly from Finnish playwrights. The intention was to become the sole American source of Finnish-language plays; if the "bourgeoisie" wanted to see a stage performance in Finnish, they would thus have to come to the workers' theaters.[62]

The Theater Alliance was founded at the point where the labor movement had started to disintegrate; thus it did not long remain the central body for all theater activity within the movement, but soon came under Communist leadership. In 1922, a competitor arose: the Finnish American theater director and playwright Lauri Lemberg became a member of the Finnish Dramatists' League in the home country (the only Finnish American to do so) and acquired the right to represent the league in the United States and Canada. The socialist-leaning Finnish Organization of Canada (Kanadan Suomalainen Järjestö) at first made use of the material offered by the Theater Alliance, but problems with long distances and customs payments, among other difficulties, led it in 1927 to establish its own agency for the acquisition of performance rights for plays. The IWW likewise established its own agency, which from 1932 to 1942 operated under the auspices of the Workers' College; later it operated in the facilities of the *Industrialisti,* the Finnish-language IWW newspaper.[63] The splitting up of the Finnish American labor movement thus meant that during the liveliest years of Finnish American theater activity, the Theater Alliance was unable to maintain any sort of monopoly. A single town might thus have two or even three different Finnish American workers' theaters, each of which acquired its plays from a different source.

The frequent turnover of plays in the Finnish American theaters did not always please the audience, since it meant that there was insufficient time for proper rehearsal. Generally speaking, it is nevertheless true to say that despite shortcomings, the audiences enjoyed what they saw. Time and again people came to see a performance, even if it had not been adequately rehearsed. The theater was a place for the community to meet; the actors were familiar; and the theater was in many cases the only form of artistic expression available. By the 1920s, however, considerable effort might be invested in making the performances a pleasurable and artistic experience; for the director, in particular, this was a question of honor. In the early 1920s, the most prestigious Finnish American workers' theaters were those belonging to the socialist branches in New York City and Fitchburg, Massachusetts; a little later they were joined by the New York Communist theater.[64] New York City was the epicenter of American theater; the immigrant theater learned from it and was able to raise its standard of ambition. This helped to maintain the point of gravity of the Finnish American theater in the eastern parts of the country, rather than farther west, where the immigrant community was perhaps larger.

Finnish American newspapers paid considerable attention to the activities of the dramatic societies. Actual critiques and reviews, however, were relatively rare; anyone presenting a critical comment would have been singled out and censured in both the dramatic society itself and the local branch under whose auspices it operated. Furthermore, a play was seen as an extension of ideology; there was a tacit agreement that one would not unduly criticize at least the performances of one's own local theater group.[65] According to Taru Sundstén, true critiques began to appear only toward the end of the 1920s, chiefly in the Communist daily *Työmies,* reviewing performances in the Finnish American Communist theater.[66]

It is difficult to say anything definite as to individual popular plays; the theaters operated over several decades and in addition were divided in the 1920s between competing organizations. Timo Riippa, however, has concluded that over the years there were certain plays that transcended all others in popularity; all of these had been written in Finland. They included classic plays by Aleksis Kivi—*Nummisuutarit* (Heath Cobblers), *Karkurit* (The Runaways), and *Kihlaus* (The Betrothal); Minna Canth's more recent but already classic *Murtovarkaus* (The Burglary), *Papin Perhe* (The Parson's Family), and *Työmiehen vaimo* (The Workingman's Wife); and Teuvo Pakkala's *Tukkijoella* (Timber River); the last of these, like certain other classic plays, is best known as a Finnish film made in 1951. Historical plays worth mentioning include in particular some of the works of Zachris Topelius.[67]

The ideological demands of the labor movement with regard to the repertoire remained in the background until the late 1920s. During the era of light comedy and operetta, the halls were constantly filled. During the 1920s, however, calls for a more ideologically sound "working-class" repertoire became stronger. The Finnish American Marxist writer and playwright Moses Hahl had been demanding such changes since the 1910s. The end result was that a popular play would have a few scenes added to it expressing a socialist ideology, after which the work could be advertised as a working-class play.[68]

A new phase began in the 1930s when the Comintern (the Communist International, based in Moscow) sent a letter to the Central Committee of the American Communist Party in reference to Finnish members of the party. Among other points made in the letter, it criticized the "bourgeois trash" presented in Communist theaters.[69] The letter had considerable consequences for Communist theaters. Previously, they had been more inclusive, with the hope of influencing an audience outside the party; the idea had been that a suitable play would bring a right-wing audience to the halls, who then might gain at least an inkling of the superiority of the Communist ideology. Such slight seeds might be retained and later bring forth fruit. As a result of the Comintern letter, the repertoire became much heavier, and the audience began to disappear from the halls.

During the 1930s, the organization was forced by circumstances to moderate its demand for ideological purity, and toward the end of the decade folk plays once again began to be performed. The old Finnish classics, by Kivi and others, also regained favor. By the end of the 1930s, however, the time of the Finnish American organizations was coming to an end in any case, since with the end of immigration there was no new blood from the home country flowing in to revitalize them. Theater activities likewise slowed down to a trickle, and second-generation Finnish Americans turned increasingly to the English-language American theater.

Throughout its existence, the labor movement theater was characterized by a debate over its primary functions: ideology, entertainment, art, or fund-raising, in varying combinations. This debate was reflected in the repertoire and in the acquisition of plays and scripts; ultimately, plays written in America by Finnish Americans tended to express the labor movement ideology. As noted above, however, such plays accounted for only about 6 percent of the total repertoire.

Especially during the 1920s and 1930s there was considerable interest among Finnish Americans in writing their own plays. Themes were derived from real life: the mines, the bunkhouses at the lumber camps, the construction sites. The wretched conditions of the Old Country were also recalled in the plays.[70] Almost all Finnish American playwrights belonged specifically to the labor movement; the notable exception was Lauri Lemberg, although he, too, began his career in the socialist theater. The titles of plays—including *Luokkaviha* (Class Hatred), *Hehkuva tulivuori* (Fiery Volcano), and *Yleislakko* (General Strike)—speak for themselves. These Finnish American plays might have been short on literary technique and sophistication, but they did not lack for enthusiasm and ambition to promote the writer's ideology.[71]

In assessing the importance of the Finnish American theater as a whole, we need to distinguish between two separate factors: on the one hand, dramatic literature; on the other, the performance of plays on stage. Finnish American dramatic writing did not achieve a particularly great mass in relation to the total size of the repertoire over the years. Likewise, its artistic quality was not particularly high. The performance of plays, and dramatic activities in general, however, was an essential component in Finnish American organizational activity over some forty years. In fact, there is good reason to consider the theater as the crucial form of artistic activity among Finnish Americans; whether as performers or as audience, it affected a very large part of the community. In an artistic sense, it created a space for creative activity for actors, directors, and playwrights. The audience in turn was given access to the Finnish theater and writers. Some plays took a stand on various current social issues; others spoke of the history of the Old Country and contributed to preserving a Finnish identity under new circumstances. Finally, the Finnish American theater was a crucial element in how Finnish Americans spent their leisure time, which from the 1920s onward was becoming increasingly available to many members of the community.

Along with many other activities, participation in the dramatic societies was thus an important expression of social cohesion and solidarity in the Finnish American immigrant community.

## Musical Pursuits

Along with amateur dramatic societies, musical pursuits played a visible role in the leisure interests of Finnish American immigrants, particularly as part of the program at various gatherings and festivities. Music, however, never gained as prominent a position in organizational activities as the theater; as noted earlier, in 1912 the socialist organizations comprised 107 dramatic societies but only twenty-three choir groups. The number of instrumental groups active at the same time has been estimated at twenty-eight.[72] Extensive musical activities, on the other hand, developed autonomously, outside ideological, religious, and other organizations. The musical pursuits of Finnish American immigrants tended to be concentrated around choir groups, brass bands, and, at a later time, orchestral groups.

Like the theater, amateur musical activities also received their original impetus from the temperance movement. Choral singing, however, was from the very beginning important in local churches as well. In the second half of the 1880s, when choral groups and bands began to be established (at first chiefly in Finnish immigrant areas in the Michigan Upper Peninsula), practice and rehearsal sessions, as well as many performances, took place on the premises of the temperance societies until the locality gradually achieved its own church.

According to Ilmonen, Finnish American brass bands had their origins in the "regimental bands": these were made up of members of military brass bands who had come to America from the home country and had become leaders of immigrant bands. The members of the bands used their own money to purchase handsome instruments; they practiced intensively, contributed to the hiring of a bandleader, and started to perform at evening gatherings and other occasions in the immigrant community. Many bands were originally independent, that is, not connected with any organization; this was the case, for instance, in Calumet, Michigan, although later the brass band joined the Good Hope temperance society.[73] All in all, immigrant musical activities were never as closely tied to ideological and/or religious organizations as was the case with the dramatic societies. There were of course exceptions: Reino Kero refers to the factions and cliques that were characteristic of the Finnish American immigrant community, and which affected musical activities as well: the workers' organizations had their own choirs and their own songbooks, as did the churches.[74]

In the early stages of musical activities—during the 1880s and 1990s—the brass bands played a more important role than the choral groups. In mining areas, for instance, with their population gender disproportionate (more men than women), it was difficult to establish mixed choirs. It was also easier to find someone with the expertise needed to direct a brass band than a choir, although the former was not always easy either; advertisements seeking a musical director sometimes had to be placed not only in Finnish American immigrant newspapers but also in the Finnish press. It was not always possible to hire a full-time director; they would have to spend their days working in the mines, at the lumbering sites, and so forth, which tended to hamper rehearsals and performances. Brass bands, however, were popular in American culture in general during the last two decades of the nineteenth century, and it is thus not surprising that the Finnish American immigrant community saw it as a matter of their own dignity and civic pride to establish such a band in their own locality.

The first bands were established during the late 1880s, with remarkable simultaneity in different parts of the country. The first band in the state of Michigan was founded in 1886 in Calumet, under the direction of Henry Haapanen. Three years later there was a band in Ely, Minnesota. The mountain states—Wyoming, Colorado, and Montana—had Finnish American brass bands by the end of the decade, despite the very modest size of the immigrant population. The first Finnish American band on the West Coast was established in Astoria, Oregon, in 1888. Two bands established in the 1890s, however, came to be most famous: Humina in Ashtabula, Ohio, and Louhi in Monessen, Pennsylvania.[75]

Singing groups and choirs began to be established during the same years as the bands. Their total number is impossible even to estimate; by the 1930s, when Salomon Ilmonen published his two-volume cultural history of the Finnish American immigrant community, hundreds of choirs had already been discontinued. In terms of different forms of cultural activity as part of the general cultural and organizational life of the Finnish American community, establishing and maintaining a musical band or a dramatic society demanded considerably more long-term attention and effort than did founding a choir. It is thus understandable that many of the choral groups had only a short life span and retained a more amateur quality than the other two.

The first Finnish American choir was founded in 1884, in Calumet in the Upper Peninsula, under the directorship of Pekka Westerinen. Westerinen was also active in establishing choirs in other Finnish immigrant localities in northern Michigan. Also active in establishing and maintaining choral activity in this area were the newly created Suomi-Opisto and its teachers. Oftentimes, an improvised choir was created out of singers who happened to be present at an evening entertainment or other gathering; the artistic ambitions of such groups were naturally not very high.[76]

In 1898, when the Temperance Brotherhood (Kansallis-Raittius-Weljeysseura) held its tenth annual general meeting, its members decided to organize various competitions in connection with their annual festivities in order to liven up their general activities. Beginning in 1899, this central organ for the various temperance societies organized competitions for both brass bands and choral groups.[77] These competitions were open to all members of the temperance societies, and the pieces that were required to be performed (whether songs or orchestral compositions) were announced in the immigrant press in good time. At the same time, the papers naturally also mentioned the abundant prizes that would be awarded.[78]

Once a certain history had grown up around musical activity, it was decided in 1911 to establish a cover organization, the Finnish Music Association of America (Amerikan Suomalainen Musiikkiyhdistys). The organization described its purpose as "uniting all Finnish singers and musicians," regardless of party or other affiliation. The aim was to organize competitions in order to raise the standard of performance; thus Finnish music could be brought to the attention of the general public in North America. Any group with at least four members was eligible for membership. Four years later, in 1915, another organization was established, the Sibelius Society (Sibelius-Seura), to make Finnish music available to Finnish American choirs and bands. The composer himself gave permission for the newly created organization to use his name, thus naturally increasing its prestige among the immigrant community.

The Finnish Music Association of America had its origins in Michigan; the Sibelius Society originated in Pennsylvania. That same year, in 1915, a third central organization was established, in Massachusetts: the Eastern Federation for Finnish Music (Idän Suomalainen Musiikkiliitto); thus each of the three central organizations had its own regional territory. Their importance grew considerably after the First

World War; especially during the 1920s and persisting into the 1930s, musical activity was very lively. Close contacts were also maintained during this period with the home country.

After the First World War, musical pursuits among the immigrant community underwent a change: traditional brass band assemblies started to give way to more complex orchestras. During the early years of the century, musical education had become widespread in the American educational system, and individual schools had begun to establish their own orchestras. They also provided instruments for the students' use. This practice would play a significant role in the transformation of musical pursuits among the Finnish American community during the 1920s and 1930s, as older players, belonging to the first generation of immigrants, began to be displaced by second-generation, younger ones. Traditions nevertheless endured in many orchestras: for instance, the former bands Humina in Ashtabula and Louhi in Monessen continued under the same name but now as full-scale orchestras, with musicians playing a variety of instruments.[79] With the change in musical repertoire, their artistic standards rose as well.

As soon as the war was over, one change was evident in the American musical scene: jazz, which until then had been entirely an African American genre, rapidly became a universal American form of music.[80] At the same time, as Finnish American music became dominated by younger players, jazz quickly gained a foothold here as well.

Another change that took place after the war was the increasing affiliation of choral groups with the church. There was a considerable rise in the number of church choirs—a tradition that continues both in the United States and Canada down to the present day. Around 1930, the Suomi Synod was home to 112 church choirs, the National Church more or less the same. The total number of Finnish American choirs at this time has been estimated at about 400, of which half were church-affiliated.[81]

From the 1920s onward, choir activity was lively among Swedish-speaking Finnish immigrants as well. As the central organization for this immigrant group, the Runebergorden was the catalyst initiating and promoting choral activity. Activity slowed down to a trickle with the worldwide Great Depression of the 1930s, but revived again toward the end of the decade, at least in the eastern parts of the country. Three examples will suffice. The celebrations held in 1938 to mark the tercentenary of the New Sweden (Nova Svecia; Nya Sverige) colony in Delaware saw a performance by the seventy-member Runeberg choir, established a few years earlier in New York. A year later, the World's Fair of 1939 included a "Finland Day," marked by the performance of another large choir, this one with 200 members. And finally, support for Finland during the Winter War of 1939–40 included a number of concerts carefully prepared for by the choir. The Swedish-language immigrant choirs active in the western parts of the country likewise played their part in raising support for Finland at the turn of the 1930s and into the 1940s.[82]

Partly as a consequence of this vigorous musical activity, both instrumental and choral, the Finnish American immigrant community also gave rise to a number of classical musicians and composers.[83] Likewise, in the domain of popular music there were many individual performers who later became favorites in different parts of the country with a large Finnish American population. Among the most productive was Hiski Salomaa, whose reputation as an "immigrant troubadour" has endured in Finland as well. Around 1920, the big recording companies established special departments to cater to the musical needs of various immigrant groups, and records were made, for instance, for Finnish American listeners. These records were not sold through the major retailers, but were marketed only in areas with a large Finnish American immigrant population. Hiski Salomaa was one of the singers whose music was thus

FIGURE 4. Among the numerous bands and music performers, accordion player Viola Turpeinen (left), John Rosendahl (center), and Sylvia Polso (right) formed an extremely popular trio. Picture ca. 1930. (Source: IMT Photo collections, USA_3206)

recorded, and he soon became one of the most popular performers among the immigrant community. His songs, like those of many other immigrant singers, told of ordinary, everyday life. Salomaa embellished his lyrics with his own personal style of singing, which has been compared to the vigorous style of violin playing typical of the *pelimanni* (musician, fiddler) form of folk music in western Finland—the part of Finland where a majority of immigrants had originated.[84]

We should also take note of the contribution to Finnish American music by Finnish composers and musicians who paid visits to North America and the immigrant community. One such was the composer, pianist, and conductor Oskari Merikanto, who visited America as early as 1900 and performed to immigrant audiences. Jean Sibelius arrived in the United States in 1914, as an already famous composer. Another composer and pianist, Selim Palmgren, taught during the 1920s at the University of Rochester in New York State. In the sphere of popular music, Pasi Jääskeläinen, the interpreter of folk music, paid two visits to the Finnish American immigrant community in the early years of the century. Likewise, Johan Alfred Tanner and Tatu Pekkarinen, already famous in Finland for their original song lyrics, toured America performing for immigrant audiences.[85] In the winter of 1937–38, the famed Finnish choir

FIGURE 5. Postcard to Finland in 1928 explaining that this was a place to dance at Williams Lake (Rosendale, New York), built by Kustaa Williams (or Stenberg from Laitila). Williams built houses, hotels, and places of amusement. Williams Lake was popular for summer vacations of Finnish Americans. (Source: America letters, Satakunta/V/Raum XX, DGH)

Ylioppilaskunnan Laulajat (University Male Voice Choir) arrived for a visit, giving rise to great enthusiasm in the Finnish American community, particularly in choral circles.[86]

These visits by musicians—of whom there has been space here to mention only a few—from the Old Country to the United States and Canada helped not only to add to a sense of national identity among immigrants but also to increase the zeal to continue to develop musical activities. It is not surprising that musical activities continued to maintain their vigor in the 1930s, at a time when organizational activity was slowing down, along with cultural activities such as the theater, which had been closely connected with ideological organizations. It was also easier to involve the second generation, since language skills—a knowledge of Finnish—played a less important role in music than in the theater or in literary pursuits.

Beginning in the 1920s, Finnish American music thus gained ground in the home country as well. The Louhi brass band from Monessen toured Finland in 1920. This was actually the first group visit by immigrants back to the Old Country, involving a total of 400 people; it went by the name of the "Louhi expedition," since the band took responsibility for organizing it. Two years later, another visit to Finland was organized by the Suomen Sävel (Melody of Finland) choir. And in 1926 it was the turn of the Finnish American Suomi orchestra. It was the musicians on this tour who created—the word is not too strong—the foundation for the development of jazz in Finland. Inspired by the orchestra, Finnish jazz bands rapidly appeared on the scene. Already in the early 1920s a degree of "jazz fever" could be perceived in Helsinki, but it was only the visit by the Suomi orchestra, in particular Wilfred "Tommy" Tuomikoski, who played the clarinet and the alto saxophone, that brought about a true breakthrough.

Tuomikoski remained in Finland for several years, contributing in concrete ways to the first baby steps of Finnish jazz.[87]

Thus Finnish American musical activities helped to build bridges between the Old Country and the immigrant community. Unlike, for instance, the dramatic societies, musical activities continued to grow even after the immigrant era as such had come to an end. Musical activities were clearly less strongly tied to organizations; it was perhaps for this very reason—standing as they did outside ideological disputes—that both the artistic and the entertainment functions of music survived for a long time among Finnish American immigrants, and that Finnish American immigrant music was also able to speak to audiences in the Old Country.

## Sports and Athletics

Organized activities among Finnish Americans in the field of sport and athletics had their beginnings in the first decade of the twentieth century, chiefly through the efforts of first-generation immigrants who had been active in this field in the home country. The earliest gymnastics clubs were founded in Finland in the mid-1870s;[88] a central organization to coordinate these activities, the Gymnastics and Athletic League of Finland (SVUL), was established in 1906.[89] In 1919, following the Civil War, a competing organization was founded, the Labor Sports League (TUL).[90] This ideological split would be clearly reflected in the forms of organization of sports and athletics in the Finnish American immigrant community in the 1920s, the decade when such activities were at their peak.

From the first decades of the twentieth century onward, the temperance societies began to establish gymnastics groups, which would perform at immigrant gatherings and festivities. At the same time, independent clubs and societies not affiliated with any other organization also began to arise. Local socialist chapters began to set up groups for sport and athletics, as, somewhat later, did some churches as well.[91] Sports were seen as a natural form of recreational activity, along with intellectual or ideological culture. Critical voices, however, were also heard: "What's the use of punishing the body!" Questions of propriety were likewise voiced: gymnastics was sometimes seen merely as "the indecent contortions of men in a state of semi-nudity."[92]

Sports and gymnastics nevertheless soon achieved a firm position among Finnish American immigrants. In 1911, for instance, the Finnish Socialist Federation included fifty-three athletic clubs.[93] Since the federation at this time had a total of some 200 chapters, this meant that athletics had achieved a visible role in one out of four of them. During the years preceding the First World War, these clubs chiefly practiced (to quote Salomon Ilmonen) "calisthenics, the performance of graceful bodily movements demanding flexibility and skill." During the period, calisthenics and acrobatic pyramids were in fact a central element in gymnastic performances.[94]

During the first decade of the twentieth century, however, competitive sports and athletics, which were popular in Finland, began to gain ground over gymnastics among the immigrant community as well, mainly in the form of track-and-field and wrestling; gymnastics remained an important third form of physical culture during the entire active immigrant era. During the same decade, a number of successful Finnish track-and-field athletes and wrestlers moved to the United States.[95]

Most sports clubs were established in the eastern parts of the country; the farther west one went, the less sports took organized form. Finnish American sports associations in the states of New York

**FIGURE 6**. Wrestling was popular in Finland and among the immigrants. Here is the successful team of the Reipas sports and gymnastics association from Fitchburg, Massachusetts, in 1921. (Source: Photo collections, DGH)

and Massachusetts arranged the earliest track-and-field and wrestling competitions during the first decade of the new century. In 1911, the Eastern Gymnastics and Athletic League (Idän Voimistelu- ja Urheiluliitto) had eleven member clubs, even the names of which sometimes expressed a love of physical culture: Pyrintö (Aspiration, Effort) in Coal Center, Riento (Swiftness, Activity) in Newport, Ponnistus (Effort, Striving) in Peabody, Toivo (Hope) in Springfield, Reipas (Vigorous, Energetic) in Fitchburg, Karhu (Bear) in Quincy, Into (Zeal, Enthusiasm) in Gardner, and Tarmo (Energy, Vigor) in Maynard. In other cases, the names expressed the members' immigrant identity: the Cambridge Pohjola (North; a name with Kalevala associations), the Worcester Suomi, and the Brooklyn Kaleva. At this point, the clubs belonging to the association had a total of about 400 members.[96]

In the Finnish American labor movement, the position from the very start was that the board of a local section would define the form of activities of the sports club. The intensive growth of the labor movement during the two decades before the First World War nevertheless meant that some independent sports clubs joined local socialist chapters. Party membership was important; for instance, the Quincy Hurja (Wild) sports club was expelled from the Eastern Gymnastics and Athletic League because it did not belong to the Socialist Party.[97] Many sports clubs joined the party apparatus in part simply because it gave them access to the local hall and financial security for their activities.

As already noted, the first two decades of the century can be seen chiefly as the period of new sports associations. At the same time, however, competitive sports began increasingly to gain ground. In particular, the move to the United States of the Finnish athlete Hannes Kolehmainen after the Stockholm Olympics of 1912 (where he had won three gold medals) provided a powerful impetus. Kolehmainen arrived in America with his brother William, also a well-known runner. On his first trip, Hannes Kolehmainen stayed in the United States until 1915; he returned for a while to Finland and then came back to New York, where he married a Finnish American woman. During these years, he appeared frequently in the American media after winning many important long-distance running competitions. At the same time, he worked in construction in New York and returned to Finland before the Antwerp Olympics of 1920.[98]

Along with Kolehmainen, several other athletes—runners and wrestlers—had made Finnish athletics famous already before the war.[99] For the Finnish American community, this had a dual importance: on the one hand, it increased interest in sports within the community; on the other, it elevated the Finnish American national identity among other immigrant groups.

At the beginning of the 1920s, Finnish American sports activity reached its apogee. At the same time, it split up on rigidly ideological grounds into two camps, the left-affiliated and the independent, following the founding in Finland of the TUL. Prior to the Finnish Civil War in 1918, Finnish American sports clubs founded under the auspices of the local socialist chapters were allowed to organize and compete in events within the United States; but from 1920 onward, members of the clubs were prohibited from participating in "external" competitions.[100] At the same time, the labor movement itself split up into socialist and Communist camps, entailing a further splitting and some degree of collapse of sports activity. Many successful athletes moved to nonsocialist clubs, so as to be able to go on competing. The splitting up of labor movement sports meant a dwindling of competitive activity. In addition to the socialist and Communist wings, the IWW also established its own sports organizations in the 1920s.[101]

Toward the end of the decade, however, labor movement sports organizations began to be less strict in their attitudes. Athletes belonging to the local socialist club, for instance, had practically no access to competitions at all. In 1926, a decision was made allowing members of the clubs once more to take part in all competitions. One explanation given was that getting top athletes to compete would lead to increased spectator interest. Another reason was the realization that many of the athletes in the socialist clubs were now second-generation immigrants, for whom the socialist ideology as such was no longer as important as it had been for the previous generation.[102] At the same time, the Communist and IWW sports organizations likewise relaxed some of their restrictions, at least with respect to each other; this led to a boom in sports activity in the labor movement compared to the first half of the decade. Contributing to this relaxation of attitudes was the visit to America by the runner Paavo Nurmi, the most successful and famous Finnish athlete of his time, and the success of Finnish athletes in general. Around 1930, sports activity in both the socialist and the Communist camps was once again relatively lively; the strength of the former was mainly in the eastern part of the country, that of the latter in the midwestern states.[103]

But the 1920s were predominantly the golden age of independent sports organizations not associated with the labor movement. In 1922, the Finnish American Gymnastics and Athletics League (Amerikan Suomalainen Voimistelu- ja Urheiluliitto) was founded at Worcester, Massachusetts, as a joint organization to coordinate the activities of sports clubs. The association maintained close contact with the SVUL in the home country, with the consequence that numerous Finnish athletes visited the United States to heighten interest in sports competition.[104]

In the area of competitive sport, the most successful club during the 1920s was the Finnish American Athletic Club (FAAC) in New York City, founded as early as 1901 among the Swedish-speaking Finnish immigrants living in the city. At first the most important competitive "event" was the rope-pull, but in the 1910s the club began to focus on wrestling. In 1917, Hannes Kolehmainen (who until then, chiefly for financial reasons, had represented an Irish American sports organization in New York) transferred to the FAAC; this signaled the start of the most flourishing era for the club. It soon became one of the best-known American athletic clubs, and for a while was a considerable financial success as well. The club had its own building, with a separate wrestling arena and bowling alley, as well as a ballroom and a bar. The Finnish American immigrant community gave the club powerful support, since its members included famous long-distance runners such as Ville Ritola.[105]

Ritola had immigrated to the United States in 1913; he began his actual competitive career in 1919, at the relatively late age of twenty-three. The Olympics in Paris in 1924 and in Amsterdam in 1928 elevated him to the apex of long-distance running, with five gold and three silver medals. He returned permanently to Finland only in 1971.[106] A number of other Finnish track-and-field athletes were also successful in the Olympics.

Particular excitement arose among Finnish American immigrants out of Paavo Nurmi's competition tour of the country between December 1924 and May 1925; Nurmi's great success received wide attention in the American media. Although Nurmi was of course not an immigrant, the Finnish American community considered him one of their own. In the 1920s, attitudes in the United States toward various immigrant groups were hostile and mistrustful, with quotas enacted to restrict further immigration; under these circumstances, Nurmi's success helped to improve self-esteem in the immigrant community. The FAAC in fact elected him an honorary member and arranged his competition in Madison Square Garden in New York City.[107]

What, then, was the significance of the athletic success of Nurmi and Finnish American athletes in the America of the 1920s? Obviously Americans had many other spectator sports besides track-and-field and long-distance running; these were not then, nor for that matter are they today, a focus of interest among the American public. According to Juhani Paasivirta, Finnish athletics did not in general offer a particularly accurate picture of Finland, since they emphasized physical performance alone. Hannu Salonen, in his study of Finnish American immigrant sports, takes a more positive stance: the success of Finnish distance runners contributed to the creation of a certain positive image, one marked by doggedness and determination—in a word, the notorious Finnish "grit" (*sisu*).[108] Finnish Americans themselves considered the runners' success to be important, as at least to some extent did Americans themselves; Nurmi, for instance, was invited to Calvin Coolidge's White House, competed again in the United States at the end of the 1920s, and in 1940, long after his competitive career was over, made a goodwill tour of the country together with Taisto Mäki, a Finnish distance runner of that period.[109]

In any case, long-distance running held a certain place in the "American dream," with its worship of heroic figures. In 1928 and 1929, a certain promoter got the idea of organizing a cross-country run, from Los Angeles to New York. The race was expected to take more than two months. The prizes were also noteworthy; the winner would get $25,000, the runner-up $10,000, and the third prize would be $2,000. In both races, the competitors included several Finnish Americans, of whom John Salo came in second in 1928 and first in 1929; in the latter case—the year of the stock market crash—the promoter was unfortunately unable to pay the prize money due to bankruptcy.

A concrete expression of the important role played by competitive sports among the Finnish American community can be seen in the fund-raising campaigns of the 1920s, aimed at subsidizing the travel of Finnish American athletes to Europe for the Olympic Games as members of the Finnish Olympic team. The first fund-raising drive took place in anticipation of the 1920 games in Antwerp; organized in New York City, the most important center of Finnish American athletics, it was carried out with the help of the Finnish American immigrant press, in particular the *New Yorkin Uutiset* (New York News). The campaign raised almost $10,000 (at the time an enormous sum), enabling the marathon runners Hannes Kolehmainen and Johan Tuomikoski, as well as the wrestler Eino Leino, to travel to Antwerp. Similar campaigns were organized before the Olympic Games of 1924 and 1928, in the name of Ville Ritola in particular.[110]

In 1932, both the winter and the summer games were held in the United States (at Lake Placid and in Los Angeles, respectively), and the Finnish American community was once again enthusiastically involved in the preparations. The Great Depression naturally left its mark on the fund-raising drive, but at the games themselves, members of the immigrant community did all they could to support Finnish athletes. A campaign was once again launched for the 1936 Olympic Games in Berlin, even though the Finnish team no longer included any Finnish American athletes.[111] By this time, sports activities among the community had taken a downturn: the first generation was aging, and the Great Depression weakened interest in sports in any case. The younger generation of Finnish Americans tended to be more interested in typical American sports, such as basketball.

Sports activities in the immigrant community had tended to take the form of competitive sports; in the 1930s, when this period began to be over, it was hard for the clubs to change their way of operating. In 1934, the female gymnasts of the best-known club, the New York FAAC, therefore established a club of their own, the New York Finnish Women Gymnasts (New Yorkin Suomalaiset Naisvoimistelijat). The club was very active; its performances raised funds for charity in Finland and for the American Red Cross.[112]

During the 1930s, competitive sports were replaced among the Finnish American community by the most popular form of "sport," spectator sports. The careers and successes of Finnish athletes were followed closely, and constant contact was maintained with the home country—for instance, in the form of fund-raising campaigns for the Olympic Games. After the announcement in 1938 that the 1940 Olympics would be held in Finland, the Finnish American community was actively involved in the initial arrangements. Funds were raised for the construction of the Helsinki Stadium, the prize money for the New York run was donated for the Sports Museum founded in 1938, and the Finnish American Society (Suomi-Seura) sent a memorial plaque to be placed on the stadium in Helsinki. Issues of *Suomen Urheilulehti* (Finnish Sports Magazine )regularly sold out in the United States.[113] When the 1940 games had to be canceled due to the outbreak of war, disappointment among the immigrant community was great.

Within the labor movement, a momentary surge occurred in sports activity toward the end of the 1920s, but here, too, the next decade brought a decline. The local socialist sections tried to defy the challenges of changing times by bringing back wrestling and by including basketball in their programs. In 1930, there were thirteen socialist sports clubs, with some 300 members. Correspondingly, the central Communist organization, the Labor Sports Union, was still envisioning lively activity during the 1930s; there were plans to bring Soviet athletes to the union's games in 1930. The Great Depression, which began in 1929, however, meant that already the following year the question arose as to whether it made sense continuing with the union's activities.[114]

Overall, competitive sports activity within the Finnish American labor movement had shrunk by the mid-1930s almost to nothing. The problem was no longer one of ideological conflicts within the movement; there were simply too few athletes competing. In Canada, on the other hand, conditions continued to be relatively favorable, due to the fact that Finnish immigration to Canada was then at its height. During the 1930s, the Finnish Canadian immigrant community was strengthened by large numbers of new immigrants arriving from the home country, and sports and athletics had an important place in the cultural life of the community, which has continued down to our own time.

Over a period of some thirty years—from the turn of the twentieth century approximately to the beginning of the Great Depression—sports competitions and show performances played a highly visible role in the cultural life of the Finnish American immigrant community. They were also characterized, more clearly than other forms of culture, by close ties with the Old Country, reflected in the American competition tours by Finnish athletes, in the quadrennial Olympic Games, and in the success of numerous Finnish American track-and-field athletes and wrestlers representing Finland in international competitions. Due to this foregrounding of competitive sports, the connection between the new country and the old was sustained even after the Second World War, primarily in the form of fund-raising campaigns for what had now become spectator sport. The annual Boston marathon remained for decades a matter of interest among the Finnish American community, who collected money to allow Finnish runners to participate.

Along with these "top-level" competitive sports, we naturally have to bear in mind that over the decades the sports clubs also organized competitive activities on a smaller scale. In addition, gymnastics and calisthenics, as "aesthetic" forms of sport, maintained their position on the program when Finnish festivities and celebrations were organized. In the 1930s, when sports activities began to diminish and there were few top runners and wrestlers, the Finnish American community found other outlets for their sports zeal—always, however, keeping their ethnic identity in mind. Boxing, for instance, had never been a leading interest among the immigrants themselves; but when the Finnish heavyweight Gunnar Bärlund started to gain fame in the mid-1930s, Finnish Americans were among his strongest supporters—professional boxing being among the most popular sports among Americans in general. The Finnish winner of the middleweight series at the Berlin Olympics, Sten Suvio, also turned professional in the United States, but he soon returned to Finland;[115] thus neither he nor (ultimately) Bärlund was able to do much to revitalize the Finnish American sports clubs.

The 1930s were a time of transition in the life of the Finnish American immigrant community, and like other forms of culture, sports did not survive; the dwindling and dying out of new immigration accelerated the process of assimilation to such a degree that by the end of the decade, older immigrants could at best look back on the "good old days," watch the involvement of their children in "American" sports, and support and cheer for the top competitive athletes of the Old Country.

### NOTES

1. Salomon Ilmonen, *Amerikan suomalaisten sivistyshistoria. Johtavia aatteita, harrastuksia, yhteispyrintöjä ja tapahtumia siirtokansan keskuudessa. Edellinen osa* (Hancock, Mich.: Suomalais-Luterilainen Kustannusliike, 1930), 49.

2. Eija Lehtinen, *Raittiusliike, osa amerikansuomalaista järjestötoimintaa (1885–1932)*. Pro gradu-tutkielma (Turku: Turun yliopisto, 1978), 113.

3. FSF Proceedings 1912. *Suomalaisten sosialistiosastojen ja työväenyhdistysten viidennen eli suomalaisen sosialistijärjestön kolmannen edustajakokouksen pöytäkirja* 1-5, 7-10 p. kesäkuuta 1912, ed. Aku Rissanen (Fitchburg, Mass. 1912), passim.
4. See Reino Kero, *Suuren lännen suomalaiset* (Helsinki: Otava, 1976), 148-52.
5. Anders M. Myhrman," The Finland-Swedish Immigrants in the U.S.A.," in *Old Friends—Strong Ties,* ed. Vilho Niitemaa et al. (Turku: Institute of Migration, 1976), 190-94.
6. See Mirja Koivunalho, *Amerikansuomalaisten näytelmäseuratoiminta työväenliikkeen piirissä viime vuosisadan lopulta toiseen maailmansotaan.* Pro gradu-tutkielma (Turku: Turun yliopisto, 1978), 73-77.
7. *Suomalaisen Sosialistijärjestön seitsemännen edustajakokouksen pöytäkirja. Laadittu* Waukeganissa, Ill. 25-31 p. joulukuuta 1920 pidetystä S. S. *Järjestön edustajakokouksesta,* ed. Aaro Hyrske (Superior, Wis.: Työmies Society, 1920) 25; cf. Riitta Stjärnstedt, *Naiset amerikansuomalaisessa työväenliikkeessä vuoteen 1920.* Pro gradu-tutkielma (Turku: Turun yliopisto, 1981), 112.
8. Stjärnstedt, *Naiset,* 39-52.
9. See Salomon Ilmonen, *Amerikan suomalaisten sivistyshistoria. Johtavia aatteita, harrastuksia, yhteispyrintöjä ja tapahtumia siirtokansan keskuudessa. Jälkimmäinen osa* (Hancock, Mich.: Suomalais-Luterilainen kustannusliike, 1931), 142.
10. Yvonne R. Lockwood, *Finnish American Rag Rugs: Art, Tradition, and Ethnic Continuity* (East Lansing: Michigan State University Press, 2009).
11. A. William Hoglund, *Finnish Immigrants in America 1880-1920* (Madison: University of Wisconsin Press, 1960), 20.
12. Ilmonen, *Amerikan suomalaisten sivistyshistoria. Edellinen osa,* 25-26; Rafael Engelberg, *Suomi ja Amerikan suomalaiset. Keskinäinen yhteys ja sen rakentaminen* (Helsinki: Suomi-Seura, 1944), 192.
13. Eija Lehtinen, *Raittiusliike, osa amerikansuomalaista järjestötoimintaa* (1885-1932). Pro gradu-tutkielma (Turku: Turun yliopisto, 1978), 62.
14. Ilmonen, *Amerikan suomalaisten sivistyshistoria. Edellinen osa,* 121; Lehtinen, Raittiusliike, 65-66.
15. Onnen Aika—temperance society, minutes April 1, 1900 (Republic, Mich.), DGH, TYYH/S/m/8/175. Microfilm collection at the Department of General History, University of Turku.
16. Lehtinen, *Raittiusliike,* 66-67.
17. Ilmonen, *Amerikan suomalaisten sivistyshistoria. Edellinen osa,* 151-62.
18. On the founding of the Suomi Synod and Suomi College, see Ilmonen, *Amerikan suomalaisten sivistyshistoria, Edellinen osa,* 73-78; Engelberg, *Suomi ja Amerikan suomalaiset,* 249-54; Ralph J. Jalkanen, "Suomi College," in Niitemaa et al., *Old Friends—Strong Ties,* 175-77; Hannu Heinilä, *Work People's College—amerikansuomalaisen työväestön oppilaitos.* Pro gradu-tutkielma (Turku: Yleinen historia, 1976), 13.
19. Suomi-Opiston *25-vuotisjuhlajulkaisu 1896-1921* (Hancock, Mich.: Suomi-Opisto, 1921), 9.
20. See Ilmonen, *Amerikan suomalaisten sivistyshistoria. Jälkimmäinen osa,* 224.
21. Jalkanen, "Suomi College," 178.
22. See Ilmonen, *Amerikan suomalaisten sivistyshistoria. Edellinen osa,* 68-69; Heinilä, Work People's College, 13.
23. Cf. Auvo Kostiainen, "Work People's College: An American Immigrant Institution," *Scandinavian Journal of History* 5, no. 4 (1980): 297.
24. Ilmonen, *Amerikan suomalaisten sivistyshistoria. Edellinen osa,* 162-63.
25. V. Rautanen, *Amerikan suomalainen kirkko* (Hancock, Mich.: Suomalais-luteerilainen kustannusliike, 1911), 197-98.
26. K. L. Haataja, "Piirteitä Kansan-Opiston toiminnasta," *Vallankumous* 1 (1908): 6; see also Ilmonen, *Amerikan suomalaisten sivistyshistoria. Edellinen osa,* 164-65; Heinilä, Work People's College, 15-16; Kostiainen, "Work People's College," 298-99.

27. Rautanen, *Amerikan,* 202.
28. Ilmonen, *Amerikan suomalaisten sivistyshistoria. Edellinen osa,* 166-67; cf. Hans R. Wasastjerna, *History of the Finns in Minnesota,* ed. and trans. Toivo Rosvall (Duluth: Minnesota Finnish American Historical Society, 1957), 227; Kostiainen, "Work People's College," 302.
29. Cf. Heinilä, *Work People's College,* 19-28; Kostiainen, "Work People's College," 299-301.
30. Minutes, People's College (Kansan opisto) board, June 4, 1908, Jack Ujanen Collection, DGH, TYYH/S/a/14/V.
31. *Kolmannen Amerikan suomalaisen Sosialistijärjestön edustajakokouksen pöytäkirja. Kokous pidetty Hancockissa, Mich.* 28-30 p. elokuuta, ed. F. J. Syrjälä (Fitchburg, Mass.: A. S. S. Järjestön toimeenpaneva Komitea, 1909), 206; see also Heinilä, *Work People's College,* 54, 67; Kostiainen, "Work People's College," 303.
32. See *Raivaaja,* June 26, 1908.
33. Heinilä, *Work People's College,* 148-59; Kostiainen, "Work People's College," 305-6.
34. Cf. Heinilä, *Work People's College,* 81-87, 99, 105-20; Douglas J. Ollila Jr., "The Work People's College: Immigrant Education for Adjustment and Solidarity," in *For the Common Good, Finnish Immigrants and the Radical Response to Industrial America,* ed. Michael G. Karni and Douglas J. Ollila Jr. (Superior, Wis.: Työmies Society, 1977), 102-9.
35. Heinilä, *Work People's College,* 56-57, 104, 172; Ollila, "Work People's College," 112; Kostiainen, "Work People's College," 307-8.
36. See Ilmonen, *Amerikan suomalaisten sivistyshistoria. Jälkimmäinen osa,* 157.
37. Yrjö Leiwo, *Hakemisto (Politiikkaa ja merkkimiehiä)* (Helsinki: SKS, 1935), passim; see Keijo Virtanen, *Finnish Emigrants (1860-1930) in the International Overseas Return Migration Movement* (Forssa: Institute of Migration, 1979), 209.
38. Ritva Heikkilä, "Kuparisaaren suomalaisia," *Oma markka 8 (1976):* 29; cf. Koivunalho, *Amerikansuomalaisten,* 21.
39. Työmies, July 7, 1927.
40. Timo Riippa, "The Finnish Immigrant Theatre in the United States," in *Finnish Diaspora II: United States,* ed. Michael G. Karni (Toronto: Multicultural History Society of Canada, 1981), 283.
41. *Ajan kaiku. CSJ:n Port Arthurin osasto 36 vuotta 1903-1939* (Sudbury, Ont.: n.p., 1939), 9.
42. Taru Sundsten, *Amerikansuomalainen työväenteatteri ja näytelmäkirjallisuus vuosina 1900-39.* (Turku: Siirtolaisuusinstituutti, 1977), 18; Koivunalho, *Amerikansuomalaisten,* 60.
43. *Industrialisti,* December 15, 1929
44. *Industrialisti,* February 6, 1930; see also Sundsten, *Amerikansuomalainen,* 19; Koivunalho, *Amerikansuomalaisten,* 61.
45. Sulkanen, *Amerikan suomalaisen,* 113
46. See Koivunalho, *Amerikansuomalaisten,* 33, 49; Riippa, "Finnish Immigrant Theatre," 278.
47. Seventieth Anniversary Souvenir Journal 1903-1973 (Superior, Wis.: Työmies Society, 1973), 31; cf. F. J. Syrjälä, *Historia-aiheita Ameriikan suomalaisesta työväenliikkeestä* (Fitchburg, Mass.: Raivaaja Publishing Company, 1925), 93.
48. Työmies, February 26, 1927.
49. Sundsten, *Amerikansuomalainen,* 22-23, see sources.
50. Riippa, "Finnish Immigrant Theatre," 278.
51. The theater club of the Gardner, Massachusetts, Finnish Socialist Society, minutes, September 1, 1912, September 17, 1916, March 6, 1921, Gardner, Massachusetts Finnish Socialist Society Collection, DGH, TYYH/S/m/8/56-59.
52. See Riippa, "Finnish Immigrant Theatre," 278-89, esp. the John Wiita memoirs.
53. Kero, *Suuren lännen,* 166.
54. *Raittius-Kalenteri vuodelle 1911,* 145; see also Hoglund, Finnish Immigrants, 1960, 96; Sundsten, *Amerikansuomalainen,* 6; Koivunalho, *Amerikansuomalaisten,* 12-13.
55. Koivunalho, *Amerikansuomalaisten,* 16-17.
56. Lehtinen, *Raittiusliike,* 85.
57. *Kalevan Naisten historian ääriviivoja 1904-1954*

(n.p.: Kalevan Naiset, 1954), 7, 34, 65, 88; also Koivunalho, *Amerikansuomalaisten,* 20–21; Riippa, " Finnish Immigrant Theatre," 280.

58. Riippa, "Finnish Immigrant Theatre," 280–81, see sources.
59. Koivunalho, *Amerikansuomalaisten,* 19–20; cf. Myhrman, "Finland-Swedish Immigrants," 193.
60. Riippa, "Finnish Immigrant Theatre," 281; see also Timo Tiusanen, *Teatterimme hahmottuu: Näyttämötaiteemme kehitystie kansanrunoudesta itsenäisyyden ajan alkuun* (Rauma: Kirjayhtymä, 1969), 154–61.
61. Sundsten, *Amerikansuomalainen,* 7–8; see also Syrjälä, *Historia-aiheita,* 110; *Neljäkymmentä vuotta. Kuvauksia ja muistelmia Amerikan suomalaisen työväenliikkeen toimitaipaleellta 1906–1946,* ed. Leo Mattson (Superior, Wis.: Finnish American Mutual Aid Society, 1946), 33, 117, 131, 157; Sulkanen, *Amerikan suomalaisen,* 347.
62. *Yhdysvaltain Suomalaisen Sosialistijärjestön viidennen edustajakokouksen pöytäkirja Chicagossa, Ill. lokakuun 25 p:stä marraskuun 3 p:ään 1919,* ed. J. F. Mäki (Superior, Wis.: S. S.Järjestön Toimeenpaneva Komitea, 1920), passim.
63. Sundsten, *Amerikansuomalainen,* 28–29; Koivunalho, *Amerikansuomalaisten,* 27–28; see Heinilä, *Work People's College,* 174.
64. Kolehmainen, *Finns in America,* 111; Koivunalho, *Amerikansuomalaisten,* 82–83.
65. Kero, *Suuren lännen,* 168; Koivunalho, *Amerikansuomalaisten,* 45.
66. See Sundsten, *Amerikansuomalainen,* 23–24; Koivunalho, *Amerikansuomalaisten,* 47.
67. Riippa, "Finnish Immigrant Theatre," 282–83.
68. Koivunalho, *Amerikansuomalaisten,* 78; Riippa, "Finnish Immigrant Theatre," 283.
69. *Taistelu oikeistovaaraa vastaan. Kominternin opetuksia Amerikan suomalaiselle työväestölle* (Superior, Wis.: Amerikan Suom. Sos. Kustannusliikkeiden Liitto, n.d.), passim; see also Sundsten, *Amerikansuomalainen,* 35; Riippa, "Finnish Immigrant Theatre," 284.
70. Kero, *Suuren lännen,* 168–69.
71. On immigrant drama literature, see Sundsten, *Amerikansuomalainen,* 43–90.
72. FSF Proceedings 1912, 54.
73. Ilmonen, *Amerikan suomalaisten sivistyshistoria. Edellinen osa,* 49–50; Lehtinen, *Raittiusliike,* 21.
74. Kero, *Suuren lännen,* 172–73.
75. Ilmonen, *Amerikan suomalaisten sivistyshistoria. Edellinen osa,* 207–12; Engelberg, *Suomi ja Amerikan suomalaiset,* 196, 199; Kero, *Suuren lännen,* 172.
76. Ilmonen, *Amerikan suomalaisten sivistyshistoria. Edellinen osa,* 213–15.
77. See SKRW Society (Republic, Mich.) minutes, January 10, 1898, DGH, TYYH/S/m/8/194.
78. Ilmonen, *Amerikan suomalaisten sivistyshistoria. Edellinen osa,* 51.
79. Ilmonen, *Amerikan suomalaisten sivistyshistoria. Edellinen osa,* 219–22; Ilmonen, *Amerikan suomalaisten sivistyshistoria. Jälkimmäinen osa,* 130–31; Engelberg, *Suomi ja Amerikan suomalaiset,* 240.
80. Veli-Matti Henttonen, "Jazz Music in Finland before the Winter War," in *The Impact of American Culture: Proceedings of an International Seminar in Turku, April 17–18, 1982,* ed. Eero Kuparinen and Keijo Virtanen (Turku: Institute of History, General History, 1983), 121–26; Keijo Virtanen and Esko Heikkonen, *Amerikkalaisen kulttuurin leviäminen Suomeen. Tutkimusraportti Suomen Akatemian tukemasta projektista* (Turku: Turun yliopiston Historian laitos, 1985), 121–22.
81. Ilmonen, *Amerikan suomalaisten sivistyshistoria. Jälkimmäinen osa,* 132–33.
82. Myhrman, "Finland-Swedish Immigrants," 194–97.
83. For more information, see Ilmonen, *Amerikan suomalaisten sivistyshistoria. Jälkimmäinen osa,* 134–38.
84. Pekka Gronow and Ilpo Saunio, *Äänilevytieto* (Porvoo: WSOY, 1970), 45–46.
85. Ilmonen, *Amerikan suomalaisten sivistyshistoria. Jälkimmäinen osa,* 138–40; Engelberg, *Suomi ja Amerikan suomalaiset,* 302–9.

86. YL Amerikassa, ed. Oiva Ruusuvuori (Helsinki: Kivi, 1939), passim; Engelberg, *Suomi ja Amerikan suomalaiset*, 307-8; Merja Dyhr, *Amerikansuomalaisten matkailu kotimaahan vuosina 1920-1947*. Pro gradu-tutkielma (Turku: Turun yliopisto, 1979), 82-87.

87. Veli-Matti Henttonen, *Jazz musiikkina ja kulttuuri-ilmiönä Suomessa ennen toista maailmansotaa. Tutkimus "mustan" musiikin ensimmäisistä vuosikymmenistä Suomessa*. Pro gradu-tutkielma (Turku: Turun yliopisto, 1983), 34-36; cf. Ilpo Hakasalo, *Malmstenista Marioniin* (Helsinki: Tammi, 1979), 10.

88. Aimo Halila and Paul Sirmeikkö, *Suomen Voimistelu- ja Urheiluliitto. Ensimmäinen osa 1900-1917* (Vammala: SVUL, 1960), 19.

89. *Suomen Voimistelu- ja Urheiluliitto vv. 1906-1926*, ed. Lauri Santala (Helsinki: WSOY, 1926), 19.

90. See Hannu Salonen, *Amerikansuomalainen urheilutoiminta Yhdysvalloissa 1900-1940*. Pro gradu-tutkielma (Turku: Turun yliopisto, 1978), 9.

91. On the founding of the clubs, see Ilmonen, *Amerikan suomalaisten sivistyshistoria. Jälkimmäinen osa*, 66-67; Engelberg, *Suomi ja Amerikan suomalaiset*, 200; Kero, *Suuren lännen*, 174; Salonen, *Amerikansuomalainen urheilutoiminta*, 17-23.

92. *Urheilu-viesti II* (1909), 15-16, 33-36.

93. Cf. Salonen, *Amerikansuomalainen urheilutoiminta*, 27.

94. Ilmonen, *Amerikan suomalaisten sivistyshistoria. Jälkimmäinen osa*, 66.

95. Engelberg, *Suomi ja Amerikan suomalaiset*, 200; Kero, *Suuren lännen*, 174; Salonen, *Amerikansuomalainen urheilutoiminta*, 18, 95.

96. *Suomen Urheilulehti,* May 23,1912; cf. Salonen, *Amerikansuomalainen urheilutoiminta*, 21-22.

97. *Urheilu-viesti 2* (1910): 11-14.

98. Ilmonen, *Amerikan suomalaisten sivistyshistoria. Jälkimmäinen osa*, 72-74; Engelberg, *Suomi ja Amerikan suomalaiset*, 241; Salonen, *Amerikansuomalainen urheilutoiminta*, 32-33.

99. Juhani Paasivirta, *Suomen kuva Yhdysvalloissa 1800-luvun lopulta 1960-luvulle. Ääriviivoja* (Porvoo: WSOY, 1962), 90-91.

100. For example, *Raivaaja*, October 11, 1916, May 29, 1920.

101. Cf. Salonen, *Amerikansuomalainen urheilutoiminta*, 64-70.

102. *Raivaaja*, January 24, 1926.

103. Cf. Kero, *Suuren lännen*, 176-177; Salonen, *Amerikansuomalainen urheilutoiminta*, 67-70.

104. Ilmonen, *Amerikan suomalaisten sivistyshistoria. Jälkimmäinen osa*, 69-70; Engelberg, *Suomi ja Amerikan suomalaiset*, 200-201; Salonen, *Amerikansuomalainen urheilutoiminta*, 42.

105. *Suomen Urheilulehti*, December 21, 1931; cf. Ilmonen, *Amerikan suomalaisten sivistyshistoria. Jälkimmäinen osa*, 68; Engelberg, *Suomi ja Amerikan suomalaiset*, 200; Salonen, *Amerikansuomalainen urheilutoiminta*, 44-46.

106. Ilmonen, *Amerikan suomalaisten sivistyshistoria. Jälkimmäinen osa*, 76-77; Salonen, *Amerikansuomalainen urheilutoiminta*, 46; Virtanen, *Finnish Emigrants*, 217.

107. Paavo Karikko and Mauno Koski, *Paavo Nurmi* (Helsinki: Weilin & Göös, 1965), 35-38, 54-66, 72; cf. Ilmonen *Amerikan suomalaisten sivistyshistoria. Jälkimmäinen osa*, 74-76.

108. Paasivirta, *Suomen kuva*, 93; Salonen, *Amerikansuomalainen urheilutoiminta*, 57-58.

109. Sulo Kolkka and Helge Nygren, *Paavo Nurmi* (Keuruu: Otava, 1974), 66-67; Karikko and Koski, *Paavo Nurmi*, 73, 106, 139-40.

110. Ilmonen, *Amerikan suomalaisten sivistyshistoria. Jälkimmäinen osa*, 71-72, 78-79; Kero, *Suuren lännen*, 175; Salonen, *Amerikansuomalainen urheilutoiminta*, 53-55.

111. For example, *Suomen Urheilulehti,* January 11, September 12 and 15, 1932, June 8, 1936; see also Ilmonen *Amerikan suomalaisten sivistyshistoria. Jälkimmäinen osa*, 72; Salonen, *Amerikansuomalainen urheilutoiminta*, 86-87.

112. Salonen, *Amerikansuomalainen urheilutoiminta*,

84, see sources.

113. *Suomen Urheilulehti,* June 9, 1938, April 14, 1939; *New Yorkin Uutiset,* June 21, 1938.

114. *Raivaaja,* January 24, 1927, January 28, 1930; cf. Salonen, *Amerikansuomalainen urheilutoiminta,* 92–93.

115. *Suomen Urheilulehti,* August 31, 1936, February 15 and October 28, 1937, May 16, 1938; cf. Salonen, *Amerikansuomalainen urheilutoiminta,* 88, see sources.

# Papers and Publications

*Auvo Kostiainen*

Many types of publishing activities flourished in the Finnish American community, thus providing the immigrants with information and possibilities of network of contacts across the extensive continent and many geographical regions. This chapter discusses the formation of publishing companies, most of which were short-lived, although a number were active even for decades. Many types of books and other publications were issued. They ranged from religious to political publications, including children's books, guidebooks, and leaflets. Mostly, the publications reflected the ideological split in the ethnic community.

Immigrants brought with them cultures of their own, which were reflected strongly in the literary interests of various ethnic groups. Newspapers meant for immigrants in North American colonies were established as early as the 1700s. The most lively period for the immigrant press occurred after the First World War; in 1917, there were a total of 1,300 newspapers and periodicals published in a great variety of languages.[1] Finnish American cultural and educational activity is to an important extent characterized by the publishing of a large variety of newspapers and periodicals, yearbooks, fiction, and other literature.

Only a few thorough studies have been done on Finnish publishing activities in North America, although there are bibliographies published on both sides of the Atlantic by John I. Kolehmainen and others.[2] The Finnish individuals and communities in the United States as well as in Canada have left a large inheritance of printed materials, and therefore I examine three main questions: Who issued the printed materials? How extensive was the volume? What was the life span of the publishing activities? Considering the publishing activities, a broad understanding of the immigrant society is needed.

Since Finnish immigrants as whole were fairly literate, they were in this sense better equipped compared to many other groups of immigrants. When Finns began to land on American shores in greater numbers during the latter half of the nineteenth century, the need for literature in the Finnish language became evident, and the number of volumes began to increase. The first works published in the Finnish language in the United States appeared, so far as is known, as early as 1858–59, but not as a product on the part of the Finns themselves. The American Tract Society came out with six small

**FIGURE 1.** Finns published a variety of newspapers and periodicals, representing a variety of ideological or societal orientations. (Source: IMT Photo collections. USA_0452)

tracts in the Finnish language dealing with religion and temperance.[3] The first publications for which the Finnish Americans themselves were responsible are thought to be a Finnish-language sermon by P. O. Grape and the newspaper *Amerikan Suomalainen Lehti* (American Finnish Journal), edited by J. A. Muikku, dating back to 1876. The first actual belletristic work was evidently a comedy titled *Kappale Kapakkaelämää* (A Piece of Saloon Life), written by K. A. Jurva, which appeared in 1889. Equivalent literary efforts were possibly made even earlier.

The energy of Finnish American publishing was concentrated mainly on the production of newspapers. These were also very suitable for spreading factual information for immigrants, to help in the organization of immigrant activities, and to help immigrants in adjusting to American culture and society. The newspapers were on the whole business ventures belonging to one or more persons or companies. According to Häkli, literature imported from Finland played a big role commercially in the Finnish American book market. In terms of their value, books shipped to America from Finland at the beginning of the century reached tens of thousands of Finnish marks annually. After Finland achieved national independence in 1917, the value was multiplied.[4]

Finnish American publishing was in general scattered in the sense that there were hundreds of publishers, with many of them being short-lived individual enterprises targeting the publication of a certain book or other publication such as a book celebrating the anniversary of a society. On the other hand, there were also numerous publishers who published many titles or issued a serial for years, in some cases even decades. The publishers may be divided into four main groups: those publishing religious, temperance, labor, and other literature. In an earlier study, I discovered information on 289 publishers. The scale of publication varied, from publishers whose career was short and may include only one piece of publication, to publishers who printed titles over several decades. Of the 289 publishers, 96 (33.2 percent) printed religious pieces, 23 (7.9 percent) temperance-related pieces, and 60 (20.8 percent) labor-related materials; the remaining 110 (38.2 percent) publishers did not have a clear connection with any of the previously mentioned groups.[5] An additional factor complementing the number of publishers were the special anniversary or commemorative publications of festive occasions by various societies.

When the geographical distribution of the Finnish publishers operating in America is considered, the state of Michigan is clearly the most heavily represented (27.1 percent), followed by Massachusetts (18.2 percent), Minnesota (17.9 percent), and New York (11.9 percent). These are precisely the states with the heaviest concentrations of Finnish Americans and also the states with the most vigorous Finnish American culture. Considering the activity of the 289 Finnish American publishers in a chronological light, only 14 publishers, or about 5 percent, were in the business before the year 1900. Activity was liveliest in the period between 1920 and 1940, when 36.6 percent of the publishers were working. The figure for the period between 1901 and 1920 was 30.4 percent, and for the post-1941 period 22.4 percent.[6] This chronology in turn reflects the "life cycle" of Finnish immigration, since the immigrant community was at its liveliest stages during the early decades of the twentieth century.

### Active Workers' Publishing Companies

One of the oldest Finnish American publishing companies was the Suomalais-amerikkalainen kustannusyhtiö (Finnish American Publishing Company), founded in 1894 in Brooklyn, New York. It was a most productive enterprise that brought out more than seventy small volumes, mainly booklets in translation of rather slight significance, but also cookbooks and historical works. Among its publications was also the literary periodical *Edistys* (Progress), which appeared in the years 1898 and 1899. Another New York–based early publisher calling itself New Yorkin Lehti (New York Journal) printed a newspaper with the same title. There was also a famous independent or liberal newspaper, *New Yorkin Uutiset* (New York News), which was started in 1906 and continued until 1996.[7] Over the years, this newspaper company also published a large quantity of other materials, mostly novels and magazines.

The concept of publisher was quite versatile. The publisher could be an individual person, a group of individuals working together, a printing house, an organization, or quite frequently a Finnish American newspaper company that carried on many activities, such as book printing and selling or the actual newspaper printing. On the other hand, there were quite a few joint operations between publishers. One example of this involved publishers who were active within the fold of the Finnish American working-class movement. They frequently operated as a team to produce various titles, such as the newspapers *Työmies* (Worker), *Toveri* (Comrade), and *Raivaaja* (Pioneer). These publishers even joined forces, and their cooperation took on established forms. Around 1910, they founded a league of Finnish American socialist publishers called Amerikansuomalaisten sosialististen kustannusliikkeiden liitto, whose membership varied from time to time, depending on the ideological and organizational developments taking place within the Finnish American labor movement.

Among the largest publishing enterprises in the Finnish American community was the Workers' Socialist Publishing Company of Duluth, Minnesota. Its main product was the newspaper *Industrialisti* (Industrialist), preceded by the *Sosialisti* (Socialist), which was founded in 1914, and due to government pressure toward the paper was printed briefly under the title *Teollisuustyöläinen* (Industrial Worker). The *Industrialisti* competed with the *Työmies* in boasting which newspaper was representative of the "true working-class movement." This publishing firm was in close cooperation with the Work People's College of Duluth. Over the decades, it printed syndicalist books, novels, and calendars as well as various kinds of periodicals.

In the West, there functioned the Western Workmen's Co-operative Publishing Company and specifically the newspaper *Toveri*, which was brought out under its wing. The company was founded in 1907 for the purpose of satisfying the needs of the Finnish working people in the western United States. It was also responsible for a number of periodicals designed for children and other young readers, as well as the women's journal *Toveritar* (Woman Comrade). The *Toveri* was discontinued in 1931 when it merged with the *Työmies,* while its printing machinery was transported to Soviet Karelia to establish Finnish-language publishing there along with the thousands of American Finns in order to build a "Republic of Work."

These developments show that the operations of the publishers representing the labor movement were quite centralized. The labor activities in general circulated around their newspaper enterprises, which in a way formed the core of their operations as a whole. In the United States, publishing activities were mostly taken care of by the newspaper publishing companies of the *Raivaaja, Työmies, Toveri, Eteenpäin* (Forward), and *Industrialisti,* and, in Canada, around the *Työkansa* (Working People), in the beginning, and, at a later date, *Vapaus* (Freedom), and even later *Vapaa Sana* (Free Press). The *Työkansan kustannusliike,* mentioned by Häkli, operated in Sudbury, Ontario, between 1907 and 1915, concentrating on the publication of *Työkansa*. The newspaper *Vapaus*, which started publication in 1917, is to be regarded as almost a direct heir to the earlier one. To a very large extent, the publication program of both ventures included the same type of material as that of the Finnish working-class newspapers on the American side of the border—namely, short stories, novels, and poetry written by Finnish Americans, along with various periodicals and socialistic literature in translation. It would also seem that the left radical newspapers *Työkansa* and *Vapaus* published more books and periodicals when compared with other publishing firms established by Finns in Canada. In 1931, *Vapaa Sana* was started as a consequence of ideological quarrels within the left-dominated *Vapaus* newspaper. It began as a social democratic media, and later became more conservative in tone. The paper continues publication today.

The Työmies Society came into existence as the organization that published *Työmies,* which was born in 1903 in Worcester, Massachusetts; moved to Hancock, Michigan, in 1904; and then to Superior, Wisconsin, in 1914, where it remained until 1998. The Työmies Society published newspapers, periodicals, and books for Finnish-speaking Americans to advance the ideas of the international working-class movement, to deliver information, and to "educate" Finnish immigrants ideologically. It also published many kinds of seasonal, humorous, and children's periodicals, as well as dozens of books and pamphlets. The most famous humorous periodical was *Lapatossu (*Henpeck Fellow*),* as well as its successor, *Punikki* (The Red), which in turn was followed by *Kansan huumori* (People's Humor) in the mid-1930s. The Työmies Society as a whole appears to be among the Finnish-language publishers with the largest

**FIGURE 2.** *Punikki* (The Red) was a popular leftist cartoon journal, by written, illustrated, and edited by K. A. Suvanto. Here, during the hard times in 1929, a worker is trying to sit on the same bench of prosperity with big capital. (Source: *Punikki,* January 15, 1929, DGH)

number of literature printed during several decades. Also, it must be remembered that the Työmies Society became a political, social, and cultural center with a lot of activities, and many political left activities were debated, planned, and put into practice from the circle of this society. It was a radical center along with the *Raivaaja* group in the East and the *Industrialisti* group in Minnesota.

There were also labor newspapers and literature appealing to women, including the newspapers *Toveritar* from 1911 to 1931, followed by *Työläisnainen* (Working Woman) from 1930 to 1936 and *Naisten Viiri* (Women's Banner) from 1936 to 1978. Several newspapers also published special women's as well as young people's or children's sections.

The "golden age" of the Työmies Society's publishing operations as well as of the newspaper itself was between 1910 and 1930. At its peak, the paper's circulation reached close to 10,000 subscribers. The retreat of the old immigrant generation began to show up first in the paper's merger with the *Toveri* of Astoria, Oregon, in 1931 and later, in 1950, with the *Eteenpäin* of New York, after which the newspaper's masthead of began to carry the name *Työmies-Eteenpäin*. It was one of the longest-running Finnish immigrant newspapers in the United States, and at its peak it had the largest circulation. Throughout its ninety-five year history, *Työmies* remained an outspoken critic of American capitalism and a community voice for left-wing Finnish Americans, advocating socialism, cooperative ideas and practices, and labor unions. The newspaper has continued from the 1980s as the *Finnish American Reporter* in English, and later began publishing in Hancock, Michigan, under the auspices of Finlandia University.[8] This turn may also refer to the new combinations of the Finnish American descendants, who are less interested in political quarrels and are more interested in Finnish ethnic activities in general. In order to survive, *the Finnish American Reporter* has thus changed its media interests to cater to its readers.

The Raivaaja Publishing Company, which is still doing business in the town of Fitchburg, Massachusetts,[9] was founded in 1905 to serve the membership of the Finnish American labor movement in the northeastern states. The heyday of this enterprise dates back to the second decade of the twentieth century. In the period between 1905 and 1954, the company was originally called the Suomalainen Sosialistinen Kustannusliike (Finnish Socialist Publishing Company) and later renamed the Raivaaja Publishing Company. The newspaper was its main product, and it brought out eight different periodicals and a total of seventy-six different books or booklets. In addition, as Kolehmainen points out, the firm published a considerable number of plays and pamphlets.[10]

Each major labor newspaper had several publications serving the Finnish American "workers' community." These included women's papers and the special agricultural paper *Pelto ja Koti* (Farm and Home) among others. The monthly *Säkeniä* (Sparks) was produced by the Raivaaja Publishing Company in Fitchburg, and the humorous *Lapatossu* had its heyday in Hancock. The literature that Finnish -American socialists printed included textbooks, fiction, poetry, essays, plays, various kinds of anniversary publications, calendars, and so forth. Perhaps the most important educational literature to be published was ideological, for the majority of the so-called classic works by socialist theorists have been published in Finnish in the United States. The fiction, whether translated or original works by Finnish American socialist authors, reflected "class consciousness." Additionally, there were a number of periodicals such as *Viesti* (Message), a theoretical labor journal published during the 1930s by the Communist Finnish Federation in Brooklyn, New York.

Finnish American cooperative societies that were closely connected to the labor movement were active in the publishing field as well as in social and cultural endeavors. The largest number of publications came from the Keskusosuuskunta (Central Cooperative Exchange or Central Cooperative Wholesale [CCE/CCW]) of Superior, Wisconsin, and its successors—with various manuals and annuals put out by the cooperative movement as well as pamphlets of an educational and political nature. The CCE/CCW published, for example, the Finnish-language newspaper *Työväen osuustoimintalehti* (Workers' Cooperative Daily) between 1930 and 1965, and the English-language journal Cooperative Builder between 1962 and 1982. They aimed at mainly spreading the idea of cooperative activities, in which they in fact were very successful, especially in the Midwest.

### Religion-Based Publishing

It would appear that the publication of a newspaper has been the point of departure from which advances have been made into other publishing activity—evidently for the reason that this was the way to lay a firmer fiscal basis for operations. The Suomalais-amerikkalainen kustannusyhtiö in Hancock, Michigan, was more clearly a publisher connected with the Suomi Synod. Even in this case, newspapers and periodicals played a fairly central role. The importance of the revenue gained from newspapers to the publishing companies is clearly indicated, for example, by the fact that the income of the Raivaaja Publishing Company from the sale of books—both its own and those imported from Finland—amounted to $1,204 in 1905, whereas income from subscriptions to the newspaper amounted to $2,888. It wasn't until 1913 that proceeds from book sales exceeded the revenue from newspaper subscriptions for the first time. The Finnish Lutheran Book Concern, on the other hand, emphasized the sale of literature, which was of central importance, whereas subscription payments for newspapers and periodicals were conspicuously less important.[11]

Hancock, Michigan, was the seat of Suomi-Opisto (Suomi College) and the most important religious center of the Finnish American community since the late 1800s when the Suomi Opisto (Suomi College) was established under its wing. The clergymen belonging to the synod engaged in newspaper publishing, producing *Paimen-sanomia* (Shepherd's Tidings) and *Amerikan Suometar* (American Finn) and established a bookstore in Hancock. The convention of the Suomi Synod held in 1900 voted to purchase the two newspapers and the bookstore, and these enterprises were all combined to operate under the Suomalainen Luterilainen Kustannusliike (Finnish Lutheran Book Concern). In addition to printing *Paimen-sanomia* and *Amerikan Suometar,* this company engaged vigorously in other publishing activity as well, and its list of publications included more than a hundred different books and booklets, Bibles, hymnbooks, religious poetry, textbooks, and guidebooks, as well as novels with a religious content. Moreover, the company issued three other religious periodicals and church calendars. The oldest appears to be *Kirkollinen Kalenteri* (Church Calendar), started in 1902, which was changed to *Suomi konferenssin kirkollinen kalenteri* (Church Calendar of the Suomi Conference) in 1962 and again in 1981 to *Suomi konferenssin vuosikirja;* at the same time, there were printed English versions of the calendar book named *Suomi Conference Yearbook.* Led by the Suomi Synod and Suomalainen Luterilainen Kustannusliike in Hancock, a remarkable number of other publishers of religious literature appeared, such as, for example, Suomi College with its annuals, the college's student body, and different associations of clergymen belonging to the Suomi Synod.

Among religious organizations involved in publishing, the other important church was the Apostolis-luterilainen kirkko (Apostolic Lutheran Church), otherwise known as Laestadians. Not much is known about the Apostolic Lutheran publishing activities. There were over 20,000 Finnish members of diverse Laestadian sects as late as 1946 in the United States, but it appears as if their publishing operations have been fairly weak. Evidently, one reason for this is the rather loose organization of their church on the national level—they did not, for instance, have any central seat corresponding to that of the Evangelical Lutherans. The best-preserved publications have been the Laestadians' accounts of "great assemblies" and their seven periodicals, as noted by Kolehmainen, as well as their newspaper *Valvoja* (Guardian). Within the Apostolic Lutheran Church there functioned the publishing company Rauha (Peace), which was responsible for the *Rauhan tervehdys* (Greeting of Peace). The founding of this publishing company dates back to 1921, and it continued until the early 1980s; the publishing company also issued an English-language monthly Greetings of Peace from 1938 until at least 1981, first in Calumet and then Laurium, Michigan. It also printed a number of hymnbooks in the Finnish language compiled by Finnish Americans. In 1932, it published a collection of songs in English and Finnish for Sunday school and confirmation school children. It seems that the Apostolic Lutherans very much followed in the footsteps of the Laestadian group in Finland, copying also the title of their most important journal, *Rauhan tervehdys*.[12]

Two other large Finnish American church organizations, Kansalliskirkko (National Church) and Lähetyskirkko (Congregational Church), were also fairly active in the publishing trade. Evidence for this is found in Kolehmainen's catalog listing fifteen periodicals published by the Kansalliskirkko. He also noted that the Lähetyskirkko was the publisher of seventeen periodicals. In the light of the information available, these two churches engaged in actual book publishing on a modest scale.[13]

## Belles Lettres and Guidebooks

As has already been noted, a special feature of Finnish American publishing was its widespread activity. At the same time, the volume of printings written in the exotic Finnish language remained quite small in North America.

Many an active society had a small library of its own, which acquired and collected various types of literature. Depending on the ideological orientation and other relevant features, the libraries were inclined to gather certain types of literature. Finnish churches or congregations held religious literature—such as Bibles, hymnbooks, and other related literature—usually following the spiritual direction of the group. Temperance groups perhaps did not have as large a collection of publications as churches and labor groups, but many active labor associations used to have quite a few publications in their libraries. There, it was possible to find a number of novels, short stories, and calendars produced by the group itself, such as the novels by Eemeli Parras or Helmi Mattson. In addition, a number of translations into Finnish included the famous classics of the working-class movement by Karl Marx, relevant novels by Jack London, or historical studies by Morris Hillquit, a leading American socialist at the time.

Helmi Mattson (1890–1974) serves as an outstanding example of the many female activists in Finnish American society in general, and particularly of the female left writer radicals. She was a member of a left labor group, and after the Communist group was established, she adopted its ideology. She was born Lampila in Finland, moved to the United States via Canada in 1911, and got involved in labor activities in International Falls in northern Minnesota, after being hired as a servant. Shortly after their marriage, she and husband, William Mattson, moved to Astoria, Oregon, where she became editor of *Toveritar*, the left women's paper. Mattson followed in the footsteps of earlier leftist editors of *Toveritar* such as Selma Jokela-McKone (or Makkonen) in Astoria, and was an important editor during the 1920s. Ida Pasanen, another well-known Finnish American immigrant woman and labor activist, strongly affected the socialist line *Toveritar* adopted.[14]

After the paper closed in 1930, Helmi Mattson and her husband moved to New York, where she was employed by the Communist paper *Eteenpäin*. At the end of 1930s, they moved to Kelso, Washington, where she lived until her death. During her life, she wrote 500 poems and published five novels in book format. Additionally, she published seven other novels in newspaper serials. In her books, she described the life of immigrant women and men, their developing class consciousness, and their fight against the capitalist society. Many of her poems also included romantic themes, and during her later years also her interest in history. Mattson was a devoted leftist, although it seems that her ideological stand was not at all times "strong enough," which apparently caused some interruptions of her editorial work, and also aroused criticism of a number of her literary works.[15]

In Finland, a number of early feminists gained attention; for example, Minna Canth became a well-known playwright whose plays were frequently discussed and performed on Finnish American theater stages. Still it seems that Finnish American women in general were not as active as writers as males, which may be a reflection even of the Old Country traditions. As shown earlier, however, quite a few women were active as speakers and organizers during the late 1800s and early 1900s. Particularly, there were labor activists such as Ida Pasanen, Helmi Mattson, and Selma Jokela-McCone who were writers and commentators. A number of others were visible in the press and at various meetings, such as businesswoman Maggie Walz (originally Margareeta Niranen), who gained position in Michigan press circles, was a publisher of the women's paper *Naisten Lehti* (Women's News) as well as business manager for the *Amerikan Suometar* (American Finn) newspaper, and was a Michigan delegate at the American Women's Suffrage Convention.[16]

Rev. Milma Lappala (1879–1950) was an active Finnish American religious leader. Born in Kuopio in Finland, she moved to the United States in 1901, studied in Boston in an evangelical institution, and later married Rev. Risto Lappala. Actually, she was the first Finnish-origin woman to be ordained as a minister (in the Unitarian group) for the Alango, Minnesota, Finnish church in 1916. If Lappala was not an active writer, she was widely known as a very gifted speaker.[17]

An example of religiously oriented writing is the autobiographical novel written by Hugo Hillilä, who completed his studies at Suomi College in 1918. He became a minister of the synod and a well-known industrious preacher, writer, and poet. His book *Valinkauhassa* (In the Ladle) describes the life of the immigrants in the country in various workplaces, along with strikes and confrontations in the immigrant communities, including confrontations between various immigrant groups. The basic tone of the text is to emphasize the importance of the spiritual and religious activities in the country.[18] A number of religious guides were also published, including works by Joseph Salmu and John Ruokasmäki. Their books were designed to follow and interpret the Bible, with frequent citations and instructions. Rev. Salmu's work, for example, demanded that the readers had to avoid a lighthearted lifestyle or being hypocritical in their religious life.[19] On the other hand, John Ruokasmäki structured his religious guide on the creation of the world by God, providing also geographical explanations for the Great Deluge and the Ice Age.[20]

The works that appeared in print have been exceedingly diverse in both character and quality. The publications varied from magazines and textbooks to novels, poetry, plays, and histories. Attention has been drawn, furthermore, to the marketing of trivial literature, especially in the early days, that is, the late 1800s and the beginning of the 1900s. Thus Elis Sulkanen, in his history of the Finnish American labor movement, complained that "the bourgeois societies and their newspapers" distributed "dream books and other curious stories"; he stressed that the publishers turning out literature for the labor movement had screened out the trash from their output.[21]

The uneven level of the Finnish writers in America, whether on the political right or the left, often caused the publishers to hesitate before taking economic risks with manuscripts. The result was frequently a falling back on translated works, and the beginners in the literary craft were obliged to publish their own writings, such as novels, historical accounts, memoirs, poems and songs, as well as prayer books.

Immigrants needed publications in their own language because of linguistic skills and also for information and other needs to be fulfilled conveniently. These publications quite often carried a lot of information dealing with the Old Country and various transnational activities. As long as works were published in Finnish, a lot of news and other information from the old homeland was available. This was especially important during times of crisis in Finland, when the emigrants longed for more exact information about what was going on in Finland. This was particularly important during the Civil War year 1918 and during the Second World War and its aftermath.

The journals and calendar books by immigrant Finns included advice on the American government, legislation, and many practical matters. Even guidebooks for various practical tasks were produced. Thus the well-known socialist agitator Moses Hahl published in 1906 a 195-page book, *Uudempi kansantalous* (New National Economics), which appears to be based on his own reading of various classics such as Malthus as well as socialist theorists. He strongly attacked the capitalist system of economics, which in his opinion was wrong "in all respects" and full of false assumptions. His book described how socialist economics aimed to help humanity and real democracy instead.[22]

Literature included advice for farming, religious practices, and cooking. In addition, there were special books on cooperative associations such as a guidebook titled *Osuustoimintaopas* by the well-known cooperative store leader and newspaperman Severi Alanne. Another cooperative guidebook translated into English with the title *Co-operative Activity and Its Importance in the Class Struggle* was produced by William Marttila, and had a very strong emphasis on political leftist activity.[23] Alanne and Marttila were also active "teachers" for the immigrant Finns. For example, Alanne produced a large English-Finnish dictionary with subsequent revised editions, and English-language guidebooks for cooperative store activities. Marttila wrote guidebooks for farmers. A large variety of other guides were also published. For example, in 1906 a legal guide for functionaries in a civic association, including directions on how meetings should be conducted, was published. Originally written by Uriah Smith in English, the Finnish translation was edited by John Stone, and became known as the founder of the Kaleva knighthood (the Knights of Kaleva and the Ladies of Kaleva).[24] A socialist newspaperman, Henry Askeli, wrote a book on eating the right kind of diet, which included information on vitamins, overweight problems, and many other problems.[25]

Children were served by various publications. There were a few children's journals such as *Lasten Lehti* (Children's Journal). Primers were prepared that reflected the ideological directions of the publisher. Thus, for example, the Lutheran publisher in Hancock printed a primer for Finnish children in America (*Lukukirja Amerikan suomalaisille lapsille*) in 1915. It was compiled by a committee nominated during the twenty-fifth convention of the Suomi Synod. The contents were made up of several Old Country children's verses or proverbs and poems, but also included short stories on Finland as well as America. An essay about an old migrant from Finland to the Delaware Colony of the 1600s was also included. In addition, some information on the traditions of the Old Country were offered as well as some lessons for the Finnish language. The book was apparently used for the nonofficial summer or Sunday school classes offered in many locations for Finnish children. This primer was compiled from the "church people's" point of view, aiming at strengthening the ethical conviction of religion but also making the Old Country traditions, customs, and even language more familiar. This was topical especially after the 1920s, because immigration from Finland became more restricted due to the new laws, and the demands for Americanization were rising.

Among the children's literature there is also another interesting primer entitled *Aakkosia sosialistien lapsille* (Socialist Children's Primer) compiled by A. B. Mäkelä in 1912. He had been the companion of Matti Kurikka in the Sointula (Harmony) utopian venture in British Columbia a few years earlier. This type of primer was actually not so rare in socialist circles at that time, and Mäkelä must have had international examples to follow and advise Finnish American children. The small book even aroused the interest of U.S. Military Intelligence during the year 1918, which deemed it a seditious book. There were ten commandments; the first one, for example, was seen very suspicious as it was translated into English: "*Ajattele itse, tutki itse. Ei kannata uskoa pappien loruja eikä porvarien jaarituksia. He eivät tiedä tulevaisista eikä salaisista asioista enempää kuin sinäkään* (Think for yourself. Examine things yourself. It doesn't pay to believe in the nonsense of the priests and capitalists. They don't know any more about future than you do).[26]

The language of most publications was naturally Finnish, but some Swedish was also used in the Finland-Swedish circles in the United States and Canada. The Finland-Swedes had quite a few successful associations, such as the Finland-Swedish Temperance Society, which organized a lot of activity. The West Coast may have had the strongest activity among the Finland-Swedes. They most likely also found more available literature and publications produced by the Swedish immigrant group in the country. One of their major publications was the newspaper *Finska Amerikanaren,* later *Norden.*

Another example of later Finland-Swedish publications is the newspaper *Canada Svensken* (Canadian Swede) published in Toronto. Founded by Finland-Swede Thorwald Wiik in 1961, the paper lasted until 1978, when it closed down due to financial constraints. Material on its existence is available at the Canadian National Archives in Ottawa, as well as the Multicultural History Society of Ontario. Very little has been written on this publication.

Beginning in the 1930s, English gradually became the standard language in the publications as well as in association life in general. This was due mainly to the aging of the immigrant generation, but of course there were also pressures from the host society, beginning during the First World War and increasing during the Second World War and its aftermath. Children became more used to reading and writing in English. This would also affect readership and meant the decline and eventual disappearance of many Finnish-language newspapers and journals. Some publications began to include certain English-language columns for the younger generation readers already in the 1920s. It seems that the cooperative movement showed the way in the use of English, due to the apparent necessity of dealing with people speaking English or even other ethnic-based languages while doing business for cooperative stores. The fact that many Finnish American organizations had essential contacts with large regional or national associations in, for example, religious activities or labor organizations made it also necessary to move to the use of English and also English-language publishing. This important move toward the English language was apparent in most of the Finnish ethnic activities either before the Second World War or during the postwar decades.

There was also a time when quite a large number of independent publishers used to function among the Finnish immigrants in North America, without any close ties to any of the aforementioned ideologically oriented groups. Some of these publishing activities were commercial, as was seen in the case of calendars such as the *Kalenteri Amerikassa asuville suomalaisille* (calendar for the Finnish population in America) issued by the Finland Steamship Company Agency of New York during the pre–World War I period. The calendar contained quite a few useful ideas and advice for the immigrants and, for example, practical advice to businessmen to be punctual, to be diligent, and to pay their bills on time. There was information on voting rights in the United States as well as a presentation of the differences between state regulations in the country. More important, there was sound advice for an arriving immigrant. Immigrants were told, for example, that they should not carry large amounts of cash; they should never show their finances to strangers; they should always be suspicious if someone wishes to be very helpful and is very eager to become friends; and they should never change dollar bills with any stranger. In New York City, they should especially beware of the so-called runners (*runnareita*), drivers, and "expressmen." And of course, the best help an immigrant in New York could find was available in the office of the Finland Steamship Company.[27] One of the guidebooks for immigrants was *Siirtolaisen opas,* printed in 1910, which also included serious advice. Produced by the Finnish Seamen's Mission and the Suomi Synod in the United States, the guidebook included, for example, an article for young migrants. It was pointed out that several young people at the time of departure forgot all the good advice of their parents as well as teachers. Some migrants get intoxicated by the freedom of flesh and many kinds of sins. Therefore, it would be best to follow the advice of Jesus, to trust him, and to find the right kind of company in the country.[28]

In all, the impression is inescapable that Finnish American publishing activities were widely scattered, with a large number of enterprises bidding for readers in a relatively small market. In size, the publishing enterprises were fairly small and, on the whole, rather short-lived. Clearly a few newspaper companies have had an important role in running many kinds of publishing activities, such as newspapers, periodicals, novels, guidebooks, calendars, and so forth. This observation is valid both for the labor and church-oriented publishers. In light of the total volume of operations, however, it would appear that the publishers connected with the labor movement were most conspicuously active in the Finnish American community beginning in the early 1900s. Evidence clearly indicates that the decline in the publishers' ranks paralleled the steady disappearance of the immigrant generation proper and a shift to English-language publishing.

The peak period of publishing activity falls between the two world wars. Social life among the Finnish American immigrants seemed to have reached full bloom in the beginning of the 1920s; hence it should be a natural consequence for publishing operations also to peak around the same time. A decline followed, however, fairly rapidly along with the effective legal obstructions to immigration set up by the U.S. government in the early 1920s. Therefore, Finnish cultural activity of every kind lost vigor.

### Toward a New Era

The post–World War II migration has produced only minor new publishing activities, although the new technology with the Internet has resulted in the technical change of publishing forums into electronic journals and books. Due to the change of migration patterns and the passing of the old immigrant generations, several changes have taken place also within the sphere of cultural organizations and their interest in issuing books and other printed materials. The most notable change is the near total closure of Finnish-language publishing. The change to the use of English started slowly during the 1920s, when, for example, some newspapers started to publish English-language columns for their younger readers. The cooperative group began to publish its English-language journal, *Cooperative Pyramid Builder,* as early as 1926, apparently aiming to reach an English-speaking clientele and new members.

With the technological changes and a new concentration of the Finnish American population in the South and West, as well as minor new immigrant streams coming to America, the publishing interests also changed. Old printing houses began to vanish and reorganize their activities. The biweekly *Amerikan Uutiset* (American News), the national newspaper for Finnish Americans, is published by Finnish Media Group, Inc. of Lake Worth, Florida, and continues to report on news, people, and events in Finland and the Finnish-related people across the United States and Canada. It is published primarily in Finnish with some English articles and has readers even in Finland.

Originally, it was founded in New York Mills, Minnesota, in 1932 under the title of *Minnesotan Uutiset* (Minnesota News) as a nonpartisan paper by printer Carl Parta and editor Arthur Lunquist. In 1965, its name was changed to *Amerikan Uutiset*. After a big domestic migration stream toward Florida, with the aging of the migrant generation and new immigration from Finland, it was moved in 1986 to Lake Worth, Florida, where a new concentration of American Finns had grown. Later on, in 1996, the famous *New Yorkin Uutiset* and *Canadan Uutiset* were incorporated into it. The paper has also published as a biweekly Internet paper, including news and contact information for Finnish-related people in North America and even in Finland.[29] Thus it seems that the last vanguard of Finnish-language publishing is located in Canada, where the last major Finnish migration wave also took place in the decades following the Second World War.

Some other new developments are the web-based forums served by the *Finnish-American Reporter* and *Raivaaja*. The descendants of Finnish migrants have began to publish novels and poetry in English, with their connecting link in the Finnish North American Literature Association (FINNALA).[30]

**NOTES**

1. Cf. Arja Pilli, "Suomalainen lehdistö Pohjois-Amerikassa: silta vanhasta maasta uuteen," in *Suomen siirtolaisuuden historia III. Sopeutuminen, kulttuuritoiminta ja paluumuutto,* ed. Keijo Virtanen, Arja Pilli, and Auvo Kostiainen (Turku: Turun yliopiston Historian laitos, 1986), 54.

2. See Olavi Koivukangas and Simo Toivonen, *Suomen siirtolaisuuden ja maassamuuton bibliografia. [A Bibliography on Finnish Emigration and Internal Migration]* (Turku: Siirtolaisuusinstituutti, 1978); Kaarina Kotiranta, "Amerikansuomalaisen kirjallisuuden yhteisluettelo," *Helsingin yliopiston kirjaston monistesarja* 3 (1970); Esko Häkli, "Amerikansuomalaisten kirjallisuudesta ja kustannusoloista," *Bibliophilos* 2 (1962): 41–54 and 3 (1962): 62–71; John I. Kolehmainen, *The Finns in America: A Bibliographical Guide to Their History* (Hancock, Mich.: Finnish American Historical Library, Suomi College, 1947).

3. Häkli, "Amerikansuomalaisten," 42.

4. Häkli, "Amerikansuomalaisten," 42–44.

5. Auvo Kostiainen, "Features of Finnish-American Publishing," *Publications of the Institute of General History* 9 (1977): esp. 57, table 1.

6. Kostiainen, "Features of Finnish-American Publishing," 68.

7. Kolehmainen, *Finns in America,* 82; cf. Häkli, "Amerikansuomalaisten," 52.

8. See *Finnish-American Reporter,* http://www.finnishamericanreporter.com/.

9. The Raivaaja Publishing Company is a web-paged forum today. It is a "not-for-profit publication owned by the Finnish American community. It strives to keep its readership informed in Finnish and in English about happenings in Finland and in Finnish communities all over the world. This kind of information is not usually found in the mainstream American press. Our *Raivaaja* staff believes publishing to be the most important way to transmit knowledge of our ethnic history and culture from one generation to the next. Publishing is also the vital way to communicate current events

and issues concerning the future of our Finnish-American cultural activities. *Raivaaja* provides a forum for this dialog." http://www.raivaaja.org/.
10. John I. Kolehmainen, *Sow the Golden Seed: History of Fitchburg (Massachusetts) Finnish-American Newspaper. Raivaaja (The Pioneer) 1905-1955* (Fitchburg, Mass.: Raivaaja Publishing, 1955), 143-50.
11. Kostiainen, "Features of Finnish-American Publishing," 64-65; cf. Taisto John Niemi, *The Finnish Lutheran Book Concern 1900-1950: A Historical and Developmental Study* (Ann Arbor: University of Michigan Press, 1960), 250-53, table 14, 258-59.
12. See Uuras Saarnivaara, *Amerikan laestadiolaisuuden eli Apostolisluterilaisuuden historia* (Ironwood, Mich.: n.p., 1947).
13. Kolehmainen, *Finns in America*, 86, 88.
14. For more on Ida Pasanen and women's active participation, see especially Gary Kaunonen, *Challenge Accepted: A Finnish Immigrant Response to Industrial America in Michigan's Copper Country* (East Lansing: Michigan State University Press, 2010), 37-44.
15. See Auvo Kostiainen, "Mattson, Helmi (1890—1974) kirjailija," in *Kansallisbiografia* (Helsinki: SKS, Biografiakeskus, 2005). http://www.kansallisbiografia.fi/kb/artikkeli/4393/.
16. For example, K. Marianne Wargelin Brown, "Three Founding Mothers of Finnish America," in *Women Who Dared, Dared: The History of Finnish American Women*, ed. Carl Ross and K. Marianne Wargelin Brown (St. Paul: University of Minnesota, Immigration History Research Center, 1986), 151-55. She came from the Tornio River valley Laestadian revivalist region. The original name correctly spelled probably was Niiranen.
17. Carol Hepokoski, "Milma Lappala. Unitarian Minister and Humanist," in Ross and Brown, *Women Who Dared*, 158-64. Actually, the first American female minister, Olympia Brown, was ordained in the 1860s, in the Unitarian Church, too.
18. Hugo Hillilä, *Valinkauhassa* (Hancock, Mich.: Suom.-Amerikkalainen kustannusliike, 1950).
19. See Joseph Salmu, *Totiset ja väärät kristityt* (Hancock, Mich.: author, 1924), 5, 20-22.
20. John Ruokasmäki, *Tunnetko jumalaa luomisen töissä?* (Hancock, Mich.: author, 1932), 219-22.
21. Sulkanen, *Amerikan suomalaisen*, 337.
22. Moses Hahl, *Uudempi kansantalous* (Fitchburg, Mass.: Sos. Kustannusyhtiö, 1906), esp. 3-4.
23. Severi Alanne, *Osuustoimintaopas: Käsikirja Amerikan Suomalaista Osuustoimintaväkeä Varten* (Superior, Wis.: Co-operative Central Exchange, 1921); William Marttila, *Osuustoiminta ja sen merkitys luokkataistelussa* (Superior, Wis.: Amerikan suomalaisten sosialististen kustannusliikkeiden liitto, 1930).
24. Uriah Smith, *Parlamenttaarinen laki ja esityslista. Amerikaan kielelle toimittanut Uriah Smith. Mukaellen suomentanut John Stone* (Duluth, Minn.: Finnish Publishing, 1906).
25. Henry Askeli, *Syökäämme oikein. Johdatus ravintotieteeseen* (Fitchburg, Mass.: Raivaajan kustannusyhtiö, 1933).
26. *Aakkosia sosialistien lapsille*, ed. A. B. Mäkelä Toinen painos (Fitchburg, Massachusetts: Suom. Sos. Kustannusyhtiö, 1913), 61. The book was probably adapted according to the socialist primer by Nicholas Klein. Cf. "Pastor Denounces Socialist Primer," *New York Times*, March 21, 1910.
27. See *Kalenteri Amerikassa asuville suomalaisille 1910* (New York: Finland Steamship Company Agency); cf. Auvo Kostiainen, "Ajan merkit. Kalenterit amerikansuomalaisten oppaina," in *Samanaikaisuuksia. Kansainvälisiä näköaloja vuoden 1911 maailmaan*, ed. Leila Koivunen ja Taina Syrjämaa (Turku: Yleinen historia, Turun yliopisto, 2010), 111-12.
28. M. J. Kuusi, "Sananen nuorille siirtolaisille," in *Siirtolaisen Opas* (Helsinki: Suomen Merimieslähetysseura ja Suomi-Synodi, 1910), 16-20.
29. See http://www.amerikanuutiset.com/.
30. See more on this organization at http://www.finnala.com/.

PART 6
# Finland's Minority Emigrants

# Finland-Swedes in North America

*Mika Roinila*

The Finland-Swedish population has provided a relatively large proportion of immigrants, since every fifth Finn going to the United States was from the Swedish-speaking regions of Finland. The economic, social, political, organizational, and cultural differences between the Finnish Finns and Finland-Swedes have been a multifaceted issue, as relations between the two ethno-linguistic groups have waxed and waned over the years. Attitudinal differences between generations, questions of ethnic self-identity, and even the place of Finland-Swedes in today's immigrant community are explored below.

The roots of the Finland-Swedes date to the twelfth century, when Swedes began their rule over Finland after the Swedish crusades brought Christianity to Finland in 1157.[1] Swedes gradually settled on the Åland Islands, as well as on the southwestern and southern coastal margins of present-day Finland.[2] By 1250, Swedish settlement had extended north along the western coast and generally extended some 30 kilometers inland. This settlement pattern remained largely intact until the 1950s.[3]

Descendants of these early settlers are today known as Finland-Swedes. They are defined as citizens of Finland whose mother tongue is Swedish.[4] They speak a dialect of Swedish, referred to as Finland-Swedish, which differs from *rikssvenska*, the "national Swedish" language spoken in Sweden.

The self-identity of Finland-Swedes is a difficult concept to grasp. Among the immigrant population in North America who arrived in the late 1800s and early 1900s, many recognized themselves simply as being Swedish, while others identified themselves as being Swede-Finns.[5] However, with the passing of language legislation and the establishment of official bilingualism in Finland in 1921, the term "Finland-Swedes" has been in use in Finland. Immigrants who arrived after this period have often preferred to identify with this officially accepted term. Linguistically speaking, the term "Finland-Swedish" "signifies both the adjective denoting the ethnicity and language spoken, and Finland-Swede(s) refers to individuals belonging to this ethnic group."[6]

While "Finland-Swede" is the officially accepted term today, there can still be some confusion in identifying members of this ethno-linguistic minority. According to Christer Lauren, numerous other terms are used that need clarification.[7] "Sweden-Finn" is a term used to describe a Finn in Sweden, and their variety of Finnish is "Sweden Finnish." The term "Swedish-speaking Finn" is a term that should never be used to describe members of this ethno-linguistic minority, since it can include a Finnish citizen whose mother tongue is Finnish but who has learned Swedish. "Swedish-Finn" or "Swede-Finn" is "hopelessly ambiguous," as it might mean almost anything: a Finland-Swede; a Finn in Sweden; or an immigrant from Sweden living in Finland. Finally, "Finnish-Swedish" is a term that should only be used in jointly organized enterprises by citizens of the two countries.

As a result, it should come as no surprise that different terms are encountered among scholars as well as the general public. Literature has focused on both Finland-Swedes[8] and Swede-Finns.[9] Notwithstanding these differences, it is most heartening to know that members of this ethno-linguistic minority can overlook these differences and continue to recognize their roots, along with the historical, linguistic, and cultural affinity to their region of origin in Finland—whether it is in the region of Österbotten, Nyland, or the Åland Islands.

### History of Migration

Migration of Finland-Swedes to North America has a long history. Initial emigration from Finland to Sweden took place during the 1500s, 1600s, and 1700s. Many of them were seasonal migrants to the copper and iron mines in the winter months, returning to Finland during the summer.[10] Between 1790 and 1867, many Finland-Swedes were involved as sailors, shipwrights, seamen, skippers, clergy, and company officials with the Russian Alaska Company. The first Finn in Russian Alaska, and perhaps in North America since the New Sweden colony of the 1600s, was Matvei Gakkorein, who worked in the Russian colonies as early as 1829, predating the main flow that began with the coming of Finland-Swedish governor Arvid Etholen in 1840.[11]

The early arrivals of Finland-Swedes occurred in coastal cities such as New York City or elsewhere along the East and/or West Coast. Still, the earliest confirmed records include Finland-Swedes found in Ludington, Michigan, in 1868;[12] Minneapolis, Minnesota, in 1869;[13] and Chicago, Illinois in 1872.[14] By the mid-1880s, Finland-Swedes were found in some numbers in New York; in Worcester, Massachusetts; in many sawmill communities of southern Michigan; in a couple of mining towns in Colorado; and in several pioneering settlements on the West Coast.[15]

Reino Kero has pointed out that the total number of emigrants from Finland before World War I was a little more than 300,000. Of these, every fifth person was a Swedish Finn. The main concentrations were in four regions: the East Coast, between Philadelphia in the south and Boston in the north, with the greatest concentrations in New York State and Massachusetts; the midwestern states bordering the western Great Lakes, namely Michigan, Wisconsin, Minnesota, and northern Illinois, as well as certain places in the Canadian prairie provinces; the Rocky Mountain region, from Arizona in the south to British Columbia in the north, with the largest concentrations in Colorado, Montana, and Utah; and the West Coast, from southern California to British Columbia, with the heaviest concentration in the state of Washington.[16]

While emigration from Finland after the First World War was more often destined to Canada, in the United States there were already many second-generation Finland-Swedish descendants who resettled elsewhere. A large number of younger people moved from the East and Midwest to the West. Still, the geographic and economic patterns of settlement of the Finland-Swedes before the turn of the twentieth century have generally remained intact into the twenty-first century.

A good analysis of the geographical and economic distribution of Finland-Swedes around 1920 is available in the book by Johannes Näse published in 1922. It is based on a questionnaire survey of 713 Finland-Swedes throughout the United States, which helped establish the numerous areas of settlement as well as the work that dominated in the areas. Näse comprised a list of fourteen occupational groups that were representative of the time period. The most dominant occupations included mining (18 percent), carpentry and construction (17 percent), factory workers (14 percent), farmers (14 percent), and lumberjacks and sawmill workers (11 percent). These occupations account for 74 percent of all occupational categories associated with the surveyed population (Table 1).[17]

In the United States, one of the most important early centers of activity was New York City and its environs. The state of Massachusetts was another important area of early settlement. The majority of the men were engaged in the building trades, while others pursued factory work.[18] In New York, Finland-Swedes were employed in numerous jobs, including in factories, offices, as well as shipbuilding, with some later immigrants establishing several well-known and respected cabinet-making and interior furnishing businesses.[19] There were workers and metal industries of various sorts, making wire, machinery, tools, and weapons in locations such as Worcester, Springfield, Fitchburg, and elsewhere in Massachusetts. Coal mining in Pennsylvania attracted some Finland-Swedes, as did quarrying in Stony Creek, Connecticut, and Quincy and North Chelmsford, Massachusetts.[20] Overall, this concentration and presence of Finland-Swedes along the East Coast has remained intact, and many Finland-Swedes can still be found in the New York City area, in Massachusetts, and in Connecticut.

Finland-Swedes settled in many towns and cities of the American Midwest, in a broad area that includes Lower and Upper Michigan, Wisconsin, Minnesota, and northern Illinois. In the early period, most of the newcomers found economic opportunities in the lumber industry. Southern Michigan attracted loggers and sawmill workers in the 1870s and 1880s. Once the forests had been cut, many moved to the north, where mining provided work. When the mines in Michigan were not providing employment, Finland-Swedes moved to Minnesota to continue their trade.[21] Iron Mountain, Negaunee, and Ironwood, Michigan, and Eveleth, Hibbing, and Virginia, Minnesota, were home to many Finland-Swedes. Smaller numbers engaged in manufacturing and the building trades. In a few places, farming and fishing quickly became the chief occupations. Finland-Swedish farming communities included Metropolitan, Michigan; Conover, Siegel, and Wentworth, Wisconsin; and Cook, Gilbert, and Palisades, Minnesota.[22] Commercial fishing was confined to the Great Lakes—namely Lake Superior and Lake Michigan. An excellent example of a Finland-Swedish fishing village is Larsmont, Minnesota, which was settled in 1909 by immigrants arriving from Larsmo, Finland.[23] Other locations with Finland-Swedish fishermen included Ludington and Manistee, Michigan.[24]

The Rocky Mountain states provided mining opportunities as well, and included positions in drilling and blasting, loading, and tunnel carpentry. The number of Finland-Swedes in these positions most likely peaked in the decades before the First World War. A concentration of Finland-Swedes lasted the longest in Butte, Montana, while centers such as Telluride and Silverton, Colorado; Eureka and Bingham, Utah; and Wallace, Idaho, had Finland-Swedes for a shorter period of time. During the war, opportunities on the West Coast attracted many to relocate, and Finland-Swedes found jobs in shipbuilding.[25]

The fourth area with large numbers of settlers was the West Coast, especially the Pacific Northwest and the states of Washington and Oregon. A few Finland-Swedes were here in the 1880s, but immigration to this region increased rapidly in the 1890s and in the first two decades after the turn of the century.

## Table 1. Finland-Swedes in America in the Early 1920s

| STATE | NUMBER* | LOCATION | DOMINANT OCCUPATION |
|---|---|---|---|
| Michigan | 17,500 | Amasa | Mining and a second job |
| | | Baraga | |
| | | Bay City | Factory |
| | | Bessemer | |
| | | Calumet | Mining |
| | | Caspian | Mining |
| | | Crystal City | |
| | | Detroit | Mining and farming |
| | | Dollar Bay | |
| | | Escanaba | Factory |
| | | Flint | Dockwork, factory, and farming |
| | | Gladstone | Various occupations |
| | | Hancock | Factory |
| | | Iron Mountain | Various occupations |
| | | Ironwood | Mining |
| | | Ishpeming | Mining |
| | | Ludington | Mining |
| | | Manistique | Mining |
| | | Marquette | Factory, farming, and a second job |
| | | Metropolitan | Mining |
| | | Munising | Various occupations |
| | | | Farming |
| | | Negaunee | Mining |
| | | North Escanaba | Mining |
| | | Norway | Mining |
| | | Ontonagon | Mining |
| | | | Dockwork/stevedore and various occupations |
| | | Quinnesee | Mining |
| | | Ramsey | |
| Minnesota | 11,500 | Biwabik | |
| | | Chisholm | Mining |
| | | Eveleth | Mining |
| | | Hibbing | Mining |
| | | Minneapolis | Factory, farming, and a second job |
| | | St. Paul | Factory, farming, and a second job |
| | | Waldeck | Farming |
| | | West Duluth | Dockwork/stevedore, factory, and various occupations |
| Washington | 5,000 | Aberdeen | Lumberjacks and sawmill workers |
| | | Cool Creek | Mining |
| | | Everett | Factory and farming |
| | | Hoquiam | Lumberjacks and sawmill workers |
| | | Lake Stevens | Various occupations |
| | | Olympia | Factory and a second job |
| | | Rochester | Farming |
| | | Seattle | Various occupations |
| | | South Bend | Lumberjacks and sawmill workers |
| | | Spokane | Farming |
| | | Yakima | Farming |

| | | | |
|---|---|---|---|
| Massachusetts | 4,500 | Boston | Various occupations |
| | | Cambridge | Various occupations |
| | | Fitchburg | Factory and various occupations |
| | | Gardner | Farming and a second job |
| | | Malden | Farming and a second job |
| | | Melrose | Farming and a second job |
| | | Norwood | |
| | | Springfield | Factory and a second job |
| | | Woonsocket | Factory and a second job |
| | | Worcester | Factory and a second job |
| New York | 4,000 | Brooklyn New York | Factory and a second job |
| | | | Factory and a second job |
| California | 4,500 | Berkeley | Factory, farming, and a second job |
| | | Eureka | Lumberjacks and sawmill workers |
| | | Fort Bragg | Lumberjacks and sawmill workers |
| | | Oakland | Factory and a second job |
| | | Reedley | Factory and a second job |
| | | San Francisco | Various occupations, farming |
| Oregon | 3,000 | Astoria | Fishing and a second job |
| | | Coos Bay | Lumberjacks and sawmill workers |
| | | Marshfield | Various occupations |
| | | Portland | Various occupations |
| Wisconsin | 3,000 | Ashland | Various occupations |
| | | Superior | Various occupations |
| Montana | 2,000 | Butte | Mining |
| Ohio | 1,500 | Toledo | Farming |
| Illinois | 1,500 | Chicago | Factory and a second job |
| | | Waukegan | Factory, farming |
| Pennsylvania | 1,500 | Philadelphia | Factory |
| | | Pittsburgh | Factory |
| Utah | 1,000 | Bingham | Mining |
| | | Eureka | Mining |
| | | Park City | Mining |
| North Dakota | 1,000 | — | Farming |
| South Dakota | 1,000 | — | Farming |
| Colorado | 1,000 | Leadville | Mining |
| | | Telluride | Mining |
| New Jersey | 1,000 | Jersey City | Factory and a second job |
| Connecticut | 500 | Brantford | Factory and a second job, farming, various occupations |
| Wyoming | 500 | New Haven | Farming and a second job |

*Estimated by Näse.
Source: J. Näse, "Finlandssvenskarna i Amerika," Svensk-Ostrobottniska Samfundet, Arkiv för Svenska Österbotten, Band 1, Häfte 3–4 (1922): 245–75.

**FIGURE 1.** Star of Wasa was a temperance society that functioned in Eureka, California, among the Finland-Swedish population. (Source: IMT Photo collections, USA_3174)

Lumbering provided the livelihood for the majority of Finland-Swedes.[26] Other early occupations included farming, fishing, and the building trades. Perhaps one of the best examples of Finland-Swedish entrepreneurship was the veneer industry, which was firmly established on the West Coast after the First World War. The founding of Olympia Veneer Company in Washington State involved many local Finland-Swedes whose efforts are well recognized. As recorded by Nelson Perkins, Finland-Swedes excelled in the business.[27]

Ed Westman, cofounder of Olympia Veneer, was a Swedish immigrant active in the Swedish fraternal lodges. He recruited men who were willing to invest in a worker-owned plywood plant. Because of his efforts, Olympia Veneer incorporated in January 1921, and the company made its start as a cooperative venture. Two hundred shares of capital stock were authorized at $500 each; 125 of Westman's friends bought shares, while 63 of these friends were Finland-Swedes.[28] Among them was "Big Bill" Gustafsson, who served for several years as the superintendent. Later on, several Finland-Swedes held manager and superintendent posts in the company. Only a few years after its founding, the company began to turn a profit. During World War II, Olympia Veneer was the largest producer of plywood in the world.[29]

In Canada, the earliest recorded Finland-Swedes arrived on the West Coast and settled in British Columbia. This province has always maintained the strongest concentration of Finland-Swedes in the country, and it is noted by the arrival of Victor Holmlund (later Jacobson), who jumped ship in Victoria in 1880 and later became a well-known sea captain.[30] Other early destinations for many Finland-Swedes in the province included Vancouver and New Westminster. Other provinces followed, with records indicating the presence of Finland-Swedes in Alberta in 1887, and in the Lakehead region of Port Arthur/Fort William, Ontario, in the 1880s.[31] In the Maritimes, Charles Magnuson of the Åland Islands arrived in Saint John, New Brunswick, in 1891. Whitemouth, located in the Canadian Shield of eastern Manitoba, was home to a Finland-Swedish family in 1892, and the earliest Finland-Swedes in the eastern Canadian prairies arrived at the New Scandinavia Colony of western Manitoba in 1893.[32]

The occupations of the Finland-Swedes in Canada followed the patterns established in the United States. Some also gained status through accomplishment in sports, such as Ray Timgren, who played for the Toronto Maple Leafs when they won the Stanley Cup in 1951.[33] Others excelled in businesses and were known for their entrepreneurship. This was exemplified by Erhard Alm, who invented the portable vulcanizing machine in 1956 and went on to revolutionize the vulcanizing industry in North America and Europe. In the 1960s, Alm's company became the largest manufacturer of vulcanizing machinery in the world.[34]

**FIGURE 2**. The Swedish pantry in Escanaba, Michigan, is a well-known restaurant founded by an early Finland-Swede immigrant named Andersson to western Michigan. The present owner is Phyllis Cossette. (Source: photo and information from Mika Roinila)

Finland-Swedish immigrants were destined to settle across North America in a manner common for all ethnicities. Historically, ethnic groups have tended to follow the pattern of chain migration, which means that there was a tendency for immigrants from a particular province or parish in Finland to group together in a certain locality in such numbers that they predominate in the local Finland-Swedish population. Much of this was caused by influential correspondence that enticed neighbors and relatives to follow their kin to the New World.

In general, it appears that immigrants from Finland-Swedish communes in southern Österbotten (south of Vasa) were concentrated in the eastern states. Those from communes in northern Österbotten generally settled in the Midwest and the West. Immigrants from the Åland Islands were attracted to New York City and Norwood, Massachusetts. According to Myhrman, the largest number of Finland-Swedish immigrants from a single commune who concentrated in any locality in the United States or Canada was surely the group from Närpes in Worcester, Massachusetts. More specific evidence of settlement concentrations also includes distinct place names that reflect the origins of the inhabitants. Some of these terms are vernacular terms heard among the public, while others appear on maps. Branford, Connecticut, was at one time called "Little Övermark" because of the fact that a great number of its inhabitants came from Övermark.[35] Larsmont, Minnesota, was home to many Finland-Swedes from Larsmo, while Lilla Munsala in New Westminster, British Columbia, was dominated by inhabitants who came from Munsala.[36]

Statistically, the number of Finland-Swedes in the United States and Canada has historically been difficult to obtain, and the numbers have varied based on estimates and available census data. The descendants of the first-generation immigrant population would undoubtedly increase in number as a result of bearing children, but the population of Finland-Swedes has historically been estimated at well below the 20 percent share who arrived as members of the total immigrant population from Finland.

Scholars have provided various estimates for the number of Finland-Swedes in North America. Based on passport records and available data, Myhrman estimated that some 73,000 Finland-Swedes immigrated to North America during the period 1871–1929. According to Nelson, the total Finland-Swedish population in the United States in 1930 was estimated at 50,000 individuals. Estimates for other periods are not available. More recently, Westerberg proposed that the number of Finland-Swedes in the United States in 1990 constituted a mere 6,000 of the total population of 660,000 Finns.[37]

In Canada, customized cross-tabulations obtained from the 1991 census revealed only some 1,000 Finland-Swedes out of a total Finnish population of 100,000 people.[38] These individuals identified themselves with their Swedish mother tongue and Finnish ethnic identity. In other words, the percentage of Finland-Swedes appeared to represent only 1 percent of the Finnish ethnic population—far from the 20 percent figure noted earlier. This has led to many questions regarding the disappearing Finland-Swedes and their lack of identity.[39] However, some revisions, based on higher representative percentages, allege that today there may be some 80,000 Finland-Swedes in the United States (15 percent of all Finns) and 10,000 in Canada (10 percent of all Finns).[40]

Today, accurate data for the United States is available through the Integrated Public Use Microdata Series (IPUMS) housed in the Minnesota Population Center.[41] This database enables researchers to analyze variables and data that are relevant to social and economic research. Detailed cross-tabulations of census data showing the number of people born in Finland with a Swedish mother tongue provide, for the first time, definitive numbers that debunk the previously alleged percentages. Data show that the number of Finland-Swedes is well below the 20 percent indicated by earlier scholars (Table

## Table 2. Finland-Swedes in the United States, 1910–2000.

| STATE OR DISTRICT | BORN IN FINLAND WITH SWEDISH MOTHER TONGUE | | | | | BORN IN FINLAND WITH SWEDISH LANGUAGE | | |
|---|---|---|---|---|---|---|---|---|
| | 1910 | 1920 | 1930 | 1940 | 1960 | 1980 | 1990 | 2000 |
| Alaska | | 202 | | | | | | 20 |
| Arizona | | 303 | 101 | | | | | |
| California | 1,605 | 1,817 | 1,818 | 800 | 1,490 | 480 | 382 | 334 |
| Colorado | 100 | 202 | 101 | 100 | | 20 | | 42 |
| Connecticut | 600 | 909 | 909 | 400 | 300 | 180 | 132 | 118 |
| District of Columbia | | | | | | | 52 | 15 |
| Florida | | | | | 99 | 120 | 152 | 98 |
| Georgia | | | | 300 | | 40 | 19 | |
| Hawaii | | | | | | | | 10 |
| Idaho | | 101 | 101 | | 99 | 20 | | |
| Illinois | 600 | 505 | 707 | 500 | 498 | 40 | 48 | |
| Indiana | 200 | | | | | | | 57 |
| Iowa | | | | | 100 | | 34 | |
| Kansas | | | | | | 20 | | |
| Kentucky | | | | | | | 4 | |
| Louisiana | | | 101 | | | | | |
| Maine | | 101 | | | 99 | 60 | 9 | 13 |
| Maryland | | | | | 200 | | | 32 |
| Massachusetts | 602 | 1,816 | 2,323 | 1,200 | 498 | 140 | 75 | 46 |
| Michigan | 2,905 | 3,232 | 2,525 | 1,100 | 399 | 80 | 53 | 82 |
| Minnesota | 1,206 | 2,222 | 606 | 700 | 996 | 100 | 74 | |
| Montana | 101 | 606 | 606 | | | | | |
| Nebraska | 100 | | | | | | | |
| Nevada | | 101 | 202 | 300 | | | | 21 |
| New Hampshire | | | | | | | | |
| New Jersey | 100 | 705 | 1,111 | 900 | 599 | 240 | 46 | 72 |
| New Mexico | | | | | | | 27 | 40 |
| New York | 2,101 | 1,616 | 1,616 | 2,200 | 2,190 | 380 | 216 | 182 |
| North Carolina | | | | | | | 48 | 47 |
| Ohio | | | 404 | | | 40 | | |
| Oregon | 2,001 | 808 | 1,414 | 500 | 499 | 60 | 103 | 48 |
| Pennsylvania | | 101 | | 300 | 100 | 80 | | 61 |
| Rhode Island | 100 | | | 300 | | | | |
| South Carolina | | 202 | | | 99 | | | 6 |
| South Dakota | | | | | | | 10 | |
| Texas | 101 | | | | | | | 36 |
| Utah | 1,401 | 1,111 | 202 | 100 | 200 | | | 16 |
| Virginia | | | | | | 20 | 24 | |
| Washington | 1,408 | 2,523 | 2,222 | 1,600 | 1,292 | 420 | 75 | 36 |
| Wisconsin | 904 | 606 | 707 | 2,000 | 998 | 80 | 44 | |
| Wyoming | | | | | | 20 | | |
| TOTAL | 16,135 | 19,789 | 17,776 | 13,300 | 10,755 | 2,620 | 1,647 | 1,402 |
| Total Finnish Born | 126,105 | 148,058 | 143,218 | 113,694 | 64,446 | 30,240 | 23,035 | 23,199 |
| Percentage Finn-Swedes | 12.8 | 13.4 | 12.4 | 11.7 | 16.7 | 8.7 | 7.1 | 6.0 |

Source: http://usa.ipums.org/usa/.

2). From data calculated for the census periods 1910–40, 1960, and 1980–2000, the percentage of all Finland-Swedes within the Finnish-born immigrant population in the United States has declined from nearly 20,000 individuals in 1920 (13.4 percent of all Finnish-born immigrants) to only 1,400 in 2000 (6.0 percent). A slight increase in concentration appeared in 1960, as 16.7 percent of the Finnish-born population identified themselves as Finland-Swedish. It must also be noted that the U.S. Census did not collect information on the 1950 and 1970 census forms that identified Finnish-born and Swedish mother tongue components. More research is needed to explain this unexpected shift.

Census data verify the distribution of Finland-Swedes across the country and support the settlement patterns noted earlier. Finland-Swedes have held the strongest concentrations in Michigan, New York, Washington, California, and Massachusetts.

Although the available census data are informative and reliable to some degree, it must also be remembered that data from 1910 to 1960 are based on a sample of only 1 percent of the total population of the United States. A somewhat better result is obtained from the 1980–2000 censuses that includes a 5 percent sample of the total population. Thus the number of Finland-Swedes in the United States in 2000—born in Finland-speaking Swedish—was only 1,402. This does not include the children, grandchildren, and great-grandchildren of many of the Finland-Swedes who came to this country decades earlier. Without accurate statistical data and lack of verifiable census tabulations that include the descendants of Finland-Swedish immigrants, the true number of Finland-Swedes may be impossible to measure.

Why the overall number of Finland-Swedes has diminished is quite difficult to determine. In studying the Finland-Swedish population in Canada, Roinila concluded that the loss of identity is the result of several factors. First, there is a high level of dissociation of Finland-Swedes from the Finnish communities in which only the Finnish language dictated interaction. In some cases, Swedes who could not speak Finnish and sought English-language usage in the early 1920s were not welcome in Finnish circles. Second, because of language, Finland-Swedes found more in common with the Swedes, and thus became more associated with the Swedes. Third, descendants of many early immigrants may not have learned about the 1917 independence of Finland, nor did they learn about the 1921 bilingual legislation of Finland. A lack of knowledge only helped push Finland-Swedes toward assimilation as quickly as possible, which led to Canadianization. Finally, historical antagonisms between groups may also have been a factor that kept the Finns and Finland-Swedes at a distance from one another. These factors are all significant in the lives of immigrants, more so in the distant past than today. However, since the largest influx of immigrants arrived prior to the 1920s, later immigrants were not as likely to follow the direction of the older immigrants. Thus there are many Finland-Swedish descendants who are unaware of their Finnish identity. These factors may well explain why the number and proportion of Finland-Swedes in the overall Finnish North American population appear so low today. Several studies that focus on interethnic attitudes and reciprocity support these findings.[42]

### Developmental Periods

The preeminent scholar who has contributed the most to our understanding of Finland-Swedes in North America was undoubtedly Anders Myhrman (1888–1972). His vast collections and materials available in archives and libraries are invaluable to our understanding of this ethno-linguistic minority. According to Myhrman, the period roughly from 1880 until 1900 may properly be called a *period of pioneering and establishment*—a time during which Finland-Swedes became established both geographically and economically in the New World. This pattern has, of course, changed greatly with the passing of time, especially because of changes in the North American economy, the increasing adjustment in the skills and ambitions of the immigrants, and the different social orientation of successive generations. A second period—beginning shortly before the turn of the twentieth century and lasting into the early 1920s—may properly be called a *period of organization,* for during these two decades the sick-benefit, temperance, fraternal, and religious organizations that played such an important part in the lives of these immigrants were founded and developed. The Finland-Swedish interest in organizations of their own and for the benefit of their fellow immigrants can in some places be traced back to the mid-1880s.[43]

As will be seen in the following accounts that deal with organizational and religious activities, it is evident that a third *period of maturity* existed between the 1920s and 1950s. During this era, large memberships were common in the Finland-Swedish organizations. Likewise, the Finland-Swedish churches were well attended, and newspapers had high subscription levels. A fourth period is evident in terms of the Finland-Swedish community from the 1960s onward. I propose this period be called the *period of decline and assimilation,* for over the past forty or so years the various organizations, originally established to support and uphold Old World traditions and practices, have declined to the point of disappearing. Few younger generation members are encountered among many of the formerly active organizations. At the same time, assimilation into North American society has occurred, and the more recent immigrants do not find value in the formerly important fraternal and ethnic associations. Finally, there has also been the assimilation of many younger generation and recently arrived Finland-Swedes into the mainstream of the Finnish-language communities.

## Organized Activities

As noted above, a number of organizations were established by Finland-Swedes who arrived on the North American continent. The first involved sick-benefit societies that provided mutual aid in times of illness and death for the immigrant community. The first such benefit society, Imatra, was organized in Worcester, Massachusetts, in 1889. In time, a federation of local societies was formed. This federation became national in scope; by 1920 there were about fifty active local sick-benefit societies with a total membership of about 3,500 in the national Svensk-Finska Sjukhjälpsförbundet Finland av Amerika (Swedish-Finnish Sick-Benefit Society in America).[44]

Aside from their sick-benefit groups, Finland-Swedes also established temperance societies. Similar societies already existed among Finns and the other Scandinavian immigrants throughout the United States. Following these examples, and after some years of discussion, the leaders among Finland-Swedes in Worcester decided to establish the Aavasaksa Society in 1892. The society became very active not only in direct temperance work but also in sponsoring other activities such as a library, a sewing society, two choirs or singing societies, and at least two "mission societies" that later became the nuclei of churches. New temperance societies were founded in different parts of the United States, as was a national body—the Svensk-Finska Nykterhetsförbundet of Amerika (Swedish-Finnish Temperance Society of America), which had a membership of over 2,600 by 1916.[45]

The membership of the sick-benefit and the temperance societies overlapped considerably, and over time the two national societies joined to form the Order of Runeberg in 1920.[46] In combining the aims of the two previous societies, the new fraternal order left the beneficial provisions intact, but the temperance requirement was considerably modified. While the new organization started with about 4,500 members, the activities of the order flourished, and its influence became most extensive during the 1920s and 1930s. At its peak, membership reached 8,500 in 1929.[47]

The monthly paper *Ledstjärnan* (Leading Star) was started in 1906 by the national temperance society Nykterhetsförbundet (Temperance League) to promote the work of that organization and temperance work in general. Its contents consisted largely of articles that dealt with various aspects of alcohol and temperance problems. It also included letters and communications from the local societies. Most of the time *Ledstjärnan* was published as a monthly that consisted of eight pages, which were half the size the pages of ordinary newspapers.[48] When the Order of Runeberg was established in 1920, it took over *Ledstjärnan* as its promotional organ, something that has continued to this day.

Several other organizations have also been established by Finland-Swedes. These include the Åland Society, which was founded in New York City in 1914. The Åland Society reached a membership of some 600 by the 1960s. Since 1947, Finland-Swedes in the New York area have held an annual Närpes Festival,[49] which helped form the Norden Society (Norden meaning North) in 1961. The membership of this society was made up of more recent arrivals, and the society was very active in the 1960s and early 1970s. With time, the nature of the society changed, and in the late 1970s the society became known as the Skandinaviska Klubben.[50]

### Religious Organizations

Following the religious practices of Finland, Finland-Swedes became associated with the Lutheran Church in the United States at an early period. According to Myhrman, the earliest Lutheran congregations were established in Marshfield, Oregon, in 1884. Others soon followed in East Tawas, Michigan (1885), Branford, Connecticut (1888), Gardner, Massachusetts (1894), and Felch-Metropolitan and Thompson, Michigan (1895). Interestingly, although New York City was home to many Finland-Swedes, the Lutheran Church did not begin its work until 1913, when a church was founded in Brooklyn. A second congregation was opened in the Bronx in 1919, and a third congregation in Jersey City, New Jersey, in 1923.[51]

In Vancouver, British Columbia, some early Finland-Swedes helped to found the First Swedish Evangelical Lutheran Church in 1903. For all intents and purposes, this was a Swedish church. Six years later, Finland-Swedes established their own congregation in New Westminster, the Immanuel Evangelical Lutheran Church, which was supported by many. By way of comparison, Finnish-speaking immigrants did not establish congregations in the Vancouver area until the 1920s.[52] All Finland-Swedish Lutheran churches joined the Swedish-American Augustana Lutheran Synod.[53]

Around 1930, there were twenty Finland-Swedish Lutheran churches, with a total of about 4,000 members, and eighteen Baptist and Congregational churches, with a total of 1,000 members between them.[54] Augustana Lutheran congregations remained dominant in the religious lives of Finland-Swedes. In the 1930s, it was estimated that twice as many Finland-Swedish immigrants belonged to Augustana Lutheran congregations compared to their own separate Lutheran churches. By the 1950s, most of the independent Finland-Swedish churches had either merged with Swedish American congregations, had become completely Americanized through the influx of outsiders, or had ceased to exist.[55]

Finland-Swedes also founded several other congregations based on their religious interests. Some of the other congregations that were established include Baptist and Covenant churches, both of which were more common in Sweden and among Swedish Americans than in Finland and among the Finnish Americans. The first Baptist church for Finland-Swedes was organized in Worcester in 1900.[56] In Chicago, Finland-Swedes formed the First Finnish Baptist Church in 1902, which became Bethel Baptist Church in the 1930s.[57]

In 1916, a total of fifteen Baptist congregations were found across the country, with only one being a Finnish-language congregation. Churches were located in New York City; Gardner and Worcester, Massachusetts; Chicago; Felch, Gladstone, and Negaunee, Michigan; Hartford, Connecticut; Seattle, and Tacoma, Washington; and Eureka and San Francisco, California. The lone Finnish congregation was located in Hancock, Michigan.[58]

In 1930, a total of fifteen active congregations existed, all of which were Swedish speaking. Although congregations in Eureka and San Francisco, California, had dissolved, new congregations had been founded in Dollar Bay and Roscommon, Michigan, as well as in Wentworth, Wisconsin.[59]

By 1957, a total of eighteen churches were affiliated with the Finska Baptist Missionsföreningen (Baptist Mission Union). Four of these congregations were Finnish (located in Toronto and Intola, Ontario; Painesville, Ohio; and Chisholm, Minnesota), and the total membership was over 1,000. The church published the *Finska Missionposten* (Finnish Mission Message), and at its height some 1,300 copies were printed. The Mission Union was dissolved in 1961.[60]

The first Covenant church organized by Finland-Swedes was established in Brooklyn, New York, in 1900. It grew out of "mission work" that had been started some years earlier. The activities of this church came to an end with the beginning of the Great Depression in 1930. To further the work of these churches, a monthly called *Svensk-Finska Budbäraren* (Swedish-Finnish Messenger) was published in New York during the years 1908–25. During its best years, the paper had about 800 subscribers. Covenant congregations were also found in locations such as Worcester and Springfield, Massachusetts; Ironwood, Michigan; and Chicago.[61]

Finland-Swedes have also been associated with the Swedish American Methodist Church as well as the Salvation Army. Aside from Finland-Swedes as members of the Swedish American Methodist churches, they have also pastored congregations within this denomination. Finland-Swedish pastors have been found in Duluth, Minnesota, and Crystal Falls, Calumet, Iron Mountain, and Ishpeming, Michigan.[62]

The impact of the Finnish Salvation Army has been minimal in the overall religious experience of Finland-Swedes. Still, from among ten corps (congregations) across the East Coast and Midwest, the presence of the Brooklyn #8 Corps during the period 1906–56 served the Finnish and Finland-Swedish community of New York. Finland-Swedes also associated themselves with the Salvation Army work that was centered on Belmont Hill in the Swedish enclave of Worcester, Massachusetts.[63]

## Decline and Assimilation

The national assimilation of immigrants, if broadly conceived, is a process that involves many factors. In terms of generations, it obviously means that native-born individuals gradually take the place of the foreign-born immigrants. Economically and vocationally it implies that immigrants, at least to some extent, and the native-born more completely, graduate from the group's early occupations and enter different vocations that usually are better paid and require more skill and knowledge. Such a change, in general, has taken place within the Finland-Swedish group. This has also brought about a membership decline in the different organizations, churches, and activities that had kept the earlier generation together.

The assimilation of Finland-Swedes into the host American society, as well as their incorporation into the mainstream of Finnish immigrant communities in the New World, fits the theory of assimilation subprocesses.[64] The theory identifies seven subprocesses of assimilation that operate simultaneously and at varying rates of speed to bring about various types of intergroup merger. Among the subprocesses that have affected the Finland-Swedes are: cultural assimilation, namely the acquisition of the host culture; structural assimilation, or engagement with outsiders in occupational, educational, civic, neighborhood, and public settings; marital assimilation, or dealing with intermarriage and exogamy; identificational assimilation, when minority group members become identified as part of the larger society; attitude receptional assimilation, when ethnic prejudice declines; behavior receptional assimilation, when ethnic discrimination declines; and civic assimilation, in which intergroup conflict over values and power declines.[65]

By the 1960s, the progressive assimilation of the Finland-Swedish immigrants and the numerical increase of the native-born in many of the lodges led to changes. Sentimental speeches about the culture and history of Finland lost their appeal, and popular songs and music of the day tended to supplant the older Scandinavian songs and melodies. Over the years, associations with the Finnish-speaking community also increased. This is part of the assimilation process as well, as members of the younger generation who now speak English have forgotten and do not even know about the linguistic divides that once kept Swedish-speaking and Finnish-speaking Finns separate. This is part of civic assimilation within the Finnish communities, and may be seen as a positive trend.[66]

By the 1930s, organizations, churches, and newspapers began to use the English language instead of Swedish. For example, the newspaper *Ledstjärnan* was renamed the *Leading Star/Ledstjärnan* in 1950. In the end, assimilation and change are inevitable. In both churches and the lodges of the Order of Runeberg, it became necessary to shift to English in order to interest the native-born generation, to secure them as members of the organization, and to encourage others' active participation in its activities. Many of them could assume responsibilities only if the English language were used.

Resistance to linguistic change, however, does exist, primarily in the world of the press. To the credit of its editor, the Swedish language predominates in the weekly paper *Norden*. Founded in Worcester in 1897 as the *Finska Amerikanaren* (Finnish American), this paper relocated to Brooklyn in 1899, where it has been published ever since. At the height of its success, there were over 6,000 subscribers to the paper during the 1908–15 period. The paper was renamed *Norden* in 1935, and by the late 1950s some 2,900 copies were printed of each weekly issue. The paper has continued to the present, but the number of subscribers has continued to decline significantly. According to editor Erik Hermans, who began working at *Norden* with some 2,200 subscribers in 1962, there are only 450 subscribers to the paper today—275 in the United States and 175 in countries such as Canada, Finland, Ireland, and Belgium.[67]

Another Swedish-language newspaper that was aimed toward the Finland-Swedish community was the *Canada Svensken* (Canadian Swedish), which was published in Toronto. Established in 1961 by Finland-Swede Thorwald Wiik, the paper was initially published semimonthly, and later became a monthly publication. The paper was provided free of charge to Finland-Swedes and others interested in a Swedish-language newspaper in the Toronto area, but as it depended almost totally on advertisements derived from businesses and private enterprise, it struggled to remain in operation without government assistance, and finally folded in 1978 after seventeen years of publication.[68]

While change is regarded as inevitable, something must be said about the general tendencies of retaining a distinct cultural and ethnic identity among Finland-Swedes, which primarily relates to the private sphere of families and households. Here, women have played a very significant part in maintaining an ethnic identity in the New World. Many Finland-Swedish women have "sacrificed their spare time and invested innumerable hours of hard work to organize and cater for Finland-Swedish gatherings."[69] The maintenance of ethnic traditions has often come to be regarded as the responsibility of women in both the public and private spheres. Cultural variables that were deemed important in maintaining Finland-Swedish identity correspond well with those of recent major studies on the ethnic identity of Americans of European descent. These include traditional foods as being of the greatest importance in maintaining a sense of identity, while interaction with relatives and visits to Finland are also seen as being very important. In the end, Finland-Swedish immigrant women and their descendants have taken a very active part in both private and public activities that promote and maintain a sense of Finland-Swedishness in North America.[70]

A final point can be made in the realm of identificational assimilation. While the terms "Finland-Swede" and "Swede-Finn" exist in North America, it is also evident that since the 1950s there has been a distinctive trend for these groups still to identify themselves simply as Finnish. This may be explained in part by the awkward explanations that many people try to avoid when explaining their double-hyphenated identity as "Finland-Swedish-Americans" or "Finland-Swedish-Canadians." Surveys reveal that the choice of identity leans more toward the use of "Finnish American" and "Finnish Canadian" when identifying an individual.[71]

## Finland-Swedes Today

Among North America's Finland-Swedes, while all indicators point to some major losses, there have also been some positive developments. As noted earlier, there has been a steady decline in membership in the number of organizations, churches, and newspaper subscriptions. This is most evident within the Order of Runeberg. Membership was highest in the 1920s, when close to 9,000 people were part of this organization within North America. Membership has declined since then. In 1944, membership was about 6,700. In 1950, membership was about 4,800. In 1965, membership had dropped to 4,000, and by 1975 membership was about 3,400. In 1995, slightly more than 1,000 members remained, and the numbers have continued to decline further since then. In 2004, a total of eighteen lodges maintained a membership of 679 individuals. By 2009, only fourteen active lodges continued, with a total of 537 members (Table 3).

The continuation of activities within the Order of Runeberg is described by Annabelle Kergan, the current Supreme Board president of the organization:[72]

> We live in a different world today. . . . Our technical world has pushed us into the 21st century with an entirely new set of needs and values. We no longer rely on one another as greatly as we did in the past for the basic social networking we valued in the past. No longer is the interest as great as it was in the past. People today do not want to commit to something that might infringe on their personal time and energy. It might require that

## Table 3. Order of Runeberg Membership, 2004–2009

| LODGE #—NAME | MEMBERSHIP 2004 | 2009 | LODGE #—NAME | MEMBERSHIP 2004 | 2009 |
| --- | --- | --- | --- | --- | --- |
| 1—Bessemer, MI | 3 | closed | 124—Vancouver, B.C. | 50 | 56 |
| 8—Dollar Bay, MI | 28 | 69 | 125—Portland, OR | 90 | closed |
| 101—Seattle, WA | 54 | 39 | 126—North Bend/Coos Bay, OR | 62 | 43 |
| 102—Eureka, CA | 145 | 124 | 129—Port Angeles, WA | 9 | closed |
| 104—San Francisco, CA | 30 | 23 | 130—New Westminster, B.C. | 16 | 11 |
| 105—Butte, MT | 28 | 31 | 132—Crescent City, CA | 32 | 21 |
| 106—Tacoma, WA | 36 | 45 | 205—New Haven, CT | 45 | 49 |
| 110—Hoquiam, WA | 15 | 11 | 211—Norwood, MA | 23 | 15 |
| 111—Everett, WA | N/A | closed | | | |
| 120—Rochester, WA | 13 | closed | TOTAL | 679 | 537 |

Source: *Leading Star* 98, no. 2 (June 2004): 8; Kergan correspondence with author, May 3, 2009.

they hold office or serve on a committee and generally speaking, today's members do not want to commit. Attend a function yes, but do not expect that they will work to make it happen. This may sound cynical but it is a true-ism.

There are lots of dedicated people out there but not in great numbers. Without strong leadership and willing members able to do the work and commit time and energy to the cause, the International Order of Runeberg will surely and steadily fade away.... Sadly we must accept this fact but I do hope that the Order of Runeberg will still remain for some time to come. Some individual Lodges are still growing and expanding in membership due to the programming and the enthusiasm of their leadership and/or the enthusiasm and commitment of their members.... We do not want to see it die.

While the Order of Runeberg is declining across the United States and Canada, a few locations have Finnish-speaking members (sometimes with no Swedish ties at all) who maintain the organization. Indeed, as the case of the Order of Runeberg in New Haven, Connecticut, attests, Swedish speakers are a distinct minority. While this lodge has mostly Finnish-speaking members, and more of the members speak Finnish than Swedish, the language of communication is simply English. Still, I have also heard some allegations of apparent resentment by Finnish-speakers toward their colleagues who have joined a "Swedish organization."

In the early 2000s, a group of Finland-Swedish women in the New York City area brought together an informal network of like-minded people who wanted to maintain their ethnic traditions and participate in some organized activities. This was the New York's Finlandssvenskar (NYFS), which established a short-lived virtual presence online, was promoted in the ethnic media, and collaborated with the American-Scandinavian Foundation, the consulate general of Finland, and other local organizations in hosting events and guest speakers. In January 2004, the club brought in guest lecturer Merete Mazzarella, renowned Swedish-Finn author, columnist, and professor, who presented a talk on "identity." Following the presentation, the NYFS invited participants for wine and cheese, and the discussion continued. About sixty people came to the event, which was arranged by the NYFS, the Finnish American Women's Network, and the American Scandinavian Foundation. Dozens of individuals participated in other events such as May Day celebrations, picnics, and crayfish parties, but since most of the participants were involved in short-term contract employment or did not have time to commit to continual activities, this cultural association is no longer active.

Today, the biggest success story of the Finland-Swedish community in North America is the Swedish-Finn Historical Society (SFHS), based in Seattle. Founded in 1991, the society maintains an archives and a library that contain material pertaining to Finland-Swedish culture, history, and tradition, and makes this material available for interpretive, educational, and research purposes.[73]

The SFHS publishes a periodical, *The Quarterly,* and maintains a very active and informative web site. The society provides genealogical information to members, arranges and participates in cultural events, and invites people from throughout the world who are interested in Finland-Swedish culture and tradition to become members. In 2002, the SFHS had a total 652 members from as far away as Finland. In terms of geographic distribution, most members came from Washington (43 percent), California (8 percent), Finland (6 percent), Oregon (6 percent), and Michigan (5 percent). In 2009, membership had climbed to some 700 people, with strongest membership being in the Pacific Northwest.[74] The society has actively promoted the culture and presence of Finland-Swedes in ethnic events, including the presentation of interesting and attractive posters that are displayed at several FinnFest events that take place annually across the United States. Unfortunately, according to the organizers, "Many Finnish-Americans spend no time at the SFHS exhibits, once they see the SFHS logo. However, if they don't notice it, they become very interested, especially in the New Sweden colony exhibit, and this year's [2004 Florida] exhibit on contributions to the American culture."[75]

The exhibit staff members often get the feeling that Swedish-Finns are not considered Finns. The Florida event was characterized by its lack of any Swedish-Finns on the program. With the lack of immigration from Finland, or the movement of highly educated Finland-Swedes who hold short-term contract positions in North America, there have been changes in the Finland-Swedish population and its interests. For many decades, there has been a clear trend in the loss of language connections within Finland-Swedish churches, organizations, and societies. On the other hand, historical animosities between the Finns and Finland-Swedes are less obvious today than during the 1920s across the continent. Tolerance appears to be a more commonly espoused characteristic among individuals. Hard feelings have given way to acceptance.

Today, differences appear to matter very little, and ancestry even less. A dying older generation may ultimately take with it the organizations that formerly provided support and identity. The changing demography of a younger generation includes widespread intermarriage, better-educated descendents, and, ironically, people who lack historical knowledge and interest in their roots. The younger generation relies less on personal interconnections than ever before. Now the focus is on high-speed Internet connections, on-demand access to Yleisradio (Finnish Broadcasting Company), and instant connections to Finland. Finland-Swedes may well remain a small, marginalized, and increasingly invisible minority that keeps treading the cultural waters of a vast continent, while simultaneously changing the characteristics of their clubs and personal interests to suit the changing times.

## NOTES

1. A shortened version of this article was published by Mika Roinila, "Finland-Swedish Experience in North America," *Journal of Finnish Studies* 13, no. 2 (2009): 58–66.
2. Hugh Shearman, *Finland: The Adventures of a Small Power* (London: Stevens and Sons, 1950)
3. Eino Jutikkala and Kauko Pirinen, *A History of Finland*, rev. ed. (New York: Praeger, 1974).
4. Christer Laurén, *Canadian French and Finland Swedish: Minority Languages with Outside Standards, Regionalisms, and Adstrata* (Quebec: International Center for Research on Bilingualism, 1983).
5. Mika Roinila, "Finland-Swedes of British Columbia," *Journal of Finnish Studies* 4, no. 1 (2000): 20.
6. Börje Vähämäki, "Footnote on Terminology Cited in Mika Roinila, "Finland-Swedes in Canada: Past and Present," *Journal of Finnish Studies* 1, no. 3 (1997): 91.
7. Laurén, *Canadian French*.
8. Johannes Näse, "Finlandssvenskarna i Amerika," Svensk-Ostrobottniska Samfundet(Vasa, Finland: Arkiv for Svenska Österbotten, Band 1, Häfte 3–4, 1922): 245–75; Anders Myhrman, "The Finland-Swedes and Their Cultural Organizations in America," *American Swedish Historical Society Yearbook*, 1957, rev. ed. by Order of Runeberg (1964), 9–25; Anders Myhrman, *Finlandssvenskar i Amerika*, Skrifter Utgivna av Svenska Litteratursälskapet i Finland, N0.453, Folklivsstudier IX, *Helsingfors (1972)*; Anders Myhrman, "The Finland-Swedes in America," *Swedish Pioneer Historical Quarterly* 31, no. 1 (1980), 16–33; Christer Laurén, *Canadian French;* Mika Roinila, "Finland Swedes of British Columbia" *Journal of Finnish Studies, University of Toronto, V01.4:1, 2000, 13-36*; Mika Roinila, Susanne Österlund-Pötzsch, and Susan Larson, "Women's Maintenance of Finland-Swedish Identity in North America," in Jarmo Lainio, Annaliina Gynne, Raija Kangassalo (eds.), *Transborder Contacts and the Maintenance of Finnishness in the Diaspora* (Eskilstuna, Sweden: Mälardalen University, 2009), 55–82.
9. C. E. Johnson, "Swede-Finns in Mason County," in *June Pelo Article Collection*, Swedish-Finn Historical Society, 1980, http://finlander.genealogia.fi/sfhswiki/index.php/Swede-Finns_in_Mason_County,_Michigan; Timo Riippa, "The Finns and the Swede-Finns," in June Holmquist (ed.) *They Chose Minnesota: A Survey of the State's Ethnic Groups* (St. Paul: Minnesota Historical Society Press, 1981), 296–322; Elizabeth Oman, "Swede-Finns on the Iron Ranges of Northeastern Minnesota," *Finnish-Americana* 7 (1986): 39–42; Norman Westerberg, "Swedish-Finns in the World Today," *Leading Star/Ledstjärnan* 101, nos. 1, 2, & 7 (2008).
10. Oman, "Swede-Finns," 39–42.
11. R. Pierce, *Russian America: A Bibliographical Dictionary* (Kingston: Limestone Press, 1990).
12. Johnson, "Swede Finns."
13. Riippa, "Finns."
14. Johnson, "Swede Finns."
15. Myhrman, "Finland-Swedes in America," 18.
16. Myhrman, "Finland-Swedes in America," 18.
17. Näse, "Finlandssvenskarna"; Myhrman, "Finland-Swedes in America."
18. Myhrman, *Finlandsvenskar,* 11.
19. Myhrman, "Finland-Swedes in America."
20. Myhrman, "Finland-Swedes in America," 19.
21. Myhrman, "Finland-Swedes in America," 20.
22. Myhrman, "Finland-Swedes in America," 20.
23. Mika Roinila, "North Shore Fishermen," *Finnish-American Reporter,* November (2003): 10–11.
24. Akseli Järnefelt, *Suomalaiset Amerikassa* (Helsinki: Otava), 1899.
25. Myhrman, "Finland-Swedes in America," 22.
26. Myhrman, "Finland-Swedes in America," 23.
27. Nelson Perkins, *Plywood in Retrospect: Olympia Veneer Company,* 1–8, no. 7 in a series of

monographs on the history of West Coast plywood plants (Tacoma, Washington: Plywood Pioneers Association, 1969), http://www.apawood.org/plywoodpioneers/pdfs/PPA_07.pdf.

28. Myhrman, *Finlandssvenskar*, 45.
29. Myhrman, *Finlandssvenskar*, 48.
30. Roinila, "Finland-Swedes in Canada: Past," 92.
31. Mika Roinila, *Finland-Swedes in Canada: Migration, Settlement and Ethnic Relations* (Turku, Finland: Institute of Migration, 2000), 82-85.
32. Roinila,
33. Mika Roinila, "Finland-Swedes in Canada: Discovering Some Unknown Finnish Facts" *Siirtolaisuus-Migration* 24, no. 1 (1997): 6.
34. Mika Roinila, "Erhard J. Alm: Inventor and Entrepreneur," *Scandinavian Canadian Studies* 17, no. 2 (2007): 72.
35. Myhrman, "Finland-Swedes in America"; Alex Lind, "Valsberg from a Historical Perspective: Are We Finns or Swedes or What?" *Valsbergs Hemsida*, 2008, http://www.freewebs.com/valsberg/inenglish.htm.
36. Roinila, "Finland-Swedes of British Columbia"; Roinila, "North Shore Fishermen."
37. Myhrman, "Finland-Swedes in America," 17; Helge Nelson, *The Swedes and Swedish Settlement in North America*, 2 vols. (Lund: Lund University, 1943); Westerberg correspondence, May 21, 2004.
38. Roinila, "Finland-Swedes in Canada: Migration."
39. Norman Westerberg, "More on the Missing Finns," *Finnish-American Reporter* 8, no. 10 (1997): 10.
40. Westerberg, "Swedish-Finns in the World Today."
41. S. Ruggles et al., *Integrated Public Use Microdata Series: Version 4.0* (machine-readable database) (Minneapolis: Minnesota Population Center), http://usa.ipums.org/usa/.
42. Roinila, "Finland-Swedes of British Columbia"; Kenneth D. McRae et al., *Intergroup Sympathies and Language Patterns in Finland: Results from a Survey* (Helsinki: Suomen Gallup, 1988); Kenneth McRae, *Conflict and Compromise in Multilingual Societies*, vol. 3, *Finland* (Waterloo, Ont.: Wilfrid Laurier University Press, 1997); Roinila, "Finland-Swedes in Canada: Migration."
43. Myhrman, "Finland-Swedes and Their Cultural Organizations," 12.
44. Myhrman, "Finland-Swedes and Their Cultural Organizations," 13.
45. Myhrman, "Finland-Swedes and Their Cultural Organizations," 14.
46. Named according to the national poet of Finland, J. L. Runeberg (1804-1877).
47. Myhrman, "Finland-Swedes in America," 32.
48. Myhrman, "Finland-Swedes in America," 17.
49. Närpes was an important departure area for the Swedish-Finnish emigration on the western coast of Finland.
50. Myhrman, "Finland-Swedes in America," 33.
51. Myhrman, *Finlandssvenskar*, 457-59.
52. Yrjo Raivio, *Kanadan Suomalaisten Historia, Osa 1.* (Copper Cliff, Ontario: Kanadan Suomalainen Historiaseura, 1975).
53. Myhrman, "Finland-Swedes and Their Cultural Organizations," 18-19.
54. Myhrman, "Finland-Swedes in America," 31.
55. Myhrman, "Finland-Swedes in America," 32.
56. Myhrman, "Finland-Swedes and Their Cultural Organizations," 19.
57. Timo Riippa, "Finns," in the *Encyclopedia of Chicago, 2004*, http://encyclopedia.chicagohistory.org/pages/456.html.
58. Myhrman, *Finlandssvenskar*, 460-62.
59. Myhrman, *Finlandssvenskar*, 463.
60. Myhrman, "Finland-Swedes and Their Cultural Organizations"; Myhrman, *Finlandssvenskar*, 464.
61. Myhrman, "Finland-Swedes and Their Cultural Organizations," 21; Myhrman, *Finlandssvenskar*, 465.
62. Myhrman, *Finlandssvenskar*, 465-67.
63. Myhrman, *Finlandssvenskar*, 465-67; Mika Roinila, "A Forgotten Outreach: The Finnish Salvation Army in North America," *Journal of Finnish Studies* 11, no. 1 (2007): 32-46.
64. Milton Gordon, *Assimilation in American Life* (New

York: Oxford University Press, 1964).
65. S. Dale McLemore and Harriet D. Romo, *Racial and Ethnic Relations in America*, 7th ed. (Boston: Pearson, Allyn & Bacon, 2004), 47–48.
66. Roinila, "Finland-Swedes in Canada: Migration," 200–201.
67. Hermans correspondence, May 7, 2009.
68. Roinila, "Finland-Swedes in Canada: Migration," 194.
69. Roinila, Österlund-Pötzsch, and Larson, "Women's Maintenance," 79.
70. Roinila, Österlund-Pötzsch, and Larson, "Women's Maintenance," 79.
71. Roinila, "Finland-Swedes in Canada: Migration," 205–6.
72. Kergan correspondence, May 3, 2009.
73. There is an evident longing for roots, seen, for example, in the search of history by Arlene Sundquist Empie's novel of her grandmother Ida Lillbroända, who came from the central Ostrobothnian coastal region of Kronoby in 1893. Arlene Sundquist Empie, *The Legacy of Ida Lillbroända: Finnish Emigrant to America 1893* (La Conner, Wash.: Boulder House Publishers, 2010), esp. 233–48.
74. Damstrom correspondence, May 7, 2009.
75. Forsman correspondence, October 6, 2004.

PART 7
# Connected to Finland

# Distant Dreams, Different Realities:
# North American Immigrants Revisit Finland

*Erik Hieta*

Many Finns who migrated to North America later either returned to Finland for good or often took part in various types of tourist trips, telling stories about the countries to which they had been and having different ideas and expectations about what exactly they were hoping to find in Finland on their return. Their various hopes and disappointments highlight the extent to which travelers transmitted information about changing historical and cultural realities and influenced the ideas that other North Americans had about Finland. This in turn affected the ways in which the immigrants adjusted to their new environment and their memories of the home country, as well as the ways in which people in the home country later perceived them. While at once part and parcel of the migration story, travel narratives are also connected to questions of multiculturalism and the shaping of ethnic identities in diverse contexts.

Travel between Finland and North America has a long history. Primarily, this history has been interconnected with the story of migration, so much so that until quite recently scholars largely treated travel narratives as an aspect of migration. Beginning in the 1970s, scholars became interested in the ways in which studies of migration and travel shed light on the cultural, economic, and political relations between nations. Scholars increasingly recognized the interdisciplinary nature of travel narratives, encompassing as they do such disciplines as anthropology, history, sociology, economics, psychology, political science, and, perhaps especially, literature. At base, the study of travel is the study of ideas about the self and others. Travel narratives provide a setting to engage in leisurely self-reflection and the chance to portray an encounter that is both global and local. Within this setting, however, much prior scholarship often constituted traditions, communities, and identities in spatial terms that excluded movements of both the traveler and of multiple cultures.[1] Many scholars failed to grasp the complex and historically contingent nature of the cross-cultural encounter. Nonetheless, in the hands of scholars, travel narratives have increasingly highlighted the shifting cultural, political, and economic compulsions that are at once a part of the migration story but also connected to questions of multiculturalism and the shaping of ethnic identities within diverse contexts. From a historical standpoint, travel has been significant for three reasons. First, it has facilitated cultural contact and the spread of cultural influences;

second, travel has influenced technological development and changes in economic life; and, third, it has influenced domestic and international politics, namely in terms of immigration.

This chapter focuses primarily on Finnish American travelers to Finland in the late nineteenth and early twentieth centuries. Though it is not about migration as such, it focuses strongly on the ideas that North American Finns had about Finland. Within the context of European migration to North America, travelers transmitted information about changing historical and cultural realities. The image of Finland held by most Americans largely evolved as a consequence of travel writing, diplomatic reports, and popular efforts by the media to fit these narratives into shifting political, cultural, and economic contexts. This in turn affected the adjustment of the immigrants to their new environment, their memories of the home country, and the ways in which people in the home country later perceived them. Starting from the common assumption that travel educates people about other cultures and helps break down prejudices, this chapter explores the extent to which travel by North American Finns, and later by people from Finland, also borrows from previous perceptions and misperceptions. It focuses on travel from both Canada and the United States to Finland, the stories the travelers told about those countries, and what exactly they were hoping to find when they returned to Finland. The chapter begins by focusing on the early years of migration and travel between Finland and the United States and the dreams that motivated many of these people, including the Communist-minded Finns' movement from North America to Soviet Karelia in the hopes of creating a workers' paradise. This is followed by a discussion of the decades after Finland gained its independence and attempted to market a particular image of itself to the world, and concludes with a discussion of changes in the last couple of decades to transcontinental travel and cultural exchanges.

### The Early Years of Migration and Travel

Technological progress, the rapid increase in the numbers of migrants to North America, and the opening up of Finnish society outwardly from the 1890s onward impacted travel tremendously. The advent of the steamship greatly facilitated travel abroad and caused a shift in the amount of information available on Finland and the United States. During the so-called Great Migration, thousands of Finns traveled to the United States every year. Many Finnish immigrants returned home to pass along stories about the "Great West" and about the fortunes of Finnish relatives who had emigrated there; approximately 20 percent of Finns who migrated to North America ultimately returned to Finland for good, while others returned once again to America.[2] Finnish American scholar John I. Kolehmainen recounts encountering a number of these "Old Yankees" on a steamship traveling between Hanko and New York, many of whom were making their third or fourth trip to the United States. He found them vainglorious about their store of "worldly" knowledge. In an evident display of one-upmanship over villagers who had stayed behind, they paraded their mastery of English and boasted of their familiarity with the United States, describing its immense size to spellbound listeners.[3] He noticed that it was primarily poor Finns who were impressed by these stories. The upper classes by and large remained hostile to immigration. At the same time that many in the Finnish working class celebrated the new opportunities to be found in the United States, the spread of American cultural features to Finland and to Europe in general gave rise to expressions of concern among the upper classes about "Americanization." Newspapers and public officials at the time began taking an interest in immigration from Finland, and Finnish scholars had begun studying

FIGURE 1. The Cunard Line offered trips in both directions across the Atlantic. Here is an advertisement from 1930, advertising modern ships and the pleasures available to each passenger during the trip. (Source: IMT Photo collections)

the economic reasons for why many chose to travel to North America, linking immigration also to the loss of economic labor for Finnish industry.

Travel between the two countries by Finnish Americans and the stories they told Finnish friends and relatives about the United States and Canada greatly influenced Finnish ideas about North America. Reino Kero, in "The Background of Finnish Emigration," studied the letters that Finns in America wrote to their families and friends in Finland describing the wonders of the new country.[4] Letters, photographs, and postcards helped spread the news among the poor rural populations of Finland that the United States was a land of great riches. For example, from letters Finns learned that "in America there were vast piles of all good things gathered together: gold, silver, wheat, punch, and whiskey"; that grain would grow in a week; that red wine flowed continuously from "between cracks in the cliffs"; and that all women, even the poor, walked the streets dressed in silk.[5] The simple, rural hometowns of the Finns paled in comparison to promises of new social, political, and spiritual opportunities at a time when many Finns were desperately poor. At the same time, just as many Finnish immigrants no doubt wanted to tell certain tall tales to impress people back home about newfound opportunities in North America, they also wanted Finland itself to remain the same: a place where the familiar home village, cottage, sauna, birch trees, and village road could be found and where they could still hear the squeak of the horse-drawn carriages.[6] Motivated by a healthy dose of homesickness, the first groups of Finnish Americans began traveling to Finland on group tours in 1912. Three different group tours, totaling more than 500 Finnish Americans, visited Finland that year, and more followed in subsequent years.[7] The group visits represented the beginning of stronger contacts between Finnish Americans and host organizations in Finland. However, at the same time, the romantic appeal of Finland as an unchanging patchwork of quaint villages and rural landscapes that contrasted easily with the United States and Canada as lands that were constantly changing and full of opportunities contributed to future misunderstandings between Finns and North Americans. This was no less true for more conservative, churchgoing Finns as it was for politically radical Finns, who traveled alternatively to the United States/Canada and to Finland and the Finnish-speaking regions of Karelia, only recently ceded to the Soviet Union, to help create societies friendly to the rights of workers.

### Idealistic "Karelian Fever" Tours

Amid the economic and political tensions in North America, some recent migrants chose to move to the Karelian region of the Soviet Union as part of a utopian socialist experiment in the early 1930s. Usually those travelers passed through Finland on their way to the "land of the future" in the East: Soviet Karelia.[8] As Peter Kivisto discusses in more detail from the point of view of transnationalism, between 1931 and 1934 approximately 6,000–8,000 men, women, and children from North American Finnish communities left to settle in Soviet Karelia and contribute to the building of Communism. Many Finns at the time believed that the national epic, the *Kalevala,* took place in Karelia and that the region represented the source of Finnish national culture.[9] Both conservative and Communist Finns believed that the stories of the *Kalevala* offered glimpses into early Finnish society; they just differed in that, whereas members of the political right wanted to preserve Karelian culture as a sort of living museum, Communists wanted to bring it into the modern world.[10] Initially, the Soviet Union supported this "Karelian Fever" and the desire to build a workers' paradise with Finnish as the national language.[11] Since the Soviet Union lacked a qualified revolutionary elite in Karelia, political leaders invited the foreigners to take over and develop the administration, educational system, and culture.[12] The Russians had long viewed the *Kalevala* and the romanticism surrounding it, not to mention Communist efforts to read the epic as something of a blueprint for a more egalitarian society, as a means by which Finns would recognize that they should be looking eastward rather than westward for their cultural, political, and economic influences.

The stories of those involved in building a Finnish workers' paradise in Karelia resonate with hope and enthusiasm. The utopian ideals were also infused with a practical desire to find a space within a society friendly to the interests of labor.[13] A fourteen-year-old girl named Irma Pohjansalo remembered fondly that all of those on the boats from Canada to Finland were waving red flags when they arrived in ports and were talking eagerly about what they would do in Karelia.[14] Other travelers also described this type of "revolutionary spirit" and the enthusiasm they felt during the trip to Soviet Karelia: many people on the ships sang revolutionary songs, while others commented on the "desperate-looking workers standing in the harbor dock yards" during the stops in the Swedish ports of Gothenburg or Stockholm, as well as the Finnish ports of Turku and Helsinki,[15] before sailing on to Leningrad.

Unfortunately, all this changed a few years later when Stalin's political police arrested and executed many of the migrants to Karelia, both from Finland and North America, for being foreigners and supposed spies. By 1933–34, hundreds of disappointed refugees were returning to Canada and the United States. Russian scholar Irina Takala estimates that approximately 1,500 North American Finns had returned by 1935,[16] and more returned later. While some were quite vocal in voicing their disappointments, many remained silent about their experiences, and many Finnish American Communists continued to maintain the party line that those arrested in the purges were American agents and spies who deserved their fate.[17] Rumors and stories about the horrible conditions in Karelia, accusations of fraud, and much misinformation in general circulated throughout Finnish communities in Canada and the United States.[18] The personal stories, like that of Irma Pohjansalo, help shed light on the complex debates that still exist in many Finnish American and Finnish Canadian communities regarding those who left and the troubled divide between more conservative churchgoing Finns and more radical Communists.

## Politics and the Well-Heeled Traveler

Even as the efforts by Communist Finns to found communities more sympathetic to labor and workers' rights ultimately failed, more conservative Finns traveled in ever greater numbers between North America and Finland. During the interwar period, traveling by ship became easier than it had been previously, and many travelers were better established financially. Whereas travel at the turn of the twentieth century had still been full of hardships, travelers could now talk easily about pleasure trips. Ships boasted nicer cabins and better food, and many ships offered different entertainment programs to travelers. Throughout the 1920s and 1930s, more well established Finnish artists, businessmen, and politicians took an interest in the United States. Finnish authorities actively marketed an image of Finland as a western European nation, indeed as "an outpost of Western culture" in the far north of Europe.[19] In the 1930s, the Finnish Foreign Ministry commissioned the propaganda film *Finland Calling*, which advertised Finland as a modern nation with the only motorway leading all the way to the Arctic Sea. To further correct any misunderstandings, the Finnish Tourist Association claimed that even the Russians had recognized the Western nature of Finnish civilization.[20] If anything, guidebooks of the time protest too much that the Finns do not have any "Eastern" influences, as if trying to wish away more than a hundred years of shared Finnish/Russian history, including the current efforts by Communist Finns and Russians in Karelia. Then again, the gambit seems to have been somewhat successful. Diplomats at the American Consulate in Helsinki reported that more and more Americans were visiting Finland and finding a country open to American ways. Diplomats attributed this to the large numbers of migrants from Finland to the United States as well as to Finnish businessmen traveling to the United States to study American industrial and commercial methods.[21] For example, more than 58,000 Finns from North America visited Finland during this period. In general, Finnish Americans and Finnish Canadians were welcome guests, and often their relatives came to meet them in Helsinki. From the Finnish point of view, the visitors brought important news about conditions in North America, and prominent conservative organizations such as the Association of Finnish Culture and Identity and representatives from Helsinki University hosted numerous groups that arrived from the United States and Canada.[22]

For Finnish and American travelers, it was important to reaffirm connections based on immigration and shared cultural values. More often than not, this involved a celebration of high culture. For instance, in 1920 the Finnish American orchestral band Louhi visited Finland and performed many concerts. This group from Pennsylvania arrived in Hanko to much fanfare, with a band and a musical choir.[23] Not to be outdone, the 300-year colonial history of Finns in the Delaware valley was celebrated in 1938, and famed Finnish artist Väinö Aaltonen was chosen to design a monument of granite to commemorate Finnish participation in the early settlement of the state. The Finnish minister to the United States, Eero Järnefelt, was an honorary guest at the ceremonies in Chester, Pennsylvania, where the monument was unveiled.[24] A year later, in 1939, the U.S. government invited Finland to take part in a world's fair to be held in New York. Famed architect Alvar Aalto prepared plans for "an American town in Finland" as an opportunity to demonstrate to the United States Finland's "ardent desire to strengthen the cultural bonds" between the two countries.[25] The Finnish tourism industry began marketing an image of sauna, *sisu*, and Sibelius to highlight tangible aspects of Finnish culture. Throughout the 1930s, Finnish choral groups and singers gave concerts in the United States, and famed distance runners Paavo Nurmi and Taisto Mäki showcased Finnish athletic prowess in a series of benefit events during the Winter War to help sell the image of Finnish culture. Their job was made easier by the fact that most Americans already had a positive image of Finland as the only European country to continue repaying its debts to the United States during the 1930s when all others had defaulted. With the Winter War, the American media celebrated both the image of "honest Finland" and "brave Finland" valiantly defending democracy against brutal Soviet repression. The media also helped coordinate massive relief efforts, which helped disseminate knowledge about Finland to the general American public. The media reports highlight the extent to which travel can be as much a literary endeavor as a material one, and, as such, the simplistic images of honest and brave Finland soon became more complicated and problematic.

The positive media coverage of Finland during the interwar period and the Winter War, and the stories brought home by well-heeled American travelers who had often met like-minded individuals in Finland, masked lingering political tensions. The later years of the Second World War, when Finland fought as a cobelligerent with Nazi Germany, caused many Americans to call into question the cultural connections between the two countries. Many felt that either way, whether by Nazi influence or renewed Soviet aggression, Finland's status as an independent democracy was all but lost. Hoping to allay apprehensions, the Finnish government enlisted the Finland Society (Suomi Seura), which had been organized in 1927 to provide expertise and service to Finns living or moving abroad or returning to Finland and an up-to-date image of Finland to the outside world, to transmit, via radio, information to Finnish Americans about their relatives and the general situation.[26] Nonetheless, the more conservative American media lamented "the tragic case of Finland," saying by the end of the war that the United States was witnessing "the crushing of a democratic outpost in Northern Europe."[27] Likewise, the Save Finland Committee published several pamphlets that asked "Is Finland Worth Saving?" and "Are the Lights Going Out in Finland?" It used firsthand accounts by travelers to argue that Finland's democratic way of life was all but "extinct."[28] As the media in both Finland and the United States focused increasingly on the complex nature of the relationship between Finland and the Soviet Union and propaganda mills on both sides of the ocean exploited Cold War tensions, many Finnish Communists reacted with distain to stories of the paranoid "Red scare" of the late 1940s and 1950s, whereas many Americans doubted Finnish claims of neutrality and saw Finland as a Soviet satellite. Though these ideas no doubt impacted the numbers of North Americans who wanted to travel to Finland and the impressions of those that did, it is still difficult to say to what extent. There are few archival materials and travel narratives by members of the lower classes and their impressions of Finland or the United States during this period. Many of the more critical Americans obviously stayed away from Finland, and those who did travel to Finland probably did not meet many Finnish Communists or political leftists.

## From Kinship Trips to Transnational Connections

Despite the shifting political context, American relief aid to Finland continued in the years after the war, and the packages and visits by relatives from North America continued to foster strong ties. Relief activities begun during the Winter War increased in the years after World War II, with American Finns sending over two million packages and large amounts of money to Finland just between the years 1945 and 1949. Both Communist Finns and more conservative churchgoing Finns participated in the relief activities, often working together for the first time, which helped bind some of the old wounds that had divided the various communities.[29] In the autumn of 1945, thirteen Finnish American groups traveled to Turku, Finland. Representatives from the Finland Society and Finland General Radio met the groups.[30] According to the Finnish media, Finns greeted the visitors enthusiastically and expressed deep gratitude for all the relief help extended them during the war years. In the years after the war, famed Finnish violinist Kerttu Wanne and opera singer Väinö Sola toured the North American continent, giving benefit concerts to help raise money for ongoing Finnish relief. The archives of the Finland Society at the Department of General History of the University of Turku contain numerous boxes of old newspaper clippings about Finnish musicians traveling to the United States and Canada, and American and Canadian choirs in turn visiting Finland. In the 1950s and 1960s, choirs from all parts of the United States and Canada traveled by plane or steamship to Finland on goodwill tours. Indeed, until the end of the 1960s the arrival of ships in Helsinki crowded with North Americans of Finnish origin was a big event at the beginning of each summer, and the Finnish press reported widely on the "smiling American singers" who came to give concerts.

During the next decades, the numbers of these so-called kinship trips grew exponentially, and, in contrast with what had taken place earlier, they also involved many Finns traveling to North America and not just North Americans traveling to Finland. In 1947, the first tourists arrived in Finland by airplane. Finnish Americans and Finnish Canadians could now travel between their home countries and Finland more easily than ever. The Finland Society organized hundreds of trips between the two countries throughout the 1960s, 1970s, and early 1980s. Aside from visiting relatives, what were these travelers hoping to find and convey to others? Many retired first-generation Finnish Americans still wanted to return to the land of their birth fifty to sixty years after leaving. Even more than before, they found a Finland that had changed tremendously. Throughout the 1960s and 1970s, Finland underwent a rapid process of urbanization. In the 1950s, Finnish Americans could not resist bragging to the press about the high standard of living in the United States, exclaiming that almost everyone had a car and that, unlike in Finland, only children rode bicycles;[31] in contrast, later groups of Finnish American travelers expressed surprise at Finland's rapid development and a certain bittersweet disappointment about the rural lifestyles that had been lost.[32] Many second- and third-generation Finnish Americans and Finnish Canadians also traveled to Finland and felt somewhat surprised that the country did not resemble the stories of their youth. But many others doubtless felt a sense of pride in what Finland had achieved. Ultimately, the 1980s represented a period of transition: the number of chartered flights and group trips diminished, and more and more Finns and North Americans began to travel independently across the

**FIGURE 2.** Among travelers visiting Finland in 1920 was the well-known band Louhi, from Ashtabula, Ohio. The band gave concerts in Finland. Picture taken in Helsinki. (Source: IMT Photo collections)

Atlantic. Though Finnish Americans and Finnish Canadians will continue to travel to Finland to meet relatives and reconnect with their heritage, the phenomenon of mass tourism has made it possible for increasing numbers of Finns and North Americans to cross the Atlantic for other reasons.

Whereas generations of Finnish and American travelers largely formed their impressions through stories of immigration and the opportunities found in America and not in Finland, a younger generation of travelers often notice the extent to which Finland, the United States, and Canada share a similar popular culture that is part and parcel of the continuing homogenization of global culture. Mass tourism may take new forms, combining earlier individualistic travel with mass travel and even, more recently, including virtual travel through online exhibitions and interactive websites, but it will continue into the foreseeable future. Indeed, developments in mass tourism have gone hand in hand with greater access to information about other cultures via music, movies, sports, food, and television. More than ever before, mass tourism helps spread technological changes and standardized economic practices.[33] Finns have long seen the United States as a site of economic modernity. For example, in the 1950s Finnish entrepreneur S. P. J. Keinänen toured the United States, studying the cars and the use of roads, and returned to Finland with the idea of starting a taxi service.[34] Numerous foreign visitors, including a large number of North Americans, took advantage of the taxi service during the 1952 summer Olympics in Helsinki. In later decades, fascination with American television and pop culture in general complemented the longer-standing fascination with automobiles. More and more Finnish young people traveled to the United States as exchange students and returned with both positive and negative impressions of the country.

The rapid changes in Finnish and American society in recent decades have facilitated a certain "false friendship," one in which the long-standing familial connections have often been replaced by ambivalence about deeper underlying social and cultural conventions. Finnish exchange students often return with the impression that Americans are superficial. For their part, while many Americans are increasingly impressed with Finnish technology and education and travel to Finland on educational exchanges, they complain that many Finns are rather unsociable. All too often earlier studies on immigration failed to adequately contextualize the ways in which Finns, Canadians, and Americans maintained strong ties while still developing in different directions as a result of different historical realities, such as the Winter War, the tensions of the Cold War, and American (and Canadian) abundance in the postwar years, which stood in stark contrast to the material deprivation in Finland and the forces of rapid Finnish urbanization.

In recent years, scholars have begun increasingly to focus on the intersection between migration and travel and the way they foster transnational connections. Current trends in research emphasize the multiple and continuous connections that occur in a transnational social space, the dimensions of cultural reproduction and the generation of novel cultural forms that are a part of such connections, and the hybrid and fluid nature of identities constructed by people participating regularly in a multicultural setting.[35] The representational process that is a part of travel writing offers many insights into these themes. Likewise, travel narratives inform questions regarding the saliency of ethnic identities within multicultural societies. As Finland receives more and more tourists and longer-term migrants from around the world, researchers are again looking to the United States and Canada for answers on how to create and sustain diverse multicultural societies. A number of the most recent studies on migration and travel focus on Finnish American and Finnish Canadian communities as case studies for addressing larger questions of multiculturalism and cross-cultural encounters. They also focus on the ways in which different generations create their own narratives of integration and belonging, separation and difference. Then again, travel continues to appeal to other impulses as well. As more and more students travel between the countries for study, as rapid airline flights facilitate cross-cultural romances, and as people in general read and surf the Internet and travel the world more, impressions of Finland and North America will continue to evolve. Just as ambivalence about other nations and tension between different points of view will likely continue, so too travel—whether as a means of facilitating cultural and political contacts and technological development, or as a means of sustaining transnational communities—has been and will continue to be one of humanity's more expansive and creative spheres of operation.

## NOTES

1. James Clifford, "Travelling Cultures," in *Cultural Studies,* ed. Lawrence Grossberg et al. (New York: Routledge, 1992), 105.
2. Keijo Virtanen, *Settlement or Return: Finnish Emigrants (1860-1930) in the International Overseas Return Migration Movement* (Forssa: Institute of Migration, 1979).
3. John I. Kolehmainen, "Hanko–Liverpool–New York," *Turun Historiallinen Arkisto* 28 (1973): 347.
4. Reino Kero, "The Background of Finnish Emigration," in *The Finns in North America: A Social Symposium,* ed. Ralph J. Jalkanen (East Lansing: Michigan State University Press, 1969), 55–62.
5. Kero, "Background of Finnish Emigration," 59–60.
6. Reino Kero, *Suomalaisina Pohjois-Amerikassa: Siirtolaiselämää Yhdysvalloissa ja Kanadassa* (Turku: Siirtolaisuusinstituutti, 1997), 335–36.
7. Kero, *Suomalaisina Pohjois-Amerikassa,* 344–45.
8. Peter Kivisto, "Finnish Americans and the

Homeland, 1918–1958," *Journal of American Ethnic History* 7, no. 1 (1987): 9–28.

9. William A. Wilson, *Folklore and Nationalism in Modern Finland* (Bloomington: Indiana University Press, 1976).

10. Paul M. Austin, "Soviet Karelian: The Language That Failed," *Slavic Review* 51, no. 1 (1992): 19.

11. Michael Gelb, "'Karelian Fever': The Finnish Immigrant Community during Stalin's Purges," *Europe-Asia Studies* 45, no. 6 (1996): 1091.

12. Paul M. Austin, "Soviet Finnish: The End of a Dream," *East European Quarterly* 21, no. 2 (1987): 188.

13. Peter Kivisto and Mika Roinila, "Reaction to Departure: The Finnish American Community Responds to 'Karelian Fever,'" in *North American Finns in Soviet Karelia in the 1930s: Proceedings of International Research Seminar Held in Petrozavodsk 22–23 May, 2008*, ed. Irina Takala (Petrozavodsk: Petrozavodsk State University Press, 2008), 17–38.

14. Irma Pohjansalo papers, Institute of Migration, Turku.

15. See especially Reino Kero, *Neuvosto-Karjalaa rakentamassa: Pohjois-Amerikan suomalaiset tekniikan tuojina 1930-luvun Neuvosto-Karjalassa* (Helsinki: SHS, 1983), 85–90.

16. Irina Takala, "From the Frying Pan into the Fire," *Journal of Finnish Studies* 8, no. 1 (2004): 120.

17. David Ahola, "The Karelian Fever Episode of the 1930s," *Finnish Americana* 5 (1983): 4–7.

18. Varpu Lindström, "'Heaven or Hell on Earth?' Soviet Karelia's Propaganda War of 1934–1935 in the Finnish Canadian Press," in ed. Takala, *North American Finns in Soviet Karelia*, 83. Much archival and historical research, including many memoirs, has been published on the topic of North American Finns in Soviet Karelia in the last ten to fifteen years. Two research projects have been organized recently: "Missing in Karelia: Canadian Victims of Stalin's Purges" was started in 2006 by an international team of researchers from Canada, Finland, and Russia, and "North American Finns in Soviet Karelia during the 1920s–1950s" was a two-year project funded by the Russian Foundation of Humanities in 2007–8. Other archival material is still being collected and published.

19. *Finland: The Country, Its People, and Institutions* (Helsinki: Otava, 1926), 5.

20. Finnish Tourist Association, *Finland: A Practical Guide-Book* (Helsinki: Finnish Tourist Association, 1931), 9.

21. Consulate of the United States of America, *Finland* (Helsinki: Consulate of the United States of America, 1928), 2.

22. Kero, *Suomalaisina Pohjois-Amerikassa*, 345–47.

23. Kero, *Suomalaisina Pohjois-Amerikassa*, 345.

24. Suomi Seura newspaper clippings, folders 12–14, Turku University Department of General History archives.

25. Finnish New York World's Fair Commission, *Finland Builds* (New York: Finnish New York World's Fair Commission, 1940), 68–75, 78.

26. Kero, *Suomalaisina Pohjois-Amerikassa*, 359.

27. William Henry Chamberlin, "The Tragic Case of Finland," *American Mercury* 59, no. 247 (July 1944): 7.

28. Save Finland Committee, *Is Finland Worth Saving?* and *Are the Lights Going Out in Finland?* (Duluth, MN: Save Finland Committee, 1940).

29. Kero, *Suomalaisina Pohjois-Amerikassa*, 342–43.

30. Kero, *Suomalaisina Pohjois-Amerikassa*, 348.

31. Suomi Seura newspaper clippings, Turku University Department of General History archives.

32. Kero, *Suomalaisina Pohjois-Amerikassa*, 354.

33. Auvo Kostiainen et al., *Matkailijan ihmeellinen maailma: matkailun historia vanhalta ajalta omaan aikaamme* (Helsinki: Suomalaisen Kirjallisuuden Seura, 2004).

34. Suomi Seura newspaper clippings, Turku University Department of General History archives.

35. Steven Vertovec, "Conceiving and Researching Transnationalism," *Ethnic and Racial* Studies 22, no. 2 (1999): 447–62.

# Help among Nations: The Humanitarian Impulse in American–Finnish Relations

*Erik Hieta*

Relief activities on behalf of Finland took place during the First World War and the Second World War, most particularly during the Winter War of 1939-40 and its aftermath, and the activities significantly impacted American–Finnish relations and Finnish American communities. This chapter explores the strong role of former president Herbert Hoover in working on Finland's behalf and the challenge this presented for American foreign policy during World War II and in subsequent decades. The chapter demonstrates that the official and voluntary efforts at providing aid, despite at times being contested, ultimately impacted political relations and social and cultural connections between peoples in the two countries.

Relations between nations are shaped in a number of ways, not least of which through official and voluntary efforts at providing material aid for the relief of suffering during catastrophes such as war, for improving living standards, and for strengthening cultural life. Scholars of diplomacy and foreign affairs have all too often studied the economic, ideological, and ethno-racial components shaping international relations, while often downplaying or overlooking the extent to which humanitarianism, whether in the form of relief efforts, private philanthropy, technical aid, or educational and cultural exchanges, also impacts relations between peoples and nations. Beginning at the end of the First World War, but especially with the Second World War, American aid abroad became increasingly intertwined with the activities of national and international agencies, both official and unofficial. To fully understand American aid to other nations, it is important to take into account both the existing international context and the reciprocal efforts undertaken by other nations, in this instance Finland. This chapter addresses relief efforts by the United States on behalf of Finland, responses by the Finns, and the ways in which the efforts have impacted Finnish and American relations. I argue that the official and voluntary efforts at providing aid significantly impacted American–Finnish political relations for the better and improved social and cultural connections between peoples and diplomatic officials in the two countries. After first explaining the role played by Herbert Hoover in particular in providing aid to Finland at the end of World War I and throughout World War II and its aftermath, I look at ways Americans and Finns in the last half-century have established numerous organizations, foundations, and exchange programs to strengthen social and cultural understandings between the two countries.

## Herbert Hoover and Relief during the War Years

The first important period of American overseas philanthropy to Finland began during the First World War and continued through the end of the Winter War in 1940. The economic growth of the United States and its new role as a world power explained the increased role of philanthropy in international affairs. Famine relief often provides new opportunities for cooperation and diplomacy. No one was more aware of this than Herbert Hoover. Few American presidents or politicians in the first half of the twentieth century possessed such an intimate knowledge of foreign peoples and their governments as Hoover. Arguably the most respected man in America in the 1920s, Hoover earned an international reputation as a great humanitarian for organizing relief efforts for the millions of starving civilians affected by World War I, including those in Finland. In March 1938, Hoover received an honorary doctorate from the University of Helsinki for his efforts, the first awarded to a foreigner in ninety-eight years. Several days after the Soviet Union attacked Finland on November 30, 1939, the Finnish government asked Hoover to again organize relief for Finland. He quickly organized the Finnish Relief Fund and appealed to newspapers, politicians, and citizens across the United States to help aid Finland. Most Americans hardly needed convincing on the importance of helping Finland: they held Finland in high regard in the 1930s as the only European country not to default on repaying its loan from the First World War. Hoover's appeal to help Finland struck the theme of sharing American bounty with war-stricken peoples as a means of spreading the faith of freedom and democracy. Hoover envisioned an organization that would provide a mass supply of food to starving people during the exceptional circumstances caused by intense warfare.

The Finnish Relief Fund proved enormously popular in the United States. In addition to stirring images of "honest Finland" always paying its debts, it also tapped into a wellspring of anti-Communist feeling. Newspapers quickly took up the cause of "brave little Finland" valiantly defending democracy and Western civilization itself against the Bolshevik menace. Numerous celebrities from the entertainment industry and famous sports stars made relief for Finland into a cause célèbre. Artists and cartoonists of national fame helped the cause as well. In a little over three months, the Finnish Relief Fund sent, in supplies and cash, a total of $3.5 million. This amount was more than half of the total amount of aid contributed by all other countries.[1] Though the Finnish Relief Fund did not act in an official government capacity, Hoover and the Finnish government enjoyed a close relationship, and he exchanged numerous cables with the Finnish president, prime minister, and other top officials. Many of the cables draw attention to shared cultural connections between Finns and Americans. Newspapers and the Publicity Division of the Finnish Relief Fund made the most of these sentiments. Varpu Lindström, in *From Heroes to Enemies: Finns in Canada, 1937–1947,* has studied how the war years impacted immigrant identities and issues of integration.[2] Scholars in the United States have not devoted significant attention to how the relief efforts impacted relations between ethnic Finns and mainstream Americans at the domestic level or the significant role played by women at the local level in working for the organizations and helping redefine their place within both Finnish American communities and mainstream society.

Materials at Stanford University's Hoover Institution on War, Revolution and Peace in particular provide much information on the relief efforts and the men and women involved in them and on their relationship to broader political and ideological discussions. The writings of Herbert Hoover provide additional information on the Finnish Relief Fund and famine relief to Finland in general. Of special

THE HONEST MAN SEEKS OUT DIOGENES.  —By Jerry Doyle

**FIGURE 1.** Political cartoons from the interwar years highlighted Finland's good reputation in the United States for repaying its loans. (Source: IMT Photo Collections)

importance are Hoover's accounts of his relief activities in *An American Epic*[3] and the *Memoirs of Herbert Hoover*.[4] Hoover also linked his ideas about giving to foreign policy and how philanthropy would help promote democracy and freedom throughout the world in *Addresses upon the American Road,* published in three volumes for the period 1940–48.[5] The Finnish Relief Fund published *Reports to American Donors, December 1939–July 1940,* which includes some of the comments of top officials involved in the relief effort in both Finland and the United States and summarizes the relief activities.[6] The Hoover Institution holds 250 boxes of archival material on the Finnish Relief Fund, which lasted from 1939 to 1946, and on the numerous national and local committees that were a part of it. It also holds another 166 boxes of material from the National Committee on Food for the Small Democracies, which was organized in 1940 but includes the years between 1932 and 1948 (such as photographs and speeches from Hoover's trip to Finland in 1938), and more than 350 boxes on Hoover's humanitarian efforts, correspondence, and writings and speeches on matters of foreign policy in the collection entitled Herbert Hoover Papers.

Within several months, twelve relief organizations had arisen, many organized and staffed by Finnish Americans, which made appeals for various forms of relief for Finland. Aside from the Finnish Relief Fund, however, other relief organizations had little time to establish themselves as anything more than a scattering of ad hoc groups before the war came to an end. For this reason, Hoover set up a special remittance division as part of the Finnish Relief Fund, which transferred all gifts and monies collected by the other agencies to Finland free of charge. Individual Finnish Americans also organized relief organizations to aid Finland. From the beginning, Finnish American relief was of several kinds: individuals sending money and goods to relatives and friends; and organizations sending clothes, shoes, food, medicines, vitamins, and cash to one or more relief organizations in Finland. Finnish American Lutheran churches in particular took the lead in relief activities. The Lutherans conducted a wide-ranging program of relief. Much of the food, clothing, and medicine provided by Lutheran World Relief went to persons displaced from their homes. Finnish American societies and organizations, such as the Finnish-American Historical Society of the West, have subsequently written about these relief efforts,[7] and many of them contain their own archives on the relief efforts. The Institute of Migration in Turku, Finland, also contains some records on the help provided by individuals and church organizations in Finland and the United States during this time.

The war and relief activities at once broke down many long-standing differences between churchgoing Finns and many left-leaning social democrats, while at the same time reinscribing new divisions between those Finnish Americans on the political right and the extreme political left that would last for many decades. In *Immigrant Socialists in the United States: The Case of Finns and the Left*[8] and "Finnish Americans and the Homeland, 1918–1958,"[9] Peter Kivisto has assessed the way the war years impacted ethnic Finnish identities on both the political right and left. In addition, Finlandia University's Finnish American Historical Archive contains materials on the Winter War in general as well as on the various socialist parties and Communist movements, the Industrial Workers of the World (IWW), and the Evangelical Lutheran churches.

### Humanitarianism and American–Finnish Relations

The politics of the Winter War and American aid to Finland has received more attention from scholars than has the popular response to the Finnish Relief Fund celebrated in the media and throughout the country at the time. In *America and the Russo-Finnish War,* Andrew J. Swartz credits American friendship with Finland as the reason so many Americans rushed to assist Finnish efforts during the Winter War,[10] whereas Benjamin D. Rhodes, in his article "The Origins of Finnish-American Friendship, 1919–1941," details how American funding of the Finnish war debt in 1922 and Finland's determination to pay the money back solidified this strong friendship.[11] More recently, scholars have turned their attention to the issue of how famine relief as an extension of foreign policy bitterly divided Herbert Hoover and his efforts from those of the Roosevelt administration. The Roosevelt administration did not entirely approve of Hoover's activities on behalf of Finnish relief. This was not out of any ill will toward Finland. Rather, the disagreements between Hoover and the Roosevelt administration spoke to the bitter partisan politics dividing the nation at the time. In September 1939, President Roosevelt had asked Hoover to assist with food relief in Europe. Hoover had refused. Believing that Roosevelt intended to lead the nation into war, Hoover wanted to be free to criticize the White House if it did anything that might jeopardize U.S. neutrality.

How did the bitter political divisions affect help to Finland? In his article "Hoover, Roosevelt and the Politics of American Aid to Finland, 1939–1940," Hal Elliott Wert argues that Finland was the ultimate beneficiary of the intense political rivalry between Roosevelt and Hoover.[12] While continuing

FIGURE 2. Before and during the Winter War (1939-40), a large number of cartoons and images were published in the Western press in favor of Finland. Here in *the Evening Telegram of Toronto,* on November 22, 1939, Stalin is accusing Finland of planning an attack on the Soviet Union. (Source: Photo collections, miscellaneous, DGH)

to appreciate Hoover's efforts with the Finnish Relief Fund, the Finnish government was also able to maintain close ties with the Roosevelt administration. In addition to the $3.5 million raised by the Finnish Relief Fund, Congress appropriated a loan of $30 million for nonmilitary relief, most of which the Finnish government used to buy food, trucks, tractors, factory machinery and parts, cotton, chemicals, and medical supplies. The Ministry of Foreign Affairs in Helsinki contains several boxes of material on the correspondence between the Finnish government and the Roosevelt administration throughout the war years. The political discussions also helped keep Finland in the spotlight after the Winter War. During the Second World War, the Roosevelt administration began to associate philanthropy more directly with national policy. The controversies surrounding providing humanitarian relief to countries at war became even more heated after the United States joined the Allied cause in 1941. In "On the Outside Looking In: Herbert Hoover and World War II," Richard Norton Smith links the politics of Hoover's Finnish Relief Fund and National Committee on Food for the Small Democracies to the controversial nature of famine relief in general and the question of whether it would be beneficial to send aid to suffering civilians in countries occupied by Nazi Germany or fighting as one of its allies.[13] Finland once again entered the headlines, with Hoover and his supporters still defending the need to send relief, and numerous other Americans, including many leftist Finnish American groups, arguing that Finland was now the enemy and needed to be punished. Organized labor set up agencies that were international in scope for promoting its own overseas programs, which no doubt helped drain off potential contributors to the ethnic and national agencies.

Nonetheless, the goodwill established between Finland and the United States during the Winter War largely carried over into the later years of the war, when Finland was fighting as a cobelligerent with Nazi Germany, and into the postwar period. Though the Roosevelt administration cut diplomatic ties with Finland in 1944, it never declared war on Finland, unlike its ally Great Britain. R. Michael Berry, in *American Foreign Policy and the Finnish Exception: Ideological Preferences and Wartime Realities,* argues that, because of the goodwill built up in the years before 1941, American–Finnish friendship not only survived the later years of World War II but also contributed to the United States officially recognizing Finland's neutrality at the height of the Cold War.[14] Despite the fact that Finland refused aid from the Marshall Plan in 1947 because of Soviet pressure, the U.S. government granted Finland more than $120 million in loans in the late 1940s and early 1950s. Finland benefited in other ways as well during the immediate postwar years. In addition to strong overseas operations administered by the Finnish Relief Fund and the Lutheran Church, the Red Cross furnished medical supplies and clothing to refugees (it sent over $1 million worth of supplies in 1940 alone and more in the years after World War II), and the Quakers, through the American Friends Service Committee, administered a program of feeding children and managed day nurseries, orphanages, and work camps in the years immediately after the end of the war. The Cooperative for American Remittance for Europe (CARE), later the Cooperative for American Relief Everywhere, sent more than two million relief packages containing food, toys, and clothing to Finnish families between 1946 and 1957. Additionally, Americans sent food, clothing, building materials, and trucks to Finland via the United Nations.

For its part, Finnish appreciation of the aid was widespread. The Finnish government created an official relief committee that worked with American representatives in helping 600,000 civilians with food, shelter, medical treatment, and family rehabilitation between 1939 and 1952. A number of Finnish refugees wrote letters of thanks to Herbert Hoover and heads of the other relief organizations for sending so many goods, much of which the recipients had never seen before. Other individuals such as Basil Robert McAllister, a New York bank teller who first fell in love with Finland at the New York World's Fair in 1939, picked up where Hoover left off and collected food and clothing for the Finns. Though he was not the head of a relief organization, McAllister single-handedly collected and sent 600 packages of food and clothing, totaling more than 6,000 pounds, to Finland. In all, he aided twenty-five families. The postage alone cost him $700 in a single year. Turku's Institute of Migration contains records on his efforts, as well as information about his travels to Finland to meet the families that he had helped. In addition to the archival materials at the Institute of Migration, Kimmo Kuikka offers an analysis of Finnish Relief Fund efforts from a Finnish perspective in his thesis study.[15] Eljas Repo has studied America's aid to Finland immediately after World War II.[16] Tomi Haapanen's thesis on the Help Finland organization, 1945–52, examines an organization that succeeded the Finnish Relief Fund.[17] In addition to focusing on the relief efforts, Finnish political historians have also noted that the Finnish government, as a calculated maneuver to further strengthen Finnish–American relations, continued making loan payments in the 1930s when other European nations had defaulted. Scholars in both countries have concluded that this strategy was for the most part successful, as evidenced by the continuous relief received by Finland in both an official and unofficial capacity long after the Second World War.

FIGURE 3. Finnish American volunteers in the Winter War gathering after the war on June 16, 1940, in Helsinki. (Source: IMT Photo collections, USA_0424)

### Relief Aid and Improved Cultural Connections

During the next important phase of philanthropy, which spans the period between the late 1940s and the present, private foundations, government-funded educational exchange programs, and corporations have channeled economic, cultural, and social support into areas such as international grants and fellowships. Friendship societies and organizations also began in the decades after the war, most notably the Finlandia Foundation. Yrjö Paloheimo, a wealthy Finn who traveled to the United States with Finland's diplomatic corps and served as field secretary for the Help Finland organization, established the Finlandia Foundation in 1953 to serve Finnish American communities at the national level and to operate as an informal arm of Finnish foreign policy, one that hoped to enhance Finland's image in the United States. According to Jon L. Saari, in *Black Ties and Miners' Boots: Inventing Finnish-American Philanthropy—A History of Finlandia Foundation National 1953-2003*, it offered material support to Finland—money for Finnish athletes, medicines, used musical instruments, hospitality for Finnish visitors, and scholarships for Finns and Americans—and ideological support for Finnish democracy.[18] The Finnish government was enthusiastic and grateful for the support during the decades of reconstruction and the Cold War as a way of combating economic and cultural marginalization from western Europe. Paloheimo in fact started the foundation and modeled it after the much larger American Scandinavian

**FIGURE 4.** Large collections and relief systems formed in the United States. The picture shows a truck being loaded with relief packages for Finland. (Source: IMT Photo collections, USA 43/1978)

Foundation because that foundation excluded Finns at the time (formal inclusion came only after 1960). The Immigration History Research Center (IHRC) in Minneapolis, Minnesota, contains several boxes of material dealing with the fifty-year history of the Finlandia Foundation and Finlandia Foundation Trust, and well as Yrjö Paloheimo's papers and the papers of other important members and leaders of the organization.

Private American foundations and government-funded exchange programs helped build goodwill between the two nations as well. Private foundations that derived their resources from American corporations played an important part in overseas technical aid. The Finnish nursing leader Venny Snellman opened the door for cooperation between Finland's health-care organizations and the Rockefeller Foundation during the time that the Finnish government began promoting social welfare policies. Ann Yrjälä has studied this issue in depth in *Public Health and Rockefeller Wealth: Alliance Strategies in the Early Formation of Finnish Public Health Nursing*.[19] Marianne Tallberg has also written about the Rockefeller Foundation's interest in Finland in her article, "Venny Snellman, Finnish Nurses, and Rockefeller Foundation Support, 1929–1956."[20] In 1947, the Ford Foundation (Henry Fordin Säätiö) also began providing Finland with technical aid. It provided funding for research into motor traffic and farming machinery. The Ford Foundation allocated nearly $6 million throughout the world in the late 1940s and 1950s for economic research pertaining to industrial as well as rural problems, including efforts to improve agricultural methods. Pioneering work at the time, the foundation has since provided more than 2 million euros to Finland for work on motor and traffic safety. Timo Juotsivuo et al. have published a work summarizing the work of the Ford Foundation in Finland called *Henry Fordin Säätiö 1947-1997—Henry Ford Stiftelsen, 1947-1997.*[21] Though the foundations did not receive financial support from the American government, they seldom initiated programs without the approval of Washington. The government even took an active role in creating and promoting some programs. In 1949, for example, Congress, recognizing the Cold War implications of Finland's debt to the United States, authorized that the remaining payments fund a joint education program. This program, known as the Fulbright Program, has since funded the exchange of numerous scholars and teachers between Finland and the United States.

With the end of the Cold War and Finland's more recent role as a prosperous and technologically advanced nation, the cultural, educational, and economic exchanges between the two countries have taken place on a more even footing. The Finnish government and private organizations mainly donate money to Finnish American organizations to maintain cultural connections and to fund research grants and further educational exchanges between the countries. Organizations such as the Finland Society (Suomi Seura), founded in 1927 to provide expertise and service to Finns living abroad and support Finnish culture, have more recently taken a stronger role in providing significant financial support to expatriate organizations and media. Suomi Seura organizes and funds Finnish summer language programs for foreigners. It also helps fund *Suomi koulut* (Finnish-language schools) throughout the country for youngsters wanting to learn Finnish. Together with the Finnish government, it helps fund FinnFest USA, a yearly festival first organized in 1983 to celebrate Finnish American culture and history. Suomi Seura and Finnish educational and government leaders also support the Salolampi Foundation, which is dedicated to sustaining Finnish language and culture through scholarships and programs such as the Salolampi Finnish Language Village in Minnesota. Each summer, young people throughout the United States reenact traditional Finnish life and culture at the Salolampi Finnish Language Village. The Finnish government and the Finnish Ministry of Education also promote scholarly exchanges between Finnish academic institutions as well as the study of the language, culture, and society of Finland through their support of Finnish study programs at American colleges and universities.

In conclusion, humanitarian efforts, including both private philanthropy and public giving as well as official and unofficial gestures, have helped create strong bonds of friendship between Finland and the United States. Still, we need to know more about the impact of such help on the American and Finnish reputation and on the lives, institutions, and culture of the recipients. At times, such as during the Finnish Winter War, American giving stands out as a heartening display of the humane instincts of the country. In many other instances, however, the American desire to help nations struggling with poverty withstand the appeals of Communism and move toward higher economic levels played a strong part in philanthropic enterprises. Though the extent to which the technical aid and exchanges of knowledge impacted ideological perspectives remains unclear, they did win significant economic successes. Nonetheless, there are downsides to tying overseas relief too closely with national policy. The relief efforts and economic aid often implied an inequality between donor and recipient, an implication that many Americans tried to minimize, but not always successfully. To what extent did Finnish Communists and other social critics discount American philanthropy during the period? How have the relief activities and current efforts at supporting Finnish American cultural identity impacted ethnic identities in the United States? How are Finnish and American organizations currently broadening the scope of giving in ways that continue to support an ethnic and national focus, while at the same time responding to the needs of an increasingly globalized and transnational world? These questions and more might be possible avenues for further study, as nations, organizations, and peoples continually find new ways to use their time, knowledge, and money to help others, redefining themselves and their place within the international community in the process.

## NOTES

1. Merle S. Curti, *American Philanthropy Abroad: A History* (New Brunswick, N.J.: Rutgers University Press, 1963), 413.
2. Varpu Lindström, *From Heroes to Enemies: Finns in Canada, 1937-1947* (Beaverton, Ont.: Aspasia Books, 2000).
3. Herbert Hoover, *An American Epic* (Chicago: Regnery, 1959).
4. Herbert Hoover, *The Memoirs of Herbert Hoover* (New York: Macmillan, 1951-52).
5. Herbert Hoover, *Addresses Upon the American Road, 1940-1941, 1941-1945, 1945-1948* (Toronto: D. Van Nostrand, 1941, 1946, 1949).
6. *Reports to American Donors, December 1939-July 1940* (New York: Finnish Relief Fund, 1940).
7. See, for example, *Finnish Relief, 1940-1952* (Portland, Ore.: Finnish-American Historical Society of the West, 1972).
8. Peter Kivisto, *Immigrant Socialists in the United States: The Case of Finns and the Left* (Rutherford, N.J.: Fairleigh Dickinson University Press, 1984).
9. Peter Kivisto, "Finnish Americans and the Homeland, 1918-1958," *Journal of American Ethnic History* 7, no. 1 (1987): 7-28.
10. Andrew J. Swartz, *America and the Russo-Finnish War* (Washington, D.C.: Public Affairs Press, 1960).
11. Benjamin D. Rhodes, "The Origins of Finnish-American Friendship, 1919-1941," *Mid-America* 54, no. 1 (1972): 3-19.
12. Hal Elliot Wert, "Hoover, Roosevelt and the Politics of American Aid to Finland, 1939-1940," in *World War II: A Fifty Year Perspective on 1939: Selected Papers*, ed. Robert W. Hoffner (Albany, N.Y.: Siena College Research Institute Press, 1992), 89-112.
13. Richard Norton Smith, "On the Outside Looking In: Herbert Hoover and World War II," *Prologue* 26, no. 3 (1994): 141-51.
14. R. Michael Berry, *American Foreign Policy and the Finnish Exception: Ideological Preferences and Wartime Realities* (Helsinki: SHS, 1987).
15. Kimmo Kuikka, *Finnish Relief Fundin huoltoapu talvisodasta kesään 1940*. Pro gradu-tutkielma (Joensuu: Joensuun yliopisto, 1990).
16. Eljas Repo, *Yhdysvaltain huoltoapu Suomelle 1945-1947*. Pro gradu-tutkielma (Helsinki: Helsingin yliopisto, 1988).
17. Tomi Haapanen, *"Niin kauan kuin tarve vaatii": Amerikansuomalainen Help Finland Inc. Suomen avustuksen keskusjärjestönä 1945-1952*. Pro gradu-tutkielma (Turku: Turun yliopisto, 2000).
18. Jon L. Saari, *Black Ties and Miners' Boots: Inventing Finnish-American Philanthropy—A History of Finlandia Foundation National 1953-2003* (Pasadena, Calif.: Finlandia Foundation National, 2010), 14-15.
19. Ann Yrjälä, *Public Health and Rockefeller Wealth: Alliance Strategies in the Early Formation of Finnish Public Health Nursing* (Åbo: Åbo Akademi Press, 2006).
20. Marianne Tallberg, "Venny Snellman, Finnish Nurses, and Rockefeller Foundation Support, 1929-1956," *Nursing History Review* 14 (2000): 175-88.
21. Timo Juotsivuo et al., *Henry Fordin Säätiö, 1947-1997. Henry Ford Stiftelsen, 1947-1997* (Helsinki: Henry Fordin Säätiö, 1997).

# The Return Migration of Finns from North America

*Keijo Virtanen*

Roughly 90 percent of the Finnish emigrants to America between 1860 and 1930 planned to make only a preliminary working trip: their purpose was to earn money and then return to Finland. Of the 380,000 emigrants, only 20 percent came back permanently. This contrast between the original motives of the migrants and the final result of the Finnish overseas emigration is examined here. The Finnish experience is analyzed as a twofold phenomenon: the adaptation of Finns to American society, and their integration into and impact on Finnish society after their return. This essay defines the central factors in the life-cycle and identity of the overseas migrants.

There are several questions to be analyzed. First, why did the great majority of Finns stay in America for good even though their original plan was different? Second, what impact did their original motives have on the willingness of Finns to integrate into American society? Third, because of this ambivalence, was the Finnish community somehow unique in its attitudes toward American society? Fourth, did they follow their original plan? Did they succeed well in America, or did they fail? Fifth, what was their cultural, political, and social impact on the Finnish society? To what extent were they able to put into practice their "American values" in the home country?

I am not going to present information about the sources of migration, the present state of research, the general causes of emigration, or the general-type (macrolevel) factors influencing the settlement or return. I have treated these questions widely in my book, *Settlement or Return: Finnish Emigrants (1860–1930) in the International Overseas Return Migration Movement.*[1] The present essay takes a more personal and cultural point of view, aiming at a synthesis on the life of the migrant.

From the point of view of an overall study of overseas migration, research must concern itself with four phases: life in the country of origin, emigration, life in the host country, and return. Return may lead to a new departure, and so on, but one day the circle comes to an end, either in the host country or in the country of origin. The emigration from Finland to overseas countries took on the nature of a mass movement at a later date (in the 1870s) than that for many central European and Scandinavian countries, but it was in full swing when the "new" immigration began to reach North America.[2] The beginnings of the emigration from Finland thus fall somewhere in the middle of the European development.

The analysis of the Finnish return migration and its comparison with the movements from the Scandinavian countries reveals considerable similarities. The Finnish return rate was about 20 percent, which is on the same scale as in Sweden and Denmark.[3] The situation was quite different in countries such as Italy and Greece, which were typical "new" migration countries, where a large proportion of the migrants returned home, perhaps subsequently to commute overseas to work again.[4]

### Adaptation to New Environments

As mentioned, the predominant motive for emigration also in Finland was the search for better earnings leading to an improved standard of living, and a subsequent return home. Consequently, over half of the Finnish migrants who returned did so within five years of emigration. Studies of migrants from other countries, both of the "old" and "new" migrations, have revealed similar patterns.[5]

But most emigrants to America settled there permanently; they did not follow their original plan. Therefore, it is no surprise that a lot has been written on immigration and assimilation of immigrants during the last 100 years. Research on the adaptation and assimilation of immigrants has been almost completely in the hands of investigators in the receiving countries. The immigrant has been seen as a stable phenomenon—that is, that he or she is ready and willing to settle permanently immediately after arrival. The motives for departure have not been taken into account in assimilation studies.

The concept "assimilation" is used differently in different contexts. Speaking of immigration, a common approach is to study the stages of adaptation, starting immediately after arrival to the new country. The assimilation process is completed when the immigrant has fully accepted the new culture—not only its external features but also its values and norms. The immigrant does not emphasize consciously his or her ethnic background any more but connects himself or herself and his or her interests to the new homeland.[6]

The assimilation research that has been accomplished in the receiving countries, especially in the United States, can be divided into three—at the same time chronological—groups. First, the advocates of Anglo-Saxon culture thought that it was possible and also necessary for the immigrant to throw out the old language and the old habits in favor of the Anglo-Saxon, Protestant core culture of America.[7] Second, a new interpretation was born at the beginning of the twentieth century when the departure area of European emigration spread to the southern and eastern parts of the continent. The rapid industrialization and urbanization of the United States needed a lot of cheap labor power. In 1909, the term "melting pot" was born.[8] It claimed that the immigrants of various nationalities and races would assimilate into one entity in the new country. Soon, however, this new wave of immigration caused a reaction in American society. It culminated in the quota system of the 1920s, which was designed to prevent the "new" immigration: Americans thought that these immigrants would not be able to assimilate nearly as well as western and northern Europeans.[9]

Third, researchers of immigration had taken for granted that various nationality groups would rapidly assimilate in the new environment after the first stage of adaptation. To their surprise, however, they found that immigrant communities were still alive decades after the great emigration period. During the last fifteen to twenty years, the melting pot theory has been put aside, and it has been replaced by a new term, "ethnicity," which refers to the maintenance and preservation of the original features of different groups.[10] Today scholars of ethnicity do not think that assimilation begins when somebody decides to emigrate, or—at the latest—when he or she arrives in the new country.[11]

Still, the common philosophy of these three approaches has been in the assumption that immigrants have come over the ocean to settle permanently. They have not paid attention to the so-called temporary labor power. While keeping this in mind and knowing that—in spite of their motives at the time of departure—only one-fifth of the Finnish emigrants returned permanently home, we can find new dimensions in the assimilation and adaptation conversation. Why has the ethnic identity of various groups survived so long? Had the immigrant any reason to try to adapt or assimilate into the new society since he or she planned to stay there only for a few years? The immigrant was an egotistical person: the strengthening of his or her own economic situation guided his or her actions almost completely. An American scholar concludes that the Finnish immigrants in the Copper Country of northern Michigan were so stubborn that they did not even want to learn the English language.[12]

On the other hand, it was necessary for the immigrant to find features that eased his or her stay in the new society. It is a well-known fact that different groups tended to settle in the same areas: Finns in the little towns and countryside in northern Michigan and Minnesota, Italians in the big cities of the eastern parts of the United States, and so forth. In these communities, immigrants founded all kinds of organizations and engaged in other activities.

For adaptation and assimilation, these group activities had a double meaning. On the one hand, they eased the cultural shock that the immigrant had to face after arrival. Immigrant communities helped immigrants to get used to the new surroundings. On the other hand, these communities were an obstacle to complete assimilation. The immigrant was isolated; his or her ability to create new contacts was limited because of language difficulties alone.

Over the years immigrants became so used to their new home, however, that they did not return to the Old Country; thus most Finnish immigrants stayed for the rest of their lives as immigrants. There were many reasons for this. One was the continuous flow of new immigrants up to the 1920s. The immigrant communities received new members; men sent tickets to their families, relatives, and friends. A counterweight to the idea of returning was also the overall situation in the country of origin—that is, economic conditions at emigration, and critical attitudes toward emigration in the home country.[13]

After the adoption of quotas in the United States, the process of assimilation changed its nature with the ending of the new flow of immigrants.[14] The immigrant community got older, and the children and grandchildren of immigrants became an important factor for assimilation. They went to English-language schools, they were able to make contacts outside their own community, and they married persons from other ethnic groups, which had been rare among the first generation of immigrants. In other words, they assimilated rapidly, and simultaneously this had a considerable impact in binding and connecting their parents to American society. It has been stated that immigrants with families assimilated faster than unmarried persons.[15]

Even though the mass emigration to the United States ended half a century ago, we still can find a lot of ethnic communities. Especially those groups that immigrated in large numbers have been able to preserve their Italys and Irelands in the new environment. But even from a small immigrant group—like the Finns—we can generalize that the first generation did not assimilate if the criterion is a complete identification with a homogeneous American community. Immigrants adapted to the new conditions, but only their children became Americans. He himself was an immigrant who attained citizenship.

The Finnish immigrant belonged to three worlds: to the immigrant world where Finnish language dominated and where all the activities were concentrated around Finnishness; to the receiving country,

**FIGURE 1** *(OPPOSITE)*. Some immigrants sent death announcements to relatives in Finland on postcards. Here is news about the passing of a young woman, Rose East, age twenty-five, on December 30, 1921. There was also a card on her brother Alfred's passing away the previous July at the age of nineteen. (Source: America letters, Varsinais-Suomi I/K-la II, DGH)

which became more familiar over decades and because of children; and to the Old Country, the home village, which he or she never could forget. Probably in most cases immigrants were able to acquire a reasonably nice standard of living in the New World. But only death cut off their Finnishness, even though they had not seen their home country in decades.[16] The immigrants had taken good care of their ethnic identity—their idea of permanent settlement in America had developed only gradually; it had not been their original purpose.

One-fifth of the Finns came back to their home country. Did they follow their original plan? Many did, but it also can be said that the achievement of their objectives was not the only motive for migrants to return, since adversities might also send them back. The most common cause mentioned by the migrants themselves was homesickness, arising from a failure to adapt to the host country, and this was at its strongest soon after arrival. These are typical expressions: "Longing for the old country brought me back to where I was born (a returnee of 1938),[17] or "I felt homesick the whole time" (a returnee of 1933).[18]

Not only did the culture of the host country cause difficulties of adaptation for immigrants, but there were also tensions operating within the ethnic groups that aroused controversy, and Finnish immigrants were very active in political radicalism. However, these tensions were probably not of great significance in relation to return; on the contrary, with the growth of the numbers of Finns in a particular area, conditions were likely to become more pleasant. The political radicalism of the Finnish immigrants, however, did cause a movement from North America to the Soviet Union in the early 1920s and early 1930s.[19]

My analysis does answer the question as to how many migrants would have returned if they had had the opportunity. However, from the point of view of the processes in deciding whether to return, this is relevant. While it is impossible to obtain any exact information, some indications are available. Migrants who were unable to afford the journey home were entitled to receive a repatriation grant from the U.S. government during the early 1930s.[20] There are no data available on how many actually applied for this assistance. We do know—on the basis of the estimate made by shipping companies—that about 10 percent of those returning had been so unsuccessful abroad that their families in Finland had to send them the money for the return ticket.[21]

In the early 1970s, there were still old Finnish lumberjacks living in the "hotels" in Duluth, Minnesota, who had stayed there for decades with no real contacts with the world outside, not even the Finnish community. We may presume that many of them would have returned to Finland during the depression years of the 1930s if they had had money for the return ticket. The purpose of these examples is only to show that the migrants had differing motives for their return—not only the one that was most common at the time of original emigration.

### Integration and Impact after Return

Where homesickness or similar reasons drove many of the migrants back to Finland, their intention in the majority of cases was, clearly, to settle permanently there. But return did not necessarily mean that the migrants would be happy back in Finland either. During their years of absence, changes had taken place in their home area, and also in the migrants themselves, sometimes creating insuperable tensions. About 10 percent of all the Finnish migrants made two or more journeys overseas in the period up to 1930.

The immigrants in North America were aware of the possible problems that might await them in the Old Country. Concrete evidence of this is to be found in plans for return in large groups, which envisaged settlement in an area entirely occupied by return migrants. During the depression years of the 1930s, there were plans for a mass movement back to Finland, to establish a lakeside community settlement somewhere near the largest cities (Helsinki, Turku, or Tampere). A community of only Finnish Americans would help the returning migrants to readapt to Finnish society more successfully.[22] Plans for common settlements of returnees were still being discussed in several places at the time of the Second World War,[23] but they were never realized.

These plans illustrate that many different problems had to be faced in connection with return, and that efforts were made to solve these in advance. One such effort in Finland was the founding in 1933 in Helsinki of Amerikan Suomalaisten Seura (the Society of American Finns). It ceased its activities very soon, however, as did a similar organization, founded in 1934, which had only thirty-eight members two years later.

After all, the returning migrants had a relatively good chance of readjusting to life back home, primarily due to the fact that in most cases they had only been abroad for a few years. The majority also tended to be fairly well-off when they returned; since they often invested their savings either in farming or some other form of real estate, this, too, was likely to strengthen their ties with the area they had settled in and to lead to the abandonment of any ideas of reemigration overseas.

It was natural that the returning migrants brought new influences back with them, which they tried to put into practice in Finland. But since the numbers returning to Finland were so small, this impact is not as clearly identifiable as, for instance, in southern Europe, where the economic significance of the return migration was considerable.[24] One Finnish returnee of 1928 states:[25] "In a town (urban) society there wasn't much chance for unskilled emigrants to have much effect on the life of the town. I'm sure that returning emigrants—despite their hard work and the bit of money they had—were on the receiving end."

In Finland, too, the most easily recognizable impact of the returning migrants was on the economy, but only in rural areas in the regions of high emigration, where the return was locally significant even in absolute terms. They bought farmland, repaired buildings, built new houses, and introduced technological (especially agricultural) innovations. There were some exceptional success stories, since a few returning migrants had earned a fortune. Thus brothers Anton Fabian Johnsson and Karl Fredrik Joutsen, from the Turku area, were successful gold miners in Alaska and the Yukon area at the turn of the twentieth century. After several years in the Klondyke, they returned home. In 1942, Karl Fredrik Joutsen donated in his will most of his property to the University of Turku. The main library building of the University of Turku was built in the 1950s with the funds willed to them by Mr. Joutsen's.[26]

The returning migrants also wanted to use the "mental capital" they had acquired abroad. Typical were opinions like "views broadened, practical experience, learned to live." The time spent abroad was "the best high school you could hope for." But their access to local influence depended on the attitude in their home area toward the various kinds of new ideas they held. Intellectual, moral, and political ideas were more likely to encounter an emotional reception than economic influence, depending on the attitudes and value judgments of the people involved.

Finnish Americans have been shown to have brought about an increase in rural radicalism in Finland; in the towns, on the other hand, socialist ideas were mainly homegrown. Between the achievement of Finnish independence in 1917 and 1933, there were at least fifteen members of the Finnish Parliament who had been migrants in North America. Several of the socialists had studied at the Finnish American institution the Work People's College in Duluth, Minnesota.[27]

It also has been shown that the returning migrants had an impact on religious life and the Church of Finland. The spread of the Free Churches, in particular, and the introduction of legislation ensuring liberty of religion have been attributed partly to the migration. A concrete example of the religious impact of the returning migrants was the founding in 1882 of the first Methodist congregation in Finland.[28] All this led the official Lutheran Church to adopt a critical attitude toward emigration as a whole.[29]

In general, however, the returning migrants do not appear to have caused much irritation in the surrounding community; with the exception of the high emigration areas in western Finland, there were simply too few returning migrants for their impact to be identifiable. A returnee of 1932 stressed the overall limitations of the new experience:[30] "Those American or Canadian emigrants who were working in the forests, or other kinds of casual work, had very limited opportunities to participate in social, political, or cultural activities, so I don't think they had anything to offer in these fields. They might have new ideas to do with the economy, though. I don't think there were any big differences in morality."

This comment, even though somewhat pointedly stated, underlines the main results derived from my analysis. Only in high emigration areas did the rural economy received a stimulus, and the returning migrants were quite active in local affairs. In general, though, the intellectual impact of the migrants remained modest or insignificant, and the same also appears to apply to nations where the return migration occurred on a much larger scale than in Finland. Those who had never been away were not willing to modify their thinking, with the result that the emigrants had to adjust, and in the course of time abandon many of their ideas.

## Final Result

In terms of the return migration in a wider context, the balance of Finnish overseas migration was definitely negative, for Finland only regained 75,000 of the 380,000 persons who had "commuted to work" overseas prior to 1930. The final balance in a "new" migration country such as Italy was quite different, where the economy visibly prospered from the busy movement back and forth between Italy and the United States and from the capital brought back by those returning. Thus the Finnish migration differed radically from the overseas migration movement in southern European countries, which was essentially a temporary phenomenon, an intercontinental working trip.

In the final analysis, for most Finnish migrants, this overseas working trip was a one-way street, which never led to a permanent return even though this had been their original idea. The investigation of the Finnish overseas migrants may offer comparative material when recent migrations are studied. For example, there has been a large amount of emigration from Finland to Sweden since the Second World War, and to a lesser extent also to Canada and Australia. These labor migrations are caused basically by similar factors and pass through similar stages even though the chronological and geographical contexts are different.

### NOTES

1. Keijo Virtanen, *Settlement or Return: Finnish Emigrants (1860–1930) in the International Overseas Return Migration Movement* (Forssa: Institute of Migration, 1979).

2. Theodore Saloutos, *They Remember America: The Story of the Repatriated Greek-Americans* (Berkeley:

University of California Press, 1956), 1–2; Arnold Schrier, *Ireland and the American Emigration 1850–1900* (Minneapolis: University of Minnesota Press, 1958), 158–59.

3. Cf. Kristian Hvidt, *Flugten til Amerika: Eller drivkraefter i masseudvandringen fra Danmark 1868–1914* (Odense, Denmark: Jysk Selskab for Historie, 1971), 327–28; Lars-Göran Tedebrand, *Västernorrland och Nordamerika 1875–1913: Utvandring och återinvandring* (Uppsala: Acta Universitatis Upsaliensis, 1972), 223.

4. Robert F. Foerster, *The Italian Emigration of Our Times* (Cambridge: Cambridge University Press, 1919), 23; John S. Lindberg, *The Background of Swedish Emigration to the United States: An Economic and Sociological Study in the Dynamics of Migration* (Minneapolis: University of Minnesota Press, 1930), 252n2; Saloutos, *They Remember*, 29–30; Betty Boyd Caroli, *Italian Repatriation from the United States, 1900–1914* (New York: Center for Migration Studies, 1973), 49–50.

5. See Foerster, *Italian Emigration*, 35; Ingrid Semmingsen, *Veien mot vest. Annen del. Utvandringen fra Norge 1865–1915* (Oslo: Aschehoug, 1950), 460; Anthony H. Richmond, *Post-War Immigrants in Canada* (Toronto: University of Toronto Press, 1967), 231; Caroli, *Italian Repatriation*, 50; Lars-Göran Tedebrand, "Remigration from America to Sweden," in *From Sweden to America: A History of the Migration*, ed. Harald Runblom and Hans Norman (Minneapolis: University of Minnesota Press, 1976), 225–27; Saloutos, *They Remember*, 51.

6. See Lawrence Guy Brown, *Immigration: Cultural Conflicts and Social Adjustments* (New York: Longmans, 1933), 369–72; William Carlson Smith, *Americans in the Making. The Natural History of the Assimilation of Immigrants* (New York: Arno Press, 1970), 114–39; Charles Price, "The Study of Assimilation," in *Migration*, ed. L. A. Jackson (Cambridge: Cambridge University Press, 1969), 181–83.

7. Price, "Study," 183.

8. Henry Pratt Fairchild, *The Melting-Pot Mistake* (Boston: Little, Brown, 1926), 9.

9. Maldwyn Allen Jones, *American Immigration* (Chicago: University of Chicago Press, 1960), 276–77.

10. Nathan Glazer and Daniel P. Moynihan, "Introduction," in *Ethnicity, Theory and Experience*, ed. Nathan Glazer and Daniel P. Moynihan (Cambridge, Mass.: Harvard University Press, 1975), 1–26; Leonard Dinnerstein and David M. Reimers, *Ethnic Americans: A History of Immigration and Assimilation* (New York: Harper & Row, 1982), 150–56.

11. See Smith, *Americans in the Making*, 124.

12. Arthur W. Thurner, *Calumet Copper and People: History of a Mining Community, 1864–1970* (Chicago: Book Concern, 1974), 18.

13. See, for example, Matti Tarkkanen, *Siirtolaisuudesta* (Mikkeli: Kansanvalistus seura, 1902), 25–26; Teo Snellman, *Ulkokansalaistoiminta ja siirtolaisten huolto I* (Helsinki: Suomi-Seura, 1929), 10.

14. Price, "Study," 209.

15. Brown, *Immigration*, 253–56; Maurice R. Davie, *World Immigration: With Special Reference to the United States* (New York: Macmillan, 1936), 490–91; Smith, *Americans in the Making*, 376–86; Dinnerstein and Reimers, *Ethnic Americans*, 146–50.

16. John I. Kolehmainen, "Americanization and the Search for Identity," in *Old Friends—Strong Ties*, ed. Vilho Niitemaa et al. (Turku: Institute for Migration, 1976), 265–66.

17. The interview questionnaire collection at the Department of General History (DGH), University of Turku, signum: TYYH/S/1 /5732.

18. The interview questionnaire collection at the DGH, TYYH/S/1/6181.

19. Reino Kero, *Neuvosto-Karjalaa rakentamassa: Pohjois-Amerikan suomalaiset tekniikan tuojina 1930-luvun Neuvosto-Karjalassa* (Helsinki: SHS, 1983); B. McNitt, "Americans in Soviet Russia: The Kuzbas Experiment" (unpublished seminar paper,

University of Michigan, 1971).
20. See Industrialisti, June 27, 1931.
21. See Engelberg, *Suomi ja Amerikan suomalaiset*, 382.
22. Lännen Suometar, July 19, 1932.
23. Engelberg, *Suomi ja Amerikan suomalaiset*, 381, 384–85, 388–90.
24. See Saloutos, *They Remember*, 117–21, 123–24, 130–31; Caroli, *Italian Repatriation*, 57–61, 93, 98–99.
25. The interview questionnaire collection at the DGH, TYYH/S/1/7149.
26. Yrjö Raevuori, *Klondiken veljekset. Alaskan kultakentiltä Turun yliopistonmäelle* (Helsinki: Weilin & Göös, 1975), passim.
27. Leiwo, "Hakemisto."
28. Sjöblom, *Kristinestads historia*, 286.
29. Widén, "De religiösa Återverkningarna," 87–89.
30. The interview questionnaire collection at the DGH, TYYH/S/1/7234.

# Deported Finns

*Auvo Kostiainen*

Although the United States was a land of dreams for immigrants, in real life it could be something else: their reception and final deportation was, to many immigrants, a nightmare. This contradictory face of the New World is seen in the formulation of the deportation policies, which were an important part of the policies of the immigrant-receiving countries, as they are in the contemporary world. It is evident that several hundred Finns entering a North American port were turned back. Of special interest, however, are deportations caused by social and economic problems, illness, criminal acts, or political activities, after these immigrants had settled in the country. Finnish Americans were in fact rarely deported for political activities, but the stories of this occurring aroused attention in the news media and within the Finnish ethnic community, especially during the Cold War years.

Attitudes toward immigrants entering the American homeland, as well as issues regulated by official legislation, have always divided people. American society and business developments have influenced the issue, because during certain periods newcomers have been viewed as a serious threat to the labor market. Ethnic and other tensions have also come to the fore.[1] The political system, economy, and labor conditions in the United States have not always embraced new arrivals, although the U.S. economy needed fuel to make use of its natural resources and to continue economic growth. These facts and the selection criteria have been demonstrated in various studies dealing with the treatment of immigrants. The Chinese, in 1882, were the first foreign group that faced the closing of immigration to the United States. This was based mainly on the competitive element in the labor market, as well as the limitations based on the idea of the "Yellow Race," which was not seen as suitable for the United States. Finally, during the Second World War the legislation was changed, and the Chinese were again allowed as migrants with a small quota. Finally the "Yellow Race" legislation was changed in 1965, when the migration was freed from quota systems, mainly as a consequence of the labor force demand.

Immigrants from various countries were turned back from control stations on an annual basis. Specific deportation cases have, of course, received publicity, but these accounted only for a small minority of all the cases. The number of deportations increased from the late 1800s. Thousands of immigrants were able to pass through Ellis Island in New York on any given day, but several hundred of them could be turned back for a variety of reasons. Perhaps they did not fulfill the criteria for a prospective immigrant, because of health or other reasons. It has been well documented that the general health condition of the immigrants was examined. A classic study carried out in the 1930s by Janet Clark found that a person was usually deported for a period of either three or five years, or even indefinitely. A person could be deported for being a beggar or becoming "a burden to the society at large" because of mental illness, or for being a member of an illegal organization, such as an anarchist group, or for being a member of a radical labor movement.[1]

No exact information has been found on early deportations of Finns from the American continent, and the means of handling the deportations varied over the decades. In general, according to Jane Clark, exclusion because of physical, mental, moral, or economic reasons gradually became more and more rare during the early twentieth century. There were also "warrant cases" for arrest, for trial, or for deportation.[2]

In this chapter, I estimate the total numbers of deported Finns from the United States and Canada. If we look at the cases in more detail, we find that not only political radicalism but also the social conditions of the individual Finnish immigrants made them the target of U.S. immigration officials. However, the Finnish American community in many locations held the "Red Finns" label from the early decades of the twentieth century. At that time, the "loyal" immigrant Finns had, for example, founded the Lincoln Loyalty League to fight the radicals and to promote the image of "good Finns" in America. It seems that during the deportation of radicals in the 1950s, Finns were again faced with the historical burden of stereotypical images of radical Finns.[3]

## Interwar Deportations

There were statutes about deportations. The laws that clearly had an effect on the Finnish population in the United States were the criminal syndicalism laws. The regulations made it a crime to defend, advocate, or set up an organization committed to the use of crime, violence, sabotage, or other unlawful means to bring about a change in the form of government or in industrial ownership or control. The laws were directed especially toward the radical labor union Industrial Workers of the World (IWW). Since this union was strongest in the West, criminal syndicalism laws appeared first in that region. The prototype was a 1917 Idaho statute. Twenty states enacted criminal syndicalism laws between 1917 and 1920, and some states, such as California, prosecuted a number of radicals for criminal syndicalism during the post–World War I "Red Scare."[4] The laws that prepared the basis for the post–World War II deportations were primarily the Alien Registration Act of 1940 and the Internal Security Act, otherwise known as the McCarran-Walter Act, of 1950. The leading person behind the raids was the Wisconsin Republican senator Joseph McCarthy.[5] At this time in the 1950s, U.S. officials reported that approximately 7,000 people were deported from the country on an annual basis.

It is possible to study the deportation of Finns with the help of public writings and diplomatic correspondence between the Foreign Ministry in Finland and the consuls and other representatives of Finland in North America. Also, the Department of Justice and Immigration and Naturalization Service papers shed some light on the topic. But, as we will see, there were quite a few interesting cases, some of them rather peculiar. The following cases may be typical of the time in reflecting the public atmosphere. With the help of these examples, we may also see the changing times and their influence on deportation policies.

As referred to earlier, there were arguments about the races and origins of people during the pre–World War I period. The discussion of the immigration policies was also connected with the heated topic of racial definitions: What ethnic groups should be welcome in America? Or was a Finn possibly "a stone age man," between an ape and a human?[6]

In general, Finnish Americans were considered to be industrious workers.[7] This was also the obvious image that Finns in America wished to have.[8] In 1911, the U.S. Immigration Commission (called also the Dillingham Commission) concluded its extensive analysis on immigrants, and published a forty-one-volume massive report. The commission had been formed in response to growing political concern about mostly southern and eastern European immigration. The report had an effect on the immigrant quota systems that were created in the 1920s. At the time, it was stated that Finnish Americans were good workers, which was an opinion represented by the well-known economic historian John R. Commons. The report included suspicions typical of the time, including the notions that the Finns were actually a "Yellow Race."[9] As Peter Kivisto and others have shown, the race issue persisted up until the beginning of the twenty-first century.[10]

Thus the early 1900s was a difficult period for Finnish Americans, with many workers joining either the radical American labor unions or parties. Quite a few of them actively participated in a wave of strikes in the northern Minnesota Mesabi Range mining district under the leadership of the syndicalist-oriented IWW. Their participation in the strikes led to furious confrontations with the employers and resulted in the blacklisting of a number of Finnish miners.[11] Other industrial confrontations occurred, and thousands of Finns joined the political parties of the left and, after 1917, the Communist movement, and even gained notable leadership positions.

An explanation for the deportations was the rising tide of radical activities inside the United States. It was a reaction to the societal problems in the country but also reflected the major events in world history, such as the birth of a socialist Soviet Russia in 1917. The most famous individual act of deportation involved the ship called *Buford,* which sailed from New York to Russia (actually via Hanko, Finland). It carried 249 deportees, such as the anarchist leader Emma Goldman. They had been sentenced because of un-American activities and ordered to be deported. "The Soviet Ark," which actually was the U.S. Army old transport *Buford,* carried these "Reds" to the Soviet state. In this shipload there were hardly any Finns.

Another interesting case involving a number of Finnish Americans was the train called "Red Express" in February 1919 going from Chicago to an East Coast harbor town with fifty-four convicted radical labor leaders from the West Coast. The train had two carloads of tightly packaged deportees, with fourteen gunmen watching them. Interestingly, it was commented in the media that the "foreign Reds" were made up of people from certain Russian provinces, some Norwegians, Scandinavians, and Finns. A guard said that the deportees were in a cheerful mood and were singing foreign songs for hours. A Finn leader of the group was eagerly waving a red flag from the window. There was one woman in the group, a Finn. The train's schedule was kept in secrecy since, as it was argued in the *New York Times,* there had already been problems with demonstrating "mobs" that might try to meet the deportees during train stops.[12] Another active IWW member was Niilo Wälläri, who was deported in 1920 due to illegal entry; in later years Wälläri rose to fame as a radical trade union leader in Finland.

In addition to the Finns sent to Finland, a number of Finnish Americans were sent to Canada, on the grounds that they had originally landed there but later arrived in the United States. For example, Jane

Clark cites in her book the case of a Finnish American woman, Mary Hanna, who was caught in a train coming from Canada without proper documents. She planned to go to Fitchburg, Massachusetts, where her three sisters already had settled. After legal process, she was deported to Canada.[13]

There are several documents from the U.S. Immigration and Naturalization Service papers showing that especially in the early 1930s, because of the Great Depression, some Finnish Americans were working illegally in the lumber camps of the Upper Peninsula of Michigan. They had crossed the border from the Canadian side, and obviously the Canadian border was easy to cross. The immigration inspectors were aware of the situation. However, one inspector knew what was going on and was not too much troubled. On the other hand, another inspector dramatically stated that there were radical tensions in the areas in question in the 1930s: the Finns were known to have excellent speakers, and Bolsheviks gave radical sermons in some of their churches. Apparently, the combination of the church and Bolsheviks was an exaggeration or a misunderstanding of the role of the Finn meeting halls owned by various societies. The Immigration and Naturalization Service did not take any major legal action toward these Finnish Canadians;[14] they were needed as labor force.

The motives for deportation of a few persons are difficult to figure out, but more detailed research materials on their cases would reveal further background factors. For example, a man named Mannisto (in Finnish, Männistö) ended up on the pages of the *New York Times*. He was in trouble because he had been a member of a radical organization in his youth. Now that he had a family with three American-born children, the newspaper felt sorry for him because there were plans to deport him.[15]

The new immigration laws were enforced more strictly in 1921 and 1924. Thereafter immigration favored particularly the "western European" element. The Finns were regarded mostly as the eastern European element, and the yearly quota for Finns was reduced to a few hundred, while earlier there used to be thousands of Finns arriving in the United States each year. As a consequence, the wave of migrants turned increasingly toward Canada. However, even Canada was quite willing to deport some immigrants, and there was quite a lot of cooperation with U.S. officials and the representatives of Finland on the new continent. Their task was mainly to figure out if the deportee candidate was a Finnish citizen. If that was the case, Finland was, according to international regulations, obliged to receive the deported Finn.

The Immigration and Naturalization Service files present information on the country of birth combined with the causes of deportation. According to the study by Carey, there were 612 cases for half a year in 1930, and fifteen people were sent to Finland, while Sweden received twenty deportees.[16] Eleven of the fifteen Finns were deported because of illegal entry.

There is also other evidence available. Table 1 shows the number of deportations according to the information found in the Foreign Ministry of Finland's correspondence files. More cases will certainly be uncovered in the future.

When looking at these numbers, we should note that these cases were under review. In addition, there were a few cases that were going through the review process but did not result in deportation. In general terms, males naturally dominated the deportation statistics because the majority of Finnish immigrants were males. In relative terms, Canada was much more eager to deport people than the United States during the interwar years. A reason for this may be the fact that Canada became the main target of migration for Finns because of the immigration laws of the United States in 1921 and 1924. After the Second World War, Canada had a more open policy toward immigrants than the United States; this

## Table 1. Deportation Cases of Finns from the United States and Canada, ca. 1919–1970

|  | UNITED STATES | | | | CANADA | | | | |
|---|---|---|---|---|---|---|---|---|---|
|  | MALE | FEMALE | CHILDREN | TOTAL | MALE | FEMALE | CHILDREN | TOTAL | GRAND TOTAL |
| 1919–40 | 26 | 4 | — | 30 | 29 | 2 | 2 | 33 | 63 |
| 1941–70 | 23 | 2 | — | 25 | 6 | 2 | — | 8 | 33 |
| Unknown | 6 | — | — | 6 | 1 | — | — | 1 | 7 |
| Total | 55 | 6 | — | 61 | 36 | 4 | 2 | 42 | 103 |

Source: Group 21,Va, 1–3, FMF.

policy changed only in 1965. When more deportation cases are found, it may be possible to draw more conclusions on the social background of the deportees.

When we categorize the deportation cases, it is possible to define four actual types: illegal entry cases, those who were considered to be "social burdens" to the host society, criminals, and political cases. When looking at the cases more closely, the illegal immigrants stand out. During the 1920s and 1930s, people who had arrived in Canada could illegally cross the border into the United States. On the other hand, it is known that even Canada had had illegal immigration cases—for example, during the World War I period, when probably hundreds of Finns from the United States crossed the border to Canada in order to avoid being taken into the U.S. military. Many of these people returned to the United States after the war ended.

As mentioned above, it was quite common, especially during the interwar period, to migrate first to Canada and then, after some months or years, cross the border to the United States. For example, in 1924 Wiljo Lindberg, age twenty-two years, and in 1925 Armas Lindfors, age twenty-one years, were deported to Finland from the United States. Both young men had the same kind of deportation history: they had arrived in Canada and illegally crossed the border to the United States, where they then were arrested.[17] In fact, during the first half of the 1920s there was a lot of illegal movement from Canada to the United States and also from the United States to Canada.

An interesting case is that of a Finnish young male with the pseudonym Lars Antikainen (wrongly misspelled Antikanen). Born in Helsinki, he went to Canada in 1924 to work in the fields. In 1925, he crossed the border at Detroit in a rowboat, having paid $30 for the crossing. He was caught immediately by the border patrol and held as a witness against his smuggler. The accusation was "likely to become a public charge" because he had arrived without inspection and without proper immigrant papers. He was denied a passport by the Finnish consulate in the United States, but was finally given a passport from the Finnish embassy in Canada. However, because of the legal charges presented, he was deported to Finland from Ellis Island.[18] There were also a few cases in which a person had arrived to a harbor with false information or had otherwise broken the immigration procedures and rules.

Quite a special case was that of Oskari Tokoi, a Finnish socialist leader and member of the government in 1918. He arrived in Canada in 1920, in the aftermath of the Finnish Civil War. After sporadic jobs in the Ontario lumber camps, he moved to Fitchburg, Massachusetts. Later, he became a leader of the *Raivaaja* group in the eastern United States. He was not deported from the United States, although he was arrested for charges of anarchism and illegal entry. However, after "careful investigation" he was released. This may have been because of his political exile role, and because he was a quite important politician in Finland. Also, several years earlier he had spent a few years as a mine worker in the United States and Canada.[19]

The second group of people were those who were deemed to a "social burden" to the host society. It was even possible to deport entire family. Some of this has been documented in the correspondence between the officials in Finland and Canada. Consul General A. J. Jalkanen, from Montreal, reported to the Finnish Foreign Ministry in Helsinki that K. G. Grönman and his whole family were deported "for reasons of undeniably legal nature." The father of the family had arrived in Canada in 1928 and the wife in 1930. Two daughters were born in Canada, Alice in 1932 and Doris in 1933. The family had become unemployed and thus depended on the support of society. Consul Jalkanen asked the governor-general of Vaasa Province not to grant a passport to Canada any more for the deported family.[20] In this case, Canadian-born children were deported; Doris was only a few months old.

The third group consists of deportees who had been engaged in criminal activity. There were quite a few persons from Canada and the United States who faced deportation because of crimes, which might include the breaking of the "moral codes," alcohol abuse, or various acts of violence. For example, Verner Enqvist had a fairly long list of crimes and other unacceptable actions. His case was discussed during several decades, and he had a lengthy criminal history. Born in Finland in 1898, he arrived in the United States in 1903 as a child. In 1917–19 he served in the U.S. Army on European fronts and applied for the "first papers" for citizenship in 1917. According to the consular's comments, the process had been interrupted because of his own fault. He never completed the naturalization process, and remained a citizen of Finland. He committed several crimes and had jail sentences: he was sentenced for grand larceny in Yakima, Washington, in 1920 for one to fifteen years; in Billings, Montana, in 1924 for highway robbery for six to twelve years; and in Quincy, Massachusetts, for bootlegging for six months, in addition to a $125 fine. It appeared that he was ordered to be deported in 1941, but he was not "available." In 1946, a new deportation order was given, but finally in 1952 he actually was deported, now under the title of an artist, and arrived in Helsinki on May 15 at the age of fifty-four.[21]

Many kinds of crimes or criminal activity could justify deportation, in addition to those assigned to Enqvist described above. For example, Johannes Backlund had arrived first in the United States, but according to consular papers, he moved illegally to Canada in 1920. He was fined several times for alcohol abuse. After repeated failure to pay fines and after short imprisonments, he was ordered for deportation in 1925 at the age of thirty-eight.[22]

## Post–World War II Deportations

After World War II, there was a lot of debate about Communism and anti-Communism, terms that were used inconsistently. For much of the decades from the 1950s through the 1970s, anti-Communism was one of the major components of the Cold War and U.S. government policy of containment against the Soviet Union. In the sphere of domestic policy, anti-Communism was an ideology of opposition to Communist organizations, governments, and ideology. It was fairly vague in the sense that it often incorporated many left radical ideologies and activities. During the Cold War era—particularly during the time of the Communist hearings under the zealous stewardship of the Wisconsin republican senator

McCarthy—it was deemed suitable to try and possibly deport Communists to Finland, and there was the question of Communist "ubiquitous infiltration" in the society.

In the following, I present a detailed analysis of some cases that gained widespread interest. In a number of cases, the legal procedures lasted for several years and often did not even result in deportation. These individuals were usually accused of carrying out un-American activities, which in many cases pointed to some activities in the 1930s. Of course, the Finnish American press keenly followed what happened to their countrymen and women. Even American papers with large circulations took notice of the cases.

It seems that ultimately the actual deportations of "politically un-American persons" were few. Several persons were tried for deportation, but it seems that only two of them were actually deported. At least the following cases were brought into discussion: Taisto Elo (labor union activist) in the years 1952–53; William Heikkilä (Communist activist) in 1949–58; K. E. Heikkinen (Communist editor, activist, and organizer) in 1949–58; William Lahtinen (Communist editor) in 1954–67; Carl Latva (Communist activist) in 1952; William Niukkanen, alias William A. Mackie (Communist organizer), in 1952–60; and Carl Päiviö (Communist writer and party organizer) in 1949–52. All of them were accused of Communist sympathies and activity. An important American Communist icon of the post–Cold War years was Gus Hall, who to some extent was also brought into deportation discussions. However, it was not really possible to deport him, since he was born in America. Of these persons, Taisto Elo was deported in 1953, and William Heikkilä was deported in 1958, although his case had a surprising ending, as described below. William Niukkanen lost a long legal battle and was deported to Finland in 1960 because of Communist activity in the 1930s and 1940s.

It is possible that there are some additional political cases. For example, there is information that in Superior, Wisconsin, there was a female Communist activist, Hanna Keskela, who was involved in the deportation process in 1952. It is not known if she was ultimately deported. There is also the case of Wäinö Nummi (Saarinen), who was deported from the United States in 1956 because of Communist Party membership.[23] His case was not widely noticed.

(Kaino) William Heikkilä was "deported" in 1958. Born in Finland in 1906, he was two and a half months old when he arrived in the United States with his parents. The charges included membership of the Communist Party in 1926–39 and the forgery of a U.S. passport in 1930. He was arrested on the streets of San Francisco on April 18, 1958, and under deportation order was taken to Vancouver, Canada, then to Amsterdam, and then to the Helsinki airport. He never left the airport, because as a result of the activity by the deportee's legal advisers, the immigration commissioner N. M. Swing ordered him to be taken back to the United States for a new legal process.[24] The case was handled in the U.S. Court of Appeals and discussed twice in 1958 in the Canadian House of Representatives because Vancouver was the stopping place for Heikkilä when he was transferred to Europe. Heikkilä died because of an illness in 1960 at the age of fifty-four, but the case was still discussed in the court while his widow, Phyllis, carried on the legal process. Thus it seems that it was a difficult task to deport a person who was a U.S. citizen. Even a number of articles were printed in the press questioning the "Gestapo mentality" of the U.S. officials as well as the role of Canadian officials in the deportation effort.

Even the deportation case of Knut Heikkinen was quite interesting. He had been the editor-in-chief of *Työmies-Eteenpäin,* the Communist newspaper in Superior, Wisconsin. He was born in Tampere in 1890, arrived in Canada in 1910, and moved to the United States in 1916. He had taken second-level education in Tampere and had worked as a journalist for socialist papers in Canada and in the United States. His case was taken up in the United States in 1949 during the rise of anti-Communist purges. His main legal problems were connected with the fact that he had earlier become a Canadian citizen. However, according to Canadian officials, after moving to the United States he had not been in contact with Canada. Therefore, Canadian officials ruled that he had lost his citizenship. Now he was in a U.S. prison asking help from the Finnish representatives in order to be able to return to Finland. But the Finns ruled that he was not welcome in Finland after taking the Canadian citizenship. Heikkinen even sent a letter to the president of Finland, J. K. Paasikivi, in October 1953 explaining the problem. In his letters to Finnish officials, Heikkinen wrote that he wanted to return to Finland and that his purpose was only to retire in a calm place on the lakes. The archives of the Finnish Foreign Ministry contain correspondence dealing with the various phases of the Heikkinen case. The ultimate result appears to be that he was sent to Canada.[25]

The political deportations have been mostly from the post–World War II period, with William Mackie Niukkanen, Wäinö Nummi, and Taisto Elo deported to Finland, and Knut Heikkinen to Canada. But there were quite a few others, too. In materials from the Foreign Ministry files are found three persons deported for social reasons such as illness, and a total of six cases because of criminal charges. In addition, there were half a dozen cases in which the reason for deportation remained unclear.[26]

### Complexity of Deportations and Deportation Politics

The period discussed here started from the World War I years and extended through to the McCarthy years into the 1960s, when the deportation policies calmed down at the same time as the Cold War passed its height. What is more, the focus of American domestic policy was no longer directed so intensively on Communists, as other kinds of trouble for the government emerged, such as the rising civil rights movement.[27]

Most of those who were deported were "ordinary" Finns who had some problems in working life, were not healthy, or had become a stress for the society. In principle, deportations from the United States and Canada were based on four factors: illegal entry, social reasons such as becoming a burden to society, criminal acts, and political reasons or participation in left political radicalism. The last-mentioned deportations gained headlines in the news media. Of course, most publicity was given to the McCarthy raids and political deportations involved with them.

The deportations were legal cases. Because of the great similarity of the deportation cases in the United States and Canada, there is good reason to believe that these two nations had a lot of joint activities on the borderline and border guarding, which is also shown in several cases discussed. Often deportations were handled jointly by the immigration officials in the two countries. It appears that in relative terms, when comparing the numbers of immigrants of Finnish descent, Canada was more active. On the other hand, it is possible that the Canadian cases were collected more carefully in the archival files and thus were preserved for future researchers.

The total number of Finns deported from the United States and Canada during the twentieth century probably amounts to a few hundred, although more exact numbers will only be ascertained after additional research. From 1919 to 1970, 103 Finns were in the process of being deported, 61 from the United States and 42 from Canada. The cases are complicated by the fact that ultimately not all of them were deported. In our materials there are a total of nine cases that did not result in actual deportation and there are also cases where the results are uncertain, but more information is needed. A political deportation often resulted in court appeals, which delayed or even prevented the deportations. Some deportations were actually show-cases, through which it was possible to point to the threats of the Cold War years. It was possible that the decision to deport these individuals was based on something that happened about twenty years earlier in the Finnish ethnic society. Perhaps this fact also tells us something about the seriousness of the activities of the legal apparatus in both the United States and Canada. The "historical burden" of the Red Finns and their experiences from the early decades of the twentieth century quite apparently made all those in the Finnish American community very sensitive to the issues of radicalism. The situation was somewhat similar to that of the Finnish "race issue"—that is, the debate on the origins of the Finns, which had persisted for decades and which had also been connected with the tangible threat of deportation.

## NOTES

1. Jane Perry Carey (Clark), *Deportation of Aliens from the United States to Europe* (New York: Arno Press, 1969), 59-69.
2. Carey, *Deportation*, 27-28. In Canada, political elements were most visible. See Barbara Roberts, *Whence They Came: Deportation from Canada 1900-1935* (Ottawa: University of Ottawa Press, 1988).
3. For actual citizenship discussion, see Auvo Kostiainen, "For or against Americanization? The Case of the Immigrant Finns," in *American Labor and Immigration History, 1877-1920s: Recent European Research: Papers Prepared for a Conference at the University of Bremen, November 1978* (Urbana: University of Illinois Press, 1983), 259-75.
4. Eldridge Foster Dowell, *A History of Criminal Syndicalism Legislation in the United States* (Baltimore: Johns Hopkins University Press, 1939); for ideas of nativism, see John Higham, *Strangers in the Land: Patterns of American Nativism, 1860-1925,* 2nd ed. (New Brunswick, N.J.: Rutgers University Press, 2002); William Preston, Jr., *Aliens and Dissenters: Federal Suppression of Radicals, 1903-1933* (New York: Harper & Row, 1966); Morton Keller, *Regulating a New Society: Public Policy and Social Change in America, 1900-1933* (Cambridge, Mass.: Harvard University Press, 1994); cf. Robert W. Dunn, ed., *The Palmer Raids* (New York: International Publishers, 1948).
5. For example, Ellen Schrecker, *Many Are the Crimes: McCarthyism in America* (Boston: Little, Brown, 1998).
6. See Auvo Kostiainen, "Deportations of Finns during the Cold War Years," paper presented at the Thunder Bay Finn Forum 8, Ms., 2010.
7. David R. Roediger, *How Race Survived U.S. History: From Settlement and Slavery to the Obama Phenomenon* (London: Verso, 2008), 153-68.
8. See Eugene van Cleef, "The Finn in America," *Geographical Review* 6, no. 3 (1918): 185-214.
9. U.S. Immigration Commission, *Reports of the Immigration Commission* (New York: Arno Press, 1970); Johanna Leinonen, "Mongolians or Whites? The John Svan Case (1908) and the Ambiguity of the Finnish Race," manuscript, University of Minnesota, 2006; Eugene van Cleef, "Finns in Ohio," *The Ohio Archaelogical and Historical Quarterly* 43 (1934): 452-60.
10. Peter Kivisto, "When Did America's Finns Become White?" in *Transborder Contacts and the Maintenance of Finnishness in the Diaspora: FinnForum VIII an Interdisciplinary Conference in Finnish, Finnish-North American and Sweden Finnish Studies, Mälardalen University, Campus Eskilstuna June*

*17-20, 2007* (Eskilstuna: Mälardalen University, 2009), 36-39.

11. See Arnold R. Alanen, "Years of Change on the Iron Range," in *Minnesota in a Century of Change: The State and Its People since 1900,* ed. Clifford E. Clark (St. Paul: Minnesota Historical Society Press, 1989), esp. 181-83; Peter Rachleff, "Turning Points in the Labor Movement: Three Key Conflicts," in *Minnesota in a Century of Change,* 196-203.
12. "54 Foreign Reds," *New York Times,* February 10, 1919.
13. Carey, *Deportation,* 231-33. The name was a pseudonym.
14. Cf. inspector in charge M. H. Powers to district director, U.S. Immigration Service, Detroit, June 8, 1931, INS reel 4, IHRC.
15. "Enrolled Red of 1925 Fights Deportation," *New York Times,* December 22, 1934.
16. Carey, *Deportation,* 13.
17. Folders Lindberg, Wiljo and Lindfors, Armas, Group 21 Va, 3, FMF.
18. Carey, *Deportation,* 441-42.
19. Auvo Kostiainen, "Oskari Tokoi (1873-1963)—senaatin talousosaston varapuheenjohtaja, kansanvaltuuskunnan jäsen, toimittaja," *Kansallisbiografia,* 2000, http://www.kansallisbiografia.fi/kb/artikkeli/241/.
20. Information is found on Karl Gunnar Grönman, b. April 2, 1910, Korsnäs, to Canada, July 14, 1928; Helen Viktoria (b. Rosenback) b. November 6, 1909, to Canada, May 4, 1930, married in Hamilton, Ont., April 1932; Alice Helene, b. Canada, June 10, 1932; Doris Inger, b. Canada, January 10, 1933. See folder Grönman, Karl, Group 21, Va, 1, FMF.
21. Folder Enqvist, Hugo Verner, Group 21, Va, 1, FMF.
22. Folder Carlson or Backlund, William, Group 21, Va, 1, FMF.
23. Folder Nummi, Wäinö, Group 21, Va, 4, FMF.
24. Several clippings and exchange of official letters on the case are found in personal folder of Heikkilä, William, Group 21, Va, 1, FMF. See also materials http://bulk.resource.org/courts.gov/c/F2/308/308.F2d.558.16158_1.html.
25. Folder Heikkinen, Knut Einar Richard, and Päiviö, Carl Einar, Group 21, Va, 1, FMF.
26. Folders in Group 21, Va, 1-6, FMF.
27. See Donna R. Gabaccia, *Immigration and American Diversity: A Social and Cultural History.* Malden, Massachusetts: Blackwell, 2002, 213-30.

PART 8
# Acculturation and Generations

# One Culture, Two Cultures? Families of Finns in the United States in the Twentieth Century

*Johanna Leinonen*

This article examines changes that have taken place in the family life of Finns in the United States over the course of the twentieth century. The following two passages reflect aptly how Finnish families in the United States have changed over the course of the twentieth century. The first quote is from a memoir written by Armas Tamminen, a Finnish American who lived his childhood in a farming community in northern Minnesota in the beginning of the twentieth century: "Growing up in two cultures? What two cultures? I was just a little Finn kid, tucked safely in the warm bosom of a good-sized Finnish family in a Finnish farming community. Until I entered school, I was, at most, but dimly aware of the existence of any other culture."[1] The second quote is from an interview that I conducted in Minneapolis, Minnesota, in 2004. The Finnish-born woman who uttered the quote—I call her "Kati"—moved to the United States in the late 1990s with her American husband, "John." When describing her family life in the United States, she explained that "we are living our own life here, there are American things and Finnish things, but it is not American life or Finnish life, it is our life."[2] The couple had met in Joensuu in eastern Finland, where they both were completing their master's degrees. At the time of the interview, Kati and John were living in Minnesota with their two small children. In the interview, Kati emphasized how she and John combined elements from both cultures in their family life, forming a "third" culture that was neither Finnish nor American.

The contrast to the depiction of family life in Armas's quote is evident. It is clear, then, that the families of Finns in the United States have changed considerably during the twentieth century. But how have they changed exactly? And why? In this chapter, I examine these questions, showing how the transformations in the family life of Finns in the United States originate largely from the changing patterns of Finnish immigration to the country during the twentieth century. The main sources of this research include thirty-five interviews conducted with Finnish women married to Americans in Minnesota, and memoirs and other writings of Finnish immigrants in the United States. I use, for example, archival materials from the Minnesota Finnish American Family History Project, which was conducted in the 1980s and yielded a large amount of material about Finnish American families in the United States.

These records are located at the Immigration History Research Center of the University of Minnesota. In addition, I analyze U.S. Census microdata from 1900 to 2000 and data from the annual American Community Survey between 2000 and 2007, as well as statistics of the U.S. Immigration and Naturalization Service (INS) from 1943 until 2008.[3]

## What Two Cultures?

The passage from Armas's memoir reflects the life patterns of Finnish immigrant families during the peak years of Finnish immigration to the United States in the late nineteenth and early twentieth centuries. At that time, Finnish communities in the United States were lively and full of social activities, and most of the families interacted mainly with other Finns. Edward Haryn, a Finnish American living in Virginia, Minnesota, reminisced in 1980 that in his youth, Finns did not mix much with other ethnic groups: "I think we left them alone more or less."[4] Marriages across ethnic boundaries were rare; only 10 percent of Finns who married did so outside of their ethnic community.[5] While it was rare for both Finnish men and women to intermarry, it seems that relationships between Finnish women and foreign men were particularly unwelcome. Finnish men sometimes actively sought to prevent romantic relationships between Finnish women and foreign men. Varpu Lindström, who has studied the social history of Finnish immigrants in Canada, quotes an interview with a Finnish woman living in Toronto: "The Finnish men set up guards by the dance hall in order to keep out the 'German engineers.' Sometimes there was serious trouble and fights, especially when the Finns were drunk. They just couldn't stomach seeing a Finnish girl under the arm of some kielinen (one who speaks the [English] language)."[6]

These gendered norms regarding interethnic dating were not enforced only by men. The following example shows how female family members could also get involved when a young female expressed an interest in non-Finnish males. Jane Piirto writes: "We were encouraged to marry and date Finnish boys because if you marry a Catholic they make you change your religion, girls. So, girls, even if those Italian boys like the Finnish girls 'stick with your own kind / cling to your own kind' as they sang in *West Side Story,* or your children will be half-breeds. I was actually told this by my aunt when I fell in love with a boy who wasn't of Finnish background."[7]

Women courting non-Finnish men were sometimes ridiculed, too. A character named Matti explains Finnish men's opinions on Finnish women dating foreigners in a radio play broadcast on Amerikan Ääni (Voice of America) in 1953: "I didn't care for those 'paradise birds' wearing heavy make-up and expensive clothes, who looked down on Finns and took a fancy to the 'yanks.'"[8] Finnish women's interest in "Irish gentlemen" also ignited scornful comments among Finnish immigrant men. Kalle Koski, a Finnish poet, wrote in 1896 about a fictional Finnish maid, Mäkelän Maria, who regretted falling for and marrying a "foreign Irishman" (*wieras airis*): "A deep sigh comes out from her chest, always when she looks at her child, as the child playing in her bosom, is of foreign Irish blood."[9]

Thus Finnish women were usually expected to marry a man from their own ethnic group. Men had more leeway when choosing a partner—their courtship of foreign women rarely aroused public disapproval. Nevertheless, marriages between Finnish men and foreign women were still few and far between. Why, then, did Finns marry almost exclusively other Finns? One reason behind these marriage patterns can be found in Finns' relationships with other ethnic groups and representatives of the dominant culture during this time period. Timo Riippa has pointed out that although Finns are often linked in the popular mind with Norwegians, Swedes, and Danes, the Finnish immigrant experience was quite different. Arriving in a later period than most Scandinavians and other northern Europeans, the milieu that Finnish immigrants faced at the turn of the twentieth century was different than previously. With free farmland no longer readily available, Finns often engaged in the most menial jobs. As nativist feelings among the "old stock" Americans rose, newcomers were not welcomed as before. In addition, radical tendencies among Finnish immigrant workers turned Americans' opinions against them.[10]

A researcher often encounters memories of ethnic discrimination and feelings of isolation when reading memoirs and other writings of Finnish immigrants in the United States. The language barrier "tended to keep many Finns isolated from the mainstream of American life and to stick with Finns and Finnish activities."[11] Furthermore, when unskilled immigrant masses poured into the United States from southern and eastern Europe in the late nineteenth and early twentieth centuries, the racial status of these "new" immigrants was often ambiguous. Many Finnish immigrant writers recollect hearing racial slurs from other immigrants and "old stock" Americans. For example, Inez Jaakkola reminisces: "Taunts such as 'dirty Finn' were hurled at us children and I could never understand that term because my mother kept us clean and well dressed as the best."[12] Sometimes children of immigrants wanted to keep distance from their parents' culture because of the tensions between immigrant communities and the dominant society. Inkeri Väänänen-Jensen, a daughter of Finnish immigrants who grew up in Ely and Virginia in Minnesota in the 1920s, writes about her feelings of shame when she was recognized as a Finn: "I felt honored when someone said, 'But you don't *look* Finnish.'"[13] Another example can be found in Valto Eetu Kirri's novel *Amerikan Vieras,* in which he narrates an exchange between a mother and a daughter:

> "Just remember not to talk Finnish to me in the street!" Irene said once to her mother when they were about to leave to the city.
> "Why not?" Mom asked, confused.
> "Because I don't want to be considered as some kind of an immigrant, let alone a Finn."
> "Oh no!" Mom exclaimed. "Is there something wrong with that?"
> "Yes, there is. All those who came from Europe are uncivilized and stupid. . . . And our school books say that Finns are Mongols and I don't want to be any kind of a slant-eyed Mongol."[14]

When considering these circumstances, it is not surprising that Finns often kept to themselves and consequently found their life spouses among fellow Finns. A majority of Finns immigrated alone; family immigration did not become common until toward the end of the period of mass immigration to the United States.[15] In the new country, single immigrants joined lively Finnish communities; temperance and workers' halls and churches became "a second home" for immigrants.[16] Feelings of common ancestry, language, and culture and experiences of marginalization tied Finns together.[17] Writings of Finnish immigrants reveal that many immigrants were not comfortable with interacting with other nationalities in the intimate sphere. The radio character Matti explains his reluctance to court "American girls": "There were of course slender American girls around but we were so slow and awkward in our speech, like Moses used to be, that we didn't dare to call for them."[18] In addition, cultural differences discouraged the forming of relationships across ethnic lines. A Finnish woman dating a Slavic man in Canada described her problems with dating a non-Finn: "On Saturday night, I took him to a sauna—well—he thought that he was in hell, and when I jumped into the icehole, he ran screaming to the house convinced that I was possessed by the devil. That ended that, you couldn't make him into a Finn and no way I was going to give up my Saturday night sauna—no, not for any man."[19]

A contributing factor to the absence of marriages across ethnic boundaries was the lack of language skills among Finnish immigrants: they rarely mastered the English language. As a consequence, their social life was restricted to the Finnish community, and many Finns never learned English well enough to be fluent in it. In tightly knit Finnish communities, learning English might not have been even necessary. For instance, a story of a "bachelor Finn" who had lived in the country for many years without learning any English goes: "When it was suggested to him that it was time he began to speak some English, he countered with, 'Why? There's really no need for it; one uses it so seldom.'"[20] Furthermore, Finnish parents often discouraged interethnic dating for language reasons: many feared that they would not be able to communicate with their children's spouse or grandchildren if they were not Finnish speakers. Inkeri Väänänen-Jensen writes: "Many Finnish parents hoped that their children would marry Finnish spouses; at least they could converse with one another instead of remaining strangers for a lifetime."[21]

Thus, because of the experiences of marginalization, lack of language skills, cultural preferences, and the tightness of Finnish communities, most Finns married inside their ethnic group in the early twentieth century. This trend started to change, however, in midcentury. The "age of immigration" from Finland to the United States came to an end in the 1920s as Finns' immigration opportunities withered with the 1924 National Origins Act. Finns were grouped together with immigrants from eastern and southern Europe, who were considered racially inferior to northern and western Europeans, and were therefore allotted fewer immigration slots. The quota for Finns was only 471 persons a year. In the 1930s, fewer than 2,500 Finns moved to the country, and the flow of immigrants ground to a halt during World War II.[22]

### From In-Marriages to Intermarriages

As the number of Finns arriving in the United States dwindled, the Finnish-born population grew older during the midcentury years. In 1940, for example, the largest age group among the Finnish-born in the United States was immigrants who were between fifty and sixty years old. The percentage of widows among Finnish-born women rose so that by 1960, more than 40 percent of adult Finnish-born women in the United States were widowed.[23] At the same time, the proportion of women among Finns in the United States started rising. During the years of mass immigration, approximately 60 percent of Finns had been men. However, men returned to their home country more often than women did, and they also usually died younger than women. As a result, since 1950 there have been more women than men among Finnish immigrants in the United States.[24] A contributing factor to the growing proportion of women among U.S. immigrants was the fact that a majority of Finns moving to the country since World War II have been women. According to the official U.S. immigration statistics, about 25,000 persons whose last country of residence before the United States was Finland have acquired permanent

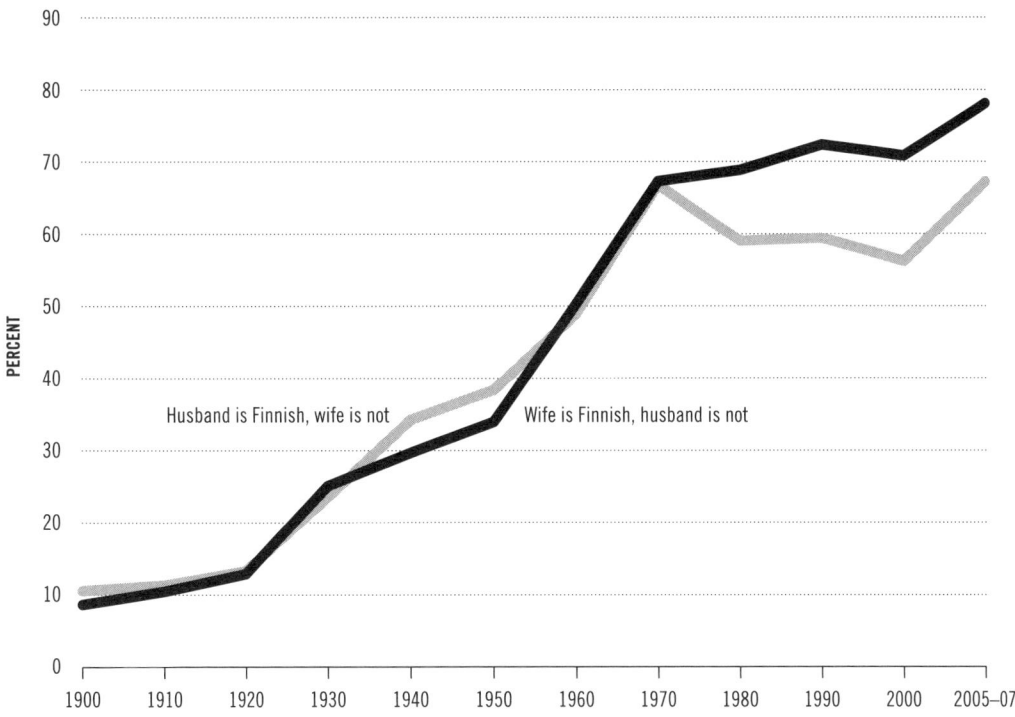

FIGURE 1. Estimated Percentage of Finnish-Born Who Were Intermarried, by Gender, 1900–2007

residency in the country between 1940 and 2011.[25] The number of men and women is available only for certain years during this time period, but in all the years when this number was available, women outnumbered the men. At the end of the 1960s, for example, three-quarters (76 percent) of admitted Finns were women. Today's immigration to the United States seems to be more gender balanced, but women still form the majority. According to Statistics Finland, in all years between 1987 and 2011 more than 50 percent of Finnish citizens who moved to the United States were women. The percentage of women fluctuated between the high of 61 percent in 1990 and the low of 51 percent in 1995.[26]

While the Finnish woman quoted above rejected dates with men who could not understand the Finnish custom so important to her (going to the sauna and jumping in the icehole in the frozen lake), a majority of married Finns in the United States have had to deal with this question of negotiating cultural differences in family life in the second half of the twentieth century. The proportion of Finns who were married outside of their ethnic group increased steadily throughout the twentieth century at the same time as the proportion of women among Finnish immigrants grew. After 1960, more than half of Finnish-born men and women in the United States have been married to a non-Finn (see Figure 1). The 1960s thus marks the beginning of a new period in the marriage patterns of the Finnish-born in the United States. As Figure 1 illustrates, the change has been quite dramatic: the percentage of Finnish-born who were out-married increased from approximately 10 percent for both men and women in 1900 to almost 80 percent for women and 70 percent for men in 2005–2007. Another new trend is the "feminization" of intermarriages of Finns: as Figure 1 demonstrates, since 1970 Finnish women, more often than men, have married a non-Finn.[27] The foreign spouse of Finnish men and women was most often a U.S.-born person with no Finnish ancestry. For example, in 2005–7 almost 60 percent of Finnish women and 50 percent of Finnish men had a spouse who was born in the United States and had no reported Finnish ancestry.[28]

Why did marriages to women and especially to men of other nationalities become much more common after 1960? Reino Kero argues in his classic 1996 study that the reason for Finnish immigration to the United States since the 1960s has been all the more often marriage to an American. This is especially true for Finnish women.[29] Under the Immigration and Nationality Act of 1952, both wives and husbands of U.S. citizens were allowed to enter the country without numerical limits (wives had been entering outside of the quota system for several years by 1952).[30] The records of the INS seem to confirm Kero's argument. The percentage of Finnish-born arriving as spouses of U.S. citizens fluctuated between 10 and 20 percent in the 1950s and 1960s. In 1971, already 34 percent of admitted Finns arrived as spouses of U.S. citizens—and the great majority as wives of U.S. citizens: from 1946 to 1971, approximately 80 percent of Finnish spouses of U.S. citizens were women.[31] We are thus talking about a female-dominated form of migration. Unfortunately, the numbers for immigrants arriving from Finland are missing from most of the 1970s (1972–79)—a drawback of studying a very small immigrant population. After 1979, additionally, the INS no longer recorded the gender of spouses of U.S. citizens. In other words, it is impossible to know how many of the spouses were wives and how many were husbands of U.S. citizens. However, the records tell us that marriage to a U.S. citizen became an even more important immigration reason by the early 1980s: in 1984, for example, 50 percent of Finns were admitted in this category. The trend seems to have remained the same up until today: from the late 1980s until the 2000s, the percentage of Finns admitted as spouses of U.S. citizens has fluctuated between 38 and 64 percent.[32]

These numbers indicate that marriage has become a central motive for immigration from Finland to the United States. Additionally, it can be argued that migration for marriage is a highly gendered form of international migration: it is still more common for a woman to follow her husband to his home country than the other way around. Of course, another half of Finnish immigrants moved to the United States for reasons other than marriage. Many planned to spend only a limited amount of time in the country because of studies, career, or travel, but some ended up staying because of marriage. Thus the increase in intermarriages among Finns living in the United States is inextricably tied to the deepening globalization processes: an ever-increasing number of people moving because of work, study, or travel and the accelerating speed of communication across borders. These processes facilitate the formation of personal relationships that transcend national borders: many migrants are young, unmarried individuals looking for education, career opportunities, or just experiences through travel, and they come into contact with others of different nationalities during a time when they are likely to form lasting personal relationships.[33] It is thus hardly surprising that marriage is sometimes the result of or the reason for migration.[34] The number of Finns arriving to the United States as nonimmigrants (students, travelers, exchange visitors, international representatives, intracompany transferees, and so on) has increased considerably during the past couple of decades: from approximately 40,000 admissions in the early 1980s to more than 148,000 in 2011. More than 3,300 students and other exchange visitors with Finnish citizenship were admitted in 2011.[35] Indeed, many of the women whom I interviewed started their stay in the United States as a university or high school student, and a majority had spent some time—studying, traveling, or working—in the country before moving there permanently. During that stay, many met their future spouses, and the temporary stays evolved into permanent ones.

The formation of personal relationships between Finns and non-Finns was facilitated by the slow disappearance of Finnish American communities and organizations during the post–World War II years. Consequently, Finns arriving to the United States were no longer able—or often even willing—to confine themselves to Finnish American circles. The number of newcomers arriving from Finland was small, and the children and grandchildren of Finnish immigrants intermarried and moved away from the areas where Finns traditionally lived. The interviewed women who arrived in Minnesota in the 1940s and 1950s were still able to find some activities in the old Finn halls and other organizations. A Finnish woman who arrived in the 1950s recalled that at that time, she only participated in activities organized by Finnish Americans. However, the remaining organizations disappeared one after another: "Still in the 1960s we had activities here in Duluth, but now we don't really have anything, and if there's something, it's done in English."[36] Furthermore, Finns who have arrived in the country during the past few decades are not necessarily even interested in traditional Finnish American organizations.

Indeed, the women I interviewed were rarely part of any larger Finnish American community. They did form informal networks among themselves, but their other reference groups consisted of people of different nationalities. Furthermore, the language barrier that prevented earlier immigrants from courting women and men of other nationalities had broken down by the end of the twentieth century. Some of the older interviewees noted that they were not fluent in English at the time of immigration. For instance, a Finnish woman who moved to the United States in 1965 was fluent in German and Swedish (in addition to Finnish), but her English was at an elementary level at the time of her immigration. She met her American husband in Germany, and during the first years of their marriage, they communicated in German. When I asked her about her English-language skills today, she stated, "I still make an awful amount of mistakes, but I just don't care, as long as I'm understood. I'm indifferent with English."[37] Most women, however, were completely comfortable with communicating in English. English became the first foreign language taught in Finnish schools in 1972 (before that, it was German), and this transition likely played an important role in the improvement of Finns' English-language skills.

A related reason for the increase of intermarriages of Finns in the United States may be the rising educational level of Finnish immigrants. U.S. census data reveals that today's Finnish-born population in the United States is highly educated: in 2007, more than three-quarters of the Finnish-born had at least some college education (30 percent had completed one to three years of college and 46 percent four years or more).[38] Some studies have found—although there are also contradicting research results—that immigrants who are well educated are more likely than those with lower education to marry outside their nationality group.[39] Matthijs Kalmijn relates the effect of education to both preference and opportunity. When it comes to preferences, Kalmijn notes that "more highly educated persons—of both majority and minority groups—have a more individualistic attitude, are less attached to their family and community of origin, and have a more universalistic view on life than lesser-educated persons."[40] These characteristics are assumed to make a person more likely to marry someone outside her or his ethnic group. Furthermore, highly educated persons may have more opportunities to meet members of other nationalities in colleges, universities, and high-status occupations. Indeed, many of the women who participated in this research had met their future spouse while studying at a university or during a work assignment abroad. While most of the couples had met in the United States, there were also couples who had met in Finland or in a third country. For example, as I mentioned in the beginning of this chapter, Kati and John met in Finland when they were both studying at the University of Joensuu. Another couple—I call them "Helena" and "Peter"—fell in love and got married in Hong Kong, where they were both working. Helena had earlier spent a year in the state of Illinois as an exchange student but did not meet her American "significant other" during her first stay in the United States. Her move to Hong Kong was affected by her exchange year in the United States: she mentioned in the interview how she wanted to experience the international lifestyle she had enjoyed in Illinois again. Helena took up the challenge of moving to and working in Hong Kong to relive the international atmosphere that she missed, and there she ended up meeting her future husband. Later on, the couple moved to Minnesota. Thus the way these relationships got started exemplifies how international mobility may produce border-crossing intimate relationships.

### What Cultural Differences?

I started this chapter with a quote from Kati's interview in which she characterized her family life as neither American nor Finnish. Many of the women whom I interviewed echoed Kati's feelings. For instance, Helena notes: "We have created our own life and lifestyle. . . . Neither my nor his family or friends meddle with our life; we are our own unit here. This has made our life easier."[41] The fact that the women's lives were no longer tied to ethnic communities or extended families seems to have given them the freedom to choose what kind of family life they built with their partners. Indeed, many women noted how the fact that they lived away from both spouses' families made it easier for them to create their own lifestyle and family traditions. Like Kati and John, most combined elements from both cultures, forming a "third" culture that was somewhere between their conceptions of "Finnish" and "American" family life.

The creation of the "third" culture is facilitated by Finnish women's privileged status as white, middle-class immigrants from Europe. The contrast to the experiences of Finnish immigrants in the early twentieth-century United States is striking: during the twentieth century, Finns became accepted as an "unquestionably white" immigrant group that is largely invisible in the fabric of U.S. society. With the ethnic revival of the 1960s, Americans of European descent started to express pride over their ethnic roots. These privileged groups of white European Americans are able to choose the extent to which they express their ethnic identity—if they decide to do so in the first place.[42] Elements from Finnish culture may, in this context, be seen as an enriching and harmless addition to everyday family life. Indeed, many women noted how their husband's family was excited to learn about Finnish culture in order to "spice up" their traditions during family holidays. Helena, for example, states: "His family doesn't have any strong ethnic heritage, and therefore we can easily bring out some Finnish things. . . . It is richness to them and they are very excited about Finland."[43]

Interestingly enough, it is not uncommon for those who are intermarried to think that cultural differences do not play a particularly important role in their marriage. Rosemary Breger and Rosanna Hill argue that "two people from different cultures may actually have more in common than they have differences, especially if they share a similar urban, highly educated, professional background."[44] Indeed, many of the women whom I interviewed found it difficult to think of any significant cultural differences in their marriage. They argued that conflicts within the marriage resulted from distinct personalities or from the differences in their gendered upbringing, rather than from the fact that they grew up in different cultures. The contrast to the opinion presented by the Finnish woman who took her Slavic boyfriend to the sauna is fascinating.

## Conclusion

Finnish immigrants in the early twentieth-century United States were, in many ways, confined to their Finnish American communities. Most of their social relationships were formed in this context, and, as a result, the majority found their life companions within the Finnish community. Many wrote about feeling inferior to "real" Americans who, if anything, thought of Finland as "a frozen wilderness . . . of Lapps peering out of their leather hoods with slanting eyes."[45] Inkeri Väänänen-Jensen recollects how she wanted to "pass" as an American but failed because of her looks: "She's got the map of Finland on her face."[46] The difference to the experiences of the women I interviewed is significant, as most of them prided themselves on their Finnish background. In addition, many women emphasized how they were able to choose how "Finnish" they were. "Anja," for example, underlined how she could define herself what exactly Finnishness meant to her: "In a way, Finland has become more important to me during these years, but I choose now, I keep few important things alive and let the rest go. But being a Finn is important to me. I don't have to nurture it all the time or be completely Finnish."[47]

The privileged social and racial status of Finns in today's United States gives them the opportunity not only to move across national borders with greater ease than many other groups but also to be creative when defining who they are or what their family life is to look like. Their marriages are inextricably tied to "the globalizing educational systems and labor markets—in other words, with rising international mobility of students and employees," as Michelle Lee and Nicola Piper put it.[48] The families negotiated their ethnic and national loyalties in a transnational space between Finland and the United States, and they combined elements from both cultures. As Helena puts it:

> It has become clearer to me, which traditions I want to keep and share with Peter and the children. It has clarified to us what is our tradition, that there are Finnish and American elements. We choose things from both and create our own traditions. It has taken years, but we have found it, our kind of life, our kind of culture. . . . It's important to me that I don't restrict myself to what I used to do; we have to find our own culture.[49]

### NOTES

1. Armas Tamminen, "What Two Cultures?" in *In Two Cultures: The Stories of Second Generation Finnish Americans,* ed. Aili Jarvenpa (St. Cloud, Minn.: North Star Press of St. Cloud, 1992), 65.
2. "Kati," interview by Johanna Leinonen, Minneapolis, July 2, 2004.
3. For more about the sources, see Johanna Leinonen, "Elite Migration, Transnational Families, and the Nation State: International Marriages between Finns and Americans across the Atlantic in the Twentieth Century" (Ph.D. diss., University of Minnesota, 2011).
4. Edward Haryn, interview by Velma Doby, November 18, 1980, Minnesota Finnish American Family History Collection (MNFAFH), Immigration History Research Center (IHRC), University of Minnesota, Minneapolis.
5. Carl Ross, "Finnish American Women in Transition, 1910–1920," in *Finnish Diaspora II: United States,* ed. Michael G. Karni (Toronto, Ont.:

Multicultural History Society of Ontario, 1981), 252; Steven Ruggles et al., *Integrated Public Use Microdata Series: Version 5.0 [Machine-readable database]* (Minneapolis: University of Minnesota, 2010).

6. Varpu Lindström-Best, *Defiant Sisters: A Social History of Finnish Immigrant Women in Canada* (Toronto: Multicultural History Society of Ontario, 1988), 64.

7. Jane Piirto, "The Finnishness of My Americanness," in *Connecting Souls: Finnish Voices in North America*, ed. Varpu Lindström and Börje Vähämäki (Beaverton, Ont.: Aspasia Books, 2000), 54.

8. "*En myöskään välittänyt vahvasti maalatuista ja kalliisti puetuista paratiisilinnuista, jotka halveksivat suomalaisia ja olivat mieltyneitä jenkkeihin.*" Papers of John I. Kolehmainen, "Tämä on Amerikan Ääni New York: Valikoima Amerikan Äänen suomenkielisistä radiolähetyksistä vuosina 1952-53," Finnish American Collection, IHRC. All translations by author.

9. "*Sywä huokaus nousewi rinnastaan, ain katsoessaan joka kerta, kun leikkiwä lapsonen helmassaan, on wierasta—'airis'-werta.*" Quoted in Reino Kero, *Suureen Länteen: Siirtolaisuus Suomesta Yhdysvaltoihin ja Kanadaan* (Turku: Siirtolaisuusinstituutti, 1996), 212.

10. Timo Riippa, "The Finns and Swede-Finns," in *They Chose Minnesota: A Survey of the State's Ethnic Groups*, ed. June Drenning Holmquist (St. Paul: Minnesota Historical Society Press, 1981), 298; Kero, *Suureen Länteen*, 76.

11. Papers of Katie Jensen, MNFAFH, IHRC. See also Inkeri Väänänen-Jensen, *My Story: Inkeri's Journey* (Iowa City, Iowa: Penfield Press, 1994), 174.

12. Inez Jaakkola, "The Story of My Life," MNFAFH, IHRC.

13. Väänänen-Jensen, *My Story*, 175.

14. Valto Eetu Kirri, *Amerikan Vieras* (Helsinki: Kustannus osakeyhtiö Smia, 1945), 241-42.

15. Kero, *Suureen Länteen*, 110.

16. Papers of Katie Jensen, MNFAFH, IHRC.

17. Varpu Lindström, "'Kodin' merkitys suomalaiselle siirtolaisnaiselle," *Naistutkimus—Kvinnoforskning* 2 (1998): 45-47. See also Väänänen-Jensen, *My Story*, 174.

18. "*Olisihan täällä noita Amerikan hoikkakylkisiä vaikka paljonkin, mutta meillä on niinkuin ennen Mooseksella hidas puhe ja kankea kieli, ettemme niitäkään uskalla avuksemme huutaa.*" Papers of John I. Kolehmainen, "Tämä on Amerikan Ääni New York."

19. Lindström-Best, *Defiant Sisters*, 65.

20. Papers of Katie Jensen, MNFAFH, IHRC.

21. Inkeri Väänänen-Jensen, "The Finnish Language Predicament in Minnesota," in *In Two Cultures*, 2-3.

22. Kero, *Suureen Länteen*, 76.

23. Ruggles et al., *Integrated Public Use Microdata Series*.

24. Kero, *Suureen Länteen*, 103; Ruggles et al., *Integrated Public Use Microdata Series*.

25. U.S. Department of Homeland Security, *Yearbook of Immigration Statistics* (Washington, D.C.: U.S. Department of Homeland Security, Office of Immigration Statistics, 2012), 8-10.

26. U.S. Department of Labor, *Annual Report of the Immigration and Naturalization Service* (Washington, D.C.: Government Printing Office, 1943-1977); U.S. Department of Justice, *Statistical Yearbook of the Immigration and Naturalization Service* (Washington, D.C.: Government Printing Office, 1978-2001); Statistics Finland, "Maahan- ja maastamuuttaneet lähtö- ja määrämaan iän, sukupuolen ja kansalaisuuden mukaan 1987—2011," http://pxweb2.stat.fi/database/StatFin/vrm/muutl/muutl_fi.asp.

27. Ruggles et al., *Integrated Public Use Microdata Series*.

28. Ruggles et al., *Integrated Public Use Microdata Series*.

29. Kero, *Suureen Länteen*, 65.

30. U.S. Department of State, "The Immigration and Nationality Act of 1952 (The McCarran-Walter Act)," http://www.state.gov/r/pa/ho/time/

cwr/87719.htm.

31. The low point for the percentage of females among spouses was 1954 when 55 percent were wives of U.S. citizens, and the high point was 1965 when almost all (96 percent) of admitted Finnish spouses were women. The numbers for Finnish-born immigrants are missing in 1969 and 1970.

32. The numbers for Finns are again missing in 1994–97. U.S. Department of Labor, *Annual Report;* U.S. Department of Justice, *Statistical Yearbook.* For more discussion on this topic, see Johanna Leinonen, "Love and Transatlantic Migration: Changing Marriage Patterns between Finland and the U.S. in the 20th Century," in *Nordic Migration: Research Status, Perspectives and Challenges,* ed. Christina Folke Ax and Nils Olav Østrem (Stamsund: Orkana Akademisk, 2011), 30–33.

33. Nicola Piper and Mina Roces, "Introduction: Marriage and Migration in an Age of Globalization," in *Wife or Worker? Asian Women and Migration,* ed. Nicola Piper and Mina Roces (Lanham, Md.: Rowman & Littlefield, 2003), 1.

34. Nicola Piper, "Wife or Worker? Worker or Wife? Marriage and Cross-Border Migration in Contemporary Japan," *International Journal of Population Geography* 9 (2003): 457.

35. U.S. Department of Homeland Security, *Yearbook 2011,* 68, 77. The number of admissions represents counts of events, that is, arrivals, not unique individuals. Thus the actual number of students and exchange visitors is somewhat smaller than 3,300—the same person may enter the country more than once a year.

36. "Helmi," interview by Johanna Leinonen, Duluth, Minn., August 16, 2004.

37. "Tarja," interview by Johanna Leinonen, Minneapolis, November 4, 2004.

38. Ruggles et al., *Integrated Public Use Microdata Series.*

39. See, for example, Delia Furtado, "Human Capital and Interethnic Marriage Decisions," *IZA Discussion Papers* No. 1989 (2006), ftp://repec.iza.org/RePEc/Discussionpaper/dp1989.pdf.

40. Matthijs Kalmijn, "Intermarriage and Homogamy: Causes, Patterns, Trends," *Annual Review of Sociology* 24 (1998): 413.

41. "Helena," interview by Johanna Leinonen, Minneapolis, July 5, 2004.

42. Mary C. Waters, *Ethnic Options: Choosing Identities in America* (Berkeley: University of California Press, 1990).

43. "Helena" interview.

44. Rosemary Breger and Rosanna Hill, "Introducing Mixed Marriages," in *Cross-Cultural Marriage: Identity and Choice,* ed. Rosemary Breger and Rosanna Hill (New York: Berg, 1998), 8.

45. Väänänen-Jensen, *My Story,* 176–77.

46. Väänänen-Jensen, *My Story,* 175.

47. "Anja," interview by Johanna Leinonen, Minneapolis, August 20, 2004.

48. Michelle Lee and Nicola Piper, "Reflections on Transnational Life-Course and Migratory Patterns of Middle-Class Women—Preliminary Observations from Malaysia," in Piper and Roces, *Wife or Worker,* 122.

49. "Helena" interview.

# The Transnational Practices of Finnish Immigrants

*Peter Kivisto*

Finns offer an instructive case of political transnationalism, particularly during the period known as Karelia fever of the 1930s, during which time several thousand Finns from the United States and Canada departed for Soviet Karelia to help the Communist regime build the "Labor Republic." While the first, and to a more limited extend, the second generations provided ample evidence of transnational activities, over time transnationalism declined as the ethnic community was transformed into American citizens, defining themselves as hyphenated Americans rather than as workers of the world.

This chapter asks whether Finnish migrants in America could be construed to be transnational immigrants. In doing so, it makes use of a concept that was introduced into immigration research in the 1990s to advance research on contemporary migration. The purpose of this research was to cast new light on a group that received considerable scholarly attention by social historians and historical sociologists during the 1970s and 1980s—a time that proved to be the zenith of scholarship focusing on the wave of immigration extending from 1880 to 1930. Rather than making use of new data, I apply the concept to this extant body of research. By using the case of Finns as a strategic research site, the chapter is intended to shed light on the debates over immigrant incorporation.

## Transnationalism

Since the early 1990s, a growing number of immigration scholars conducting research on contemporary labor migrations from the nations of the South and East to those of the North have begun to use the term "transnationalism" in order to specify what might be the distinctive features of this immigrant wave. In particular, this theorizing has sought to explore the rise of transnational immigrant *communities*. Such communities are treated as a parallel phenomenon to other manifestations of transnationalism, such as those related to global corporate capitalism,[1] entrepreneurs,[2] the emergence of international nongovernmental organizations (NGOs), social movements,[3] research think tanks,[4] and the increased hybridization of popular culture.[5] The earliest formulation of transnationalism as it applies to immigration was developed by cultural anthropologists Linda Basch, Nina Glick Schiller, and Christina Szanton Blanc, who defined it as "the processes by which immigrants forge and sustain multi-stranded relations that link together their societies of origin and settlement."[6] Put simply, transnational immigrants are seen as attempting to live with one foot in the homeland and the other foot in the host society, in the process creating an ethnic community that transcends national boundaries. Employing a language borrowed from Pierre Bourdieu or from that of social geographers, they refer to this transcendence in terms of the construction of transnational social fields or social spaces. This concept is akin to the idea of the ethnic global village.[7] The assumption of the earliest formulations of transnational immigration was that it distinguished contemporary immigrants from those who migrated during the preceding great migratory wave that occurred between 1880 and 1930. The former were potentially transnational, while the latter were not, chiefly because of the impact of improved communications technologies and transportation systems in the current era.[8]

Not all agree that transnationalism is a useful concept for immigration research. Indeed, Ninna Nyberg Sørensen has posed the question in stark terms: is it a "useful approach or trendy rubbish?"[9] Few have gone as far as David Fitzgerald in proposing that "the term as it is generally used in migration research should be retired."[10] Nonetheless, critics have questioned the conceptual inflation contained in those formulations.[11] Of particular salience for the topic at hand in this essay, some of these critics have questioned the assumption that immigrants from an earlier era were not transnational. Just how significant the differences are between immigrants past and present in this regard is an empirical question that is only now beginning to receive scholarly attention.[12] There is an increasing concession on the part of scholars of transnationalism that the early formulation overstated the differences.[13] In fact, the back-and-forth movement of immigrants in the past was far more common than is often appreciated and the numbers of those who ultimately opted to return to the homeland permanently are much higher than previously thought, as Mark Wyman's research makes clear.[14]

In an effort to refine the term and to translate it into operational terms, Alejandro Portes, Luis E. Guarnizo, and Patricia Landolt have identified three discrete but often interrelated types of transnationalism: economic, political, and sociocultural. From their perspective, economic transnationalism involves entrepreneurs whose network of suppliers, capital, and markets crosses national borders. Political transnationalism refers to "the political activities of party officials, government functionaries, or community leaders whose main goals are the achievement of political power and influence in the sending or receiving countries." Finally, sociocultural transnationalism entails activities designed to reinforce homeland culture and adapt it to new circumstances.[15] While this form of transnationalism is broad, primary research attention to date has focused on religion and thus on religious transnationalism as a subset of sociocultural transnationalism.[16]

### Were Finns Transnational?

Tracing the movement of Finns between Finland and North America has proven to be a difficult task. Some of the factors making it difficult to ascertain with real precision the transborder movements of Finns include the fact that Finns entering the United States were not always listed as Finnish, some traveled without passports, and some first entered Canada before crossing the porous border between the two nations. What is clear is that for a variety of reasons, ranging from political events to economic interests to homesickness, Finns were like most other ethnic groups insofar as many immigrants decided at some point to return to their homeland. A. William Hoglund estimated that somewhere between 30 and 40 percent of Finns returned to Finland.[17] Anna-Leena Toivonen concurred, concluding that one-third of the immigrants ultimately returned to the homeland.[18] Since those estimates, subsequent researchers have lowered the percentage figure of returnees. Reino Kero, for example, estimated that 25 percent of immigrants repatriated,[19] while in what would become the most exhaustive and authoritative study of return settlement, Keijo Virtanen lowered the figure to 20 percent.[20] Even with this lower figure, what is clear is that a substantial number of Finns—at a minimum one in five—did not settle permanently in the United States. Wyman contends that Finns were like other immigrant groups insofar as remigration was "tilted heavily toward land-hungry farmers,"[21] and thus those who returned had, or thought they had, prospects of acquiring land in Finland.

However, transnational immigrants are different from those immigrants who simply made a round-trip to America. They, instead, are expected to maintain contact with the homeland while maintaining a place of operation in the destination country. There is abundant anecdotal information about Finnish birds of passage, those who moved back-and-forth between Finland and North America. Virtanen refers to Juho Antinpoika Paavola, who departed from Finland for overseas destinations five times between 1888 and 1902, and never returned permanently to his homeland.[22] How many Finns made repeat trips between Finland and America? According to Virtanen, the figure did not exceed 10 percent.[23]

While this would suggest that the percentage of Finnish migrants who could as individuals be described as transnational immigrants was quite small, they may have been sufficient to forge a transnational social field. Portes contends that the number of actual transnational immigrants among contemporary immigrants is typically quite low.[24] Nonetheless, as few as 5 percent is sufficient to forge a transnational social field. Such a field is composed of an institutional structure that transcends the political boundaries of nation-states. The question we turn to, then, is whether in the economic, political, or religious realms one can point to evidence of such institutions.

## Economic Transnationalism

If we use Portes, Haller, and Guarnizo's definition of economic transnationalism as those economic transactions involving entrepreneurs engaged in border-crossing exchanges,[25] the secondary literature would suggest that Finns were not economic transnationals. It would suggest this because to a large extent the literature is silent on the topic. While this might simply mean that scholars have neglected the topic, being more concerned, for instance, with labor history, gender history, and religious history, the fact that Finns were overwhelmingly labor migrants who gained entrée into the American working class would lend credence to this conclusion. However, it would be surprising if the more filiopietistic writings of amateur scholars did not mention transnational entrepreneurs, since such individuals would typically be viewed as ethnic success stories. It is thus reasonable to conclude that there was little such transnational economic activity among Finns—even taking into account the rather low threshold required for such a transnational social space to emerge.

Reino Kero provides evidence of the role played by return migrants in the cultural diffusion of American technology into Finland. For example, George Holm introduced the wood pulp thermal-mechanical process into Finland's wood-processing industry, a technological innovation he had learned about when he worked as a laborer in a mill in Massachusetts. He also was responsible for introducing American paper-making machinery. Likewise, the techniques used in Chicago to produce agricultural cultivation implements were transferred to Finland by Jaakko Vassi, who worked for many years in American industry before returning to his homeland.[26] These and similar examples of the impact of American technology on Finnish industrialization might point to a phenomenon that looks in many respects like transnationalism. However, it is worth stressing that this amounted to a one-way transmission of technological innovation and did not involve or require the establishment of a transnational business network. Indeed, as far as we know, Holm, Vassi, and others like them created successful businesses in their homeland, but these businesses were strictly national rather than transnational in nature.

One might object to Portes and associates' definition of economic transnationalism for being overly limited by looking only at entrepreneurial activity.[27] Perhaps it ought to be expanded to include workers. If one does, is there evidence that Finnish labor migrants were enmeshed in a transnational economic circuit? Birds of passage, those immigrants willing to move again and again across the Atlantic and within North America, by moving between Canada and the United States, could reasonably be viewed as transnational immigrants. Indeed, for them to time their moves in economically rational terms, such migrants would have required networks of support. Transnational networks would consist in part of well-positioned individuals in various locales capable of providing useful information that could inform the timing of a move. It would also consist of institutions that could help to support and sustain recurrent transborder crossings. This would include newspapers influencing people about staying versus moving, steamship companies with cheap fares, boardinghouses, labor recruitment offices, and so forth. Recall that Virtanen concluded that only 10 percent of Finnish immigrants made repeated journeys. Thus the total number of Finnish laborers who might be defined as transnational immigrants was relatively low. Nonetheless, building on the argument of Portes et al., these immigrants can be seen as instrumental to the construction of a transnational social space, a space that involves both those exhibiting high levels of geographic mobility and those who remain in place. In other words, not everyone in a transnational social space is necessarily a transnational immigrant.

Two empirical questions arise. First, was there a critical mass of transnational labor migrants to make possible such a social space? Here I think the evidence is spotty and needs to be dealt with fairly circumspectly. Nonetheless, it does not seem unreasonable to assume that something resembling a transnational social space existed during the heyday of Finnish immigration. This leads to the second question. If such a space did exist, how long did it persist? Was it primarily a first-generation phenomenon, or did it continue into the second and third generations? I would argue that there is little reason to conclude that a transnational economic space existed by the beginning of World War II. This is a point that I make, with greater empirical support, when turning to the topic of political transnationalism.

### Political Transnationalism

Contrary to the claims made by the earliest exponents of transnationalism that immigrants in the past tended to make a clean break with their ancestral homelands, in fact they often took considerable interest in events in the homeland, including political events. In an article that appeared in the *Journal of American Ethnic History,* I attempted to trace Finnish American interest in the homeland and involvement in Finnish politics during the four-decade period between 1918 and 1958.[28] This article appeared prior to the introduction of the concept transnationalism into immigration studies. In

**FIGURE 1.** International exhibitions were a forum of transnational relations. Depicted here is Finland Day at the New York World's Fair 1939–40. Note the giant wall hanging on the stage based on one of Akseli Gallen-Kallela's famous national romantic paintings named *Kullervon sotaan lähtö* (Kullervo Goes to War). (Source: IMT Photo collections, USA_1287)

retrospect, I think that the evidence I brought to bear on this subject supports the claim that Finns were in significant ways political transnationals up through World War II, with a subsequent decline in both interest and involvement.

Much has been made of the divided nature of the Finnish American community, frequently depicted in terms of the split between conservative "Church Finns" and radical "Red Finns." During the ethnic community's formative period, these two warring camps competed to win the hearts and minds of the uncommitted. The ideological chasm between the two sides resulted at the institutional level in a system of dual halls. The first instance in which this situation spilled out of the ethnic enclaves and into the international arena was during the Finnish Civil War. Finland was divided along similar lines to the Finnish American community. In the wake of the Russian Revolution, both the question of independence and the nature of what an independent Finland might look like became very real political concerns. They also served to divide the nation, which on January 27, 1918, was plunged into a bloody civil war.

Finns in the United States followed events in Finland closely, and the protracted battles between the Reds and Whites provoked strong responses from both sides of the Finnish American political spectrum. Thus the editors of the conservative newspaper *Päivälehti* wrote, "*Shame to them: the Red revolution in*

*Finland is the most shameful deed ever done in Finland."* In reply, radicals described the Whites variously as "Finno-German junkers," "a butcher bund," and "reactionary lickspittles."²⁹

Both sides of the immigrant community mobilized in an attempt to shape American public opinion and to influence the U.S. government. In the case of the leftist community, the role of a transnational leadership stratum was crucial to their efforts. Thus Yrjö Sirola, who served as the Red Guard provisional government's foreign minister, contacted Santeri Nuorteva and asked him to establish and run a Finnish Information Office. Nuorteva was, at the time, the editor of the social democratic newspaper *Raivaaja*. Sirola had spent time in the United States developing his socialist credentials, in part by serving as an instructor at the Work People's College. Around the same time that he was in the United States, Nuorteva was serving as a member of the Finnish Parliament. The threat of imprisonment by the czarist government forced him into exile, landing in Fitchburg, Massachusetts. Sometime thereafter, Sirola returned to Finland and became immersed in the Finnish Left. Given Nuorteva's close ties to prominent leaders in the Socialist Party, he was able to use these connections in advancing the cause of the Left. He managed to receive a hearing at the State Department and was pleased when the United States adopted a policy of official neutrality. He was less pleased about its refusal to provide relief to hard-pressed revolutionaries.³⁰

Rank-and-file leftists in the immigrant community followed events in Finland with keen interest. They also participated in the Million Mark Fund, a campaign uniting socialists, Communists, and industrial unionists, which was intended to help facilitate the rejuvenation of the Finnish trade union movement in the aftermath of the short-lived Civil War. The fact that the campaign reached its monetary target speaks to the desire of Finnish Americans to maintain and enhance bonds of solidarity with fellow ethnic workers on the other side of the Atlantic. The campaign also highlighted the internal divisions within the Left in Finland and America. A battle ensued over which leftist parties in Finland should be the recipients of these funds.

What is evident in this episode is that the ideal of socialist internationalist solidarity fused intriguingly with ethnic loyalties to create and sustain a transnational political space. There is evidence of considerable back-and-forth movement of leaders. For example, Niilo Wälläri had honed his radical credentials as a student at the Work People's College and as an Industrial Workers of the World (IWW) activist. At the height of the "Red Scare" era in the aftermath of World War I, he was deported in 1920. He resumed his work as a labor activist in Finland, eventually rising to the presidency of the Finnish Seaman's Union.³¹ Virtanen identifies several other Finns who spent time working as editors of leftist newspapers in the United States before returning to their homeland prior to World War I: Kaapo Murros, A. B. Mäkelä, Väinö Riippa, Leo Laukki, and Alex Halonen.³²

Perhaps the most interesting—and ultimately the most influential—was Oskari Tokoi. After spending years as a miner in the United States, he returned to Finland in 1900, rose to prominence as a social democrat, entering parliament, becoming its Speaker, and ultimately being elected prime minister. In the wake of the Civil War and the defeat of the Left, he reemigrated in 1921. Settling in Fitchburg, he became a principal leader within reform socialist ranks, serving as editor of *Raivaaja*. He played a major role in efforts to elicit American support for Finland during World War II. He thought about returning to Finland after 1945, but circumstances prevented him from doing so.

To a lesser extent, rank-and-file workers also moved within this transnational social space. Moreover, and more significant than the number of individuals involved, there was an exchange of ideas and ideals. I argued in my homeland politics article that those in the Finnish American Left knew conditions in Finland quite well and participated in or supported sectors of the Finnish Left accordingly. I should add that the exchange of information worked both ways. Finnish leftists had a fairly good grasp of the political climate in America.

In the immediate aftermath of the Civil War, a large contingent of the defeated Red Guard went into exile. Thousands went to Soviet Russia. Prior to the passage of the Immigration Restriction Act of 1924, approximately 14,000 Finns entered the United States and Canada, among them probably hundreds of former Red Guards. They entered a social milieu in which they found like-minded comrades, and this helped to reinforce the transnational political character of Finnish and Finnish American radicalism.

A complicating twist to political transnationalism occurred during the dislocations brought about by the Great Depression. Economically distressed and disillusioned with the prospects for revolutionary change in the United States, several thousand Finns in North America returned to Europe—not to Finland proper, but to Soviet Karelia. Though not a return to what was then Finland, the move to Karelia was infused with a frequently unacknowledged sense of nationalism on the part of those who claimed to be internationalists. That is to say, Karelia was contested territory, containing largely speakers of Russian and Karelian, a language close to Finnish. It became an important cause within sectors of the Finnish right wing. After the civil war, some defeated leftists fled to Karelia, joined later by some Finnish American radicals fleeing the repressive climate of the "Red Scare" era. These migrants, along with the Finnish Communist Party operating at the time from the Kremlin, considered the region to be a base for the eventual seizure of power in Finland.

Thus the move to assist in the construction of the Labor Republic, as advocates defined this transnational migration, involved a complex set of motives. Those caught up in "Karelia fever" did so typically with an admixture of utopian motives of Communist visionaries and the practical interests characteristic of birds of passage.[33] The choice of locale was significant insofar as the region could simultaneously evoke images of successful proletarian revolution and deep-rooted ethnonationalist attachments to the soil.

The migration was organized by Soviet authorities, directed by O. W. Kuusinen, the head of the Finnish Communist Party in exile and a member of the Comintern. He believed that Finnish American radicals would bring not only the requisite revolutionary élan but also technical skills that were in short supply in the Soviet Union. In order to attract Finns in America to move, he created a labor recruitment agency known as the Technical Aid of Soviet Karelia, which was run by two Finnish American radicals, Matti Tenhunen and Oscar Corgan. The Communist press, particularly *Työmies* and *Eteenpäin,* actively promoted the plan, encouraging workers to leave "the land of rhinoceroses." The estimates on the Finns from North America vary quite a lot. Reino Kero has estimated in his 1983 study that a total of 6,000 Finns from the United States and Canada were ultimately swept up in the "fever."[34] More recently, as a result of the path-breaking research project directed by Varpu Lindström, the general consensus is that the actual number of emigrants was higher, perhaps in the vicinity of 8,000.

The initial enthusiasm of these migrants changed to disappointment and disillusionment. Not only were living conditions difficult at best, but they found the plodding Soviet bureaucracy and the general technological backwardness of the nation to be distressing. Their growing litany of complaints made the Finns suspect in the eyes of Soviet authorities. Though accurate figures are difficult to come by, it is assumed that several thousand Finns, those who arrived illegally from Finland and others from North America, became the victims of Stalinist purges. Many others fled. In fact, Kero estimated that at the most, half of the North American Finns ultimately left the Soviet Union.³⁵ They did so typically by slipping into Finland, where many remained. Of those who continued on to North America, many opted to locate in places where nobody knew them in order to hide the fact that they had been part of this misadventure.

This episode can be seen as representing the beginning of the end of the transnational political space that the Finnish American Left had created less than two decades earlier. This was evident by the time of the Winter War (1939–40) and Continuation War (1941–44). The Finnish American Left had begun its decline; the ethnic community as a whole was more Americanized; and the younger generations of Finns, lacking direct contact with and involvement in Finnish social, cultural, and political life, viewed Finland increasingly in symbolic terms—reflective of what Herbert Gans described as "symbolic ethnicity."³⁶ The cessation of immigration from 1924 forward meant that the ethnic community no longer was infused with newcomers who could reacquaint those born in the United States with Finland.

Despite these changes, Finnish Americans rallied to Finland's cause, portraying especially the Soviet invasion in 1939–40 as a battle pitting David against Goliath. While the moderate Left made common cause with the center and political Right, those leftists who still supported the Soviet Union were increasingly marginalized within the ethnic community and elsewhere. By the end of the war and by the time the process of postwar reconstruction had begun, the transnational political space linking the North American ethnic Left to the Left in the homeland had become highly constricted and fragile.

Another intriguing example of political transnationalism was the participation of a large group of leftist volunteers in the Spanish Civil War (1936–39). There were around 4,000 volunteers from North America on the republican side, "defending democracy." It has been found that around 200 of them were Finns from the United States and Canada; mostly they served in the ranks of the Abraham Lincoln or Mackenzie-Papineau battalions, in which they even had a machine-gun company unit named Jaakko Ilkka (according to legend, he was the Finnish peasant rebel leader of the 1500s). There were also about a hundred Finns from Finland on the republican side and twenty-five on Franco's nationalist side. A fourth of the North American Finns either died or disappeared during the conflict.³⁷

### Religious Transnationalism

What can we say about transnational practices within the other sector of the Finnish American community: Church Finns? Sociologists of religion have recently focused on the religious beliefs and practices of the new immigrants to the world's liberal democracies and in so doing have begun to pay increased attention to the frequently transnational nature of religious affiliation and practice.³⁸ With this body of research in mind, it is worth asking whether earlier waves of immigrants also provide evidence of religious transnationalism. Specifically for the topic at hand, could Finnish immigrants be construed to be religious transnationals?

I contend that for a period of approximately two decades, from roughly the beginning of the twentieth century to the 1920s, they could be so defined. Most religious Finns were Lutheran, though small numbers affiliated with Congregationalism and Unitarianism. In the early years of immigrant settlement they confronted the following realities: the Finnish Lutheran state church was unremittingly hostile to the immigrants, viewing them as traitors to the homeland; there was a scarcity of ordained clergy speaking the Finnish language; and the United States, free from the influence of an official state church, contained a highly competitive religious marketplace.[39] This was conducive in the early years to the growth of various lay-dominated sectarian groups, including Apostolic Lutherans and Laestadians. One of the consequences of this situation was a willingness on the part of many religious Finns to join either the Swedish Augustana Synod or pan-Scandinavian religious institutions.

This situation would change with the birth of the Suomi Synod in 1890 under the direction of the émigré pastor N. K. Nikander. He was intent on replicating as far as possible the Finnish state church in America. To do so required resources, some of which were available within the immigrant community. However, at least at the outset he needed financial support and an infusion of pastors from Finland. The state church shifted its position regarding immigrants, ceasing condemning them and instead seeking to find ways to encourage them to be faithful Lutherans. For example, the church encouraged pastors, particularly young ones, to do a tour of duty in the United States. However, Nikander planned for a future in which Finns in the United States would have to become self-sustaining. The creation of Suomi College, a liberal arts undergraduate institution and theological seminary, was intended to make this possible.[40]

In short, during the formative period of the Suomi Synod, characterized as it was both by resource dependency on the Finnish state church and by a desire to transplant its theological tradition in the new homeland, a lively transnational social network was forged and sustained. The key transnational actors included Finnish pastors who either spent time serving churches in America before returning to Finland or who remained in the immigrant community. It also included the hierarchies of both the Finnish church and the Suomi Synod. In addition, laypersons who returned to Finland were part of this mix, one that the church hierarchy in Finland did not always appreciate. This was particularly the case when immigrants brought ideas of democratic church governance and congregational autonomy back with them. The result was that the influence of the transatlantic networks was not simply one-sided but in fact reciprocal.

However, evidence that the network was weakening could be seen as early as the 1920s. The end of mass immigration was a major factor in eroding the transnational religious space. The Suomi Synod under the leadership of John Wargelin (whose thinking had been shaped by the Chicago school of sociology's understanding of assimilation) began the process of Americanization. Synod members were asked to distinguish two heritages, the ethnic and the religious, and they were informed that the latter was more important than the former.[41] This period saw the commencement of the move from Finnish to English religious services. Intermarriage began to reshape the ethnic character of those in the pews. As the impact of these changes became more consequential, the leadership of the synod entered into discussions with other ethnically based Lutheran denominations about the desirability and the feasibility of merger into a larger denomination. Although it would take four more decades for a merger to finally occur, for some time the religious space occupied by Finnish Americans affiliated with the Suomi Synod was being transformed from a transnational space to a decidedly American space. Religious transnationalism never disappeared. Rather, it became an increasingly smaller and less consequential space.

## Conclusion

One of the questions scholars of transnationalism ask is whether this phenomenon, to the extent that it exists, can be expected to persist over time or instead should be seen as characteristic of the immigrant first generation. If I am correct that Finns can be appropriately seen as transnational immigrants, forging both political and religious transnational spaces (if not economic spaces), can their example help us to answer the question? The evidence from the secondary literature as I have interpreted it in this essay would suggest that the two types of transnational social spaces were consequential, vibrant, and relatively short-lived. Indeed, if the beginning of the end for both can be seen to unfold as early as the 1920s, perhaps it is true that transnationalism is simply a phenomenon of the immigrant generation. In other words, the notion of inevitable generational change—be it the famous thesis of Marcus Lee Hansen or other subsequent arguments about generational succession—may be an adequate explanation for the fate of Finnish American transnationalism. While this might be the case, I would caution against being overly hasty in jumping to this conclusion. One other factor that must be accounted for in assessing transnationalism's fate in this particular case—and I would surmise in the fate of other immigrant groups from the same era—is that mass immigration ended with the passage of the Immigration Restriction Act of 1924. To the extent that the flow of immigrants to and fro across the Atlantic is a vital aspect of transnational social practices, the end of that flow can signal a critical closure on the ability of immigrants to sustain transnational ties. We are left pondering one of history's "what if" questions: what would have happened to second- and third-generation Finnish Americans coming of age between the two world wars if they had lived in an ethnic community containing substantial numbers of new immigrants from Finland? Might their transnational practices have persisted beyond the middle of the twentieth century?

## NOTES

1. Leslie Sklair, *The Transnational Capitalist Class* (Oxford: Blackwell, 2001).
2. Ivan Light, "Transnational Entrepreneurs in an English-Speaking World," *Die Erde* 141, nos. 1-2 (2010): 1-16.
3. Jackie Smith, "Global Civil Society? Transnational Social Movement Organizations and Social Capital," in *Beyond Tocqueville: Civil Society and the Social Capital Debate in Comparative Perspective*, ed. Bob Edwards et al. (Hanover, N.H.: New England Press for Tufts University, 2001), 194-206.
4. Raymond J. Struyk, "Management of Transnational Think Tank Networks," *International Journal of Politics, Culture, and Society* 15, no. 4 (2002): 625-38.
5. Arjun Appadurai, *Modernity at Large: Cultural Dimensions of Globalization* (Minneapolis: University of Minnesota Press, 1996).
6. Linda Basch, Nina Glick Schiller, and Cristina Szanton Blanc, *Nations Unbound: Transnational Projects, Postcolonial Predicaments, and Deterritorialized Nation-States* (Basel: Gordon and Breach, 1994), 27.
7. Thomas Faist, *The Volume and Dynamics of International Migration and Transnational Social Spaces* (Oxford: Oxford University Press, 2000); Alejandro Portes, "Conclusion: Theoretical Convergences and Empirical Evidence in the Study of Immigrant Transnationalism," *International Migration Review* 37, no. 3 (2003): 874-92; Alejandro Portes, "Introduction: The Debates and Significance of Immigrant Transnationalism," *Global Networks* 1, no. 3 (2001): 181-94.
8. Nina Glick Schiller, "The Situation of Transnational Studies," *Identities* 4, no. 2 (1997): 155-66; Nina Glick Schiller, Linda Basch, and Cristina Szanton Blanc, "From Immigrant to Transmigrant: Theorizing Transnational Migration," *Anthropological Quarterly* 68, no. 1 (1995): 48-63.
9. Ninna NybergSørensen, "Notes on Transnationalism to the Panel of Devil's Advocates: Transnational Migration—Useful Approach or Trendy

Rubbish?" Paper presented at the Conference on Transnational Migration, Oxford University, June 6, 2000.

10. David Fitzgerald, "Beyond 'Transnationalism': Mexican Hometown Politics in an American Labour Union," *Ethnic and Racial Studies* 27, no. 2 (2004): 228.

11. Elliot Barkan, "Introduction: Immigration, Incorporation, Assimilation, and the Limits of Transnationalism," *Journal of American Ethnic History* 25, nos. 2-3 (2006): 7-32; Nancy Foner, *In a New Land: A Comparative View of Immigration* (New York: New York University Press, 2005); Nancy Foner, "Immigrant Commitment to America, Then and Now: Myths and Realities," *Citizenship Studies* 5, no. 1 (2001): 27-40; Peter Kivisto, "Theorizing Transnational Immigration: A Critical Review of Current Efforts," *Ethnic and Racial Studies* 24, no. 4 (2001): 549-77; Ewa Morawska, *A Sociology of Immigration: (Re)Making Multifaceted America* (New York: Palgrave Macmillan, 2009); Ewa Morawska, "Immigrants, Transnationalism, and Ethnicization: A Comparison of This Great Wave and the Last," in *E Pluribus Unum? Contemporary and Historical Perspectives on Immigrant Incorporation* (New York: Russell Sage Foundation, 2001), 175-212; Roger D. Waldinger and David Fitzgerald, "Transnationalism in Question," *American Journal of Sociology* 109, no. 5 (2004): 1177-95.

12. Foner, *In a New Land*; Morawska, "Immigrants, Transnationalism"; Peter Kivisto, "Social Spaces, Transnational Immigrant Communities, and the Politics of Incorporation," *Ethnicities* 3, no. 1 (2003): 5-28.

13. Peggy Levitt and B. Nadia Jaworsky, "Transnational Migration Studies: Past Developments and Future Trends," *Annual Review of Sociology* 33 (2007): 129-56.

14. Mark Wyman, *Round-Trip to America: The Immigrants Return to Europe, 1880-1930* (Ithaca, N.Y.: Cornell University Press, 1993).

15. Alejandro Portes, Luis E. Guarnizo, and Patricia Landolt, "The Study of Transnationalism: Pitfalls and Promise of an Emergent Research Field," *Ethnic and Racial Studies* 22, no. 2 (1999): 217-37.

16. See, for example, Richard D. Alba et al., eds., *Immigration and Religion in America: Comparative and Historical Perspectives* (New York: New York University Press, 2009); Peggy Levitt, *God Needs No Passport: Immigrants and the Changing American Religious Landscape* (New York: New Press, 2007).

17. A. William Hoglund, *Finnish Immigrants in America 1880-1920* (Madison: University of Wisconsin Press, 1960), 8.

18. Anna-Leena Toivonen, *Etelä-Pohjanmaan valtamerentakainen siirtolaisuus 1867-1939* (Seinäjoki: SHS, 1963).

19. Reino Kero, "The Return of Immigrants from America to Finland," *Publications of the Institute of General History, University of Turku* no. 4 (1972): 9-29.

20. Keijo Virtanen, *Settlement or Return: Finnish Emigrants (1860-1930) in the International Overseas Return Migration Movement* (Forssa: Institute of Migration, 1979).

21. Wyman, *Round-Trip to America*, 132.

22. Virtanen, *Settlement or Return*, 71-72.

23. Virtanen, *Settlement or Return*, 71.

24. Portes, "Conclusion."

25. Alejandro Portes, William J. Haller, and Luis E. Guarnizo, "Transnational Entrepreneurs: An Alternative Form of Immigrant Economic Adaptation," *American Sociological Review* 67, no. 2 (2002): 278-98.

26. Reino Kero, "American Technology in Finland before World War I," *Turun Historiallinen Arkisto* 42 (1987): 160-61.

27. Portes et al., "Transnational Entrepreneurs."

28. Peter Kivisto, "Finnish Americans and the Homeland, 1918-1958," *Journal of American Ethnic History* 7, no. 1 (1987): 9-28.

29. Quoted in Peter Kivisto, *Immigrant Socialists in the United States: The Case of Finns and the Left* (Rutherford, N.J.: Fairleigh Dickinson University

Press, 1984), 159.
30. Nuorteva's office and other activities are discussed in detail in Auvo Kostiainen, *Santeri Nuorteva: Kansainvälinen suomalainen* (Helsinki: SHS, 1983), 89-121.
31. Wyman, *Round-Trip to America,* 156.
32. Virtanen, *Settlement or Return,* 214-16.
33. Peter Kivisto and Mika Roinila, "Reaction to Departure: The Finnish American Community Responds to 'Karelian Fever,'" in *North American Finns in Soviet Karelia in the 1930s* (Petrozavodsk: Petrozavodsk State University Press, 2008), 17-38.
34. Reino Kero, *Neuvosto-Karjalaa rakentamassa: Pohjois-Amerikan suomalaiset tekniikan tuojina 1930-luvun Neuvosto-Karjalassa* (Helsinki: SHS, 1983), 57-58.
35. Kero, *Neuvosto-Karjalaa rakentamassa,* 199.
36. Herbert J. Gans, "Symbolic Ethnicity: The Future of Ethnic Groups and Cultures in America," *Ethnic and Racial Studies* 2, no. 1 (1979): 1-20.
37. See Marja-Liisa Pohjanvirta, *Amerikansuomalaiset ja Espanjan sisällissota.* Pro gradu-tutkielma (Turku: Turun yliopisto 1975), 67-68.
38. Alba et al., *Immigration and Religion in America;* Levitt, *God Needs No Passport.*
39. R. Stephen Warner, "Parameters of Paradigms: Toward a Specification of the U.S. Religion Market System," *Nordic Journal of Religion and Society* 21, no. 2 (2008): 129-46.
40. Douglas J. Ollila Jr., "The Formative Period of the Finnish Evangelical Lutheran Church in America, or Suomi Synod" (Th.D. diss., Boston University School of Theology, 1963).
41. John Wargelin, *The Americanization of the Finns* (Hancock, Mich.: Finnish Lutheran Book Concern, 1924).

# Who Is a "Real" Finn? Negotiating Finnish and Finnish American Identity in the Contemporary United States

*Johanna Leinonen*

This chapter focuses on the processes of defining and redefining Finnish identity and traditions that are taking place among recent immigrants from Finland and American-born descendants of earlier Finnish immigrants in the present-day United States, utilizing oral history interviews that I conducted with thirty-five Finnish-born women living in Minnesota. By pointing to theories of ethnicity formulated by U.S. migration scholars, I examine how these processes of redefinition sometimes create frictions within an ethnic community and between different immigrant generations. The tradition invented by Finnish Americans in Minnesota—St. Urho's Day—serves as a lens through which I discuss these points.

The following quote is from an interview that I conducted in Minnesota with a Finnish woman who immigrated to the United States in 2000. The woman expressed her opinion on the tradition of St. Urho's Day, popular in many North American communities with Finnish roots. She also reflected her relationship with the Finnish American community in Minnesota—that is, the community formed by American born descendants of Finns who had immigrated to the country during the years of mass immigration in the late nineteenth and early twentieth centuries. "It's like that 'old-country culture,' like an ideal of what the forefathers had, . . . they don't necessarily even want to hear that in Finland we don't anymore dance in rhythm of the Finnish zither around birch trees wearing birch bark shoes and national costumes, that [modern Finland] is more like Nokia and Bomfunk MC's. . . . St. Urho? Oh, well, the joke is a joke."[1] As the quote reveals, the woman expressed frustration over how Finnish Americans imagined "Finnish culture" to be—for her, their vision was stuck in the national romantic ideals of an agricultural Finland that had nothing to do with the images that modern Finland (Nokia, Bomfunk MC's) invoked in her.

### Constructed and Contested Ethnicity

Like the woman quoted above, many recent immigrant women who participated in my research believed that their understandings of what it meant to be Finnish did not correspond with Finnishness represented in the remaining Finnish American organizations. This was also the reason why they rarely became active participants in them. Other researchers of Finnish American communities in the United States have made similar observations. Anja Hellikki Olin-Fahle, for example, exposed tensions between later arrivals and "old-timers" (that is, the earlier immigrant generation of Finnish Americans) in her study of a small Finnish enclave, the Finnhill, in a city on the eastern seaboard of the United States. One of Olin-Fahle's interviewees, an "old-timer," complained: "We want Finns to buy vacated co-op apartments but look what we get! These educated Finns look down upon us or do not join our activities." A response by a "newcomer" reflected the negative feelings of the "old-timer": "We got more education and training in Finland than the old Finns here. . . . . I think our interests and values are different. I think the old people's idea of being a Finn is old-fashioned. People in Finland today do not read Kalevala."[2] Similarly, Sinikka Grönberg Garcia, a Finn who immigrated to the United States in the 1950s, described the separateness of Finnish and Finnish American identities in her book *Suomi Specialties: Finnish Celebrations, Recipes and Traditions* as follows: "Among the first generation of Finns in America there is a strong reluctance to being labeled 'Finnish American.' You are a Finn and want to remain one for a long time. After all, you didn't come here to escape poverty or to avoid being drafted into the Russian Army. You came as a visitor, as a bride or groom, as au pair, or an exchange student on a scholarship. You came to learn the language. You did not need to leave Finland."[3]

For Garcia, what really separated Finns from Finnish Americans was the fact that unlike earlier immigrants who were part of the proletarian mass migrations of the late nineteenth and early twentieth centuries, later immigrants did not leave Finland out of necessity: they *chose* to come to the United States voluntarily. In effect, she referred to differences in class and social status of different generations of Finnish immigrants as the main dividing factor between them.

These kinds of tensions between immigrant generations are not limited to Finnish Americans. Donna R. Gabaccia has noted that new immigrants from Europe are often uncomfortable with European-American culture; cultural and class differences between new immigrants and European Americans discourage the formation of a coherent or unified identity.[4] For instance, Mary Patrice Erdmans found in her study on the relationship between later-generation Polish Americans and recent immigrants from Poland in Chicago that the definition of a "Polish identity" was a highly contested issue among these two groups of Poles. Migration scholars tend to portray ethnic groups as homogeneous, "smoothing over differences within groups in order to compare differences between groups."[5] However, as my interviews and Erdmans's study show, there may be considerable heterogeneity and tensions within an ethnic group.

The disagreements over what constitutes a Finnish or Polish identity highlight the dynamic, ever-changing nature of ethnicity. The term "ethnicity" has been one of the most important concepts in U.S. immigration history. In the first half of the twentieth century, ethnicity was largely seen as a primordial attachment; it was "fixed, fundamental, and rooted in the unchangeable circumstances of birth."[6] As a consequence, scholars did not spend much time studying how ethnic identities were formed. Rather, they focused on the *content* of ethnicity: on the "cultural stuff" that were supposed to form ethnic identities.[7] At the same time, American immigration scholars firmly believed in the assimilatory power of American society and culture: they presumed that distinct characteristics of ethnic groups would gradually disappear as the groups assimilated into the American mainstream. These views concerning the nature of ethnic identities started to change in the 1960s, the decade that witnessed the rise of identity awareness not only among racial minorities in the United States but also among descendants of European immigrants, assumed to have lost the memory of their ethnic backgrounds for good.[8] This unexpected persistence of ethnicity as a source of group identity stimulated an enormous amount of research on the subject not only in the United States but also in Europe. For example, Norwegian anthropologist Fredrik Barth made an important contribution to the field by shifting the research focus from the study of "contents" of ethnic identities to an examination of boundaries between ethnic groups and of the ways these boundaries were constructed and maintained.[9]

Since Barth, the idea of constructed ethnicity has become prevalent among scholars in different disciplines. For instance, an influential article by Kathleen Neils Conzen et al. defines ethnicity as a constructed rather than an essential or unchanging phenomenon: "Ethnicity is not a 'collective fiction,' but rather a process of construction or invention which incorporates, adapts, and amplifies preexisting communal solidarities, cultural attributes, and historical memories."[10] Ethnic groups are constantly re-creating themselves in response to changing realities both within the group and in the host society.

### St. Urho's Day—A "Real" Finnish Tradition or "Total Nonsense"?

Finnish immigrants and their descendants in the United States are also constantly re-creating their ethnic identities and traditions, and as the quotes above reveal, these processes can create divisions within the community and between generations. Unlike immigrants of the late nineteenth and early twentieth centuries who joined lively Finnish American communities in the United States, immigrants who have arrived from Finland during the past few decades have no longer been able to stay within the ethnic enclave, even if they had wanted to do so. Due to the small number of newcomers, Finnish communities in the country dissolved during the midcentury years. However, it seems that many recent immigrants, including the Finnish-born women whom I interviewed, were rarely interested in the activities of existing Finnish American organizations. Most thought that the Finnish American culture that the remaining organizations promoted was quite different from the "modern Finnish culture" with which they were familiar. At the same time, the newcomers' idea of "Finnish American culture" as stagnated and stuck in the idealized "Old Country culture" does not exactly hold true either. Finnish Americans have actively created new traditions in the United States, the best known of which is likely St. Urho's Day. However, the case of St. Urho's Day is also a prime example of a Finnish American tradition that creates tensions between different generations of Finns.

There are various versions of the origin of the myth of St. Urho. Most stories place the origin in Virginia, Minnesota, where in 1956 a Finnish American man named Richard L. Mattson, store manager at the Ketola's Department Store, was frustrated that none of his colleagues took seriously his stories about the mythical St. Urho. To console their coworker, Mattson's colleagues organized the first St. Urho's Day party on May 24, 1956. Later on, the date was changed to March 16—just one day before St. Patrick's Day. Indeed, it has been claimed that one reason behind the creation of the myth was the Finns' desire to compete with the Irish St. Patrick's Day celebrations.[11] According to the myth of St. Urho (as it is known now), in prehistoric times, "wild grapes grew with abundance in the area now known as Finland. . . . The wild grapes were threatened by a plague of grasshoppers until St. Urho banished the lot of them by chanting: *'Heinäsirkka, heinäsirkka, mene täältä hiiteen'*—or 'Grasshopper, grashapper [sic], go away.'"[12] Sulo Havumäki, professor at Bemidji State College in Bemidji, Minnesota, has been credited for creating this incantation St. Urho used to chase away grasshoppers from Finland. St. Urho's Day is supposed to be celebrated by wearing the colors royal purple and Nile green—the colors of grapes and grasshoppers.[13]

Today, the festival is celebrated annually on March 16 in many communities with Finnish roots in the United States and Canada. The myth is particularly well known in Minnesota, the state in which it was created. There was even a dispute between the towns of Bemidji and Menahga in Minnesota over the issue of which town can "rightfully call itself the 'home' of St. Urho." For what it is worth, Menahga erected a statue of the saint on the outskirts of the town, which was formally dedicated in 1982.[14] Also in the town of Finland, Minnesota, there is a chainsaw-carved statue of the patron saint, made by Irish American sculptor Donovan Osborn in 1982.[15]

The myth of St. Urho is a good example of ethnic groups inventing traditions to amplify communal solidarity and feelings of belonging to the group. During the ethnic revival of the 1960s and 1970s, when Americans of European descent began to express pride in their ethnic roots and chose to identify themselves in ethnic terms, St. Urho's Day festivities became more widespread across the country as well.[16] While many scholars have seen this kind of renewed interest in "homeland cultures" as a sign of surprising vitality of ethnic identities and an argument against the assimilation theory, others have been more skeptical about the deeper meaning of this renewed interest. For example, Herbert Gans argues that there has been no ethnic revival at all: grandchildren and great-grandchildren of European immigrants are merely expressing *symbolic* ethnic identity needs. By this Gans means that instead of investing time and other resources in ethnic cultures and organizations, later-generation European Americans express their ethnic identities in "easy and intermittent" ways—in ways that do not take too many resources and are not in conflict with other interests and activities. Third- and fourth-generation "ethnics" use ethnic symbols—such as wearing royal purple and Nile green on St. Urho's Day—to occasionally express their identification with the ancestral group. According to Gans, these intermittent ethnic identity needs are not in conflict with the processes of assimilation and acculturation into the American mainstream.[17]

Whether interpreted as a sign of vitality of ethnic identities or merely as occasional expressions of symbolic ethnicity that are in line with the assimilation process, the myth of St. Urho holds the power of creating resentment among "later arrivals" from Finland against the third- and fourth-generation "ethnics." My interviews provided ample evidence of these feelings. Many women who participated in my study expressed rather negative feelings toward St. Urho's Day. One of the interviewees was "Tarja," who had met her American husband in Finland and moved with him first to Germany in the early 1960s and from there to the United States in 1965. By the time of the interview in 2004, she had lived in Minnesota for thirty-five years (since 1969). When I asked what she thought about St. Urho's Day, she answered: "Um, I don't really know what to think about it, it is just somehow weird. It's bogus, weird. We never had any trouble with grasshoppers, and of course I have a view of a person from Northern Finland. I never saw grapes in trees, so it is just very weird."[18] Interestingly, Tarja was thinking about the actual natural conditions in northern Finland and relating her reluctance to understand the tradition to the fact that the mythical events could not have taken place in the conditions of her home country.

Many women draw a clear border between themselves ("real" Finns) and Finnish Americans. The most extreme example may have been "Kaisa," who moved to Minnesota to marry her American husband in 1991. She was visibly annoyed when I asked about her interest in St. Urho's Day: "It's complete rubbish, I feel a little indignant about the whole thing. The whole celebration has been created out of thin air. I

**FIGURE 1.** St. Urho's Day parade and celebration in Finland, Minnesota, on March 16, 2004. The balloons in the picture are green and purple, symbolizing the "official" colors of St. Urho's Day. (Source: photo by Johanna Leinonen)

absolutely do not celebrate it. We real Finns [*oikeat suomalaiset*] don't celebrate it; it's a celebration of Finnish Americans. I stay away from their festivities. I avoid contact with Finnish Americans."[19]

Few were as adamant about keeping away from Americans of Finnish descent as Kaisa was, but still many made a clear distinction between Finnish culture and Finnish American culture. In the quote at the start of this chapter, for example, "Kaija" was pointing out how Finnish Americans, in her view, tried to preserve a folkloric version of Finnish culture—a version that did not fit with her ideas of modern Finnish culture (which included things such as Nokia cell phones and the band Bomfunk MC's). When asked about St. Urho's Day, she responded:

> It's total nonsense! Well, it's a fun story, like the way the tradition was invented in the 1950s . . . , but if the essential part of the celebration is to drink grape juice, I say hey hello [*hei haloo*]! . . . One thing I learned when I was working at the office of FinnFest . . . is that I understood very clearly that Finnish and Finnish American cultures are two very different things, and it's probably easier to say that aloud to a Finn rather than to a Finnish American, who thinks of it as the "Old Country culture."[20]

Thus Kaija suggested that Finnish Americans would not necessarily understand or accept that their "Old Country culture" was not "real" Finnish culture. In contrast, she assumed that she and others who were born in Finland would instinctively know the difference between "real" Finnish culture and Finnish American culture.

Also "Helena," who had lived in Hong Kong for years (since 1981) before moving to Minnesota with her American husband in 1996, commented on how "outdated" Finnish Americans' knowledge of modern Finland was: "For me, it [St. Urho's Day] doesn't say anything, it's not really Finnish. I never heard anything of it in Finland. . . . Their [Finnish Americans'] knowledge [of Finland] is based on the old days. They act like they know so much about Finland but they don't. I haven't lived in Finland in a long time, so even I don't know."[21] In Helena's view, it was not possible for Finnish Americans to know much about modern Finland; even she, despite being born in Finland, did not know so much about the country and culture anymore, after having lived in Hong Kong and the United States for over twenty years.

The women who had sometimes attended St. Urho's Day festivities and expressed more positive opinions on the tradition were all older women who had arrived in the United States in the 1950s or the 1960s. I asked "Leila" about the festival, her first comment was that it was "a little silly." However, she immediately backpedaled and noted in a more positive tone, "Well, why not!" Having moved to the United States in 1968, she had participated in activities organized by Finnish American communities during her first years in the country, including St. Urho's Day celebrations. She pointed out: "They must have something equivalent to St. Patrick's Day!"[22] Similarly, a woman who moved from Finland to Minnesota in 1967 because of her marriage to a Finnish American man told me that her family used to celebrate St. Urho's Day regularly. Her husband was a son of Finnish immigrants, born in northern Minnesota. Therefore their contacts with the Finnish American community were frequent. Another woman, who had first moved to Canada with her family in 1951 and from there to the United States in 1957, noted that "I think it [St. Urho's Day] is a fun thing to have!"[23] She was a teenager when the family moved to North America, and she spent her adolescence participating actively in the cultural life of the Finnish community in Thunder Bay, Ontario, and, to a lesser degree, in Ashtabula and Cleveland, Ohio. This may be at least partly the reason why her opinion on the festival was much more enthusiastic than that of many other women whom I interviewed.

Overall, my older interviewees, who immigrated in the 1940s, 1950s, and 1960s, were still often able to get some support from Finnish communities when settling in the United States. A woman who arrived in the 1950s recalled that during her first years in the country, she participated almost exclusively in activities organized by Finnish Americans in her new hometown of Duluth, Minnesota. Perhaps the reason why some of the older women were more understanding of the tradition of St. Urho was the fact that many of them had lived in a Finnish community in the United States, and therefore had become familiar with Finnish American traditions. In contrast, more recent immigrants rarely became active participants in Finnish American organizations, even in Minnesota, a state with a long history of Finnish presence. Instead, they tended to form their own networks; for example, most of the younger women I interviewed organized activities among themselves. These activities often took a more informal form than the festivities of Finnish American organizations. For many recent immigrants, the possibility to speak the Finnish language was an essential part of these informal meetings. Today's Finnish American organizations largely function in English, and thus are not able to meet the newcomers' need to occasionally communicate in their native language.

## Conclusion

The myth of St. Urho provides an interesting case for exploring how ethnic groups constantly mold their traditions to meet the contemporary needs of the group. During the ethnic revival of the 1960s and 1970s, this newly created tradition offered many Finnish Americans a way to express their ethnic belonging through attending parades, wearing purple and green, or in some other, less visible ways. As I witnessed myself a few years ago in the town of Finland, Minnesota (Figure 1), the tradition is still alive and well in many communities with Finnish roots. However, as my interviews with Finnish women who immigrated to the United States in the past few decades reveal, there are tensions within ethnic groups and between generations over what can be seen as a "Finnish tradition." Many Finnish-born women claimed the right to define what is Finnish and what is not, and explicitly drew a boundary between themselves (the "real" Finns) and Finnish Americans who, in their view, did not know or understand modern Finland. For these women, St. Urho's Day was just an oddity created by Americans—a tradition that had nothing to do with present-day Finland. Some of my older interviewees, on the other hand, expressed more understanding views of the tradition. Many mentioned that as they aged, they had become more interested in activities of Finnish American organizations. Sinikka Grönberg Garcia, whom I quoted in the beginning of this chapter, writes about her "becoming Finnish American" over time: "Slowly, . . . almost unnoticed, I 'let go' and got involved in activities [of Finnish American clubs]. . . . I was revitalized and understood the importance of knowing my identity as a Finnish American—a recognizable strand in the tapestry of ethnicity in America."[24] Older and younger Finns, as well as later-generation Finnish Americans, are all constantly redefining the meaning of Finnish traditions and their Finnish—or Finnish American—identity in the United States.

## NOTES

1. "Kaija," interview by Johanna Leinonen, Coon Rapids, Minn., July 17, 2004.
2. Anja Hellikki Olin-Fahle, "Finnhill: Persistence of Ethnicity in Urban America" (Ph.D. diss., New York University, 1983), 202–3.
3. Sinikka Grönberg Garcia, *Suomi Specialties: Finnish Celebrations, Recipes and Traditions* (Iowa City, Iowa: Pennfield Press, 1998), 10.
4. Donna R. Gabaccia, "Europe: Western," in *The New Americans: A Guide to Immigration since 1965*, ed. Mary C. Waters and Reed Ueda (Cambridge, Mass.: Harvard University Press, 2007), 421–22, 425.
5. Mary Patrice Erdmans, *Opposite Poles: Immigrants and Ethnics in Polish Chicago, 1976–1990* (University Park: Pennsylvania State University Press, 1998), 3.
6. Stephen E. Cornell and Douglas Hartmann, *Ethnicity and Race: Making Identities in a Changing World* (Thousand Oaks, Calif.: Pine Forge Press, 1998), 48.
7. Fredrik Barth, "Introduction," in *Ethnic Groups and Boundaries: The Social Organization of Culture Difference*, ed. Fredrik Barth (Bergen: Universitetsforlaget, 1969), 15.
8. Kathleen Neils Conzen et al., "The Invention of Ethnicity: A Perspective from the U.S.A.," *Journal of American Ethnic History* 12 (1992): 3–41.
9. Barth, "Introduction," 15.
10. Conzen et al., "Invention of Ethnicity," 4–5. When talking about ethnicity as "a collective fiction," Conzen et al. refer to Werner Sollors's "Introduction: The Invention of Ethnicity," in *The Invention of Ethnicity*, ed. Werner Sollors (New York: Oxford University Press, 1989). Sollors's idea of ethnicity

as a fiction has been criticized by many scholars, including Conzen et al., for obscuring the political nature of ethnicity and the very real impact ethnicity can have on people's status in society.

11. Börje Vähämäki, "Pyhä Urho: Amerikan ja Kanadan suomalaisten oma suojeluspyhimys," *Amerikan Uutiset,* March 9, 1995.

12. Don Wegars, "A Saint Who Plagued the Grasshoppers: Finns Set to Honor St. Urho," *San Francisco Chronicle,* March 15, 1980.

13. Vähämäki, "Pyhä Urho."

14. Rob Hotakainen, "The Making of a Saint," *Emphasis* (July 1982): 42–48.

15. Lynnell Mickelsen, "Osborn Gets His Irish Up with St. Urho Totem Pole," *News-Tribune & Herald* (Duluth, Minn.), 1982.

16. Mary C. Waters, *Ethnic Options: Choosing Identities in America* (Berkeley: University of California Press, 1990).

17. Herbert J. Gans, "Symbolic Ethnicity: The Future of Ethnic Groups and Cultures in America," in *On the Making of Americans: Essays in Honor of David Riesman,* ed. Herbert J. Gans et al. (Philadelphia: University of Pennsylvania Press, 1979), 193, 202–3.

18. "Tarja," interview by Johanna Leinonen, Minneapolis, November 4, 2004.

19. "Kaisa," interview by Johanna Leinonen, Mound, Minn., July 13, 2004.

20. "Kaija" interview.

21. "Helena," interview by Johanna Leinonen, Minneapolis, July 5, 2004.

22. "Paula," interview by Johanna Leinonen, Farmington, Minn., August 6, 2004.

23. "Marketta," interview by Johanna Leinonen, Edina, Minn., July 21, 2004.

24. Grönberg Garcia, *Suomi Specialties,* 11–12.

PART 9
# Turning to Americans

# Adjustment and the Future

*Mika Roinila*

The immigrant Finns have always represented a relatively small population, roots of which come from a largely agricultural environment in northern Europe, with specific linguistic and cultural features. Work was usually found in the expanding industrial America, although many longed for farmland. In facing problems of integration, the typical immigrant solution was to build a strong societal life of their own, which often echoed the norms of the Old Country.

Immigrant generations played an important role in the development of ethnic life. The first generation had strong roots in either the Finnish or Swedish languages or the corresponding cultural heritage that defined the people of Finland. Much of this remained among the first generation, but many also wanted to learn the way of the new land, led by the desire to learn English. The second generation in turn was much more likely to adapt completely to the American way of life. Only a part of this population, and in turn their descendants, preserved the language and cultural ways of their ancestors. While a small proportion of the later generation Finnish Americans remained in the immigrant social circles, it seems quite clear that the American way of life and society successfully influenced the lives of the majority of the later generations.

In spite of a seemingly "vanishing Finnish American" trend, we must recognize the importance of several former "nesting places," the most important ones of which were found in Michigan, Minnesota, Massachusetts, New York, the western and northwestern states, as well as the retirement settlements of Florida. In these regions, Finns left a particularly strong imprint on the population structure and cultural heritage, which is expressed in the form of Finn halls, churches, cooperative stores, or the sauna buildings that dot the towns and countryside. A keen observer may even find traces of ideological and political splits that strongly influenced the Finnish American community, particularly during the first four decades of the twentieth century. This specific feature heavily influenced the Finnish American community and its community interactions, reflecting the hot issues of the "Reds" and "Whites." The "political trend" of the Finns may be interpreted as a posthumous effort in addressing problems of societal change in Finland, while simultaneously reacting to the problems they saw in their surrounding environment. Conflicts were born both within the immigrant group itself and with the political system of the United States. However, problems between immigrant factions have faded in recent decades and turned into joint activities predicated upon the preservation of Finnish American culture and history.

Throughout the decades there also existed some transnational features. While one-fifth of all immigrants from Finland returned to the Old Country, and a few thousand socialist idealists moved to build the new workers' society in the Soviet Union during the Great Depression, the great majority remained in North America. But despite the separation from the Old Country, links have existed between various organizations, families, and individuals, particularly in the form of cultural, economic, and political contacts over the Atlantic.

But what about the present status and future challenges for Finnish Americans? Current conditions in the economic, social, political, and cultural sphere of the Finnish American community are something that every generation is eager to analyze and discuss. Some of the earliest scholars believed that the Finnish culture would disappear within a short period of time after Finns immigrated to America. This has yet to happen. The imported Finnish culture and the current Finnish American culture are well maintained and promise to continue. Still, there are questions that need to be asked about future trends of Finnishness in America.

What does the future hold for the Finnish American population? Some work on this has already been done, and more is forthcoming.[1] Perhaps the hardest question for researchers interested in Finnish Americana to answer is why countless individuals in the Finnish American and even Finnish Canadian immigrant communities choose not to associate with "things Finnish"? Over the past several years, some observations and thoughts may be indicative of the only possible response—a lack of interest.

There are numerous people of Finnish ancestry who remain marginal or completely ignorant of Finnish ethnicity and uninterested in maintaining and/or perpetuating anything related to Finnishness. This includes the language, religion, culture, traditions, sauna, and other aspects of Finnishness. It may be ironic, yet understandable, to find that food is the most often mentioned feature of Finnishness among people. This basic need for life seems to be, for many people, the last remaining vestige that keeps a small connection to Finnishness.[2] While circumstances are different among all people, it is apparent that many people have no desire to stay connected to Finnishness. This speaks loudly to the desire for complete assimilation that entails the adoption of the language, culture, and way of thinking among the dominant American society. In the end, I have come to understand better the Finnish sentence *"Maassa maan tavalla, tai maasta pois!"* (Live in the land the way of the land, or get out of the land). Living in the New World includes the English language in most regions of the continent, a plethora of North American religious views, and the traditions of the North American culture and society. There are simply more individuals who desire to associate themselves with this New World connection rather than maintain the Old World connection. The result is an alienation and/or rejection of their roots.

Several negative responses from prospective respondents were received as part of a project that collected data on the current lives and thoughts of Finnish Americans and Finnish Canadians.[3] A respondent with a Finnish surname who was contacted by phone in Florida for a possible interview responded with an abrupt *"I'm not interested. I'm American!"* But why do some Finns respond in this fashion, and why don't they seem to care about Finnishness? Finding them and learning their raison d'être is a hard question that still eludes scholars. Rejection of one's true origins is not uncommon to anyone. Every ethnic group experiences this in a multicultural society where many immigrants have come to begin a new life and change their future for the better. While some remain nostalgic and even serious about maintaining their Finnish ancestry and identity, the majority of Finns seem to think differently. Norman Westerberg has shown in his work that many immigrants from Finland have "disappeared" in census counts.[4] Why indeed are there so few Finns tabulated on the census? The most obvious response is that they simply do not want to identify themselves as Finns. They have chosen a different identity.

An area that deserves much more attention is the change in languages spoken at home. While the U.S. Census has provided data on birthplace and mother tongue until the 1970 census, the 1980–2000 census provides social scientists an opportunity to discover the trends in language use that exists at home. Thus it comes as a surprise to many that there is a significant rise in Spanish-speaking Finnish Americans in the United States. In 2000, some 540,000 (86.4 percent) Finnish Americans spoke English as their main language. This concentration had steadily increased since 1980, while the Finnish language declined. In 2000, some 34,000 (5.4 percent) Finnish Americans spoke Finnish at home. To their credit, this proportion of language maintenance is the highest among all Nordic groups in the United States. The third most common language spoken by Finnish Americans was Spanish, as over 6,000 (1.0 percent) of the ethnic population spoke this language. Thus a dramatic increase in the number of Spanish-speaking Finnish Americans took place between 1980 and 2000, as the number increased from nearly 2,000 individuals to just over 6,000. If these numbers are indicative of trends to come, it will come to pass in perhaps twenty years or so that there will be more Spanish-speaking Finnish Americans than Finnish speakers. This has already happened among Norwegian Americans and Swedish Americans.[5]

Several reasons for the above may help explain the decline of a Finnish identity and culture in the New World. Intermarriage and the choice of dominant language spoken at home may be a reflection of the ancestry of a spouse and the increased importance of the Spanish language throughout the country. Intermarriage to non-Finnish speakers may decrease the association to Finnishness, and in some cases the lack of Finnish-language skills thwarts any real commitment or link to a Finnish connection. On the other hand, children may keep their parents busy at home. Families with young children often find little time or interest in ethno-cultural activities after school days. While decline is often the easiest to see, analyze, and criticize, there are some definite positives that can also be seen. These include many exciting changes that have affected our society in the past several decades, which have led to some new and different ways of thinking.

Similar to other ethnic groups that have gone through immigration and assimilation in North America, there are two possible reactions to the future of Finnish American existence. On the one hand are the *pessimists,* who see the eventual assimilation and loss of ethnic identity, culture, and language in future generations. On the other hand are the *transformationalists,* who believe that the ethnicity—the Finnish ethnicity—will survive into the future, albeit possibly in a different way.[6] With modern technology, hi-tech computers, and Internet connections, and a renewed interest in heritage and roots, many people have returned to rediscover themselves. According to Rapaport:

> Transformationalists suggest that rather than being grounded in institutions or networks of interaction, ethnicity has become transformed into a voluntary affiliation based on personal concerns for identity, an awareness of one's origins, notions of a common past, and pride in the group's cultural heritage, history, and people.

In lieu of institutions and social networks, the use of ethnic symbols satisfies the primordial need for affiliation, and enables its members to distinguish themselves from a homogenized host society.[7]

In the *pessimist* vein of thought were comments made by the late A. William Hoglund (1926–2008) to the author. When asked about the future of Finnishness in America, he responded:

I don't think it is a long-term process; it's going to go up and down, but I've a feeling that Finnishness will disappear as Finnish-American descendents intermarry with other groups. [Of the] 600,000 [Finnish] people, half I suspect have intermarried and are not fully pure Finn ancestry. And I think that a survey should try to find out why it is that these fourth, fifth, sixth generation descendants don't participate in FinnFest and so on. FinnFest only attracts, in all honesty, only a fraction of Finnish population. That's why I'm not sanguine about it.[8]

Hoglund also noted that there are major differences between the older- and younger-generation Finns living in America today. There isn't enough recognition given to the older Finns in terms of their accomplishments and contributions to community life among the younger generation, who are better educated, more established, and ignorant of the earlier immigrant generation. According to Hoglund: "There's no recognition of the cultural contribution of the immigrants. Who made Finns known in America? Without them we wouldn't have 600,000 descendents. I suspect there's a class difference."[9]

A less pessimistic opinion comes from professional photographer Eero Sorila in Vancouver, British Columbia. When asked about the future, he responded candidly:

In my opinion the Finnishness in North America is faced with the writing on the wall translating to diminished profile. Why? Very few people from Finland are currently immigrating to North America. The standard of living in Finland has risen to a level in which there is no reason to leave Finland in search of economic advancement in North America as the case was in the past. . . . Without new immigrants from Finland to the United States and Canada [a] majority of the second-generation Finnish people adapt English as their only language of communication. Language and Finnishness among other cultural factors in my opinion is a cornerstone for perpetuating Finnishness anywhere in the world. When that cornerstone is eradicated the reality of Finnishness has no leg to stand on. The responsibility and the privilege of perpetuating Finnishness in Canada and the USA then rests with the minority of Finnish people who are compassionate about preserving and fomenting the richness of Finnishness. It seems that most such people seek membership in societies such as the Finnish Heritage Society of B.C., The Vancouver Finlandia Club and hundreds of other institutions around the world with the objective of supporting, advancing and perpetuating Finnishness.[10]

Opinions in the *transformationalist* vein include comments from several people, such as the current president of Finlandia Foundation USA, Anita Häkkilä Smiley. In responding to the question on the future, she noted:

I see a future, because I see a lot of people who are working hard, and I see younger people getting involved with our Finlandia Foundation Board . . . there's an effort to get younger people in and we're doing that. And there's an effort to get cohesiveness among the groups so that they can help each other out. I think that if we can do that, there's a positive future. Finnish language may not be as strong, but if we introduce them to the Finnish culture, I think it will be there.[11]

A second example, showing a move to a new paradigm of ethnic awareness, comes from Andy Heiniluoma, who represents the younger generation of Finnish Americans. Although he is not fluent in Finnish, he has some knowledge of the language and is trying to improve this by taking language classes with the Suomi Koulu through the Boston chapter of the Finlandia Foundation. This is also another example of intermarriage, and the willingness of some to learn the Finnish language and culture. He also stresses the willingness of voluntary teachers to pass on the language to others, noting that most of his classmates were American men married to Finnish women.[12]

Heiniluoma is grateful for organizations such as the Finlandia Foundation, and noted that they are "very useful and practical"—where he meets others interested in learning the language, making plans for travel to Finland, and sharing practical information about visa issues, green cards, or bringing or shipping cars from or to Finland. He advocates the use of the Internet to listen to YLE radio and download Finnish music and news. He doesn't need this input from a local Finnish club. This was noted when Heiniluoma made comparisons to the older generation. While not directly saying so, the following statement also gives credit to parents who are willing to expose their children to Finnish culture. Without such parental influence and involvement, Andy Heiniluoma may not have developed any interest in his roots. And truly, how many teenagers are interested in activities that the older generation grew up enjoying? The current options for entertainment and enjoyment are very different from those of the past. The upkeep of traditions and heritage simply changes in form. As Heiniluoma noted:

> The ones that are of my parent's generation and older, it's just a lot different and [they] look at Finland in a completely different way. They don't have to deal with immigration, and even if they did, everything's changed since then. So I really don't find a purpose in . . . you know I'm not really at home at Sovittaja, I don't go out of my way to go to Saima Park and be with people who are 80 years old. It just doesn't make sense.[13]

The final comment comes from Jim Kurtti, the editor of the *Finnish American Reporter*. After spending years in his editorial post, he is well capable of measuring the barometer dealing with Finnishness in America. According to Kurtti,

> In the past decade we have increased Finnish-related activities to the point it's not possible to go to them all. Annual events such as Finnish Music Festival in Covington, Heikinpäivä, Sibelius Academy Music Festival, Viola Turpeinen Days, Heikki Lunta Fest, etc. Also Finnish language courses, Finnish language in public schools, kantele classes, Finnish film series. In the past five years we have three new Finnish performance groups—Kivajat Dancers, The Pasi Cats and the Suomalainen Sisters. So, I've stopped worrying about Finnish-America's impending death. Of course, things are changing, but just like Christianity in Soviet Russia, here always seems to be another generation to take on the effort. It's got to be AOF.[14]

AOF is the abbreviation for "Adult Onset of Finnishness," which was first explained in a 2003 *Finnish American Reporter* article written by David Maki. AOF is defined as the sudden interest in Finnish ethnicity and culture that takes place later in life—often following childrearing and when the "nest" is empty. This relates directly to my earlier comments on a person's stage in family life, and shows a renewed respect for the culture that had not been there earlier. As Maki wrote in 2003: "There's no known cure, but the symptoms are such that the patients never complain. The best line of therapy is constant doses of Finnish culture—music and the like—applied in ample doses. The real question is not how to develop a cure, but how to infect a greater portion of the population of Finns in North America."[15]

It becomes evident from the above comment that Finns simply won't disappear, as many have feared. There is simply more proof to support the *transformationalist* argument among the Finnish ethnic community. Many Finnish Americans will continue their efforts to maintain their identity by practicing the distinct traditions of Finland. Finnish Americans and Finnish Canadians have added their own ethnic festivals such as St. Urho's Day, and will upkeep the culture through venues such as the American FinnFests, Finn Forums, and the Finnish Canadian Grand Festivals. Ethnic awareness will continue in different ways, including online programming, YouTube video clips, social networking, and direct connections to Finnish radio programs and television shows that have all moved Finnish Americans in a new direction. Similar to many North Americans, descendents of Finnish immigrants have shown a great interest in discovering their roots through genealogical sources that are available online and through other venues. Genealogical research is growing and has become very popular. Finally, interactive Skype connections between Finns in Finland and Finnish North Americans are possible, which may help enhance a sense of Finnishness among the ethnic population living here. More research is needed in order to understand how this may affect the sense of Finnish ethnic identity and its importance in America.

While changes are inevitable, it is also important to remember the past and learn from what has gone before. It is important to recognize the early pioneers who came to this continent and toiled so hard to ensure their survival. We must respect the legacy they have left for everyone, and we must hold their collective accomplishments in high esteem. It is also very important to know where we are today, and I hope that this book presents a good reflection of the past and the present. Even more appropriate will be our look into the future, which will continue with much optimism and excitement. We are living in changing times, and change is good. This is good to remember as the Finnish American and Finnish Canadian communities continue to develop and change.

## NOTES

1. Jouni Korkiasaari and Mika Roinila, "Finnish North Americans Today," in *Finnishness in Finland and North America: Constituents, Changes, and Challenges.* Special Issue, *Journal of Finnish Studies* 9, no. 2 (2005): 98–116.

2. Mika Roinila, Susanne Österlund-Pötzsch, and Susan Larson, "Women's Maintenance of Finland-Swedish Identity in North America," in *Transborder Contacts and the Maintenance of Finnishness in the Diaspora: FinnForum VIII an Interdisciplinary Conference in Finnish, Finnish-North American and Sweden Finnish Studies, Mälardalen University, Campus Eskilstuna June 17–20, 2007* (Eskilstuna: Mälardalen University, 2009), 55–81.

3. Korkiasaari and Roinila, "Finnish North Americans Today," 98–116.

4. Norman Westerberg, "624,000 Claim Finnish Ancestry in the USA," *Siirtolaisuus-Migration* 29, no. 4 (2002): 8; Norman Westerberg, "Missing: One Million Finnish Americans," in *Melting into Great Waters: Papers from FinnForum V,* ed. Varpu Lindström, Oiva Saarinen, and Börje Vähämäki.

Special Issue, *Journal of Finnish Studies* 1, no. 3 (1997): 79–89.
5. Mika Roinila, "Habla Español? The Growing Number of Spanish Speaking Nordic Americans," *Siirtolaisuus-Migration* 37, no. 4 (2010): 13–15.
6. The terms "pessimist" and "transformationalist" date back to the late 1950s as social scientists tried to understand the changing identity and cultural upkeep among the American Jewish population. See, for example, Steven M. Cohen, *American Assimilation or Jewish Revival* (Bloomington: Indiana University Press, 1988).
7. Lynn Rapaport, *Jews in Germany after the Holocaust: Memory, Identity, and Jewish-German Relations* (Cambridge: Cambridge University Press, 1997), 25.
8. A. William Hoglund, interview by Mika Roinila, Fort Lauderdale, Fla., March 25, 2005.
9. Hoglund interview.
10. Eero Sorila, interview by Ron Ericson, Vancouver, B.C., September 6, 2008.
11. Anita Häkkilä Smiley, interview by Mika Roinila, Preston, Conn., August 6, 2004.
12. Andy Heiniluoma, interview by Mika Roinila, Gardner, Mass., August 1, 2004.
13. Heiniluoma interview.
14. Jim Kurtti, correspondence with Mika Roinila, July 16, 2008.
15. David Maki, "What's Wrong with You?" *Finnish American Reporter* (September 2003).

# For Further Reference

### Archival Sources

**Finlandia University, Finnish-American Historical Archive, Hancock, Michigan (FAHA)**

O'Meara, James. Oral history interview by Arthur Puotinen, July 13, 1972. Rev. Edward Isaac Collection.
"Letters to Aberdeen-Naselle, Washington, 1948-49." Suomi Synod Collection.
Scandinavian Evangelical Lutheran Church Records, Finnish American Churches Box B-3, Manuscripts Collection.

**Foreign Ministry of Finland, Helsinki (FMF)**

Ryhmä 21, Osasto Va. 1-6. Maastakarkoitukset. (Group 21, Dept. Va. 1-6. Deportations.)
Relations between Finland and the United States.

**Hoover Institution on War, Revolution and Peace, Stanford University, Stanford, California (Hoover)**

Finnish Relief Fund. Herbert Hoover Papers. National Committee on Food for the Small Democracies.

**Immigration History Research Center, University of Minnesota, Minneapolis (IHRC)**

Central Cooperative Wholesale, Records.
John I. Kolehmainen papers.
John Wiita papers. Minnesota Finnish American Family History project (MNFAFH). Riippa, Timo.
   *Finnish American Writers on the Left.* Manuscript, ca. 1995.
Riippa, Timo. Inventory to the Records of Central Cooperative Wholesale.
United States Immigration and Naturalization Service papers (Reels 1-4).

Institute of Migration, Turku, Finland (IMT)

Photographic Collections. Laine, Edward. *History of the Finnish Organization of Canada, 1911–2000.* Manuscript.
Irma Pohjansalo papers.

University of Turku, Finland, Department of General History, Migration History Collections (DGH)

America Letters: Varsinais-Suomi; Satakunta.
Gardner, Massachusetts Finnish Socialist Society Collection, TYYH/S/m/8/56–59.
The interview questionnaire collection, TYYH/S/1 /5732, 6181, 7149, 7234.
Jack Ujanen Collection TYYH/S/A14/V.
*Keskusosuuskunta.* Pöytäkirja, liikkeenhoitokomitea. TYYH/S/m/8/940.
*Keskusosuuskunta.* Pöytäkirja, toimeenpaneva komitea. TYYH/S/m/210.
*Onnen aika* temperance society (Republic, Mich.) TYYH/S/m/8/175.
Photographic Collections. SKRW society (Republic, Mich.) TYYH/S/m/8/194.
*Suomi Seura* newspaper clippings collection, 1921–1967.

## Documents

*Are the Lights Going Out in Finland?* Duluth, Minn.: Save Finland Committee, 1945.
*The Cooperative League Year Book 1936.* Superior, Wis., 1936.
*Finland.* Helsinki: Consulate of the United States of America, 1928.
*Finland: The Country, Its People and Institutions.* Helsinki: Otava, 1926.
*Finland Builds.* New York: Finnish New York World's Fair Commission, 1940.
*Finnish Pioneer Day: A Minnesota Territorial Centennial Celebration, St. Paul, August 21, 1949,* ed. Tom Hiltunen. Duluth: Minnesota Finnish-American Historical Society, 1949.
Hoover, Herbert. *Addresses Upon the American Road, 1940–1941, 1941–1945, 1945–1948.* Toronto: D. Van Nostrand, 1941, 1946, 1949.
*Is Finland Worth Saving?* Duluth, Minn.: Save Finland Committee, 1945.
*The Fourteenth Census of the United States Taken in the Year 1920, II: Population 1920. General Report and Analytical Tables.* Washington, D.C.: Government Printing Office, 1922. ).
*Juice Is Stranger Than Friction: Selected Writings of T-Bone Slim,* ed. and intro. Franklin Rosemont. Chicago: Charles H. Kerr, 1992.
*Käsikirja: Perustuslaki, Siwulait, Paikallis-Yhdistysten Säännöt. Järjestys- Ja Työ-Ohjeet, Lasten Raittiusosaston Säännöt, Sairastus-Apuyhdistyksen Säännöt,* 7th ed. Hancock, Mich.: Amerikan Suomalainen Kansallis-Raittius Weljeysseura, 1906.
*Keskusosuuskunnan Vuosikirja 1920.* Superior, Wis., 1920.
*Kolmannen Amerikan Suomalaisen Sosialistijärjestön Edustajakokouksen Pöytäkirja. Kokous Pidetty Hancockissa, Mich. 23-30 Pvä Elok. 1909.* Ed. F. J. Syrjälä. Fitchburg, Mass., n.d. (*FSF Proceedings 1909*)

*Minnesotan Suomalaisten Juhla-Albumi Minnesotan Valtion Täyttäessä 100 Vuotta,* ed. E. A. Pulli. Duluth: Minnesotan Amerikkalais-Suomalainen Historiallinen Seura, 1949.

*New Sweden in Documents: 1638—March 29, 1988: Exhibition in the Swedish National Archives.* Catalog Text: Kari Tarkiainen, trans. Inga Offerberg and Carol Adamson, drawings by Bror Jacques De Waern, photos by Kurt Eriksson. Stockholm: Allmänna Förlaget, 1988.

*The Palmer Raids,* ed. Robert W. Dunn. New York: International Publishers, 1948.

*Pöytäkirja, Keskusosuuskunnan Johtokunta 21.4.1947.* Superior, Wis., 1947.

*Pöytäkirja, Keskusosuuskunnan Toimeenpaneva Komitea 11.10.1948.* Superior, Wis., 1948.

*Pöytäkirja, Keskusosuuskunnan Vuosikokous 18.-19.3.1963.* Superior, Wis., 1963.

*Pöytäkirja, Keskusosuuskunnan Vuosikokous 21.-22.3.1920.* Superior, Wis., 1920.

*Pöytäkirja, Keskusosuuskunnan Vuosikokous 22.-23.4.1947.* Superior, Wis., 1947.

*Pöytäkirja Amerikan Suomalaisten Socialistiosastojen Edustajakokouksesta, Hibbingissä, Minn., Elokuun 1-7 Päivänä 1906.* Hancock, Mich., 1907.

"Report of the Finnish Translator-Secretary to the Socialist Party National Convention 1912." In *National Convention of the Socialist Party Held at Indianapolis, Ind. May 12th to 18th, 1912,* ed. John Spargo, 237-39. Chicago: n.p., n.d.

*Reports to American Donors, December 1939-July 1940.* New York: Finnish Relief Fund, 1940.

*Suomalaisen Sosialistijärjestön Seitsemännen Edustajakokouksen Pöytäkirja. Laadittu Waukeganissa, Ill. 25-31 P. Joulukuuta 1920 Pidetystä S. S. Järjestön Edustajakokouksesta.* Ed. Aaro Hyrske. Superior, Wis.: Työmies Society, 1920.

*Suomalaisten Sosialistiosastojen Ja Työväenyhdistysten Viidennen Eli Suomalaisen Sosialistijärjestön Kolmannen Edustajakokouksen Pöytäkirja 1-5, 7-10 P. Kesäkuuta, 1912.* Ed. Aku Rissanen. Fitchburg, Mass.: S. S. Järjestön Toimeenpaneva Komitea, N. D. (*FSF Proceedings 1912*).

*Taistelu Oikeistovaaraa Vastaan. Kominternin Opetuksia Amerikan Suomalaiselle Työväestölle.* Superior, Wis.: Amerikan Suom. Sos. Kustannusliikkeiden Liitto, N. D.

UNESCO. *The Race Concept: Results of an Inquiry.* Paris: UNESCO, 1952.

United States Department of Homeland Security. *Yearbook of Immigration Statistics.* Washington, D.C.: U.S. Department Of Homeland Security, Office Of Immigration Statistics, 2002-2011.

United States Department of Justice. *Statistical Yearbook of the Immigration and Naturalization Service.* Washington, D.C.: Government Printing Office, 1978-2001.

United States Department of Labor. *Annual Report of the Immigration and Naturalization Service.* Washington, D.C.: Government Printing Office, 1943-77.

United States Department of State. "The Immigration and Nationality Act of 1952 (The McCarran-Walter Act)." 2009. http://www.state.gov/r/pa/ho/time/cwr/87719.htm.

United States Immigration Commission. *Reports of the Immigration Commission.* 1910. Reprint, New York: Arno Press, 1970.

U.S. Census Manuscripts. 1850-1930.

*Yhdysvaltain Suomalaisen Sosialistijärjestön Viidennen Edustajakokouksen Pöytäkirja Chicagossa, Ill. Lokakuun 25 P: Stä Marraskuun 3 P: Ään 1919.* Ed. J. F. Mäki. Superior, Wis.: S. S. Järjestön Toimeenpaneva Komitea, 1920.

## Newspapers and Periodicals

*Amerikan Suomalainen Lehti* (Calumet, Mich.), 1879, 1880
*Amerikan Suometar* (Hancock, Mich.), 1908, 1936
*Amerikan Uutiset* (Lake Worth, Fla.), 1995
*Astoria Budget* (Astoria, Ore.), 1904
*Cooperative Builder* (Superior, Wis.), 1961
*Co-operative Pyramid Builder* (Superior, Wis.), 1928
*Duluth (Minn.) News Tribune*, 1908
*Finnish-American Reporter* (Hancock, Mich.), 1997, 2003
*Industrialisti* (Duluth, Minn.), 1929, 1930, 1931
*Kalenteri Amerikassa asuville suomalaisille vuodelle* (New York), 1910
*Lännen Suometar* (Astoria, Ore.), 1932
*Ledstjärnan/Leading Star* (Portland, Ore.), 2008
*Morning Astorian* (Astoria, Ore.), 1914
*News-Tribune & Herald* (Duluth, Minn.), 1982
*New Yorker*, 2007
*New Yorkin Uutiset* (New York), 1938
*New York Times*, 1910, 1919, 1934
*Oma markka* (Helsinki), 1976
*Paimen-sanomia* (Hancock, Mich.), 1915
*Pelto ja Koti* (Superior, Wis.), 1914–20
*Raittiuskalenteri* (Hancock, Mich.), 1911
*Raivaaja* (Fitchburg, Mass.), 1908, 1916, 1920, 1926, 1927, 1930
*San Francisco Chronicle*, 1980
*Seventieth Anniversary Souvenir Journal 1903–1973* (Superior, Wis.), 1973
*Suomen Silta* (Helsinki), 1971
*Suomen Urheilulehti* (Helsinki), 1912, 1931, 1932, 1936, 1937, 1938, 1939
*Toveri* (Astoria, Ore.), 1922, 1924, 1925, 1926
*Työmies* (Superior, Wis.), 1927
*Urheilu-viesti* (Hancock, Mich.), 1909, 1910
*Vallankumous* (Hancock, Mich.), 1908
*Veljeysviesti* (Superior, Wis.), 1929
*Wyoming Semi-Weekly Tribune* (Cheyenne, Wyo.), 1904

## Memoirs, Travel Descriptions, Belles Lettres

Dana, Richard. *Two Years before the Mast: A Personal Narrative of Life at Sea.* New York: Harper, 1840.
*Finland: A Practical Guide-Book.* Helsinki: Finnish Tourist Association, 1931.
Hillilä, Hugo. *Valinkauhassa.* Hancock, Mich.: Suom-Amerikkalainen Kustannusliike, 1950.
Hoover, Herbert. *The Memoirs of Herbert Hoover.* New York: Macmillan, 1951–52.
Kirri, Valto Eetu. *Amerikan Vieras.* Helsinki: Kustannus Osakeyhtiö Smia, 1945.

Leinonen, Artturi. *Atlanttia ja Amerikkaa katselemassa.* Porvoo: WSOY, 1938.

London, Jack. *The Mutiny of the Elsinore.* New York: Macmillan, 1914.

Mattson, Helmi. *Lännen auringon alla.* N.p.: Amerikan Suomalaiset Sosialistiset Kustannusliikkeet, 1926.

*Narratives of Early Pennsylvania, West New Jersey, and Delaware 1630–1707,* ed. A. C. Myers. New York: Barnes & Noble, 1953.

Pälsi, Sakari. *Suuri, Kaunis Ja Ruma Maa: Kuvia Ja Kuvauksia Kanadan Matkalta.* Helsinki: Otava, 1927.

Parras, Eemeli. *Jymyvaaralaiset.* Superior, Wis.: Työmies Society, 1933.

*Pehr Kalms Resa till Norra Amerika.* Red. Fredr. Elfving & Georg Schauman. Helsingfors: Svenska Litteratursällskapet in Finland, 1929.

Rauanheimo, Akseli. *Kanadan-kirja.* Porvoo: WSOY, 1930.

Sevander, Mayme, with Laurie Hertzel. *They Took My Father: Finnish Americans in Stalin's Russia.* Minneapolis: University of Minnesota Press, 2004.

Taylor, Bayard. *Northern Travel: Summer and Winter Pictures: Sweden, Denmark, and Lapland.* New York: G. P. Putnam, 1857.

*YL Amerikassa.* Helsinki: n.p., 1939.

# Contributors

**Arnold R. Alanen** is an emeritus professor at the University of Wisconsin–Madison. His extensive list of publications includes the books *Finns in Minnesota* and *Morgan Park: Duluth, U.S. Steel, and the Forging of a Company Town*. He has been both a Fulbright graduate fellow and visiting professor at the University of Helsinki, and was the Finlandia Foundation National Lecturer of the Year in 2009–10.

**Hannu Heinilä** received his Ph.D. in history from the University of Turku. He is currently a principal lecturer and head of the degree program at HAMK University of Applied Sciences.

**Erik Hieta** has a Ph.D. in history from the University of California, Davis. He is currently a researcher at the University of Turku.

**Paul George Hummasti** was a professor of history at the University of Missouri. He is well known for his research on Finnish immigration and socialism. He published a book, *Finnish Radicals in Astoria, Oregon, 1904–1940: A Study in Immigrant Socialism*, as well as numerous articles in various publications.

**Gary Kaunonen** is a labor, immigration, and social historian. He once served as assistant director of Michigan Technological University's Writing Program. He has published *Finns in Michigan*; *Challenge Accepted: A Finnish Immigrant Response to Industrial America in Michigan's Copper Country* (2010 Historical Society of Michigan Book Award); and *Community in Conflict* (with Aaron Goings).

**Reino Kero** is emeritus professor of history at the University of Turku. He has published numerous books and articles on the Finnish emigration overseas and the Finnish immigrants in North America.

**Peter Kivisto** is the Richard A. Swanson Professor of Social Thought at Augustana College and recently served as Finland Distinguished Professor at the University of Turku. He is the author of more than twenty-five books, including *Beyond a Border: The Causes and Consequences of Contemporary Immigration* (with Thomas Faist).

**Auvo Kostiainen** is a professor of history at the University of Turku. He has published more than 200 articles and books on migration history and the history of tourism.

**Johanna Leinonen** holds a Ph.D. Degree in History from the University of Minnesota. Her areas of specialization include international marriage migration, transnational families, gender and migration, and highly skilled migration. She is currently a postdoctoral researcher at the Turku Institute for Advanced Studies at the University of Turku. Her publications include articles in the *International Migration Review*, *Journal of American Ethnic History*, and *Social Science History Journal*.

**Mika Roinila** has more than twenty years of experience in the field of Finnish immigration studies. He has published three books and numerous academic articles dealing with his research on Finns in North America. He is the International Baccalaureate Program Coordinator at John Adams High School in South Bend, Indiana.

**Jon Saari** is an emeritus professor of history at Northern Michigan University in Marquette, Michigan, where he taught, researched, and wrote about modern China, ecological history, historiography, and Finnish immigrants in America. .

**Keijo Virtanen** is emeritus professor of cultural history at the University of Turku and served as the rector from 1997 to 2012. His research activities concentrate on transatlantic migration movements, American cultural impact on Europe, and Finland and European integration processes. He holds honorary doctoral degrees from the University of Tartu (Estonia) and the University of Klaipeda (Lithuania).

# Index

**A**

adaptation to American society, 263–67
Alabama, 58
Alanne, V.S. (Severi), 164–67, 214
Alaska, 56, 57; Klondyke, Yukon Territory, 268
alcohol and alcoholism. *See* temperance movement
Alien Registration Act of 1940, 274
"America Fever" (*Amerikankuume*), 59
American Indians, 80, 81; Chippewa, 81; culture, 117; Finndians, 117; Ojibwa legends, 81; smokehouse, 83. *See also* Delaware
Americanization, 214, 305; attitudes to, 99, 102, 120, 121, 151–52, 244; process of, 14, 84, 108, 127, 165–66, 177
Amerikan Suomalainen Kansanvallan Liitto (Finnish American League for Democracy), 143–44
Amerikan Suomalainen Työväenliitto, 134
Antikainen, Lars (pseudonym), 277
Apostolic Lutherans. *See* religion; Laestadian movement
assimilation process, 14, 102, 310, 312, 320–21. *See also* adaptation to American society
athletics. *See* sports

**B**

Bärlund, Gunnar, 198
Blumenbach, Johann Friedrich, 78
Boman, Eero, 182
Book Concern. *See* Finnish Lutheran Book Concern
boxing, 198
Brask, Andrew I., 76
brass bands, 188–89, 192
Brown, Charley (Charles Newman), 58, 63
Bush, George W., 27

**C**

California, 57, 63, 64, 68; and gold finds, 41, 55, 58; Los Angeles, 196; San Francisco, 185
Canada, 44, 48–49, 52, 133, 147, 148; deportations and, 275–77; Lutheranism in, 126–27
Cant, William A., 76, 80
Canth, Minna, 186
Castrén, David, 175
caucasian, 77, 78, 80
Cephalic Index, 77
charmed knots, 81
*Chicago Tribune,* 174
Chinese, 79
choirs, 248–50
choral groups, 188–90, 192
Christopher, Peter, and Mary, 62

335

churches and Church Finns. *See* religion

citizenship: first papers, 76, 148–51

Civil War (Finland), 9, 41, 132, 140, 144, 174, 193, 195, 214, 277, 301–3

Civil War (US), 41, 57, 58, 79

class, 310

Cold War, 21, 51, 248, 251, 258, 259, 261, 273, 278–81

Comintern (Communist International), 140, 144, 151, 187

commemoration of immigration history, 15–17

communists: Communist Party (US), 85, 187; Finnish American, 84, 132, 142–43, 212, 246–47, 248–49, 256, 261; Finnish Workers Federation, 144; reorganization, 144; Workers Party of America, 132, 144, 164, 244; Yhdysvaltain Suomalainen Työväen Järjestö, 144. *See also* socialism

Congress of Industrial Organization (CIO), 146

Connecticut, 69

Coolidge, Calvin, 196

Cooperative League of the United States of America (CLUSA), 164

cooperative movement, 136, 157–68; Central Co-operative Exchange (Keskusosuuskunta), 163–66; Central Co-operative Wholesale, 157–58, 160, 163–68; educational department, 160, 165, 167

Corgan, Oscar, 164

cossacks, 80

criminal syndicalism, 274

culture, 173–98; heritage, 18; pessimist and transformationalist views in maintaining culture, 321–22, 324; traditions, 20–21. *See also* Delaware; ethnicity; families; identity; literature; organizations; press; theater

Cuvier, Baron Georges de, 78, 80

**D**

dating: interethnic, 286–88; cultural differences in, 288, 289, 292; gender norms regarding, 286–87. *See also* intermarriage; marriage

Delaware: Finns in the Delaware, 29–40; founding of, 29–30; heritage of, 31–35, 148, 190, 214;

importance of, 14–15, 18; New Sweden colony, 56, 57; Tricentennial celebration, 31–33.

Davis, Angela, 145

Democratic Farmer-Labor Party, 146

deportation of Finns, 273–84 "Buford," 275; "Red Express," 275

discrimination, 287

DNA studies and genealogy, 34

drama. *See* theaters

**E**

Eastern Federation for Finnish Music, 189

Eastern Gymnastics and Athletic League, 194

education: impact on intermarriage rate, 291; level of Finnish immigrants, 291, 310. *See also* schools

Eisenhower, Dwight D., 148

Elo, Taisto, 279–80

Eloheimo, J.W., 117–18, 121–22

Enqvist, Verner, 278

Estonians, 84

ethnicity, 310–11, 312; revival of, 292, 311, 312, 315; symbolic nature of, 312

European Indians, 84

**F**

families: Finns in the United States, issue of multiple identities of, 285–96. *See also* traditions

Farmers' Union Central Exchange, 168

farms and farming, 55, 59, 79, 260, 319; export of skills to Finland, 268, 299; farmer background in Finland, 29, 30, 34, 47, 96, 146; Farmer-Labor Party, 146–47; farming districts and communities, 59, 63–69, 112, 124, 139, 157, 159, 180, 223, 226, 285, 287; farmsteads, 10, 57, 63

feminization, of migration, 288–89

Finland, 77; Catholic, 110; contacts with, 243–82; early religious history of Finland: pagan, 109–10; industrialization in, 92; Orthodox, 110, 124; Reformation in, 107, 109, 110–11, 114, 126–27; socialist movement in, 132 . *See also* communism; migration; temperance;

transnationalism; travels; wars
Finland Society (Suomi Seura), 248, 249, 261
Finlandia Foundation National, 7-8, 11 (n. 1), 17, 259-60
Finlandia University. *See* Suomi College
Finland-Swedes, 221-42, 57, 58, 62, 63, 65, 66, 67, 124, 215; Order of Runeberg, 63, 173, 185, 190
Finnish American Athletic Club (FAAC), 196-97
Finnish American Society, 197
Finnish American Evangelical Lutheran National Church, 177, 190
Finnish American Gymnastics and Athletics League, 195
Finnish Lutheran Book Concern, 76, 109, 118-19, 211
Finnish Music Association of America, 189
Finnish Organization of Canada, 185
Finnish People's College and Theological Seminary, 177
Finnish Relief Fund, 254-58; relief aid, 249, 254-58, 260; *See also* help to Finland
Finnish Socialist Federation (Suomalainen SosialistiJärjestö; Yhdysvaltain Sosialistipuolueen Suomalainen Järjestö), 76, 132-40, 143, 144, 150, 159, 164, 173-74, 179, 182-83, 193
Finnish Workers' Club in Harlem, 85
Finnish American history, themes in: development of, 13-18; ethnic cleansing, 9-10; hybridization, 7; themes as predicaments, 6; themes of interest to non-Finns, 10-11
Finnish-American Publishing Co., 207, 210
FinnFest USA, 20, 71, 261
FinnForum, 19-20
Finnishness: as liveliness, 8; and authenticity, 8. *See also* identity
Finntown/Finntowns, 55, 56, 57, 59, 62, 63, 64, 66-67, 68, 69, 70, 71
Finno-Ugric, 75, 78, 84
fishing and fishermen, 50, 63-66, 112, 125, 223, 226, 237
Florida, 58, 70; Finnish American IWW in, 141-42
Flynn, Elizabeth Gurley, 138

Ford Foundation, 260-61
Freemasons, 95
future: challenges, 320; of Finnishness, 322; generations, 321; trends, 320

## G

Gallen-Kallela, Akseli, 174
generations, vii, 4, 7-8, 9, 10, 19, 20, 32, 43, 44, 47, 101-2, 121, 150-51, 216, 221, 231, 233, 250, 251, 297, 300, 304; effect of 1924 immigration law on, 10; in literature, 11; postwar new immigrants, 7-8; tensions between, 309-14. *See also* identity; migration organizations; St. Urho's Day
Georgia, 70
*Gloucester Fisherman,* 82
Good Templars, 94-97
Grönman, K.G., family deportation of, 278
gymnastics, 193-94, 198
Gymnastics and Athletic League of Finland (SVUL), 193, 195

## H

Haanpää, Ella, 182
Haapanen, Henry, 189
Hahl, Moses, 132, 186, 214
Hall, Gus (Arvo Kustaa Hallberg), 4, 131, 145, 146, 148, 279
Halonen, Alex, 132
Halonen, George (Yrjö), 164-65
Heikkilä, William, 278
Heikkinen, Knut, 279-80
help to Finland: during and after World War II, 253-62. *See also* Finnish Relief Fund
Hendrickson, Martin, 132
Hoover, Herbert, 253, 254-56; and Roosevelt, Franklin D., 256-58
heritage, 18
Hillilä, Hugo, 213
Hillquit, Morris, 212
historical associations by the Finns, 16
Holberg, Ludvig, 184

Hurja, Emil, 36 (n. 12), 148
Hyrske, Felix, 182

**I**

identity: as an issue, 309–18; adult onset of Finnishness, 323; decline of, 324; of Finns and Finnish Americans, 309–15, 321; Finnish identity: ability to choose, 293, 310; generational differences, 309, 310, 311, 312–14. *See also* ethnicity; generations; organizations; traditions
Illinois, 64, 68; Chicago, 174
Ilmonen, Salomon, 15, 61, 63, 66
Imatra (Amerikan Suomalainen Työväenliitto Imatra, American Finnish Labour League Imatra), 133–34
immigrants, Finns. *See* migration
Immigration Act of 1924, 184, 265; and National Origins Act of 1924, 288
Immigration and Nationality Act of 1952, 290
Immigration History Research Center (Minneapolis, MN), 18
Immigration Commission (Dillingham Commission), 80, 149, 275
immigration restrictions, 273–74
Indo-European, 75
Industrial Workers of the World (IWW): and Finnish Americans, 69, 83, 84, 132, 135–42, 146, 151, 179, 186, 195
Inberg, E. H., and Mary, 58
Institute of Migration (Turku, Finland), 18
integration. *See* adaptation to American society
interethnic relations, 286–87. *See also* dating
intermarriage: cultural differences in, 292–93; increase of, 289–91; rarity of, 286, 287, 288. *See also* dating; marriage
Italians, 80

**J**

Jääskeläinen, Pasi, 191
jazz, 190, 192–93
Jalkanen, A.J., 278

Jasberg, J.H., 68
Jim Crow laws, 9
Johnson, A., 58
Johnson, John Henrik, 62
Johnsson, Anton Fabian, 268
Jokela-McKone (Makkonen), 137, 212–13
Joutsen, Karl Fredrik, 268
Jones, Mother, 138
jurva, K.A., 206

**K**

*Kalevala*, 81, 151, 246
Kannasto, Sanna, 137
Kansalliskirkko. *See* religion
Knights and Ladies of Kaleva (Kaleva Brotherhood), 151, 173, 184–85; Knights of Kaleva, 76, 77, 84; Ladies of Kaleva, 84
Kalm, Pehr, 34
Karni, Michael, 84
Kasurinen, Lyyti, 175
Kekkonen, Urho, 18
Kero, Reino, 67
Kirri, Valto Eetu, 83
Kivi, Aleksis, 184, 186–87
Knights of Labor, 95
Kolehmainen, Hannes, 195–97
Kolehmainen, William, 195
Kosonen, Vihtori, 132
Kurikka, Matti, 132, 133, 158, 215
Kuusinen, Aino (A. Morton), 145
Kuusinen, Otto Ville, 145
Kvens (Quaener), 58, 114–15, 128 (n. 20)

**L**

Labor Sports League (TUL), 193, 195
Laestadius, Lars Levi, 59, 115, 117
Laestadian movement, 110–11, 115–17
Lahti, Carl, and Peter, 59
Lahtinen, William, 279
language: English skills of Finns in the United States, 215, 288, 291; changes at home, 321; Finnish, 319,

321, 323; Spanish, 321; Swedish, 319
Lappala, Milma (and Risto Lappala), 213
Lapps, 78
leadership, political: left groups, communist, 146; Anderson, A.A., 148; Anderson, Elmer, 148; Canada, 147; Democratic and Republican Parties, 147; Hellberg, G.A., 148; Hurja, Emil, 148; Jasberg, J.H., 147; Larson, Oscar J., 147–48; Saari, John, 148
Leinonen, Alexander, 55, 56, 62
Linnaeus, Carl, 78
Lapua movement, 85
Lemberg, Lauri, 183, 185, 187
Lincoln Loyalty League, 139, 147, 151, 274
Linn, Charles (Charles Erik Englebrekt Sjödahl), 58
literacy: Finnish Americans and, 175
literature: Finnish-North American literature, 11, 205–15; belles lettres, 212–16; calendars, 208–12; children's, 214; guide books, 215; libraries and, 212
Louhi brass band, 192
Louisiana, 58
lumbering and forestry, 63, 67, 81, 82, 140, 142, 146, 157, 159, 179, 187–88, 223, 226, 267, 276, 277
Lutheran Book Concern (Hancock, MI). *See* Finnish Lutheran Book Concern
Lähetyskirkko. *See* religion, Congregational Churches.
Lönnrot, Elias, 81, 92

# M

McAllister, Basil Robert, 258
McCarran-Walter Act (1952), 274
McCarthy, Joseph, 145, 274, 279, 280
Magyars, 78, 79, 80; Hungarian, 84
Maine, 69
Mäkelä, A.B., 132, 214–15
Mäki, Taisto, 196
Manner, Kullervo, 145
Mårtensson, Mårten, 34
Massachusetts, 58, 64, 65, 69; Fitchburg, 82, 181, 186, 194; Gardner, 134, 182, 194; Maynard, 184, 194; Rockport, 132; Worcester, 184, 194–95
marriage, patterns of Finns in the United States, 286, 288–90. *See also* dating; intermarriage
Marttinen, Alpo, 52
Marx, Karl, 212
Mattson, Helmi (and Wm. Mattson), 137, 212–13
Melody of Finland choir, 192
Merikanto, Oskar, 191
Michigan, 56, 58, 59, 62, 64, 65, 70, 71; Calumet, 175, 188–89; Crystal Falls, 148; Hancock, 175–76; Marquette, 81; Republic, 175; Tapiola, 180; Upper Peninsula of, 14, 77, 81, 82. *See also* strikes
Midland Cooperative Wholesale, 168
migration: Finnish emigration: arriving as families, 287; arriving as non-immigrants, 290–1; arriving as spouses of U.S. citizens, 290; background and destinations, 47–49; cycles, 46; early sailor migration, 41; from Finland, 41–54, 57, 58, 59, 63, 64, 70; from Norway, 58, 59, 62; from Sweden, 56, 57, 58; immigrants, Finnish: arrival after World War II, 288–91; numbers, 42–44, 51; old and new, 263–64, 269; proportion of women, 288–89; structure, 47–49. *See also* return migration; transnationalism
mines and mining: 64, 65, 69, 82, 83, 93, 108, 138, 147, 157, 160, 188, 222, 275; Mesabi Iron Range, 15, 17, 62, 67, 73, 75, 76, 83, 132, 134, 139, 193, 275; Rocky Mountains, 64, 69, 223; Upper Peninsula of Michigan, 14, 62, 69, 77, 81, 82, 83, 112, 114, 125. *See also* strikes
Minnesota, 56, 57, 58, 59, 64, 65–66, 67, 68, 70, 71, 83; Duluth, 76, 134, 177, 267–68; Ely, 177; Finnish communities in, 285, 286, 309, 311–12, 314; Hibbing, 134; International Falls, 212; IWW in, 141–42; Mesabi Range (Iron Range), 15, 17, 73, 134; Minneapolis, 177; Smithville, 177; Virginia, 182–83. *See also* strikes
Mongolian, 75, 76, 77 78, 79, 80, 83, 149; eyefold, 77; spot, 77 287
Montana, 69

Morton, John, 17. *See also* Delaware
Mullika (Mullikka), Eric Pålsson, 57
Museum of the American People, 11
music activities, 188–93
Myrsky, association, 132

## N

National Committee on Food for the Small Democracies, 255, 257
nativism, 287
naturalization. *See* citizenship.
Negro question, 85
nesting places (pesäpaikat), 55, 56, 57, 58
New Ethnicity (1970–2010), 10–11, 18–21
New Jersey, 57, 58
New York, 58, 64, 69; New York City, 27, 186, 195–97; Rosendale, 192
New York Finnish Women Gymnasts, 197
Nikander, Juha K., 117–18, 120
Niukkanen, William (Mackie), 279–80
Noppa, Johan Peter, 62
North Dakota, 64, 65
Northern Michigan University, 3, 6
Northern States Cooperative League, 167
Norway, 42, 112, 114–15, 128 (n. 20)
Norwegians, 59, 62
Norwegian Americans, 94
Nummivuori, John, 162
Nuorteva, Santeri, 132, 302
Nurmi, H. V., 165
Nurmi, Paavo, 195–96

## O

Ohio, 63, 64; Ashtabula, 189–90
Oldenberg, John, 68
Oregon, 58, 63, 64; Astoria, 185, 189
organizations, of Finnish Americans, 291, 310, 314; disappearance of, 291, 311; Finns' attitudes about, 291, 309–11. *See also* generations; identity

## P

Paasikivi, J.K., 280
Pakkala, Teuvo, 186
Palmer, A. Mitchell, 150
Palmgren, Selim, 191
Paloheimo, Yrjö, 259–60
Pasanen, Ida, 137, 213
Pekkarinen, Tatu, 191
Peltoperä (Johnson), Elias, 63
Pennsylvania, 58, 64; Monessen, 189–90, 192
Polso, Sylvia, 191
press: papers and journals, 205–20
prohibition, 102–3
Protestant work ethic, 107–8, 112–14, 127
publishing activities, 205–21; religious, 210–13; workers' movement and, 207–10

## Q

Quincy Mining Company, 62

## R

race, 75–87, 287, 293. *See also* Mongolian language question; Svan, John; Yokinen, August
Raittiuden Ystävät, 97
Raivaaja Publishing Co., 211
"Red and White divide," 100–1; Red Finns, 75, 83, 84
religion, churches: Baptists, 124; Church Finns, 75, 246–47, 249, 256; Congregational Churches, 121, 123, 125, 212; Finnish American Catholics, 125–26; Finnish American Evangelical Lutheran National Church, 121–23, 177, 190, 212; Laestadian/Apostolic Lutheran, 59, 62, 63, 71, 115–17, 211; Lutheran church, 256, 258; Methodists, 124–25; Pentecostal churches, 124, 125. *See also* Suomi Synod
return migration, 263–72; impact after return to Finland, 263, 267–69
revival movements: in Canada, 126; in Finland, 110–11, 115; in the United States, 115–17
Ritola, Ville, 196–97
Rockefeller Foundation, 260
Rönn, Eskel, 164–65

Rosendahl, John, 191
Russia, Russians: 56, 57, 58, 59, 78, 80, 110, 111, 115; and Russification 110; Russian Revolution and Finnish Americans, 140

**S**

Saarinen, Eliel, 174
Salo, John, 196
Salolampi Foundation, and Salolampi Finnish Language Village, 261
Salomaa, Hiski, 190–91
Salvation Army, 125
Sami, 115, 117
sauna, 83, 85
scholars: as insiders and outsiders, 4–5
Schoolcraft, Henry Rowe, 81
schools, 175–80, 190, 265; Sunday schools, 175–76, 211
Sibelius, Jean, 75, 189, 191
Sibelius Society, 189
Sirola, Yrjö, 144, 302
Snellman, Venny, 260
socialism: the Suomi Synod and, 108, 120; associations founded, 132–34; "hall socialism," 131, 136, 138, 140–41, 143, 145; Laestadian churches and, 117; National Church and, 122–23; preventing religious work in Canada, 126–27; Socialist Party of America, 134, 147, 164; Work People's College, 123
Society of American Finns, 268
Soini, Yrjö (Agapetus), 184
Sointula (Harmony), utopian colony, 133
*Song of Hiawatha* (Henry Wadsworth Longfellow), 81
*Sosialisti (Teollisuustyöläinen),* 141
South Dakota, 64, 98, 113
Soviet Karelia: "Karelia fever" to, 145, 244, 246–47
Soviet Union, 21, 246, 248, 254, 258; and Stalin, 247, 257
sources: repositories in United States and Finland, 5–6; dead vs. living, 3
sports, 193–98
St. Urho's Day, 309–15; creating tensions between generations, 311, 312–4, 315; origin of the myth, 311–2. *See also* generations; identity; traditions
steamship, travel by, 244–48, 249
Steenroos, Carl Johan, 95
strikes: Copper Mining Strike (1913), 83; Mesabi strike (1907), 76, 83, 132, 139; Mesabi strike (1916), 83, 275
Sulkanen, Elis, 164
Suomalainen SosialistiJärjestö. *See* Finnish Socialist Federation
Suomi band, 192
Suomi koulut, 261
Suomi College (Suomi-Opisto), 18, 84, 112, 118–19, 122, 176–77, 179–80, 189, 211
Suomi Seura. *See* Finland Society
Suomi Synod, 76, 77, 176–77, 180, 190, 210, 214; as associates of American capitalism, 108–10, 112–14, 127; in Canada, 126–27; history of, 117–21
Suvanto, K.A., 209
Suvio, Sten, 198
Svan (Swan), John, 75, 76
Sweden, 110, 112, 115, 123, 125; Delaware, migration to, 21, 42, 52
Swedes, 59, 62, 79, 80
Swedish Americans, 94
Swedetown, 62
Sweet, John C. 76
*Sven Tuuva,* 62
Svensk-Finska Nykterhetsförbundet, 99
syndicalism. *See* Industrial Workers of the World
Syrjälä, Frans Josef, 132

**T**

Tafte, Christian, 62
Tanner, Anton Ferdinand, 132
Tanner, Johan Alfred, 191
temperance movement: active societies, 173, 175, 184, 188–89, 193; Amerikan Suomalainen

Kansallis-Raittius Weljeysseura, 96–99; ideological fights in, 100–1; need for, 92–93; saloons, 93–94; societies founded, 95, 99
Tenhunen, Matti, 164
Teutonic race, 80
theaters, 180–88
Thorne, Larry (Lauri Törni), 52
Tokoi, Oskari, 277
Topelius, Zachris (Sakari), 184, 186
Tornio River valley, 59
track and field, 193–98
traditions, 292, 293; recreation of, 311, 312, 315
transnational practices, 91, 297–308
travels to Finland, 243–52
Turks, 80
Turpeinen, Viola, 191
Tuomikoski, Johan 197
Tuomikoski, Wilfred "Tommy," 192–93
Työmies Society, 209
Työväen Opisto. *See* Work People's College
*Työväen Osuustoimintalehti*, 165, 210

## U

UNESCO, 77
United Co-operative Society, 161–62
University Male Voice Choir (Helsinki), 192
University of Michigan, 180
University of Minnesota, 71. *See* Immigration History Research Center
University of Turku: immigration scholars, 4; Alaskan gold, 268; graduate theses, 6, 18; Vilho Niitemaa, 6
U.S. Census, 56, 57, 58, 59, 61, 63, 64, 67, 71
Utah, 64
*Uusi Kotimaa*, 59

## V

Valon Tuote Temperance Society, 70
Viapori Mutiny, 134

## W

Wälläri, Niilo, 275
Walz, Maggie (Margareeta Niranen), 213, 218 (n. 16)
wars. *See* Cold War; help to Finland; Civil War (Finland); Civil War (US); migration; Winter War; World War II
Wargelin, John, 84, 108, 113
Washington (state), 63, 64; Kelso, 212; Seattle, 185
Westerinen, Pekka, 189
Western Federation of Miners (WFM), 134
white chauvinism, 85
whiteness: Finnish Americans and, 9, 75–87, 292; privileges attached to, 291
widows, 288
Wiita, John (Henry Puro), 134, 146, 183
Williams, Kustaa, 192
Winter War, 190, 248, 249, 251, 253, 254–58, 261
Wisconsin, 64, 68; Superior, 185
women, 47–49, 136–38; activists and organizers, 212–13; women's history, 20. *See also* migration
Work People's College (Workers' College, orig. Työväen Opisto), 65, 141, 142, 176, 178–80, 186, 268
World War II, 253–62
wrestling, 193–96, 198
Wyoming, 64
Wälläri, Niilo, 275

## Y

Yhdysvaltain Sosialistipuolueen Suomalainen Järjestö. *See* Finnish Socialist Federation
Ylönen, Taavi Vilho (Taavetti Sylvesteri), 184
Yokinen, August (Jokinen), 85